Project Management Essentials
Therese Linton

Project Management Essentials

Therese Linton

Project management essentials
1st Edition
Therese Linton

Publishing manager: Dorothy Chiu
Publishing editor: Sophie Kalienicki
Developmental editor: James Forsyth
Senior project editor: Tanya Simmons
Permissions manager: Helen Mammides
Cover design: Santiago Villamizar
Text designer: Aisling Gallagher
Art direction: Danielle Maccarone
Editor: Sylvia Marson
Proofreader: Paul Smitz
Indexer: Julie King
Cover: Getty Images/Michael Murphy
Cenveo Publisher Services

Any URLs contained in this publication were checked for currency
during the production process. Note, however, that the publisher
cannot vouch for the ongoing currency of URLs.

Acknowledgements

Cengage Learning would like to thank the Project Management
Institute for their permission to reference and reproduce text
content from *A Guide to the Project Management Body of Knowledge*
(PMBOK^R Guide), Fifth edition. This content appears on the
following pages of this book: Chapter 3, pp. 65-9;
Chapter 4, pp. 74-5, pp. 86-8; Chapter 5, pp. 106-8;
Chapter 6, p. 113, pp. 127-8; Chapter 7, pp. 133-4, pp. 157-8;
Chapter 8, pp. 164-5, pp. 194-5; Chapter 9, p. 200, pp. 225-7;
Chapter 10, pp. 234-5, pp. 253-4;
Chapter 11, pp. 259-60, pp. 261-2, pp. 291-2;
Chapter 12, pp. 297-8, pp. 323-4; Chapter 13, pp. 330-1, p. 356;
Chapter 14, pp. 362-3, pp. 379-80;
Chapter 15, p. 387, pp. 388-9, pp. 417-9;
and Chapter 16, pp. 427-9, p. 449.

Cengage Learning would also like to thank The Northern Sydney
Institute, Part of TAFE NSW, for their permission to use text
content from their copyrighted material. This content appears on
the following pages of this book: Chapter 1, p. 3;
Chapter 2, p. 11; Chapter 3, p. 40, p. 42; Chapter 4, p. 78;
Chapter 5, p. 95; Chapter 10, p. 245; Chapter 11, p. 262, p. 263;
Chapter 12, p. 297; Chapter 14, pp. 378-9;
Chapter 15, pp. 410-11;
and Chapter 16, p. 441, p. 443, p. 445.

For product information and technology assistance,
in Australia call **1300 790 853**;
in New Zealand call **0800 449 725**

For permission to use material from this text or product, please email
aust.permissions@cengage.com

National Library of Australia Cataloguing-in-Publication Data

Linton, Therese, author.
Project management essentials/9780170237062 (paperback)
Includes index.
Project management--Australia.
658.404

Cengage Learning Australia
Level 7, 80 Dorcas Street
South Melbourne, Victoria Australia 3205

Cengage Learning New Zealand
Unit 4B Rosedale Office Park
331 Rosedale Road, Albany, North Shore 0632, NZ

For learning solutions, visit **cengage.com.au**

Printed in Singapore by 1010 Printing International Limited.
4 5 6 7 8 9 10 23 22 21 20 19

Brief contents

Contents

1 **PROJECT MANAGEMENT LIFECYCLE**

2 PROJECT MANAGEMENT KEY KNOWLEDGE AREAS 131

Preface

Project Management Essentials is designed to provide both the novice and experienced project manager with frameworks to improve their ability to deliver successful project outcomes. It is full of tips and techniques from the real world which will help make you a smart project manager able to decide which project management processes are valid in different contexts.

The text is an essential tool for the following groups:

- people studying project management for the first time
- experienced project managers wishing to enhance their capability or knowledge of real world and advanced project management practices
- project managers wishing to understand how the Project Management Body of Knowledge (PMBOK® Guide) underpins all project management practices
- students of the Certificate IV in Project Management
- students of the Diploma of Project Management
- teachers of the Certificate IV and Diploma of Project Management
- university students studying project management wishing to understand the practical applications of the key knowledge areas
- project sponsors wishing to understand the concepts of project management in order to more effectively support project managers in the delivery of outcomes.

Structure of the text

Project Management Essentials is split into two parts. Part 1 consists of six chapters which focus on the phases of the project management lifecycle with additional chapters covering processes for monitoring and controlling project work, as well as improving overall project outcomes. The chapters in Part 2 are aligned to the key knowledge areas of the Project Management Body of Knowledge (PMBOK® Guide).

This structure increases the flexibility and usability of the text. Experienced practitioners can refresh their overall knowledge of the project lifecycle by reviewing Part 1, or concentrate on a specific knowledge area using Part 2. Students of the Certificate IV and Diploma of Project Management will find Part 2 useful as it aligns to the units of study within these courses. In practice, they can then move on to use Part 1 to assist with managing their first projects. Since the text is written with real-world project management insights in mind, the scope of project management in practice is provided in the appendices. Appendix 1 outlines the role of certification and professional bodies, and Appendix two describes the relationship between project management, programs and portfolios.

Therese Linton

Resources guide

FOR THE STUDENT

This text has a vast array of features in every chapter to enhance your study of the principles of project management and to help you understand its real-world application.

Learning objectives introduce each chapter and give you a clear sense of what the chapter will cover.

Research and reflection activity boxes are presented throughout the chapters to encourage you to consider, apply or further extend the theory you have learnt.

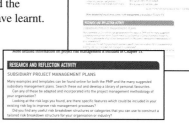

Real-world experience boxes are examples and mini case studies that link the theory mentioned in the chapter to real-world situations.

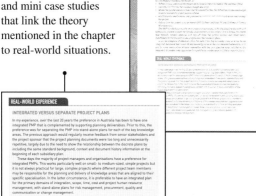

This **PMBOK® Guide icon** appears in the margin alongside important cross-references to sections of the Project Management Institute's A Guide to the Project Management Body of Knowledge. The key knowledge areas of this guide underpin the project management practices mentioned.

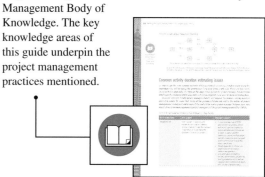

These boxes provide a practical grounding from which to approach project management and are especially useful for a beginning practitioner. There are also additional real-world experience cases available online.

Project management mastery boxes provide advanced concepts in detail by outlining their application to real-life situations. These sophisticated reflections provide the experienced practitioner with additional tips that often modify and extend the basic theory.

The **training package icon** provides a convenient link to the current training.gov.au unit of competency. The icon shows which questions are mapped to required elements and performance criteria of the named unit.

Key terms throughout the chapters are bolded in orange. A full list of key terms is available in the glossary, which can be found at the back of the book.

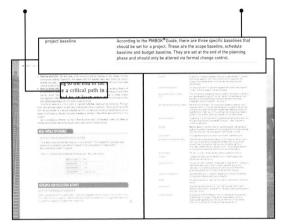

project baseline — According to the PMBOK® Guide, there are three specific baselines that should be set for a project. These are the scope baseline, schedule baseline and budget baseline. They are set at the end of the planning phase and should only be altered via formal change control.

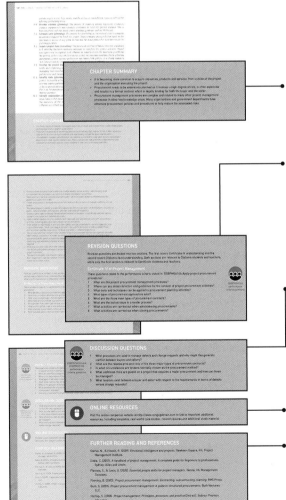

END-OF-CHAPTER MATERIAL

CHAPTER SUMMARY

The end-of-chapter summary provides a review of the chapter's main concepts and reflects the chapter's learning objectives.

REVISION QUESTIONS

The revision questions at the end of every chapter provide you an opportunity to reinforce and test your knowledge of the material covered in that chapter. The revision questions are categorised as being most applicable to the Certificate IV and the Diploma of Project Management.

DISCUSSION QUESTIONS

You can use these discussion questions to help you prepare for class or to assist in your understanding of the application and critical analysis of the issues arising in project management practice.

ONLINE RESOURCES

A reminder of the relevant online resources is found at the end of every chapter.

FURTHER READINGS AND REFERENCES

The further readings are references section lists key texts, helpful sources for further study and additional information.

ONLINE STUDENT MATERIAL

This book's student companion website provides a host of additional features to assist your study of this book, such as revision quizzes, flashcards, crosswords and video activities. These are available at http://www.cengagebrain.com.

PROJECT MANAGEMENT TEMPLATES

The ready-to-use project management templates, pre-formatted and styled, will enable you to begin and practise project management stages. These templates provide an understanding of the basic requirements of various forms and processes mentioned in the text.

ONLINE CASE STUDIES

There are additional online case studies of an experienced project management practitioner's real-world experience available.

These online case studies will help you to see the real-life application of project management theory, and how to negotiate challenges that may arise. The case studies have been written to illustrate an example of the key theoretical material contained in each chapter, so they include short-answer questions to help you engage with the key material.

FOR THE INSTRUCTOR

Cengage Learning is pleased to provide you with an extensive selection of online supplements to help you prepare your classes. These tools are available on the companion website, accessible via http://login.cengage.com.

INSTRUCTORS MANUAL

The instructor's manual provides a wealth of content to help set up and administer your subject. It includes learning objectives, chapter outlines, key teaching points, adjunct teaching and warm-up activities, lesson plans and tips, as well as solutions to all problems in the text (including revision questions, suggested answers to discussion questions and research and reflection activities).

POWERPOINT PRESENTATIONS

PowerPoint presentations cover the key concepts addressed within the text and can be edited to suit your specific teaching requirements. Use these slides to enhance your presentations and to reinforce key principles of each topic; they can also be provided as student handouts.

COMPETENCY GRIDS

Competency grids appear online to provide a simple overview of the training package units and elements covered in each chapter.

TESTBANK

An additional testbank of questions is provided in Word format to enable you to use with your LMS to set examinations, test competency or customise your students' revision.

ARTWORK

The artwork includes digital files of graphs, pictures and flow-charts from the book that can be used in a variety of media. Add them into your course management system, use them with student handouts or copy them into lecture presentations.

About the author

Therese Linton has been working as a project manager for leading corporations in Australia for more than 30 years. Her background spans a range of industries, including banking and finance, ecommerce, IT, wealth management, telecommunications, manufacturing and legal services. She also has extensive experience working as a program director, leading enterprise project management offices and in the design and delivery of training programs.

She has been lucky enough to supplement her project management training and work experience with complementary education and experience in the fields of change management and business transformation (including Lean Six Sigma).

Her education sector experience includes:

- design and delivery of the Certificate IV and Diploma of Project Management for the Northern Sydney Institute of TAFE, including face-to-face and online programs
- Unit of Study Coordinator for both the Masters of Project Management and the Masters of Project Leadership for the University of Sydney
- creation of tailored in-house training programs for project managers, project sponsors, senior managers and key stakeholders
- design and delivery of ongoing coaching programs.

She is passionate about project management education and professional certification and started her journey as an educator when she realised that she had interviewed more than 200 project management candidates in the assembly of various project teams, most of whom did not have basic project management competencies and had never heard of the PMBOK® Guide.

She decided that the only way to improve the project management competencies of potential candidates was to get out there and train the next generations of project managers. Her rationale was that this would make it easier to reliably select appropriately qualified and competent project management candidates in the future. This decision has provided some of the most rewarding experiences of her career.

Acknowledgements

I would like to thank the following important people – my husband, Edward Fairleigh, for his encouragement and assistance with diagrams and templates; Sophie Kalinecki for her faith in the text; and my students who have given me the opportunity to improve my teaching skills and to share my stories.

Cengage Learning would like to thank:

- Project Management Institute for their permission to reference and reproduce illustrated and text content from *A Guide to the Project Management Body of Knowledge (PMBOK® Guide)*, fourth and fifth editions.
- The Northern Sydney Institute, Part of TAFE NSW, for their permission to use illustrated and text content from their copyrighted material.
- The following reviewers who provided helpful and useful feedback and comments while this edition was being developed:
  - Ray Roche, Canberra Institute of Technology
  - Kelly Black, The Bremer Institute of TAFE
  - Phillip Johnston, TAFE Sydney Institute
  - Bruce Cowled, TAFE/OTEN
  - Logesvary Krishnasamy, Victoria University
  - Joel Schreiber, Pilbara Institute
  - Jacqueline Jepson, UniSA and TAFESA
  - David Kirkby, Churchill Education
  - Damian Smith, Prime Learning
  - Mark Hollis, Sunshine Coast TAFE.
- Angeline Lalini (Central Institute of Technology) for the Instructor resource PowerPoint presentations.
- Adam Leiws (Vision Quest Enterprises for the student quizzes and Ray Roche (Canberra Institute of Technology) for the student Real-world experience case studies.

Project Management Body of Knowledge

When published in 2014, Project Management Essentials was based on the 5th edition of the Project Management Body of Knowledge (PMBOK).

PMBOK is published by the Project Management Institute (PMI). First published in 1996, PMBOK has been updated every four to five years since. The current version, 6th edition, was released in September 2017 after the publication of Project Management Essentials.

The purpose of this information is two-fold:

1 Summarise the 6th edition changes
2 Provide a translation guide to the 6th edition PMBOK processes that correspond with the 5th edition processes referenced in Project Management Essentials.

PMBOK 6th edition changes

PMBOK Appendix X1 provides an overview of the 6th edition changes. The significant changes are:

The role of the project manager

The role of the project manager is new to the PMBOK guide and outlines the project manager's role from three perspectives:

- Strategic and business management skills
- Technical project management skills – the 49 processes of the 10 knowledge areas
- Leadership skills and styles
  The skill of the project manager is to integrate all three dimensions seamlessly.

Knowledge area front material

Four new standardised sections in the knowledge areas have been introduced and they precede the first process of each knowledge area:

- Key concepts, a summary of which is contained in PMBOK appendix X4.
- Trends and emerging practices that may be occurring but not practiced on lost projects.
- Tailoring considerations that accounts for the variables encountered in various contexts. PMBOK appendix X5 is a compilation of such considerations.
  Considerations for Agile/Adaptive environments where predictive approaches do not satisfy the requirement adapt to unique circumstances.

Knowledge areas and processes

Two knowledge areas were renamed:

- Project Time Management was changed to Project Schedule Management.
- Project Human Resource Management was changed to Project Resources Management.
  One process was removed, one process moved, and three processes added:
- Removed: Close procurements (section 12.4)
- Moved: Estimate Activity resources (Section 6.4)
- Added: Manage project knowledge (Section 4.4)
- Added: Control resources (section 9.6)
- Added: Implement Risk Responses (Section 11.6)
  Nine processes were renamed, and these changes are contained in the table contained the second part of this chapter.

5th edition processes	6th edition processes
8.2 Perform quality assurance	8.2 Manage quality
9.1 Plan human resource management	9.1 Plan resource management
9.2 Acquire project team	9.3 Acquire resources
9.3 Develop project team	9.4 Develop team
9.4 Manage project team	9.5 Manage team
10.3 Control communications	10.3 Monitor communications
11.6 Control risks	11.7 Monitor risks
13.2 Plan stakeholder management	13.2 Plan stakeholder engagement
13.4 Control stakeholder engagement	13.4 Monitor Stakeholder engagement

Tools and Techniques

The 6th edition attempts to reduce the number of tools and techniques and has grouped commonly used ones as follows:

- Communication skills
- Data analysis
- Data gathering
- Data representation
- Decision making
- Interpersonal and team skills.

PMBOK Appendix X6 cross references all tools and techniques against the processes they are used for.

PMBOK 5th edition to 6th edition translation

Note: When accessing a chapter, it is advisable to check this table first and note any changes to the PMBOK 6th edition. If you are using the ebook version of this text you can highlight and annotate 5th edition references with the updated 6th edition changes.

The changes in the previous table are for section numbers only. Where the term 'PMBOK' is used in in the body of the text but without an accompanying PMBOK section number it is not included in the table.

Linton chapter	Page	PMBOK 5e references	PMBOK 6e	Comment
1 Introduction	3	Project definition	Pp 13 and 716	Unchanged
1 Introduction	3	Project management definition	Pp 10 and 716	Unchanged
1 Introduction	4	Project Integration Management	P 23	Unchanged
1 Introduction	4	Project Scope Management	P 23	Unchanged
1 Introduction	4	Project Time Management	P24 Project Schedule Management	Changed
1 Introduction	4	Project Cost Management	P24	Unchanged
1 Introduction	4	Project Quality Management	P24	Unchanged
1 Introduction	4	Project Human Resource Management	P24 Project Resource Management	Changed
1 Introduction	4	Project Communications Management	P24	Unchanged
1 Introduction	4	Project Risk Management	P24	Unchanged
1 Introduction	4	Project Procurement Management	P24	Unchanged
1 Introduction	4	Project Stakeholder Management	P24	Unchanged

(*Continued*)

Linton chapter	Page	PMBOK 5e references	PMBOK 6e	Comment
2 Project initiation	13	Process groups referred to as phases	P23 Clarification Process groups are independent of project phases and are different to project phases. Table 1-4 (p 25) illustrates the interaction of the knowledge areas, the process groups and the project lifecycle. The four PMBOK phases use different terminology to initiation, planning, executing and closure but their meanings are the same.	Unchanged
2 Project initiation	13	Only two processes identified for project initiation	P 25 Table 1-4	Unchanged
2 Project initiation	22	Project Scope Definition	P 131 & 717	Unchanged
2 Project initiation	29	Identification of stakeholders is the second major process group of the initiation phase	P 25 Table 1-4	Unchanged
2 Project initiation	29	See PMBOK Guide Figure 13.2 Identify Stakeholders	P 516 PMBOK 13.2 Identify Stakeholders	Changed
2 Project initiation	29	Stakeholder Analysis Definition	P 723	Unchanged
2 Project initiation	32	Three-step Process for Stakeholder Analysis	PP 511, 512, 527	Unchanged
2 Project initiation	33	PMBOK Figure 2-7 Stakeholder Analysis Process	Does not exist. Refer instead to P 524 Figure 13-8	Changed
2 Project initiation	33	Stakeholder Power and Interest Grid	Referred to in P 513 without a graphic	Unchanged

(Continued)

Linton chapter	Page	PMBOK 5e references	PMBOK 6e	Comment
3 Project planning	41	Project Time Management	P 25 Table 1-4 Project Schedule Management	Changed
3 Project planning	42	Project Human Resource Management	P 25 Table 1-4 Project Resource Management	Changed
3 Project planning	42	Plan Human Resource Management	P 25 Table 1-4 Plan Resource Management Estimate Activity Resources	Changed
3 Project planning	42	Develop the Project Management Plan definition	P 82	Unchanged
3 Project planning	42	Perform Integrated Change Control	P 616	Unchanged
3 Project planning	42	The Project Management Plan is the primary output of the planning processes	P 565	Unchanged
3 Project planning	43	PMBOK Figure 3-1 includes 9.1 Plan Human Resource Management and Human Resource Plan	P 312 9.1 Plan Resource Management P 318 9.1.3.1 Resource Management Plan	Changed
3 Project planning	45	No reference in PMBOK to a deliverable called a 'Project Plan'	Correct term is 'project management plan'.	Unchanged
3 Project planning	58	Supplementary deliverables and other documents kept apart in order to differentiate them.	'Supplementary Deliverables' not referred to but keeping documents apart is usual practice.	Unchanged
3 Project planning	65	4.2 Develop the project management plan	82	Unchanged
3 Project planning	66	5.4 Create WBS	156	Unchanged

(Continued)

Linton chapter	Page	PMBOK 5e references	PMBOK 6e	Comment
3 Project planning	66	6.1 Plan Schedule management	179	Unchanged
3 Project planning	66	6.2 Define Activities	183	Unchanged
3 Project planning	67	6.3 Sequence activities	187	Unchanged
3 Project planning	67	6.4 Estimate activity resources	P 320 9.2 Estimate Activity Resources	Changed
3 Project planning	67	6.5 Estimate activity durations	P 195 6.4 Estimate Activity Durations	Changed
3 Project planning	67	6.6 Develop schedule	P 205 6.5 Develop schedule	Changed
3 Project planning	67	7.1 Plan cost management	P 235	Unchanged
3 Project planning	67	7.2 Estimate costs	P 240	Unchanged
3 Project planning	67	7.3 Determine budget	P 248	Unchanged
3 Project planning	67	8.1 Plan quality Management	P 277	Unchanged
3 Project planning	68	9.1 Plan human resource management	P 312 9.1 Plan resource management	Changed
3 Project planning	68	10.1 Plan communications management	P 366	Unchanged
3 Project planning	68	11.1 Plan risk management	P 401	Unchanged
3 Project planning	68	11.2 Identify risks	P 409	Unchanged
3 Project planning	68	11.3 Perform qualitative risk analysis	P 419	Unchanged
3 Project planning	68	11.4 Perform quantitative risk analysis	P 428	Unchanged
3 Project planning	68	11.5 Plan risk responses	P 437	Unchanged
3 Project planning	69	12.1 Plan procurement management	P 466	Unchanged

(*Continued*)

Linton chapter	Page	PMBOK 5e references	PMBOK 6e	Comment
3 Project planning	69	13.2 Plan stakeholder management	P 516 13.2 Plan Stakeholder Engagement	Changed
4 Project execution	73	4.3 Direct and Manage Project Work	P 90	Unchanged
4 Project execution	73	8.2 Perform Quality Assurance	P 271 8.2 Manage Quality	Changed
4 Project execution	73	9.2 Acquire Project Team	P 328 9.3 Acquire Resources	Changed
4 Project execution	74	9.3 Develop Project Team	P 336 9.4 Develop Team	Changed
4 Project execution	74	9.4 Manage Project Team	P 345 9.5 Manage Team	Changed
4 Project execution	74	10.2 Manage Communications	P 379	Unchanged
4 Project execution	74	12.2 Conduct Procurements	P 482	Unchanged
4 Project execution	74	13.3 Manage Stakeholder engagement	P 523	Unchanged
4 Project execution	80	10.2 Plan Communications Note: Should have been recorded as 10.1	P 359 Plan Communications Management	Unchanged
4 Project execution	80	10.2 Manage Communications	P 379	Unchanged
4 Project execution	80	10.3 Control Communications	P 388 Monitor Communications	Changed
4 Project execution	80	13.3 Manage Stakeholder Engagement	P 523	Unchanged
5 Project monitoring and controlling	83	8.1 Plan quality Management	P 277	Unchanged
5 Project monitoring and controlling	85	10.1 Plan Procurement Management Note: should have been recorded as 12.1	P 466 12.1 Plan Procurement Management	Changed

(*Continued*)

Linton chapter	Page	PMBOK 5e references	PMBOK 6e	Comment
5 Project monitoring and controlling	86	4.3 Direct and Manage Project Work	P 80	Unchanged
5 Project monitoring and controlling	All Knowledge Areas	New Process	P 90 4.4 Manage Project Knowledge	Changed
5 Project monitoring and controlling	86	4.4 Monitor and Control Project Work	P 105 4.5 Monitor and Control Project Work	Changed
5 Project monitoring and controlling	86	4.5 Perform Integrated Change Control	P 113 4.6 Perform Integrated Change Control	Changed
5 Project monitoring and controlling	86	5.2 Collect Requirements	P 138	Unchanged
5 Project monitoring and controlling	93	4.4 Monitor and Control Project Work	P 105 4.5 Monitor and Control Project Work	Changed
5 Project monitoring and controlling	93	4.5 Perform Integrated Change Control	P 113 4.6 Perform Integrated Change Control	Changed
5 Project monitoring and controlling	93	5.5 Validate Scope	P163	Unchanged
5 Project monitoring and controlling	93	5.6 Control Scope	P 167	Unchanged
5 Project monitoring and controlling	93	6.6 Develop schedule	P 205 6.5 Develop schedule	Changed
5 Project monitoring and controlling	93	7.4 Control Costs	P 257	Unchanged
5 Project monitoring and controlling	93	8.3 Quality Control	P 298 8.3 Control Quality	Changed
5 Project monitoring and controlling	93	10.3 Control Communications	P 338 10.3 Monitor Communications	Changed
5 Project monitoring and controlling	93	11.6 Control Risks	P 453 11.7 Monitor Risks	Changed
5 Project monitoring and controlling	93	12.3 Control Procurements	P 492	Unchanged

(*Continued*)

Linton chapter	Page	PMBOK 5e references	PMBOK 6e	Comment
5 Project monitoring and controlling	93	13.4 Control Stakeholder Engagement	P 530 13.4 Monitor Stakeholder Engagement	Changed
5 Project monitoring and controlling	94	5.6 Control Scope	P 167	Unchanged
5 Project monitoring and controlling	94	6.6 Develop schedule	P 205 6.5 Develop schedule	Changed
5 Project monitoring and controlling	94	7.4 Control Costs	P 257	Unchanged
5 Project monitoring and controlling	94	8.3 Control Quality	P 298 8.3 Control Quality	Changed
5 Project monitoring and controlling	94	10.3 Control Communications	P 338 10.3 Monitor Communications	Changed
5 Project monitoring and controlling	94	11.6 Control Risks	P 453 11.7 Monitor Risks	Changed
5 Project monitoring and controlling	95	4.4 Monitor and Control Project Work	P 105 4.5 Monitor and Control Project Work	Changed
5 Project monitoring and controlling	95	5.6 control Scope	P 167	Unchanged
5 Project monitoring and controlling	97	8.3 Quality Control	P 298 8.3 Control Quality	Changed
5 Project monitoring and controlling	98	4.5 Perform Integrated Change Control Process	P 113 4.6 Perform Integrated Change Control Process	Changed
5 Project monitoring and controlling	100	4.5 Perform Integrated Change Control Process	P 113 4.6 Perform Integrated Change Control	Changed
5 Project monitoring and controlling	103	8.2 Perform Quality Assurance	P 288 8.2 Manage Quality	Changed
5 Project monitoring and controlling	104	11.2 Identify Risks	P 409	Unchanged
5 Project monitoring and controlling	104	11.5 Plan Risk Responses	P 437	Unchanged

(Continued)

Linton chapter	Page	PMBOK 5e references	PMBOK 6e	Comment
5 Project monitoring and controlling	104	4.5 Perform Integrated Change Control Process	P 113 4.6 Perform Integrated Change Control	Changed
5 Project monitoring and controlling	106	4.2 Develop the project management plan	82	Unchanged
5 Project monitoring and controlling	107	4.3 Direct and Manage project Work	P 90	Unchanged
5 Project monitoring and controlling	107	5.1 Plan Scope Management	P 134	Unchanged
5 Project monitoring and controlling	107	5.3 Define Scope	P 150	Unchanged
5 Project monitoring and controlling	107	6.1 Plan schedule management	179	Unchanged
5 Project monitoring and controlling	107	6.6 Develop schedule	P 205 6.5 Develop schedule	Changed
5 Project monitoring and controlling	107	7.1 Plan cost management	P 235	Unchanged
5 Project monitoring and controlling	107	7.3 Determine budget	P 248	Unchanged
5 Project monitoring and controlling	107	8.1 Plan Quality Management	P 277	Unchanged
5 Project monitoring and controlling	107	10.1 Plan communications management	P 366	Unchanged
5 Project monitoring and controlling	107	10.3 Control Communications	P 388 Monitor Communications	Changed
5 Project monitoring and controlling	108	11.2 Identify risks	P 409	Unchanged
5 Project monitoring and controlling	108	11.5 Plan risk responses	P 437	Unchanged
5 Project monitoring and controlling	108	12.1 Plan procurement management	P 466	Unchanged
5 Project monitoring and controlling	108	13.1 Identify Stakeholders	P 507	Unchanged
6 Project Closure	112	4.6 Close project or phase	P 121 4.7 Close project or phase	Changed

(Continued)

Linton chapter	Page	PMBOK 5e references	PMBOK 6e	Comment
6 Project Closure	112	12.4 Close Procurements	P 492 12.4 Close Procurements	Changed
6 Project Closure	127	4.5 Perform Integrated Change Control	P 113 4.6 Perform Integrated Change Control	Changed
6 Project Closure	128	8.3 Quality Control	P 298 8.3 Control Quality	Changed
6 Project Closure	128	Monitoring and Controlling Process Group does not have a process for Project Human Resource Management	Knowledge area now known as Project Resource Management and has on monitoring and controlling process. P 352 9.6 Control Resources	Changed
7 Project scope management	P133	5.1 Plan Scope Management	P 134	Unchanged
7 Project scope management	P133	5.2 Collect Requirements	P 138	Unchanged
7 Project scope management	P133	5.3 Define Scope	P 150	Unchanged
7 Project scope management	P134	5.4 Create Work Breakdown Structure (WBS)	156	Unchanged
7 Project scope management	P134	5.5 Validate Scope	P163	Unchanged
7 Project scope management	P134	5.6 Control Scope	P 167	Unchanged .
7 Project scope management	P155	8.2 Perform Quality Assurance	P 288 8.2 Manage Quality	Changed
7 Project scope management	P155	8.3 Quality Control	P 298 8.3 Control Quality	Changed
7 Project scope management	P155	4.5 Perform Integrated Change Control	P 113 4.6 Perform Integrated Change Control	Changed
7 Project scope management	P157	4.1 Develop project charter	75	Unchanged
7 Project scope management	P158	4.2 Develop the project management plan	82	Unchanged

(*Continued*)

Linton chapter	Page	PMBOK 5e references	PMBOK 6e	Comment
7 Project scope management	P158	5.3 Define Scope	P 150	Unchanged
7 Project scope management	P158	4.5 Perform Integrated Change Control	P 113 4.6 Perform Integrated Change Control	Changed
7 Project scope management	P158	5.6 Control Scope	P 167	Unchanged
7 Project scope management	P158	5.1 Plan Scope Management	P 134	Unchanged
7 Project scope management	P158	8.2 Perform Quality Assurance	P 288 8.2 Manage Quality	Changed
7 Project scope management	P158	5.5 Validate Scope	P163	Unchanged
7 Project scope management	P158	8.2 Perform Quality Assurance	P 288 8.2 Manage Quality	Changed
7 Project scope management	P158	5.5 Validate Scope	P163	Unchanged
7 Project scope management	P160	4.1 Develop project charter	75	Unchanged
7 Project scope management	P160	4.2 Develop the project management plan	82	Unchanged
7 Project scope management	P160	4.5 Perform Integrated Change Control	P 113 4.6 Perform Integrated Change Control	Changed
7 Project scope management	P160	8.2 Perform Quality Assurance	P 288 8.2 Manage Quality	Changed
7 Project scope management	P160	8.3 Quality Control	P 298 8.3 Control Quality	Changed
8 Project time management	P164	6.1 Plan schedule management	179	Unchanged
8 Project time management	P164	6.2 Define Activities	183	Unchanged
8 Project time management	P165	6.3 Sequence activities	187	Unchanged

(*Continued*)

Linton chapter	Page	PMBOK 5e references	PMBOK 6e	Comment
8 Project time management	P165	6.4 Estimate activity resources	P 320 9.2 Estimate Activity Resources	Changed
8 Project time management	P165	6.5 Estimate activity durations	P 195 6.4 Estimate Activity Durations	Changed
8 Project time management	P165	6.6 Develop schedule	P 205 6.5 Develop schedule	Changed
8 Project time management	P165	6.7 Control Schedule	P 222 6.6 Control Schedule	Changed
8 Project time management	P172	9.1 Plan human resource management	P 312 9.1 Plan resource management	Changed
8 Project time management	P172	9.2 Acquire Project Team	P 328 9.3 Acquire Resources	Changed
8 Project time management	P173	9.2 Acquire Project Team	P 328 9.3 Acquire Resources	Changed
8 Project time management	P188	4.5 Perform Integrated Change Control	P 113 4.6 Perform Integrated Change Control	Changed
8 Project time management	P194	4.1 Develop project charter	75	Unchanged
8 Project time management	P194	4.2 Develop the project management plan	82	Unchanged
8 Project time management	P194	4.5 Perform Integrated Change Control	P 113 4.6 Perform Integrated Change Control	Changed
8 Project time management	P194	5.1 Plan Scope Management	P 134	Unchanged
8 Project time management	P194	5.4 Create work Breakdown structure	156	Unchanged
8 Project time management	P194	8.2 Perform Quality Assurance	P 288 8.2 Manage Quality	Changed
8 Project time management	P194	8.3 Quality Control	P 298 8.3 Control Quality	Changed

Linton chapter	Page	PMBOK 5e references	PMBOK 6e	Comment
8 Project time management	P194	9.1 Plan human resource management	P 312 9.1 Plan resource management	Changed
8 Project time management	P195	9.2 Acquire Project Team	P 328 9.3 Acquire Resources	Changed
8 Project time management	P196	10.3 Control Communications	P 388 Monitor Communications	Changed
9 Project cost management	200	7.1 Plan cost management	P 235	Unchanged
9 Project cost management	200	7.2 Estimate costs	P 240	Unchanged
9 Project cost management	200	7.3 Determine budget	P 248	Unchanged
9 Project cost management	201	7.4 Control Costs	P 257	Unchanged
9 Project cost management	218	4.5 Perform Integrated Change Control	P 113 4.6 Perform Integrated Change Control	Changed
9 Project cost management	220	4.5 Perform Integrated Change Control	P 113 4.6 Perform Integrated Change Control	Changed
9 Project cost management	222	4.5 Perform Integrated Change Control	P 113 4.6 Perform Integrated Change Control	Changed
9 Project cost management	225	4.2 Develop the project management plan	82	Unchanged
9 Project cost management	225	4.5 Perform Integrated Change Control	P 113 4.6 Perform Integrated Change Control	Changed
9 Project cost management	226	5.1 Plan Scope Management	P 134	Unchanged
9 Project cost management	226	5.4 Create Work Breakdown Structure	156	Unchanged
9 Project cost management	226	5.6 Control Scope	P 167	Unchanged

(*Continued*)

Linton chapter	Page	PMBOK 5e references	PMBOK 6e	Comment
9 Project cost management	226	6.4 Estimate activity resources	P 320 9.2 Estimate Activity Resources	Changed
9 Project cost management	226	6.5 Estimate activity durations	P 195 6.4 Estimate Activity Durations	Changed
9 Project cost management	226	8.2 Perform Quality Assurance	P 271 8.2 Manage Quality	Changed
9 Project cost management	226	8.3 Quality Control	P 298 8.3 Control Quality	Changed
9 Project cost management	226	9.1 Plan human resource management	P 312 9.1 Plan resource management	Changed
9 Project cost management	226	9.2 Acquire Project Team	P 328 9.3 Acquire Resources	Changed
9 Project cost management	227	10.3 Control Communications	P 388 10.3 Monitor Communications	Changed
9 Project cost management	227	11.5 Plan risk responses	P 437	Unchanged
9 Project cost management	227	12.1 Plan procurement management	P 466	Unchanged
10 Project quality management	234	8.1 Plan quality Management	P 277	Unchanged
10 Project quality management	234	8.2 Perform Quality Assurance	P 271 8.2 Manage Quality	Changed
10 Project quality management	235	8.3 Control Quality	P 298 8.3 Control Quality	Changed
10 Project quality management	239	4.5 Perform Integrated Change Control	P 113 4.6 Perform Integrated Change Control	Changed
10 Project quality management	253	4.2 Develop the project management plan	82	Unchanged
10 Project quality management	253	5.2 Collect Requirements	P 138	Unchanged
10 Project quality management	254	5.3 Define Scope	P 150	Unchanged

(*Continued*)

Linton chapter	Page	PMBOK 5e references	PMBOK 6e	Comment
10 Project quality management	254	6.2 Define Activities	183	Unchanged
10 Project quality management	254	6.6 Develop schedule	P 205 6.5 Develop schedule	Changed
11 Project human resource management	259	9.1 Plan human Resource Management	P 312 9.1 Plan Resource Management	Changed
11 Project human resource management	259	9.2 Acquire Project Team	P 328 9.3 Acquire Resources	Changed
11 Project human resource management	259	6.4 Estimate activity resources	P 320 9.2 Estimate Activity Resources	Changed
11 Project human resource management	259	6.5 Estimate activity durations	P 195 6.4 Estimate Activity Durations	Changed
11 Project human resource management	260	9.3 Develop Project Team	P 336 9.4 Develop Team	Changed
11 Project human resource management	260	9.4 Manage Project Team	P 345 9.5 Manage Team	Changed
11 Project human resource management	275	4.5 Perform Integrated Change Control	P 113 4.6 Perform Integrated Change Control	Changed
11 Project human resource management	277	9.1 Plan human Resource Management	P 312 9.1 Plan Resource Management	Changed
11 Project human resource management	277	6.4 Estimate activity resources	P 320 9.2 Estimate Activity Resources	Changed
11 Project human resource management	291	4.3 Direct and Manage Project Work	P 90	Unchanged
11 Project human resource management	291	4.4 Monitor and Control Project Work	P 105 4.5 Monitor and Control Project Work	Changed

(Continued)

Linton chapter	Page	PMBOK 5e references	PMBOK 6e	Comment
11 Project human resource management	291	4.5 Perform Integrated Change Control	P 113 4.6 Perform Integrated Change Control	Changed
11 Project human resource management	291	6.4 Estimate activity resources	P 320 9.2 Estimate Activity Resources	Changed
11 Project human resource management	291	6.5 Estimate activity durations	P 195 6.4 Estimate Activity Durations	Changed
11 Project human resource management	291	7.2 Estimate costs	P 240	Unchanged
11 Project human resource management	291	10.2 Manage Communications	P 379	Unchanged
11 Project human resource management	292	10.3 Control Communications	P 388 10.3 Monitor Communications	Changed
11 Project human resource management	292	11.2 Identify risks	P 409	Unchanged
12 Project communications management	298	10.1 Plan communications management	P 366	Unchanged
12 Project communications management	298	10.2 Manage Communications	P 379	Unchanged
12 Project communications management	298	10.3 Control Communications	P 388 10.3 Monitor Communications	Changed
12 Project communications management	310	13.1 Identify Stakeholders	P 507	Unchanged
12 Project communications management	310	13.2 Plan stakeholder management	P 516 13.2 Plan Stakeholder Engagement	Changed
12 Project communications management	323	4.2 Develop the project management plan	82	Unchanged

(*Continued*)

Linton chapter	Page	PMBOK 5e references	PMBOK 6e	Comment
12 Project communications management	323	4.3 Direct and Manage Project Work	P 90	Unchanged
12 Project communications management	323	4.4 Monitor and Control Project Work	P 105 4.5 Monitor and Control Project Work	Changed
12 Project communications management	324	4.5 Perform Integrated Change Control	P 113 4.6 Perform Integrated Change Control	Changed
12 Project communications management	324	9.4 Manage Project Team	P 345 9.5 Manage Team	Changed
12 Project communications management	324	13.1 Identify Stakeholders	P 507	Unchanged
12 Project communications management	324	13.2 Plan stakeholder management	P 516 13.2 Plan Stakeholder Engagement	Changed
12 Project communications management	324	13.3 Manage Stakeholder engagement	P 523	Unchanged
13 Project risk management	331	11.1 Plan risk management	P 401	Unchanged
13 Project risk management	331	11.2 Identify risks	P 409	Unchanged
13 Project risk management	331	11.3 Perform qualitative risk analysis	P 419	Unchanged
13 Project risk management	331	11.4 Perform quantitative risk analysis	P 428	Unchanged
13 Project risk management	331	11.5 Plan risk responses	P 437	Unchanged
13 Project risk management	331	11.6 Control Risks	P 453 11.7 Monitor Risks	Changed
13 Project risk management	353	11.2 Identify risks	P 409	Unchanged
13 Project risk management	353	11.5 Plan risk responses	P 437	Unchanged

(*Continued*)

Linton chapter	Page	PMBOK 5e references	PMBOK 6e	Comment
13 Project risk management	353	4.5 Perform Integrated Change Control	P 113 4.6 Perform Integrated Change Control	Changed
13 Project risk management	356	4.4 Monitor and Control Project Work	P 105 4.5 Monitor and Control Project Work	Changed
13 Project risk management	356	4.5 Perform Integrated Change Control	P 113 4.6 Perform Integrated Change Control	Changed
13 Project risk management	356	5.5 Validate Scope	P163	Unchanged
13 Project risk management	356	5.6 Control Scope	P 167	Unchanged
13 Project risk management	356	6.7 Control Schedule	P 222 6.6 Control Schedule	Changed
13 Project risk management	356	7.4 Control Costs	P 257	Unchanged
13 Project risk management	356	10.3 Control Communications	P 388 10.3 Monitor Communications	Changed
14 Project procurement management	362	12.1 Plan procurement management	P 466	Unchanged
14 Project procurement management	362	12.2 Conduct Procurements	P 482	Unchanged
14 Project procurement management	363	12.3 Control Procurements	P 492	Unchanged
14 Project procurement management	363	12.4 Close Procurements	P 492 12.4 Close Procurements	Changed
14 Project procurement management	379	4.1 Develop project charter	75	Unchanged
14 Project procurement management	379	4.2 Develop the project management plan	82	Unchanged

(*Continued*)

Linton chapter	Page	PMBOK 5e references	PMBOK 6e	Comment
14 Project procurement management	379	4.5 Perform Integrated Change Control	P 113 4.6 Perform Integrated Change Control	Changed
14 Project procurement management	379	6.4 Estimate activity resources	P 320 9.2 Estimate Activity Resources	Changed
14 Project procurement management	379	6.5 Estimate activity durations	P 195 6.4 Estimate Activity Durations	Changed
14 Project procurement management	380	6.6 Develop schedule	P 205 6.5 Develop schedule	Changed
14 Project procurement management	380	7.2 Estimate costs	P 240	Unchanged
14 Project procurement management	380	9.2 Acquire Project Team	P 328 9.3 Acquire Resources	Changed
14 Project procurement management	380	9.3 Develop Project Team	P 336 9.4 Develop Team	Changed
14 Project procurement management	380	11.2 Identify risks	P 409	Unchanged
14 Project procurement management	380	13.1 Identify Stakeholders	P 507	Unchanged
15 Project stakeholder management	387	13.1 Identify Stakeholders	P 507	Unchanged
15 Project stakeholder management	387	13.2 Plan stakeholder management	P 516 13.2 Plan Stakeholder Engagement	Changed
15 Project stakeholder management	387	13.3 Manage Stakeholder engagement	P 523	Unchanged
15 Project stakeholder management	387	13.4 Control Stakeholder Engagement	P 530 13.4 Monitor Stakeholder Engagement	Changed

(Continued)

Linton chapter	Page	PMBOK 5e references	PMBOK 6e	Comment
15 Project stakeholder management	404	13.2 Plan stakeholder management	P 516 13.2 Plan Stakeholder Engagement	Changed
15 Project stakeholder management	404	10.1 Plan communications management	10.1 Plan communications management	10.1 Plan communications management
15 Project stakeholder management	417	4.1 Develop project charter	75	Unchanged
15 Project stakeholder management	417	4.2 Develop the project management plan	82	Unchanged
15 Project stakeholder management	417	4.3 Direct and Manage project Work	P 90	Unchanged
15 Project stakeholder management	417	4.4 Monitor and Control Project Work	P 105 4.5 Monitor and Control Project Work	Changed
15 Project stakeholder management	417	4.5 Perform Integrated Change Control	P 113 4.6 Perform Integrated Change Control	Changed
15 Project stakeholder management	417	5.2 Collect Requirements	P 138	Unchanged
15 Project stakeholder management	417	8.1 Plan quality Management	P 277	Unchanged
15 Project stakeholder management	417	9.4 Manage Project Team	P 345 9.5 Manage Team	Changed
15 Project stakeholder management	417	10.1 Plan communications management	P 366	Unchanged
15 Project stakeholder management	417	11.1 Plan risk management	P 401	Unchanged
15 Project stakeholder management	417	11.2 Identify risks	P 409	Unchanged

(*Continued*)

Linton chapter	Page	PMBOK 5e references	PMBOK 6e	Comment
15 Project stakeholder management	417	12.1 Plan procurement management	P 466	Unchanged
16 Project integration management	427	4.1 Develop project charter	75	Unchanged
16 Project integration management	427	4.2 Develop the project management plan	82	Unchanged
16 Project integration management	428	4.3 Direct and Manage Project Work	P 90	Unchanged
16 Project integration management	428	4.4 Monitor and Control Project Work	P 105 4.5 Monitor and Control Project Work	Changed
16 Project integration management	428	4.5 Perform Integrated Change Control	P 113 4.6 Perform Integrated Change Control	Changed
16 Project integration management	429	4.6 Close project or phase	P 121 4.7 Close project or phase	Changed
16 Project integration management	432	4.2 Develop the project management plan	82	Unchanged
16 Project integration management	439	4.5 Perform Integrated Change Control	P 113 4.6 Perform Integrated Change Control	Changed
16 Project integration management	439	5.6 Control Scope	P 167	Unchanged
16 Project integration management	439	8.2 Perform Quality Assurance	P 271 8.2 Manage Quality	Changed
16 Project integration management	439	8.3 Control Quality	P 298 8.3 Control Quality	Changed
16 Project integration management	442	4.4 Monitor and Control Project Work	P 105 4.5 Monitor and Control Project Work	Changed
16 Project integration management	442	5.6 Control Scope	P 167	Unchanged
16 Project integration management	446	4.6 Close project or phase	P 121 4.7 Close project or phase	Changed
16 Project integration management	446	12.4 Close Procurements	P 492 12.4 Close Procurements	Changed
16 Project integration management	446	5.6 Control Scope	P 167	Unchanged

Project management lifecycle

PART OVERVIEW

RELATIONSHIP WITH THE PMBOK® GUIDE

Part 1 of this text follows the PMBOK® Guide project management lifecycle. The PMBOK® Guide contains process groups which align to each of the phases within the standard project management lifecycle. I like to deviate slightly from the standard and include an additional process group for directing and managing the project. The figure below shows my preferred adaptation to the standard PMBOK® Guide lifecycle.

I am a keen advocate of the use of the PMBOK® Guide as the project management standard that underpins any particular methodology or framework that an organisation wishes to develop or adopt.

See PMBOK® Guide Figure 0-1 Project management process groups

FIGURE 0.1 PROJECT MANAGEMENT LIFECYCLE

Monitor and control

Initiation › Planning › Execution › Close ›

Direct and manage

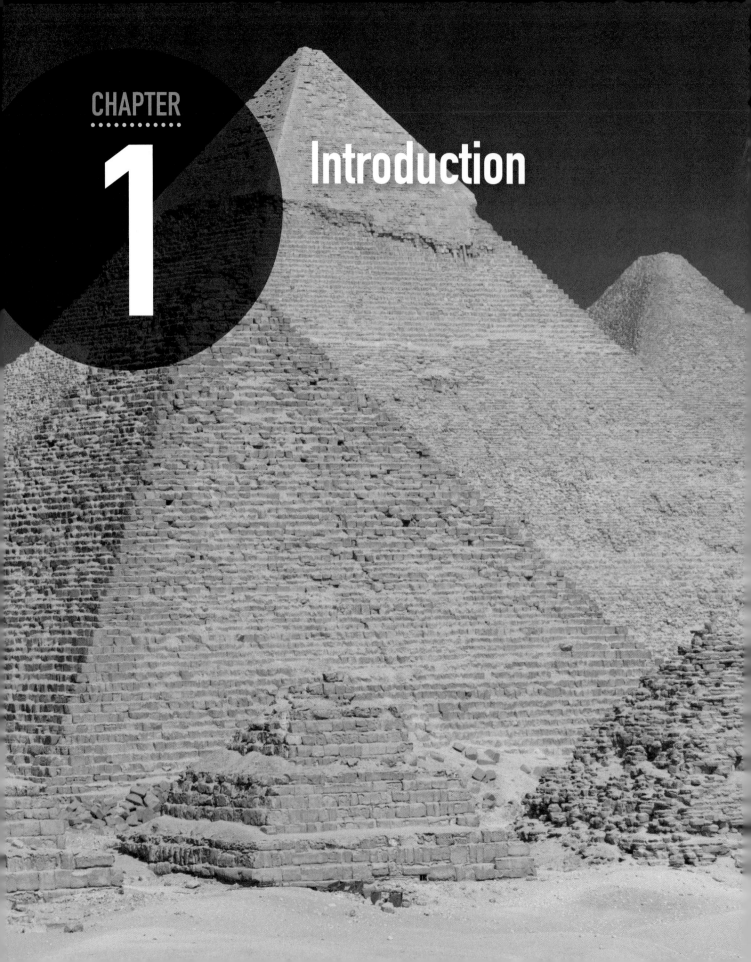

CHAPTER
1

Introduction

What is a project?

All texts on project management usually start with the definition of a project. This seems unbelievable, as the word *project* is so commonly used that it would be reasonable to assume that businesspeople would have a common definition and, therefore, an understanding of this basic concept. They do not. Businesspeople often confuse projects with operational work, processes or activities.

So, in keeping with tradition and according to the Project Management Body of Knowledge (PMBOK® Guide), a project is 'a temporary endeavour undertaken to create a unique product, service or result' (PMI, 2013, p. 553).

To facilitate a deeper understanding of this basic concept, characteristics of projects include:
- a definite beginning and end
- bringing about some form of changed state
- a scope, including all deliverables that must be executed in order to meet the project objectives
- an end result which is often permanent or ongoing.

Projects can create and deliver products, services, capabilities or other defined outcomes. These outputs can be as tangible as a new building or as intangible as a process improvement or change in organisational culture.

What is project management?

Project management is both a profession and a set of tools and techniques that can be applied to the delivery of defined outcomes.

Once again, according to the PMBOK® Guide, *project management* is 'the application of knowledge, skills, tools and techniques to project activities to meet the project requirements' (PMI, 2013, p. 554).

The role of the project manager

The project manager is the person responsible for making sure the project objectives are achieved. Managing projects typically involves the following activities:
- defining the project scope, agreeing objectives and identifying requirements
- undertaking detailed planning in order to deliver the requirements and outcomes
- directing and managing project resources (people, equipment, funds)
- monitoring progress against plans and taking corrective action as required
- applying the 10 key knowledge areas defined in the PMBOK® Guide
- balancing competing project constraints and managing variations during execution

- facilitating decision making, negotiation and conflict resolution
- ensuring the project is completed on time and within the allocated budget
- managing stakeholder expectations to ensure required outcomes are understood and delivered.

Project managers are required to achieve competency in the application of the 10 key knowledge areas, as defined by the PMBOK® Guide:

1 Project Integration Management
2 Project Scope Management
3 Project Time Management
4 Project Cost Management
5 Project Quality Management
6 Project Human Resource Management
7 Project Communications Management
8 Project Risk Management
9 Project Procurement Management
10 Project Stakeholder Management.

In addition to technical expertise, the most successful project managers also exhibit higher-order skills in the following related areas:

- people management and team building
- leadership and motivation
- communication and influencing
- decision making and negotiation
- political and cultural awareness
- change management
- emotional intelligence and resilience
- prioritisation.

Several professional bodies have developed excellent competency frameworks for the role of project manager, as well as other roles within the job family, such as project coordinator and program director.

A set of the national competency standards for project management are included on the companion website to this book. These have been developed by the Australian Institute of Project Management and map to the Certificate IV and Diploma of Project Management.

PROJECT MANAGEMENT MASTERY

CHANGE MANAGEMENT

Projects always create change and change is usually always accompanied by conflict. The most successful project managers incorporate change management into their practices, as the success of a project is enhanced when key stakeholders are supportive of the resulting changes. I recommend that experienced project managers enhance their skills by undertaking formal change management education or training.

There is little point adding to your skill set in the early stages of your project management career as it will potentially confuse or overwhelm you, making it difficult to incorporate the new skills and thereby diminish your existing project management skills. I recommend waiting until you have at least five years of project management experience before expanding your knowledge into related disciplines.

For related information and readings please refer to the following sources:

- http://www.beinghuman.com.au – information and training in Prosci's change management framework
- http://www.change-management-institute.com – international change management organisation (originating in Australia) that promotes change management accreditation and processes
- http://www.kotterinternational.com – John Kotter is considered one of the founders of the field of change management
- *The theory and practice of change management*, 3rd edition by John Hayes (see references at the end of the chapter).

PROJECT MANAGEMENT MASTERY

ADAPTABILITY

One of the first things I emphasise to my students is the need to be flexible and to be willing to adapt your preferred project management practices to suit the particular context of your project. The context of a project includes many factors, such as the characteristics of the organisation in which you are delivering the project, especially in terms of culture and project management maturity levels; the style, experience and preferences of the project sponsor and key stakeholders; the organisation's industry can also influence the expected project management approaches; and, lastly, the influences arising from the previous training and experiences of the project manager.

Project managers need to understand the context of each project in order to adapt their approach to each circumstance; this in turn will increase the chances of success for each project. If we automatically execute our projects using the same practices and style regardless of the context, then we will often fail.

The following example will assist with your understanding of this important point.

REAL WORLD EXPERIENCE

PROFESSIONAL SERVICES INDUSTRY

While establishing the project management office (PMO) and project delivery framework for a leading Australian law firm, I confirmed my belief that emerging project managers require coaching in order to adapt project management practices to suit each project. Without guidance, people exercising formal project management practices for the first time will slavishly adhere to the prescribed project management methodology and attempt to execute all the defined deliverables, even if they have no relevance to the scope of the particular project.

As part of the establishment of a large IT program, I designed and delivered tailored training for all the 'workstream leaders' – a term adopted for the mid-level IT managers who were taking on new project management responsibilities, but only on a part-time basis as they still had their pre-existing roles to fulfil. This program was the first to completely adopt the new project methodology that my PMO team had been working on for several months. About a month after conducting the first training workshop, when all the IT workstream leaders were developing their detailed planning and scoping deliverables, we had a mini-revolution. They threw their hands in the air in frustration and refused to go on as they felt they were drowning in unnecessary project management administration.

I conducted one-on-one sessions with each of the workstream leaders in order to understand their frustration and to determine a resolution so that the program could continue. It became immediately apparent that they had assumed that each workstream, no matter how small, would need to complete each and every project management deliverable. This was puzzling to me as the methodology clearly indicated the minimum mandatory deliverables and these were only six out of the potential full suite of over 50 deliverables. I then sat down with each of them and we agreed which deliverables would be required and we established regular reassessment check-in points. Naturally, the larger and more complex workstreams required the majority of deliverables, while the smaller and less risky workstreams were pared back to the basics.

This clearly emphasised to me the need to coach emergent project managers in the use and application of project management methodologies, as new project managers can often lack the experience to confidently exercise their judgement.

I also observed the reverse situation on another project that was being run by the Library Team Leader. His natural style was to cut corners and look for the easy way out, so he was attempting to execute a tender without having first completed his scoping and requirements gathering. I worked with him and his upline manager to reintroduce mandatory deliverables into his project plan. This extended the delivery timeframe of the project but greatly reduced the execution risk, and enabled a speedy approval process for the final request for tender that was issued.

The role of the project sponsor

The project sponsor becomes very important during the development of project scope and has a key role to play during project execution. They are the person for whom the project is being undertaken and they will directly benefit from the deliverables and outcomes of the project. Often they are a senior manager, customer or external client.

The relationship between the project manager and the project sponsor is the most critical relationship within the project structure. Any difficulties within this relationship will erode the project manager's ability to deliver outcomes.

Establishing ground rules and expectations with the project sponsor is a great way to start, as some sponsors are too hands-off and others are too hands-on. Always ensure that the sponsor is involved in the following activities and conversations.

What does the project manager need from the project sponsor?

- Direction on the project objectives and success criteria.
- Support with critical decision making.
- Assistance in the management of key stakeholders.
- Guidance on the resolution of risks and issues.
- Contribution to the management of scope and changes to scope.

What does the project sponsor expect from the project manager?

- Project management competency.
- Involvement in key decision making.
- Regular updates on progress, risks and issues.
- Escalation of risks and issues that will impact project outcomes.
- Successful project delivery.

Evolution of the project management profession

The field of project management is in transition between a set of skills and a recognised profession. I describe project management as both a profession *and* a set of processes and techniques that can be applied in the execution of a project. My summary of the past, present and future for the project management profession is shown below in Table 1.1.

TABLE 1.1 THE PROJECT MANAGEMENT PROFESSION

Past	Present	Future
» Poor understanding of the key knowledge areas and competencies » Thought anyone who was highly organised could be a project manager » Emerging professional bodies » No formal standards » Anyone could call themselves a project manager	» Better understanding of the key knowledge areas and competencies » Specific skills and experience expected of project managers » Strong professional bodies » Emerging standards and competencies » Formal certification and registration of project managers » Can still be a project manager without certification	» Formal acceptance of the key knowledge areas and competencies » Specific skills, experience, certification and professional membership expected » Formal recognition of standards and competencies » Compulsory certification and continuing professional development » Unable to be a project manager without certification

Source: The Northern Sydney Institute, Part of TAFE NSW.

No-one should be awarded the title of Project Manager unless they hold professional certification with one of the major professional bodies. This practice is becoming more prevalent in the US, which is home to the Project Management Institute (PMI). The PMI has a very strong professional certification program and is the largest professional project management body with more than 700 000 members and 184 chapters worldwide.

Similar to the accounting profession, there are several professional bodies in the project management industry. In addition to the PMI, the other major body in Australia is the Australian Institute of Project Management (AIPM). The AIPM was accepted as a member of the International Project Management Association (IPMA) in September 2009. The IPMA was founded in 1965 and is the world's oldest project management association.

Project management cannot be considered a true profession until certification is required in order to be a project manager, just as medical doctors must be licensed and solicitors must be certified in order to practise.

Methodologies versus standards

Students are always asking for an explanation of the differences between a standard and a methodology. This question mainly arises when you have a mix of project management experience, with some people having undertaken Prince2 training and others having an awareness of the PMBOK® Guide.

A *methodology* is:

> a set or system of methods, principles, and rules for regulating a given discipline, as in the arts or sciences.

Source: http://www.dictionary.com.

A *standard* is:

> something considered by an authority or by general consent as a basis of comparison; an approved model.

Source: http://www.dictionary.com.

REAL WORLD EXPERIENCE

ICE-CREAMS AND METHODOLOGY

My answer to the question regarding the differences between methodologies and standards is best described by using an analogy. The PMBOK® Guide is a standard and is equivalent to vanilla ice-cream. Prince2 is a methodology; it is still ice-cream but just a different flavour. You can use the PMBOK® Guide to underpin your project management practices no matter what particular methodology (or flavour) you are being asked to apply.

The most important thing to learn from the above distinction is that it is important to be flexible in both the application of the PMBOK® Guide as the standard for project management and in the application of your preferred methodology. There is no point having a debate about the benefits of one methodology over another, or of a standard over a methodology. Be prepared to adopt and adapt components from all of these to tailor your project management practices to deliver the best outcomes for each project in every context.

Flexibility and standardisation to reduce conflict

At first these two concepts (flexibility and standardisation) may appear mutually exclusive. In the early stages of project establishment they are indeed critical and operate together to reduce conflict within the project team and among key stakeholders.

The concept of flexibility is illustrated in the previous real world examples. It is important to understand the context and specific characteristics of your project in order to determine the ideal approach and the specific deliverables that will be required in order to achieve the project objectives.

The concept of standardisation is best illustrated by another example. This particular example also reinforces the need for personal flexibility.

REAL WORLD EXPERIENCE

NOT FOR PROFIT

Several years ago I took a career break and spent six months working with a not-for-profit medical research organisation to establish a program to design and deliver a new business model for their administrative and finance functions. This involved a new structure, new business processes and new systems capability. I was able to establish the project and see it through to the tender stage.

The first task was to assemble a small project team of project managers and business analysts who could execute the project. I quickly selected two project managers and two business analysts with backgrounds in finance and administration, and client relationship management, as these were the primary areas of focus for the project. As is usual in the *forming* and *storming* phases of team development, there was a certain degree of professional conflict and confusion over different terminology. I therefore established the definition of the specific deliverables for our project as quickly as possible so that the team could commence delivery.

Unfortunately, one of the analysts was not willing to accept the standard definitions and was wasting time arguing with other team members on the difference between a business process and a process map, and a business requirement versus a business specification. This went on too long and was eroding both productivity and morale. Even more troubling was his inability to align with the overall objectives of the project.

It had been established with the project sponsor and steering committee that the ideal approach for the provision of the required systems was to tender for software packages, and this was made clear to the new team members during recruitment. Even after the first month, this analyst was still advocating bespoke software development and refused to support the chosen approach of selecting and implementing packages. Luckily, he was a contractor and we were able to terminate his contract immediately so as to remove the distraction. This was an extreme case of an individual's inability to be flexible undermining the performance of the entire project team.

CHAPTER SUMMARY

» Project management is both a profession and a set of tools and techniques that can be applied to the delivery of defined outcomes.

» A project is 'a temporary endeavour undertaken to create a unique product, service or result'.

» The project manager is the person responsible for achieving the project objectives. They require competency in the application of the 10 key knowledge areas as defined by the PMBOK® Guide, as well as excellent skills in a range of modalities, including leadership, people management and communication.

» The project sponsor is the person for whom the project is being undertaken and they will directly benefit from the deliverables and outcomes of the project.

» The relationship between the project manager and the project sponsor is the most critical relationship within the project structure. Any difficulties within this relationship will erode the project manager's ability to deliver outcomes.

» The field of project management is in transition between a set of skills and a recognised profession.

» Projects always create change and change is usually always accompanied by conflict. The most successful project managers incorporate change management into their practices.

» The PMBOK® Guide is a standard while Prince2 is a methodology. You can use the PMBOK® Guide to underpin your project management practices no matter what particular methodology you are being asked to apply.

» Project managers need to be flexible in the early stages of project establishment and need to also quickly establish standard project management practices and terms in order to reduce conflict within the project team and among key stakeholders.

ONLINE RESOURCES

Visit the online companion website at http://www.cengagebrain.com to link to important additional resources, including templates, real-world case studies, revision quizzes and additional study material.

FURTHER READING AND REFERENCES

Hayes, J. (2010). *The theory and practice of change management* (3rd ed.). New York, NY: Palgrave Macmillan.

Project Management Institute (PMI). (2011). *2011 Annual report: Delivering value*, available at http://www.pmi.org/About-Us/About-Us-Annual-Report.aspx

Project Management Institute (PMI). (2013). *A guide to the Project Management Body of Knowledge* (PMBoK® Guide) (5th ed.). Newtown Square, PA: author.

Project initiation

1 learn about the specific processes undertaken by project managers during the initiation phase of a project

2 learn about the major project management deliverable that is produced during the initiation phase – the project charter

3 become familiar with the key components of the project charter

4 develop an understanding of the importance of determining the project objectives and high-level scope

5 consider the importance of key concepts, such as SMART objectives, project success criteria, scope inclusions and exclusions, and business cases

6 learn about the importance of identifying project stakeholders and understanding their expectations

7 understand the importance of the project kick-off meeting.

Context

Project initiation is generally the shortest phase of the project management lifecycle. However, it is the most important as the foundation that is established can set your project up for success or failure right from the outset.

FIGURE 2.1 PROJECT INITIATION

PMBOK® Guide processes for project initiation

The Project Management Body of Knowledge (PMBOK® Guide) has only two processes identified for project initiation:

4.1   Develop project charter

13.1   Identify stakeholders.

This is a very simplistic view of project initiation. It assumes that no project team members, apart from the project manager, have commenced the project. However, in many project-based organisations, or where there is a project management office (PMO), project team members have often already been assigned at this stage. If so, then a competent project manager will commence some of the human resource management processes from the planning and execution phases early. Activities such as joint planning workshops, project scoping and objective setting, team building and project kick-off meetings are, therefore, highly recommended.

See PMBOK® Guide Table Project management process groups and knowledge area mapping

Developing the project charter

First, it is important to recognise that the project charter is not always called the project charter. This can be a major source of confusion for inexperienced project managers and sponsors, and can create disharmony within the project team. Some common alternative terms for this primary initiation document are project brief, concept paper, high-level plan and statement of work. The context for your project, based on the industry or the particular methodology, will often determine the specific term that is used for the project charter.

The Northern Sydney Institute (NSI) Online Certificate IV and Diploma of Project Management defines this process as:

See PMBOK®
Guide Figure 4-2
Develop project
charter: inputs,
tools and
techniques, and
outputs

developing a document that formally defines and authorises a project by documenting the initial requirements that will satisfy the needs of the project sponsor and key stakeholder. The project charter establishes a partnership between the project sponsor, or client, and the project manager by establishing the high-level project scope and critical success factors for the project.

Source: The Northern Sydney Institute, Part of TAFE NSW.

Note: this is the first process within the Project Integration Management key knowledge area.

Contents of the project charter

Please visit www.
cengagebrain.com
to see a project
charter template

The specific content of the project charter varies across methodologies, industries and templates. Many templates can be found online and this is a good place to start if you don't have a standard template.

Inexperienced project managers will benefit from reviewing several examples as previous content is often a useful guide.

The common contents of a project charter are:

- project background
- project description
- project purpose or justification
- project objectives
- high-level scope, including what's in and out of scope
- assumptions, dependencies, constraints
- unresolved issues
- high-level risks or overall risk analysis
- preferred timeframe
- estimated high-level budget
- high-level project structure.

THE CASE FOR NOT HAVING A BUSINESS CASE

It is interesting to note that the business case has been identified as a common input when developing a project charter.

REAL-WORLD EXPERIENCE

BUSINESS CASES

My students always ask about the need for business cases, and it is a much debated deliverable. Having seen far too much time wasted in the production of unachievable business cases, I strongly believe that business cases should generally be avoided.

PROJECT MANAGEMENT MASTERY

WHEN IS A BUSINESS CASE USEFUL?

There *are* specific circumstances in project environments when business cases are extremely useful. High-level business cases are often used by large organisations for project prioritisation when there are lots of projects and a finite pool of funding. They can also be useful for decision making in the following circumstances.

FIGURE 2.2 NEW PRODUCT DEVELOPMENT PROCESS

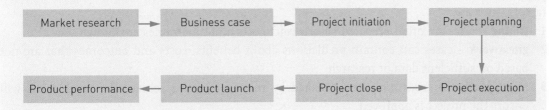

FIGURE 2.3 PROJECT BENEFITS UNCLEAR

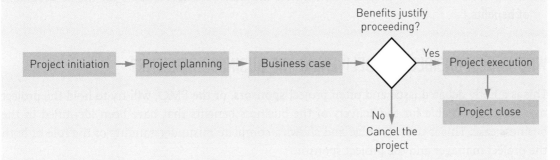

FIGURE 2.4 PROJECT REQUIREMENTS AND DELIVERY OPTIONS UNCLEAR

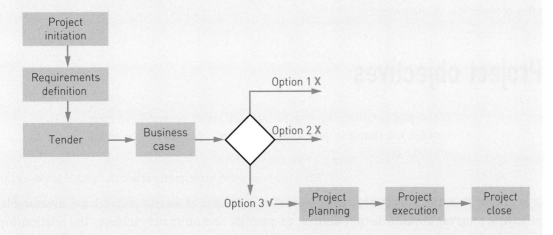

Unfortunately, I have seen many organisations enforce business cases for all projects because of the belief that these will encourage improved project delivery. Some projects are

just not negotiable, so why waste time preparing business cases (which very often contain guesses for the costs and benefits)? There is no point spending valuable time preparing business cases for projects that are:

- critical to the achievement of strategic objectives
- mandated due to regulatory changes
- required due to expiring support for a critical software application.

One major issue with business cases is that they can be influenced by many subjective factors, such as:

1 **timing** – cases are often prepared before exact costs and timeframes are known
2 **guesswork** – cases can contain predictions about benefits, costs and outcomes that are not based on sufficient data or research
3 **manipulation** – cases are often tweaked by management to achieve the results that will ensure the project is approved
4 **unclear accountability** – cases are often prepared by senior management who are then not directly involved in the project's results, nor are they held accountable for the achievement of benefits.

WHO IS RESPONSIBLE FOR DELIVERING THE BUSINESS BENEFITS?

This is a hotly debated issue and often project sponsors, or the PMO, will try to hold the project manager accountable for the delivery of the business benefits that have been identified in the business case. This is unreasonable and shows a complete misunderstanding of the role of both the project manager and the project sponsor.

Primarily, project managers need to deliver the project according to the agreed objectives and success criteria, while project sponsors need to ensure that on-going benefits are achieved after completion of the project.

Project objectives

> Many people fail in life, not for lack of ability or brains or even courage, but simply because they have never organised their energies around a goal.
>
> Elbert Hubbard, writer, artist, publisher and philosopher (1856–1915).

It is critical that the project objectives (sometimes known as *success criteria*) are measurable, otherwise progress towards them is difficult to quantify and ultimately achieve. The relationship between the project manager and the project sponsor can become strained if there is a misunderstanding about a project objective or objectives.

REAL-WORLD EXPERIENCE

SMART PREFERENCES

The **SMART framework** is considered the standard for the definition of measurable objectives. Its origins have been lost, but it is still the preferred framework of most large organisations for the setting of both project and personal performance goals. There are many slightly different interpretations of the framework and my preference is shown below.

- *Specific* – well defined objectives, clear to anyone who has a basic knowledge of the project.
- *Measurable* – for example: percentage reduction in defects, perceptions about ease of use, faster performance, or some form of monetary target.
- *Agreed* – by both the project manager and the project sponsor.
- *Realistic* – not fabricated to improve a business case; objectives that can be achieved within the expertise, knowledge, timeframe and resources of the project.
- *Timeframe* – normally upon delivery of the project or within a specified timeframe after completion; this should be challenging but not impossible.

Examples of SMART objectives

After 30 years in practice, I am still surprised by how difficult it is for many project managers and sponsors to clearly define the SMART objectives for the project. The best way for project managers to improve in this area is to consider examples of both well-constructed objectives and poorly constructed objectives.

TABLE 2.1 GOOD AND BAD PROJECT OBJECTIVES

Poor project objectives	Good project objectives
Reduce home loan approval timeframes by 50%	Design and implement process changes and system enhancements to enable home loan processing staff to reduce average home loan approval timeframes by 50%
Reduce IT infrastructure costs by 10% by establishing a centralised data centre	Consolidate all existing data centres into a new centralised data centre and ensure that new contracts achieve a 10% reduction in overall costs without compromising existing services
Reduce hard copy storage by 30% for head office by moving to a new building	Design and deliver processes and storage reduction activities to enable a 30% reduction in hard copy storage prior to moving to the new premises in December 2013
Reduce errors to an acceptable level in the rolled steel production process	Design and implement improved processes for the production of rolled steel to reduce error rates to less than 1 per 1 million metres within the four major production cycles

Poor project objectives	Good project objectives
Implement a new payroll system to increase employee satisfaction	Understand the root cause of employee dissatisfaction with payroll processes; design and implement new payroll processes to resolve the major sources of employee dissatisfaction
	Select and implement a new payroll system based on employee requirements that addresses the primary sources of employee dissatisfaction
Sell as many new snowmobiles as possible	Design and implement new marketing and sales processes and systems in order to increase sales of snowmobiles by 8% every year

PROJECT MANAGEMENT MASTERY

CLARIFYING QUESTIONS

A set of clarifying questions that can be used in conversations about the project objectives with project sponsors is very useful. These are also valuable when reviewing and refining the project objectives.

TABLE 2.2 SMART CLARIFYING QUESTIONS

SMART framework element	Clarifying questions
Specific	» Is the objective precise and well defined? » Is it clear for the project manager, project sponsor, project team and key stakeholders? » Can everyone understand it? Have they all understood it the same way?
Measurable	» How will the project manager and project team know they have achieved the objective? » What evidence is required to determine successful completion? » How will success be judged and by whom?
Agreed	» Is it within the capabilities of the project manager and project team? » Are the project manager, project sponsor and key stakeholders in agreement with the objective?
Realistic	» Are there sufficient resources and time to achieve the objective? » Is it generally feasible? Can it be done at all? » Is the objective aligned to the overall organisational goals?

SMART framework element	Clarifying questions
Timeframe	» Is there a deadline? Is the deadline feasible given the constraints and overall context? » Is there a preferred completion timeframe? » Is it the best time to do this work? Would another time of the year/month be more feasible?

Project success criteria

Defining project success seems simple; it is about delivering on time and on budget. These are important success criteria, but in most cases there are additional criteria that are of equal, or higher, importance to the project sponsor. It is often more important that the project deliver tangible business results, as defined by the project objectives.

Project success occurs when the:

- expectations of the project sponsor or client are met
- agreed project objectives have been met
- business outcomes have been realised
- timeframe and budget have been delivered
- quality and scope requirements have been delivered.

Project trade-offs and the triple constraint

During project initiation, it is useful to introduce the concept of the triple constraint, otherwise known as project trade-offs. Scope is related to time, cost and quality and this relationship is often referred to as the 'triple constraint'. Scope expansion and contraction has flow-on impacts on time, cost and quality, with trade-offs possible between all three relationships.

There are two versions of the triple constraint in common use. In Figures 2.5 and 2.6, the central triangle demonstrates the relationships between project time, project cost and project

FIGURE 2.5 THE TRIPLE CONSTRAINT

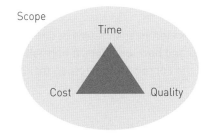

Source: The Northern Sydney Institute, Part of TAFE NSW.

quality, all of which are related to, and constrained by, the overall boundaries of the project as defined in the project scope.

The triple constraint is often communicated by the project sponsor in very simple (and somewhat contradictory) terms. Project success is often reliant on the project manager's ability to manage stakeholder expectations and make trade-offs between the key project dimensions comprising the triple constraint (see Figure 2.6).

FIGURE 2.6 PROJECT TRADE-OFFS

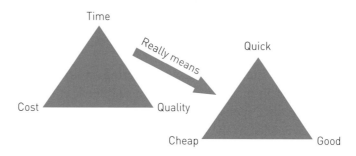

Source: The Northern Sydney Institute, Part of TAFE NSW.

PROJECT MANAGEMENT MASTERY

CLARIFYING EXPECTATIONS

Great project managers take the time to understand and document the success criteria. This ensures that the project delivers whatever is required and also meets the underlying business drivers. This is as simple as defining clear project objectives and agreeing these with the project sponsor. There is little point in having a separate set of statements about success criteria, business drivers or key performance indicators. All of these concepts can be accommodated and captured in the project objectives.

Ask your project sponsor clarifying questions about their goals and expectations so that you can set agreed and reasonable objectives for the project. My recommendations for these questions are in the following list.

- What does success look like?
- What are the critical priorities and what areas could be compromised?
- How do I know I've completed the project?
- How do I know I've done a great job?
- How will all this be measured?
- Are there any restrictions or preferences in terms of timeframes or budgets?
- What is the approval process and how long does it normally take?
- Who else will be involved in the approval and decision making processes?

REAL-WORLD EXPERIENCE

INTERRELATIONSHIPS WHEN SCOPE INCREASES

Source: The Northern Sydney Institute, Part of TAFE NSW.

If the project scope is increased but the project costs must remain fixed, then the timeframe will need to be extended to allow extra time for the additional work to be undertaken (this assumes that there is no cost involved in extending the resources for a longer period). It may also be possible to compromise on quality in order to speed up execution so that no additional time is required, thereby reducing pressure on the budget.

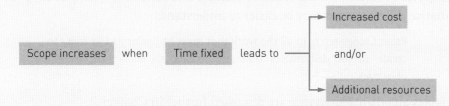

Source: The Northern Sydney Institute, Part of TAFE NSW.

If the project scope is increased and the project timeframe must remain fixed, then the overall cost will need to increase as more resources are added in order to complete the additional work.

REAL-WORLD EXPERIENCE

INTERRELATIONSHIPS WHEN SCOPE DECREASES

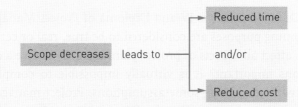

Source: The Northern Sydney Institute, Part of TAFE NSW.

When scope is decreased then it may be possible to reduce both the project cost and timeframe. Scope reduction is a common reaction to overall budget cuts within an organisation.

RESEARCH AND REFLECTION ACTIVITY

CONTROLLING SCOPE CHANGES

Consider instances where the scope has changed on past projects, or imagine typical scope changes that could occur on future projects.

Work through and discuss the flow-on impacts on time, cost and quality and the options that are available in managing these impacts.

What processes can you implement to manage and control scope changes?

High-level project scoping

Defining the scope is one of the hardest and most important activities in project management. Project scope, according to the PMBOK® Guide, is the work that must be 'performed to deliver a product, service or result with the specified features and functions' (PMI, 2013, p. 555). Here is an alternative definition that may be easier to understand:

> Project scope refers to *all* the work that must be performed in order to create *all* the deliverables that are required to deliver the project objectives.

Deliverables and their importance are discussed further in Chapter 7.

When developing the high-level project scope, which is required for the project charter, we focus on defining the boundaries of the project in terms of assumptions, dependencies and constraints. It is also recommended that the in-scope and out-of-scope elements are specifically defined.

Defining the project scope is critical as it gives the project manager concrete goals, ensures the objectives of the project sponsor are met, and provides the basis for expectation management, monitoring and reporting.

Assumptions

According to the NSI Online Certificate IV and Diploma of Project Management, assumptions are factors that for planning purposes are considered to be true, real or certain with no proof of certainty. Assumptions affect all aspects of project planning and involve a degree or risk.

Why are assumptions important? It is virtually impossible to complete the scoping and planning for a project without making some assumptions. Project managers need to take risks and assume certain conditions to be true in order to complete detailed project plans.

What do we do with them? Given that assumptions are both essential to the project planning process and also involve a degree of risk, it is recommended that all assumptions are documented in the project charter or project management plan (PMP) and also entered into the project control log. Some project managers prefer to record all major planning assumptions in the PMP and then record them in both the assumption log and the risk log. When entering assumptions into the risk log, they are expressed in terms of the negative impacts that might occur to the project if the assumptions are proven to be untrue.

Dependencies

Dependencies, as defined by the NSI Online Certificate IV and Diploma of Project Management, are relationships between the current project and other activities which are external to the project. The term is also used to define relationships between specific tasks which are internal to the project; these are of less interest to the project manager as these intra-project relationships are generally within the project manager's control.

Why are dependencies important? External dependencies generally represent higher risks as they are outside the control of the project manager.

What do we do with them? Record all major external dependencies in the project charter and then expand on their relationship with the project in the PMP. Dependencies should also be represented in the project schedule via the use of milestones, which ensures their progress is tracked regularly with the person, or organisation, that carries the responsibility for that dependency. Also enter them into the risk log with an explanation of the negative impact on project objectives if the dependency is late or delivers less than expected.

REAL-WORLD EXPERIENCE

NEW PRODUCT DEVELOPMENT – RETAIL SUPERANNUATION

It may aid your understanding of this concept to review some examples of dependencies that I have experienced in my time as a project manager.

During my time with a major wealth management company, I was program director for the development and release of a new online retail superannuation product which fully integrated into the parent company's internet banking capability. The product was the first of its kind and was designed to take advantage of new superannuation regulations that were being launched by the Australian Government in mid-2007. The dependency was both in terms of the timing of the enactment of the regulations and also in the specific design of the regulations.

If the regulations were delayed then our project would be delayed and would cost more than originally budgeted, thus impacting the business case and future profitability of the product. We responded to this dependency by ensuring that we had flexibility in all our contracts and by closely monitoring the status of the regulations.

If the regulations were changed from our original expectations then this would impact on the design of our product and create extra work, potential delays and definitely additional cost. We responded to this dependency by engaging a lobbyist to regularly meet the relevant government ministers to assess any pending changes and to champion our expectations as a major wealth management organisation.

REAL-WORLD EXPERIENCE

CABLE TELEVISION ROLLOUT

In the 1990s I joined a start-up company charged with rolling out cable television in Australia. The company was competing with Foxtel to install and deliver Australia's first pay TV services. It no longer exists (due to a merger with Foxtel) as the Australian market was too small to support two competing organisations in this area.

Under a government contract, the company had specific obligations and needed to deliver specific services to specific areas within predetermined timeframes. Naturally, these were top of mind for all the project managers within both the business services and construction arms of the company. Severe financial penalties were applicable if we didn't meet our obligations. This is an example of a circumstance when the external dependencies also involved the imposition of time constraints.

Constraints

Constraints are restrictions, or limitations, that will affect the performance of the project. They can be internal to the organisation or imposed by external bodies such as regulators, governments, etc. Constraints most often relate to fixed timeframes or fixed budgets.

Source: The Northern Sydney Institute, Part of TAFE NSW.

Why are constraints important? Constraints are critical as they can set limitations on the scope that can be achieved by the project. As we learnt with the triple constraint, scope is a product of the time, cost and quality expectations of the project sponsor. If there is a specific limitation to either the timeframe or the cost of a project then the scope will naturally be limited. If there are constraints on both time and cost then the scope will be limited further. This will place even more importance on careful scope control.

What do we do with them? Always document constraints in the project charter and then expand on the impacts of the constraints in the PMP. It is also a good idea to detail any specific monitoring and control activities or procedures that will be required in order to deliver within the constraints.

REAL-WORLD EXPERIENCE

ISSUES AT A MAJOR BANK

Most large organisations place an absolute limitation on the amount of funds that will be allocated to projects every year. This upper budgetary limitation becomes a constraint on the overall project portfolio and then for each project within the portfolio once the budgets have been agreed. This was certainly the case when I was running the Enterprise PMO for one of Australia's largest banks. Our portfolio of projects at the time represented an annual expenditure of approximately $400 million.

This was an absolute upper limit, so once the suite of projects was prioritised and confirmed each year, my team had to carefully monitor individual and collective project budgets. If a high-priority project required additional funds then we would need to identify lower-priority projects for cancellation, or delay, in order to provide the funding required by the higher-priority project.

In scope and out of scope

It is often more important, or at least of equal importance, to document what is out of scope as well as what is in scope. The concept of *out of scope* is vital to the setting and management of stakeholder expectations, especially those of the project sponsor.

PROJECT MANAGEMENT MASTERY

DEFINING 'OUT OF SCOPE'

Many students struggle to understand why it might be important to define what is out of scope. Surely this is obvious; whatever is not included in scope is by definition out of scope. However, it's not so clear for project sponsors and key stakeholders, who might spend five minutes flicking through the project charter, project management plan, scope statement or requirements, but not think to check that something they have assumed to be in scope has specifically been included because from their perspective it's just as obvious that it should be in scope.

If I'm conducting a project kick-off meeting (more on this later in the chapter) then I always include a review of in scope versus out of scope. If I don't have the opportunity to conduct a project kick-off meeting then I will always have an informal meeting with the project sponsor to discuss in scope versus out of scope. On most occasions, many items which are proposed as out of scope will end up moving into scope. This provides the basis for further discussions around the triple constraint and the fact that the additional scope items are likely to have an impact on the project budget and timeframe.

REAL–WORLD EXPERIENCE

TENANCY AND FACILITIES MANAGEMENT SYSTEM

As part of a large office relocation program, one of my project managers was scoping the requirements for a new tenancy and facilities management system. The organisation had not had any systems functionality in this area previously, although we were using a very old meeting room booking system to manage meeting and resource booking. It is important to note that we had two project sponsors for the project – one from IT and the other from Facilities Management. This situation is never ideal as you can often end up managing conflicting expectations and priorities.

It took several months to finalise the scope of the project and hence the functionality that would be required within the system. Most of the packages that were available included a module for meeting room and resource bookings and this was very attractive to our sponsor from IT as they integrated with all other modules; it was also attractive to the project team who could see process efficiencies and improved service level. Unfortunately, the Facilities Management sponsor refused to consider a new solution as he was the one who had chosen and installed the previous system. No logical discussions about improved integration, processes or service levels would sway him from this view. This was a case of a sponsor wishing to exclude something from scope that the project team and other key stakeholders felt needed to be included in scope.

The situation was finally resolved when further technical investigations were undertaken and it was found that the old meeting room booking system was not capable of interfacing with the room control panels.

RESEARCH AND REFLECTION ACTIVITY

DEFINING OUT OF SCOPE

Can you think of any past projects where this concept may have helped to achieve more successful outcomes, or to manage the expectation of the project sponsor more effectively?

Timeframe and budget

Timing and costs are often required in a project charter. These can be challenging to estimate in the initiation phase, as an accurate timeframe and budget are developed as part of the planning phase. A strong recommendation is that these two concepts are repositioned as the 'preferred timeframe' and 'indicative budget'. Changing the frame of reference for both timeframe and budget at this stage opens the door for meaningful discussions with the project sponsor and provides a foundation for the management of stakeholder expectations.

Preferred timeframe

Many sponsors have a preferred timeframe for project delivery which hasn't been validated yet via detailed planning. This is preferably expressed as:
- 'The preferred timeframe as advised by the project sponsor is six months.'
- 'The project must be delivered by day/month/year' – this indicates that there is a constraint of some form on the delivery date.
- 'The estimated delivery date for the project is between month/year and month/year.'

Indicative budget

There is often a specific upper cap, or constraint, on the budget which is dependent on the funding available, or the overall value of the project to the organisation. It is recommended that the budget is expressed as:
- 'The preferred budget as advised by the project sponsor is $150 000.'
- 'The project must be delivered for a cost of less than $500 000.'
- 'The estimated cost of the project is between $800 000 and $1 million.'

Expressing ranges

It has become common practice to express ranged estimates for timeframes or budgets as an absolute numeric value, qualified with a percentage estimate of 'plus/minus'. These are often misinterpreted by project sponsors as being definitive estimates, whereas the project manager actually means that the project is likely to cost between the absolute figure and the upper range as defined by the plus. Rarely do projects come in at the lower end of the range.

Communication between the project manager and the project sponsor around these dimensions can be greatly improved by avoiding the 'plus/minus' terminology. For example: *The estimated budget for the project is between $200 000 and $240 000* is a vast improvement over the alternative of *The estimated budget for the project is $220 000 +/− 10%*. The latter is often perceived by the project manager to mean $220 000 to $240 000 and interpreted by the project sponsor as an absolute $220 000, but between $200 000 and $240 000 is accurate.

High-level risks or project risk assessment

It is worth including a summary of the risks associated with the project as it assists with managing the expectations of the project sponsor and key stakeholders from the outset. This is an area where the good judgement and past experience of the project manager are critical in identifying the major risks to the project. These need to be selected based on the project environment, the specific requirements of the project, the risk framework of the organisation, and the risk appetite of the project sponsor.

Many project managers make a critical error of judgement here and include the detailed project risk log (more on this in Chapter 13). It is too early during project initiation to have completed the detailed risk log as this is one of the activities to be undertaken during planning. Also, the extent of the log, which often includes up to 100 risks for a medium-sized project, can be very intimidating for the sponsor.

Just because something is high risk doesn't mean we shouldn't do it. Sometimes the highest-risk projects are mandatory; we simply seek to identify and understand the specific risks so that we can reduce their impact and thereby increase the chances of success.

The following approaches to the documentation and discussion of high-level project risks during the initiation phase are recommended.

- *Major risks only:* include a short paragraph on the major risks to the project that will be of interest to, or can be influenced by, the project sponsor. This requires good knowledge of the project characteristics and the project context and good judgement as to how many risks and how much detail is included. As a rule of thumb, include three or four major risks and relate these back to standard risk categories such as project management, organisational, external and technical.
- *Top 10 risks:* if the quality and quantity of the high-level risks included in various project charters is too variable then it can be useful for the PMO to prescribe a template which has a table for the top 10 risks. This will naturally limit the number of risks presented and increase the confidence of less experienced project managers as they will not have to rely so much on their judgement.
- *General project risk assessment:* this approach can work very well in an organisation with a PMO and formal risk management procedures. Typically a standard template will be used that has been developed for the specific organisational context and areas of interest with respect to risk. This can be filled out by the project manager in consultation with the project sponsor and PMO and then included as an attachment to the project charter. These normally combine the responses to provide an overall risk rating for the project such as high, medium or low.

Project risk assessment templates

A project risk assessment template with instructions can be found online at www.cengagebrain.com.

Unresolved issues

It is good practice to include a section for unresolved issues in the template for the project charter. The rationale is that there are bound to be one or two major issues that have not been resolved at the end of a short project initiation phase. These are important if the resolution of these issues will impact on the scope, or other key element, of the project.

Many unresolved issues can be dealt with by making and documenting an assumption. This is a normal part of project management and the methods to manage these are discussed earlier in the chapter. The unresolved issue category should be reserved for those issues that will have a major impact on the project and require the specific attention of the project sponsor.

For example, in the tenancy and facilities management project that was discussed earlier with respect to in scope and out of scope, we had documented the disagreement over the inclusion or exclusion of the meeting room and resource booking functionality as an unresolved issue. There was also another unresolved issue on that project with respect to which department would have the ongoing operational responsibility for audiovisual presentation and video conference support.

Identifying stakeholders and expectations

According to the PMBOK® Guide, the identification of stakeholders is the second major process of the project initiation phase. It is the process of identifying all the people and organisations involved in, or impacted by, the project. It is the first process within the Project Stakeholder Management key knowledge area.

Gather stakeholder information including their interests, involvement and their potential impact on project success. Project stakeholders can include diverse groups such as customers, sponsors, impacted management, impacted staff, external organisations and sometimes even the public or press. These stakeholders can positively or negatively impact the project, hence it is important to understand their interests so these can be managed in order to increase the chances of success.

See **PMBOK®
Guide Figure 13-2**
Identify
stakeholders:
inputs, tools and
techniques, and
outputs

The project team and the project sponsor are also considered stakeholders but they tend to require different management to stakeholders who are not on the project team. The project team are managed by the project manager using the processes, tools and techniques encompassed by the Project Human Resource Management key knowledge area.

The project sponsor is the most critical stakeholder and they are almost always positive towards the project, given that they generally have the most to gain from the outcomes. There are, however, rare circumstances where the project sponsor may be considered negative as they can exert a negative influence over the project. Let's explore some examples.

Inexperienced project sponsor

Project managers will often be working with sponsors who are inexperienced in the practices of delivering projects. Many project sponsors are function area heads or senior line managers who have never sponsored a project before. In these circumstances it is critical that the project manager quickly develop a rapport with the sponsor. It is very useful to document the respective roles and responsibilities of both positions and to discuss these with the sponsor; this can also be a good time to ask for the support that will be required along the way. Another recommendation is that the project manager and project sponsor get together for regular one-on-one catch-ups outside of the normal project status, steering committee and working sessions.

Change of project sponsor

It can be incredibly disruptive to a project when the sponsor changes within the project timeframe. As the new sponsor gets up to speed they will often question the original scope, requirements and objectives. This is a perfectly legitimate process but it can be difficult for the project manager to view this positively due to the potential impact on the project. Many project managers find this process very frustrating and this frustration can set up barriers in their relationship with the sponsor. It is recommended that the project manager attempt to be as calm and objective as possible and to use integrated change control processes to manage any major elements of the project that need to be adjusted. It is important that the project sponsor understands that any changes they need to make will likely have flow-on impacts on the project objectives, scope, time and cost. It is good practice to provide them with options to assist with their decision making, as ultimately it is the project sponsor who needs to approve changes to the original project baselines. Integrated change control is covered in Chapter 16.

'Last person standing' project sponsor

This most often occurs in the public sector. It has similar characteristics to the change of project sponsor scenario above but with the added complication that the project sponsor doesn't want the role. They may have been lumbered with the project sponsor role due to senior staff turnover or because it is a difficult project and senior staff are actively avoiding any involvement due to possible negative repercussions. In these circumstances, it is recommended that the project manager should try to be reassigned to a new project or to move on. These types of projects with this type of sponsor are never easy and very rarely deliver successful outcomes.

Project sponsor and project manager incompatibility

Sometimes the project sponsor and the project manager are unable to develop a good working relationship. This can occur when working styles and expectations are not aligned, or if the project sponsor doesn't trust the project manager to deliver the project objectives.

REAL-WORLD EXPERIENCE

EXPERIENCING DIFFICULTIES

I am sure that many people will go through their careers without an incident like the one I am about to relay, or perhaps I am being too optimistic and many of you have, or will, encounter a similar circumstance. I have worked for more than 40 different project sponsors and senior line managers during my career and one particular project sponsor stands out as being very notorious and difficult. The specific project and context are not important, but it is useful to be aware that I was a program director at the time and the project team and I delivered a world-first program. The independent post-implementation review (covered in detail in Chapter 6) rated the program as a huge success and complimented the team on the professionalism of the delivery in some very challenging circumstances. We delivered on budget and one month later than originally planned due to a major delay in the delivery of an outsourced component of software that was the specific responsibility of one of the IT managers.

The first few months on the project underwent the normal fluctuations as the team and the ground rules were established during the planning phase. I felt that my relationship with the project sponsor was developing well even though he was more hands-on than I had experienced with previous sponsors. Suddenly, at the three month mark, everything changed. I needed to escalate the poor performance on the part of the IT manager mentioned above. Many of his deliverables were running late and I sought guidance from my sponsor as I knew that they had a good relationship. I hoped that he may be able to use his influence to improve the IT manager's performance and reduce execution risk. It ended up with my sponsor screaming at me that he didn't trust me and I realised later that the IT manager was a close friend of his. It was not specifically declared, but very obvious, that the sponsor would rather see the program fail than address the poor performance of his friend. Out of professional pride I stayed to the end of the program but it was the worst 12 months of my life. If this ever happened to me again I would not continue with the project even if it meant resigning.

The moral to the story is . . . just because you take on a project doesn't mean you need to see it through to the end. If the situation is untenable then the best outcome is to move on.

Who are the project stakeholders?

Stakeholders are persons or organisations who are actively involved in the project or whose interests may be positively or negatively affected by the performance or completion of the project. Stakeholders may also exert influence over the project, its deliverables and the project team members.

Stakeholders with positive expectations of a project will usually assist the project, while the interests of stakeholders with negative expectations are often served by seeking to hinder the progress of the project, or even by attempting to have the project cancelled.

The project management team must identify both internal and external stakeholders in order to determine the project requirements and expectations of all parties involved. The project manager must manage the influence and expectations of the various stakeholders to ensure a successful project outcome.

See PMBOK®
Guide Figure 2-7
The relationship
between
stakeholders and
the project

Identifying stakeholders and understanding their relative influence on a project is critical and can be difficult; they may not all be obvious at the beginning of a project. Stakeholder identification and expectation management are continuous processes that must be undertaken by the project manager throughout the project. It is also a good idea to enlist the support of the project sponsor in these processes.

Stakeholders can change over time and new ones can be identified during the project, and stakeholder expectations and power can also change during the project. Stakeholders identified later in the project can severely disrupt the project by impacting scope, timeframes and success measures.

Stakeholder analysis

Stakeholder analysis is defined by PMBOK® Guide as 'the process of systematically gathering and analysing information to determine whose interests should be taken into account throughout the project' (PMI, 2013, p. 563). This analysis identifies the interests, expectations and influence of the stakeholders, and considers stakeholders with both positive and negative feelings towards the project.

Positive stakeholders can be leveraged to enhance project success and negative stakeholders need to be encouraged to support the project, or at least be neutral in their impact.

Use the three-step process outlined in the PMBOK® Guide:

- **Step 1:** identify all potential project stakeholders
- **Step 2:** analyse the potential impact of each stakeholder
- **Step 3:** assess likely stakeholder reactions and plan to get support.

First, identify all the potential stakeholders and gather basic information about them, such as their role and position within the organisational hierarchy, their authority levels and any specific interests or expectations.

The key stakeholders are easily identified as they appear in the project governance and structure chart, if one has already been developed. This group includes anyone in a decision-making or management role that will be impacted by the project.

It can be difficult to identify all the stakeholders and additional stakeholders can often emerge later in the project. This always presents difficulties and often leads to delays as additional expectations are woven into the project. The more comprehensive is the stakeholder identification during project initiation, the better.

Stakeholders are often uncovered through discussions with the initial key stakeholders and the list should be expanded until all potential stakeholders are identified – for example, staff or customers impacted by the project, third party suppliers or finance and legal departments. It is a good idea to consult other experts within the organisation, such as the sponsor, other project managers and the PMO, who may be able to identify other stakeholders.

FIGURE 2.7 STAKEHOLDER ANALYSIS PROCESS

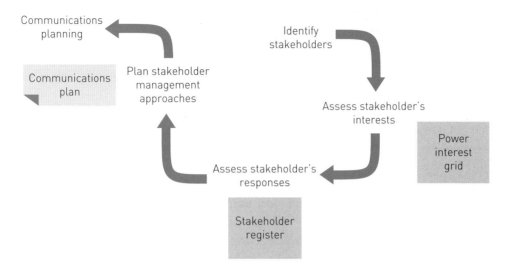

Developing the stakeholder register

STAKEHOLDER POWER AND INTEREST

The stakeholder register is a key deliverable during project initiation. The process of developing the stakeholder register carries on from stakeholder analysis and includes the identification of the power and interest of each stakeholder. Introduce specific groups of stakeholders during this process but it is critical that they have a homogenous set of expectations – if not then they need to be called out individually. This stakeholder classification information is normally captured in the stakeholder power and interest grid. There are several different forms of this grid, but the recommended one is the power and interest grid found in the PMBOK® Guide (see PMI, 2013, p. 397).

FIGURE 2.8 STAKEHOLDER POWER AND INTEREST GRID

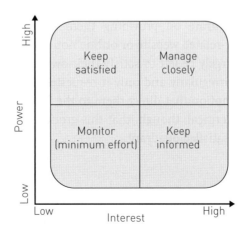

**See PMBOK®
Guide Figure 13-4**
Example power
and interest grid
with stakeholders

RESEARCH AND REFLECTION ACTIVITY

STAKEHOLDER POWER AND INTEREST GRID

Although it isn't shown in Figure 2.8, where would you typically expect to see the project sponsor plotted on the stakeholder power and interest grid? Remember that the relative position within the quadrant is important.

What are the possible implications for the project if the project sponsor was found to have low power and low interest?

Once you have completed the stakeholder power and interest grid, the next step is to determine your specific approach to stakeholder management and communication for each key stakeholder or group of stakeholders. The amount of effort and type of communication mechanisms will vary depending on their power and interest. Let's explore the four quadrants.

- **Manage closely:** the expectations of and relationships with this set of stakeholders are the most critical to achieving the project objectives. More effort will go into communicating with this group and more interactive communication methods will be used.

- **Keep satisfied:** this group are the next in order of importance due to their level of power. It is necessary to monitor their level of interest; if it increases then the level of attention and communication needs to increase. While in this quadrant, the emphasis will be on regular but less interactive communication. This is often called PUSH communication, as it is directly addressed to the recipient but doesn't always require a more time intensive form of interactive communication such as a face-to-face meeting. Choose PUSH mechanisms as the primary mode of communicating with this group and always offer to follow up with a meeting or phone call if they require more information or have questions.

- **Keep informed:** this group can often have very high interest but almost no power or influence over the project. They need to be monitored because if they move into the keep satisfied or manage closely quadrants then the approach to communicating with them and managing their expectations needs to be taken up a level. Generally, use a combination of PUSH and PULL communication mechanisms. Send them occasional specifically addressed emails (PUSH) but concentrate on providing them with the opportunity to self-serve information from a project-related website or online noticeboard.

- **Monitor:** this group can largely be left to satisfy their own communication requirements. It is best to meet with them irregularly and only if requested. Send this group general updates designed for public consumption that direct them to the PULL mechanisms provided for the keep informed group. It is critical, though, that this group is regularly monitored, especially if they move into the keep satisfied quadrant.

STAKEHOLDER ANALYSIS MATRIX

Now that the key stakeholders have been identified and classified according to their power and interest, the next step is to assess their likely reactions to the project and to determine engagement strategies to leverage the positive influence of some, and to reduce the negative influence of others.

FIGURE 2.9 STAKEHOLDER ANALYSIS MATRIX

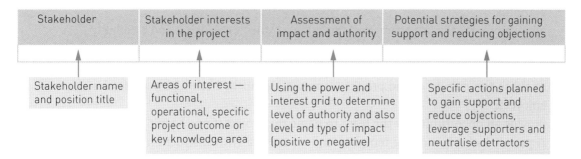

Stakeholder	Stakeholder interests in the project	Assessment of impact and authority	Potential strategies for gaining support and reducing objections
Stakeholder name and position title	Areas of interest — functional, operational, specific project outcome or key knowledge area	Using the power and interest grid to determine level of authority and also level and type of impact (positive or negative)	Specific actions planned to gain support and reduce objections, leverage supporters and neutralise detractors

Source: The Northern Sydney Institute, Part of TAFE NSW.

A stakeholder analysis template with instructions can be found online at www.cengagebrain.com.

Take this opportunity to identify any major project risks that relate to stakeholders and to commence populating the risk register. The completion of the stakeholder analysis matrix is the first step in communication planning. Both of these are explained more in Chapters 3, 12 and 13.

Both the position of stakeholders on the power and interest grid and the content of the stakeholder analysis matrix can be very sensitive. It is strongly recommended that these deliverables are treated as confidential and only shared with the core project team, and potentially the project sponsor.

Stakeholder analysis templates

The project kick-off meeting

The project kick-off meeting is one of the most important activities that the project manager conducts during project initiation. It may not be the first meeting with the project team, but it is a critical session as it sets the framework and objectives for the project. Some or all of the following objectives can be achieved through a well-planned and executed project kick-off meeting:

- direction and expectation setting by the project sponsor, including confirmation of project success criteria
- alignment of the project team around the project objectives via discussion of any differing views and acknowledgement of major priorities
- review and refinement of major in-scope and out-of-scope elements

- resolution of unresolved issues which will have a major bearing on the project approach and execution
- revelation and resolution (or at the minimum, acknowledgement) of areas of disagreement
- forum for key stakeholders to raise questions and to provide input into the design of the project prior to the planning phase
- management of expectations around the preferred timeframe and indicative budgets developed during project initiation and how these will be developed further during project planning
- opportunity for the project manager to establish their credentials and credibility
- opportunity to set expectations around project management practices, including risk management, status reporting and integrated change control
- establish the culture of the project team, which can be both highly professional as well as enjoyable
- provide an opportunity for the team to name the project if one hasn't been allocated.

A project kick-off meeting template and an agenda with instructions can be found online at www.cengagebrain.com.

Project kick-off meeting template and agenda

Project team charter

It is good practice to use the project kick-off meeting as an opportunity to undertake one of the first team building activities – the development of the project team charter.

REAL-WORLD EXPERIENCE

MICROSOFT OFFICE AND WINDOWS UPGRADE PROJECT

This example is from a major project to upgrade Microsoft Office and Windows. We had a large project team that was very technically skilled but largely inexperienced in project management and they had never worked together before. The 1.5-hour session was formally facilitated by our People and Development Manager and visualisation techniques were used in the form of picture cards to tap into the creative side of the brain. Participants were split into small groups and asked to focus on their positive experiences in previous teams; they then had to discuss and summarise these into seven major elements that were critical to their enjoyment and productivity within these teams. The facilitator then led a discussion session whereby all elements from each group were discussed in turn and classified according to how they best supported each of the firm's key values. Concepts were de-duplicated and enhanced via the discussion so that a set of team behaviours was agreed by the team. These were then refined and developed as a poster that every team member signed. The project went for 18 months and the project charter was just as relevant at the end of the project as it was at the outset. It was proudly displayed by all project team members in their work areas and regularly used to remind individuals about expected behaviours. It became the standard from which all subsequent project team charters were developed.

Examples of team charters can be found online at www.cengagebrain.com.

Team charter

CHAPTER SUMMARY

» Project initiation is generally the shortest phase of the project management lifecycle. It lays the foundation for the project's success.

» The two primary processes undertaken during initiation are developing the project charter and identifying stakeholders.

» Business cases are seen as a common input into the development of the project charter. There are limited circumstances when business cases are extremely useful. Many organisations misguidedly enforce business cases for all projects.

» It is critical that the project objectives (sometimes known as success criteria) are measurable, otherwise progress towards the specified purpose of the project is difficult to achieve and measure. The SMART framework is useful for the definition of objectives.

» Defining the scope is one of the hardest and most important activities in project management. Project scope is the work that must be performed to deliver a product, service or result with the specified features and functions. It encapsulates the work that must be performed in order to create all the deliverables that are required to deliver the project objectives.

» The project charter always includes a high-level scope statement. The focus is on defining the boundaries of the project in terms of assumptions, dependencies and constraints.

» It is equally important to document what is out of scope, as well as what is in scope. The concept of out of scope is vital to the setting and management of stakeholder expectations, especially those of the project sponsor.

» Scope is related to time, cost and quality. This relationship is often referred to as the 'triple constraint'. Scope expansion and contraction have flow-on impacts on time, cost and quality, with trade-offs possible between all three relationships.

» Timing and costs are often required in a project charter. These can be challenging to estimate in the initiation phase, as an accurate timeframe and budget are developed as part of the planning phase. It is recommended that these two concepts are repositioned as the 'preferred timeframe' and 'indicative budget'.

» A summary of major risks can be useful in the project charter. These need to be selected based on the project environment, the specific requirements of the project, the risk framework of the organisation and the risk appetite of the project sponsor.

» It can be important to document unresolved issues in the project charter, especially if the resolution of these issues will impact the scope, or other key elements, of the project.

» Stakeholders are persons or organisations who are actively involved in the project, or whose interests may be positively or negatively affected by the performance or completion of the project. In turn, they can exert positive and negative influences on the project itself.

» It can be difficult to identify all the stakeholders. The key stakeholders are easily identified as they appear in the project governance and structure chart, while additional stakeholders can often emerge later in the project.

» Stakeholder analysis is the process of systematically gathering and analysing information to determine whose interests should be taken into account throughout the project. The results of this process are captured in the power and interest grid and the stakeholder analysis matrix.

» The project kick-off meeting is one of the most important activities to occur during project initiation. It is a critical session as it sets the framework and objectives for the project and provides an opportunity to resolve issues and understand areas of disagreement.

» The development of a project team charter is often the first team building activity undertaken by the project team. It can be developed during the project kick-off meeting.

REVISION QUESTIONS

See detailed mapping grid for performance criteria covered

1 What does 'SMART' stand for?
2 Why are the objectives so important to project success?
3 What concepts does a project manager use to determine the boundaries of a project?
4 What are the typical contents of a project charter?
5 Why is it important to describe both the in-scope and out-of-scope elements?
6 How can a project manager best express time and cost when completing the project charter?
7 What steps are involved in identifying and analysing stakeholders?
8 Why is it often difficult to determine the project objectives?
9 What typically happens when the project manager discusses in scope and out of scope with the project sponsor?
10 What is the triple constraint and how are the concepts of time, cost and quality related to scope?
11 What are the benefits of a project kick-off meeting?
12 What is a project team charter?

DISCUSSION QUESTIONS

See detailed mapping grid for performance criteria covered

1 Why is it so difficult to clearly document detailed project objectives?
2 What are some of the issues that may be encountered on projects when the objectives have not been clearly documented and understood?
3 Why is it important to describe both the in-scope and out-of-scope elements?
4 What is the difference between an assumption and a dependency?
5 What impacts can occur if an assumption made for planning purposes is found to be untrue and how can these be managed?
6 What impacts can occur to a project as the result of external dependencies and how can project managers reduce these impacts?
7 In what circumstances are business cases useful?
8 Who is responsible for achieving the business benefits and why?
9 What are the benefits of conducting a project kick-off meeting?

10 What is the first team building exercise often undertaken on projects and why is this beneficial?

11 What happens when an assumption made in the initiation phase is proven to be untrue in later phases of project execution?

ONLINE RESOURCES

Visit the online companion website at http://www.cengagebrain.com to link to important additional resources, including templates, real-world case studies, revision quizzes and additional study material.

FURTHER READING AND REFERENCES

Dobie, C. (2007). *A handbook of project management: A complete guide for beginners to professionals.* Sydney: Allen and Unwin.

Hartley, S. (2008). *Project management: Principles, processes and practice* (2nd ed.). Sydney: Pearson Education.

Kerzner, H. (2007). *Project management: A systems approach to planning, scheduling, and controlling* (9th ed.). Brisbane: John Wiley & Sons.

Kloppenborg, T. J. (2012). *Contemporary project management* (2nd ed.). Melbourne: Cengage Learning.

Mulcahy, R. (2006). *PM crash course – Real-world project management tools & techniques.* Minnetonka, MN: RMC Publications.

Portny S. E., Mantel, S. J., Meredith, J. R., ... Sutton, M. M. (2008). *Project management – Planning, scheduling and controlling projects.* Brisbane: Wiley.

Project Management Institute (PMI). (2013). *A guide to the Project Management Body of Knowledge* (PMBOK® Guide) (5th ed.). Newtown Square, PA: author.

Schwable, K. (2014). *Information technology project management* (revised 7th ed.). Brooks/Cole, a part of Cengage Learning.

Verzuh, E. (2005). *The fast forward MBA in project management.* Brisbane: John Wiley & Sons.

3 Project planning

LEARNING OBJECTIVES   IN THIS CHAPTER YOU WILL:

1   become familiar with the processes and activities performed when planning a project

2   realise that half of the processes contained in the PMBOK® Guide make up the planning process group

3   appreciate the primary function of a project manager in the early stages of the project management lifecycle

4   consider different approaches to the construction and organisation of the project management plan

5   describe the differences when developing a project management plan for a small, simple project compared with a large, complex project

6   understand that project management plans may be consolidated or split into discrete separate plans for different knowledge areas

7   appreciate the benefits of applying a flexible and iterative approach to project planning

8   understand the concept of a baseline and the importance of this for scope, time and cost

9   understand that integrated change control is important when managing changes following approval of the project management plan.

Context

Project planning is the primary function of the project manager in the early phases of the project management lifecycle. The project planning process groups contain all the activities required to develop plans for the 10 key knowledge areas. These processes develop the project management plan and other related project deliverables that will be used to manage the execution of the project.

Project planning requires lots of processes to be undertaken in parallel and there will be many times when you will need to loop back and revisit the draft outcomes due to information that is revealed by other project planning activities. To get the best possible project management plan (PMP), the project manager must be able to handle complexity during this phase and approach the development of the PMP in a flexible manner that enables several rounds of refinement before the project baselines are established.

In short, the planning process group contains the processes required to establish the scope of the project, refine the objectives and deliverables, and define the overarching plan for the execution of the project outcomes. The goal is to develop a detailed PMP that covers all 10 key knowledge areas and ensures the project has the best possible chance of success.

This chapter brings together the primary techniques underlying the project planning processes. More details are in Chapters 7–16 which cover the 10 key knowledge areas separately.

PMBOK® Guide processes for project planning

The PMBOK® Guide covers the project planning process group in the most detail, with around half of the total processes falling into this phase of the project management lifecycle. The processes are:

4   Project integration management
    4.2   Develop project management plan
5   Project scope management
    5.1   Plan scope management
    5.2   Collect requirements
    5.3   Define scope
    5.4   Create work breakdown structure (WBS)
6   Project time management
    6.1   Plan schedule management
    6.2   Define activities
    6.3   Sequence activities
    6.4   Estimate activity resources
    6.5   Estimate activity durations
    6.6   Develop schedule

See PMBOK®
Guide Table A1-1
Project
management
process groups
and knowledge
area mapping

Developing the project management plan

According to the PMBOK® Guide, this is the process of defining and documenting the actions necessary to prepare and integrate all subsidiary plans for all key knowledge areas of project management (PMI, 2013, p. 72).

As detailed in the Northern Sydney Institute (NSI) Online Certificate IV and Diploma of Project Management, good practice dictates that the project management plan is baselined at the end of the planning phase, particularly in the areas of scope, cost and time. It is progressively updated during project execution via the 'perform integrated change control' process (refer to Chapter 4 of the PMBOK® Guide for more detail on managing variations).

The PMP is the primary output of the planning phase and it is the result of a complex interplay between more than 20 processes in the PMBOK® Guide. But it is not the only critical deliverable that is produced during this phase. There are many discrete deliverables that form part of the PMP although they have independent uses during the project, such as project controls logs for risks and assumptions, quality management plans, procurement planning registers and so on. These will be covered in more detail later in this chapter.

FIGURE 3.1 PMBOK® GUIDE'S 'DEVELOP PROJECT MANAGEMENT PLAN DATAFLOW' DIAGRAM

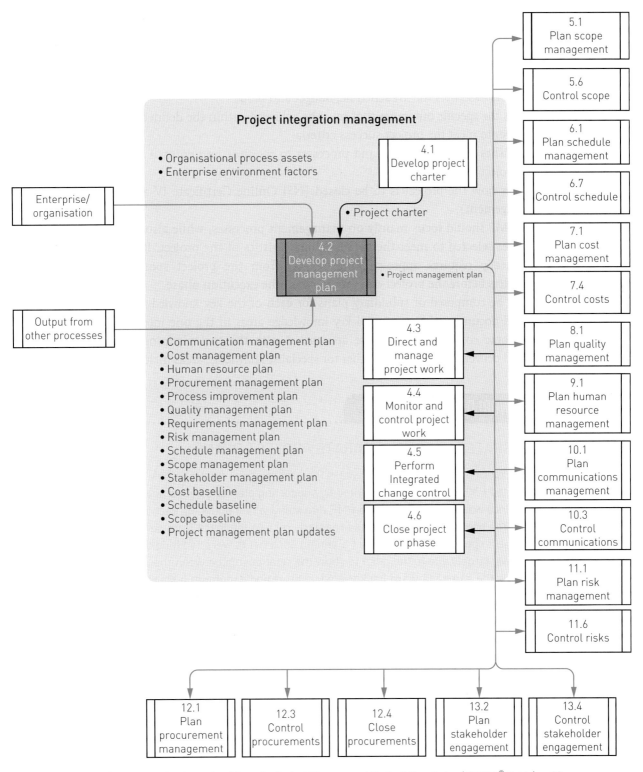

Understanding the project management plan

The project management plan is the primary output of the planning process group and provides the roadmap for executing the project. It:

- defines how all aspects of the project are to be undertaken through to the execution phase
- contains baselines for the schedule, budget and scope
- details the specific outcomes that must be achieved within the defined timeframe and budget in order to meet the project success criteria
- establishes the mechanisms and processes to monitor and control and direct and manage the project
- defines how the project is to be closed (NSI Online Certificate IV and Diploma of Project Management).

The PMP should focus mainly on management processes, while also detailing the tools and techniques selected to meet the specific characteristics of the project. It is a formal document that typically requires approval and sign-off from the project sponsor and other senior stakeholders before the project can progress into the execution phase.

It can be composed of subsidiary plans for each of the key knowledge areas; or it can be an integrated document that covers all key knowledge areas in the one integrated deliverable; or it can be some combination of these approaches with the core planning areas included in the integrated deliverable (with approaches for specialist knowledge areas included in separate plans).

REAL-WORLD EXPERIENCE

INTEGRATED VERSUS SEPARATE PROJECT PLANS

In my experience, over the last 20 years the preference in Australia has been to have one integrated PMP that is complemented by supporting planning deliverables. Prior to this, the preference was for separating the PMP into stand-alone plans for each of the key knowledge areas. The previous approach would regularly receive feedback from senior stakeholders and the project sponsor that the project planning documents were too long and unnecessarily repetitive, largely due to the need to show the relationship between the discrete plans by including the same standard background, context and document history information at the beginning of each subsidiary plan.

These days the majority of project managers and organisations have a preference for integrated PMPs. This works particularly well on small- to medium-sized, simple projects but it is not always practical for large, complex projects where different project team members may be responsible for the planning and delivery of knowledge areas that are aligned to their specific specialisation. In the latter circumstance, it is preferable to have an integrated plan for the primary domains of integration, scope, time, cost and project human resource management, with stand-alone plans for risk management, procurement, quality and communication or change management.

For very small, simple projects sometimes the initiation and planning phases are combined and the project charter and PMP are combined into one high-level planning deliverable.

The specific structure and contents of the PMP are determined by a combination of the following:

- the particular methodology and templates within the executing organisation
- the preference of the project manager and project sponsor
- the characteristics of the project in terms of size, complexity and duration
- the industry and the country in which the project is being executed.

PROJECT MANAGEMENT MASTERY

WHAT IS A PROJECT PLAN?

I am no longer surprised by naive project sponsors and inexperienced project managers who refer to the project schedule as the project plan. The project schedule only represents the detailed plan for the time dimension of the project and by itself is insufficient to effectively manage the entire project.

Whenever any of my stakeholders or project team refer to a project plan, I always clarify their meaning and then reinforce the discipline of referring to either a project management plan or a project schedule. In the PMBOK® Guide there is no formal deliverable known as a 'project plan'.

PROJECT MANAGEMENT MASTERY

WHEN DOES THE PROJECT MANAGEMENT PLAN CHANGE?

Many project management practitioners describe the PMP as a living document that is updated throughout the execution of the project. Personally, I believe this is a waste of time and imposes an administrative burden on the project manager that takes them away from critical monitoring and controlling and directing and managing tasks.

My preference is to maintain the PMP once it has been approved by the project sponsor and baselines are set for scope, time and cost at the end of the planning phase. Once execution has commenced then the integrated change control process takes over to manage ongoing change requests. I save all approved change requests in the same electronic file as the signed-off PMP, along with any related change impact assessment documentation, schedules, budget spreadsheets and so on. The PMP and the approved change requests then become the overall scope and approach for the project and they are then used to determine if the project has been successfully delivered.

Inputs into the project management plan

Inputs into the PMP include:

- the project charter
- subsidiary plans developed in other planning processes
- industry standards and regulations
- organisational policies and procedures
- project management methodology
- project management tools
- planning templates
- knowledge from past projects
- expert judgement and advice.

PROJECT MANAGEMENT MASTERY

KNOWLEDGE FROM PAST PROJECTS AND EXPERTS

The last two points in the above list are often overlooked, which is unfortunate as they are particularly powerful. Utilising knowledge and lessons learned from past projects can accelerate the planning of a new project by leveraging previous project management deliverables from projects with similar characteristics. It also increases the chances of success by highlighting issues that contributed to the success or failure of previous projects within the same organisational context.

Tapping into the knowledge and advice from experts can provide a valuable source of information on how to (1) structure a project for success within the current context; (2) tailor the methodology and approach for the specifics of the project; and (3) ensure that there are no gaps or weaknesses within the overall PMP.

Smart project managers always look for ways to leverage learnings, deliverables and successful techniques from previous projects. It is much more efficient and effective than starting each project with a clean slate.

RESEARCH AND REFLECTION ACTIVITY

KNOWLEDGE FROM PAST PROJECTS AND EXPERTS

Activity 1

Consider the availability of lessons learned from previous projects within your organisation and answer the following questions.

1 Are post-implementation reviews conducted?
2 Can you search and find lessons learned from previous projects?

3 Do you have access to a methodology with templates and project management policies and procedures?

4 Do you have access to examples of project management deliverables from past projects?

If any of these areas are weak, come up with suggestions on how these gaps can be addressed.

Activity 2

Consider the project management and organisational experts you could ask to review your project management plans and also to provide guidance on issue resolution during execution. The two most obvious sources of expertise are other project managers and the project management office (PMO). Are there other experts you can consult?

The contents of the project management plan

The primary contents of the PMP are outlined in Table 3.1. If supplementary deliverables, such as subsidiary plans, are developed then they must be referenced in the PMP. It is best to include these as links in a table of supplementary deliverables and related documents. If organisational policies and procedures exist which will be utilised as part of the project management activities, then these must also be referenced in the PMP, with links to these documents supplied. This is more effective than inserting the contents into the PMP as this would make it unnecessarily long and the policies and procedures may become out of date. By supplying a link then the latest version of related documents and supplementary plans can be easily accessed.

Subsidiary management plans

Project management plans often include support documents called subsidiary management plans. This is common for large projects where different project professionals are responsible for the planning and delivery of specific key knowledge areas, such as risk, quality and procurement. Like a project management plan, these can be developed at either a summary or detailed level, depending on the requirements of the project. A critical function of the PMP is to integrate and consolidate all the subsidiary plans, either as sections of the overall project plan or as attachments to the project plan.

The most common subsidiary plans are:

- communications management plan
- procurement management plan
- quality management plan
- requirements management plan
- risk management plan.

TABLE 3.1 CONTENTS OF THE PROJECT MANAGEMENT PLAN

Primary contents			
Project scope and requirements			
Description	**Detailed contents**	**Supplementary deliverables**	**Related documents**
» This section should include the detailed project scope including a list of major deliverables and requirements. » Many software development and process improvement projects will produce the requirements documentation as the first deliverable from the execution phase, while many construction projects, especially where the plan is in response to a tender, will refer to detailed supplementary requirements documents that have already been issued. More detail is included in Chapter 7.	» Project scope definition including what is in and out of scope. » Project objectives and requirements. » Project success criteria. » Constraints and assumptions. » Major external dependencies. » Outstanding or unresolved issues. » Scope management process (change control).	Links to any of the following are recommended: » requirements documentation » business requirements » technical requirements » specifications and design drawings » project control logs containing assumptions.	Links to any of the following are recommended: » tender documents if applicable » requirements management plan » configuration management plan » document control policies and procedures » document naming conventions and version control.
Primary contents			
Project methodology and approach			
Description	**Detailed contents**	**Supplementary deliverables**	**Related documents**
» This section details project management methodology that will be applied to the project, including project phases and major deliverables, as well as references to any project management standards that will be followed. » This is a critical section as many projects fail due to a poor selection of the approach.	» Project phases. » High-level deliverables. » Outline of the review and approval gates.	Links to any of the following are recommended: » project governance and approval processes » detailed review and sign-off authority.	Links to the following are recommended: » intranet websites detailing the project management methodology » relevant internal and external project management standards.

(Continued)

Primary contents

Project schedule

Description	Detailed contents	Supplementary deliverables	Related documents
» This section contains the detailed project timeline, most often presented in the form of a summary GANTT chart, with links to a supplementary detailed GANTT chart. » It is also useful to include summary information about high-level timelines, start and end dates for major phases, lists of major external dependencies and agreed milestones.	» Work breakdown structure including deliverables and activity duration. » Baselined GANTT chart indicating the critical path.	Links to the following are recommended: » detailed project schedule in MS Project or other scheduling software.	Links to any of the following are recommended: » time recording or timesheet capture standards and processes » time recording system » timesheet templates » standard time capture codes.

Primary contents

Project budget

Description	Detailed contents	Supplementary deliverables	Related documents
» Project budget based on project sponsor's preference and some form of quantitative estimation. » Rationale for overall cost including best case, likely and worst case. » Month-by-month breakdown by major categories.	» Detailed project budget. » Budgeting assumptions.	Links to any of the following are recommended: » detailed project cash flow projection » detailed budget tracking and cost capture spreadsheets » project control logs containing budget assumptions.	Links to any of the following are recommended: » project cost management procedures » relevant accounting and financial management procedures » purchase ordering and accounts payable processes.

(Continued)

Primary contents			
Project quality requirements			
Description	**Detailed contents**	**Supplementary deliverables**	**Related documents**
» This section includes the quality requirements for all deliverables stated in terms of any relevant quality assurance and quality control activities that are to be applied, as well as any performance measures that must be achieved. » It is also useful to list and provide links to all relevant quality and testing methodologies, standards and regulations.	» Quality requirements. » Quality assurance and quality control activities for each deliverable. » Quality definition table – see Chapter 10 for more detail.	Links to any of the following are recommended: » project-specific quality management processes » project-specific testing processes » defect capture logs.	Links to any of the following are recommended: » quality standards » applicable legislation and regulations » quality management standards » testing standards and procedures.

Primary contents			
Project team			
Description	**Detailed contents**	**Supplementary deliverables**	**Related documents**
» This section includes the project team structure and the roles and responsibilities for each project team member. It is also useful to show governing bodies such as the project sponsor, steering committee and any other related approval forums. » One of the most critical components of this section is the responsibility assignment matrix (I recommend the use of the RASIC version. More detailed information can be found in Chapter 11).	» Work breakdown structure including human resource assignments. » Basic roles and responsibilities listed for each role within the project. » Summary responsibility assignment matrix.	Links to any of the following are recommended: » project resource schedule » detailed position descriptions » detailed responsibility assignment matrix including each deliverable.	Links to any of the following are recommended: » resourcing calendars » project team code of conduct » conflict resolution processes » performance management procedures.

(Continued)

Primary contents			
Project communication			
Description	Detailed contents	Supplementary deliverables	Related documents
» This section needs to contain the communication plan for the major project stakeholders. It covers the communication requirements of the project sponsor, senior stakeholders involved in project governance (often known as the steering committee) and the project team.	» Major project stakeholder identification. » Details of primary communication channels. » Stakeholder communication table. » Project communication table. » Project performance reporting.	Links to any of the following are recommended: » project stakeholder analysis using the power and interest grid, as well as strategies to move from current to future states of support » detailed stakeholder communication plan including all communication activities and deliverables.	Links to any of the following are recommended: » stakeholder or change management plan for the project – not to be confused with change control (this plan covers the activities that assist project stakeholders to embrace the changes being delivered by the project and significantly improves the chances of success) » organisational change management methodologies.

Primary contents			
Project risk management			
Description	Detailed contents	Supplementary deliverables	Related documents
» This section details the major risks that may impact successful project delivery and the specific management strategies that will be used to reduce the negative impacts of these risks.	» Summary of the overall risks to the project. » Detailed risk descriptions and action plans for major risks. » Overall project risk assessment.	Links to the following are recommended: » detailed risk register contained within the project control logs.	Links to any of the following are recommended: » risk rating matrix » risk rating categories » risk management » Australian Risk Standards » organisational risk management procedures.

(Continued)

Primary contents			
Project procurement			
Description	**Detailed contents**	**Supplementary deliverables**	**Related documents**
» This section details the major procurement activities and requirements for the project.	» Procurement items and required procurement processes. » Procurement roles and responsibilities.	Links to any of the following are recommended: » procurement planning register » assessment and selection approach.	Links to any of the following are recommended: » Structure charts » Stakeholder context diagrams » Stakeholder roles and responsibilities » Stakeholder management frameworks.

Primary contents			
Project shareholders			
Description	**Detailed contents**	**Supplementary deliverables**	**Related documents**
» This section contains stakeholder management plans. This is different from the formal project management and progress meetings which are covered in project communications.	» Stakeholder identification and analysis. » Stakeholder impact assessments and communication requirements. » Change management plans covering communication, training and stakeholder engagement activities.	Links to any of the following are recommended: » stakeholder analysis matrix » stakeholder communication schedule » stakeholder training needs analysis » stakeholder training schedule.	Links to any of the following are recommended: » Structure charts » Stakeholder context diagrams » Stakeholder roles and responsibilities » Stakeholder management frameworks.

(*Continued*)

Primary contents			
Project integrated change managment			
Description	Detailed contents	Supplementary deliverables	Related documents
» This section contains the integrated change management processes that will be followed for the project.	» Integrated change management process. » Change control flowchart.	Links to the following are recommended: » change control roles and roles and responsibilities.	Links to any of the following are recommended: » change control forms » change impact assessment templates » change management procedures.

PROJECT MANAGEMENT MASTERY

CHANGE CONTROL AND METHODOLOGIES

Many project management planning templates do not contain sections for either the project methodology and approach or integrated change management. The inclusion of these sections by a project manager shows a genuine understanding of how to give projects the highest chance of success.

The adaptation and synthesis of the best methodology and approach for a project is dependent on the specific characteristics of the project in the following areas:

- objectives of the project
- required end outputs and products
- industry and organisational context.

Integrated change control is one of the most important project management processes as it provides a framework for the management of additional scope items and impacts that result from planning assumptions that are found to be invalid once the project is in execution phase. Unfortunately, it is often omitted as it is dismissed by the project sponsor as being too administratively demanding and a waste of time, or the project manager is not comfortable having the potentially difficult conversations around controlling scope.

COMMUNICATIONS MANAGEMENT PLAN

The purpose of the communications management plan is to define the communication requirements, resourcing and processes for the project and how information will be distributed. The primary focus needs to be on communicating with key project stakeholders and then on the project management communication processes for project team members.

The communication plan for large projects with many different stakeholder groups can be long and so it has become common practice to develop it as a discrete stand-alone planning document. The communications management plan should include:
- communication requirements for all project stakeholders
- what information will be communicated (including the level of detail and format)
- how the information will be communicated – meetings, email, telephone, internet or intranet, staff briefings, etc.
- the frequency of project communications, both formal and informal
- who is responsible for communicating project information.

The above content often takes the form of a communication table or matrix, but this is insufficient on its own as it doesn't call out the specific communication deliverables in a schedule with timeframes. The following additional inclusions are recommended:
- resource allocation for communication activities – if this is omitted then the project will suffer due to insufficient resources to execute all deliverables
- approval and sign-off processes for sensitive or confidential communication, as well as any communication that may find its way into the public domain
- any standard templates, formats or documents the project must use for communicating
- an escalation process for resolving any communication-based conflicts or issues
- project team and key stakeholder directory and contact information, especially if they are external to the organisation.

Communication planning table template

TABLE 3.2 COMMUNICATION PLANNING TABLE

Target audience	Communication needs	Messenger	Approval	Media/ channel	Frequency
Who to	What	Who from	Who approves	How	When

Source: The Northern Sydney Institute, Part of TAFE NSW.

More detailed information on project communications management is included in Chapter 12.

PROCUREMENT MANAGEMENT PLAN

The purpose of the procurement management plan is to define the procurement requirements for the project and how these will be managed, from developing procurement documentation such as tenders, through contract negotiations and acquisitions, and on to contract closure or asset disposal.

Some projects have no procurement requirements, while others have large and complex requirements in this area, and yet other projects are specifically established in order to execute a major procurement. When major procurement activity is required, it is common for this to be planned in a stand-alone procurement management plan. The typical inclusions in the procurement management plan are:

- identification of items to be procured
- procurement methods – e.g. tender, preferred supplier, comparison of quotations, etc.
- evaluation and selection criteria
- type of contract to be used
- contract approval process
- budget allowances
- timeframe requirements.

It is useful to organise this information into a table called the procurement planning table.

FIGURE 3.2 PROCUREMENT PLANNING TABLE

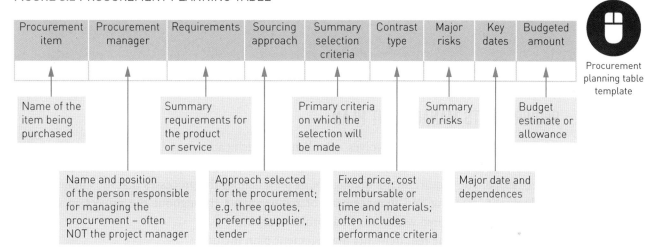

Procurement planning table template

Procurement item	Procurement manager	Requirements	Sourcing approach	Summary selection criteria	Contrast type	Major risks	Key dates	Budgeted amount

Name of the item being purchased

Name and position of the person responsible for managing the procurement – often NOT the project manager

Summary requirements for the product or service

Approach selected for the procurement; e.g. three quotes, preferred supplier, tender

Primary criteria on which the selection will be made

Fixed price, cost reimbursable or time and materials; often includes performance criteria

Summary or risks

Major date and dependences

Budget estimate or allowance

Source: The Northern Sydney Institute, Part of TAFE NSW.

More detailed information on project procurement management is included in Chapter 14.

QUALITY MANAGEMENT PLAN

The quality management plan defines the acceptable level of quality for a project in terms of the deliverables, products and outcomes that are to be achieved. Ideally, it specifies the quality assurance and quality control activities and techniques that will be allied to each deliverable. Quality management activities ensure that the products are built to meet agreed standards and requirements, work processes are performed efficiently and as documented, and defects are identified and corrected. Chapter 10 gives a real-world experience of a software quality plan; see page 236.

Quality assurance activities monitor and verify that the processes used to create the deliverables have been effective. Quality control activities monitor and verify that project deliverables meet defined quality standards.

The contents of the quality management plan are:
- quality standards that must be followed
- quality assurance activities and techniques
- quality control activities and techniques
- quality roles and responsibilities
- defect resolution processes.

It is useful to organise this information into a table called the quality planning register.

Quality planning
register template

TABLE 3.3 QUALITY PLANNING REGISTER

Project deliverable	Quality assurance activities	Quality control activities	Quality requirements	Quality standards

Source: The Northern Sydney Institute, Part of TAFE NSW.

More detailed information on project quality management is included in Chapter 10.

REQUIREMENTS MANAGEMENT PLAN

Requirements management involves establishing specifications and ensuring that these are delivered at the end of the project. It is good practice to set baseline requirements as part of the project scope. The requirements management plan defines the processes that are applied to the development, tracking and management of requirements throughout the project in order to ensure they are delivered within the final project outputs.

The contents of the requirements management plan include:
- details on how the requirements phase will be run
- the selected techniques and processes for defining and controlling the requirements
- requirements management roles and responsibilities.

More detailed information on requirements management is included in Chapter 7.

RISK MANAGEMENT PLAN

The risk management plan documents the processes, tools and procedures that will be used to manage and control risks that may have a negative impact on a project. It typically includes:
- risk identification and categorisation processes
- risk likelihood and impact assessment processes
- risk management approaches
- specific risk plan for high-priority risks
- risk monitoring and controlling processes
- relevant risk standards and methodologies.

It is common practice to present the information for each risk in the form of a table. These can be quite lengthy for large or complex projects, which explains why this is often developed as a subsidiary plan.

FIGURE 3.3 BASIC RISK LOG

Risk ID	Risk category	Risk description	Risk owner	Likelihood	Impact	Risk rating	Management strategies	Residual likelihood	Residual impact	Residual rating	Status	Priority
1	2	3	4	5	6	7	8	9	10	11	12	13

1
- Can be as simple as a number
- May relate to the risk category
- Used as a unique identifier
- May be an internal standard

2
- Can be taken from industry frameworks
- Can be set at internal standards
- May need to be developed/tailored
- Ensures identification of all risks
- Assists with monitoring and control

3
- Plain English explanation of the risk
- One to two sentences in length
- Ensures common understanding

4
- A specific person or role
- Ensures clear ownership of the risk
- Responsible for monitoring and control

5
- Probability of the risk occurring
- Typically defined in a risk rating matrix
- Has both a number scale and definition
- Requires judgement and prediction
- More accurate if can leverage lessons learnt

6
- Consequences of the risk occurring
- Impacts one or more project objectives
- Includes scope, time, cost and quality
- Has both a number scale and definition
- Requires judgement and prediction
- More accurate if can leverage lesson learnt

7
- Combines likelihood and impact
- Normally multiplied together
- Enables overall prioritisation of risks

8
- **Avoid** – remove entirely
- **Mitigate** – reduce likelihood or impact
- **Accept** – normally for LOW risks
- **Transfer** – to another party; e.g., contract or outsource

9
- Probability of risk occurring after management or mitigation actions

10
- Impact of risk occurring after management or mitigation actions

11
- Revised risk rating
- Most important for risk monitoring

12
- Typically RED, GREEN, AMBER

13
- Typically HIGH, MEDIUM, LOW

Basic risk log template

Source: The Northern Sydney Institute, Part of TAFE NSW.

More detailed information on project risk management is included in Chapter 13.

RESEARCH AND REFLECTION ACTIVITY

SUBSIDIARY PROJECT MANAGEMENT PLANS

Many examples and templates can be found online for both the PMP and the many suggested subsidiary management plans. Search these out and develop a library of personal favourites.

Can any of these be adapted and incorporated into the project management methodology of your organisation?

Looking at the risk logs you found, are there specific features which could be included in your existing risk log to improve risk management processes?

Did you find any useful risk breakdown structures or categories that you can use to construct a tailored risk breakdown structure for your organisation or industry?

Supplementary deliverables and related documents

Other documentation is often included as part of a PMP to support the development of the plan and the management of the project. The PMBOK® Guide has set these documents apart in order to differentiate them and it is recommended that links to all of these are included in the PMP. Also, as discussed earlier, provide links to relevant internal and external standards, policies and procedures.

Typical supplementary project deliverables include:
- project budget spreadsheets
- project control logs
- risk log
- procurement contracts.

Typical related documents include:
- project methodologies
- change control forms
- position descriptions
- performance management procedures
- cost management and financial tracking procedures
- time recording procedures.

Project control
log templates

PROJECT CONTROL LOGS

Establishing project control logs during project initiation is important so as to keep track of assumptions that impact scoping and risks that are established in the early stages of project formation. If this has not yet been done, then they must be set up in the project planning phase as they form the backbone of the monitoring and controlling processes.

Here is a list of the common control logs, not all of which will be required for small or simple projects:
- **Assumption log** (mandatory) – this log allows for the collation of assumptions that have been made during scoping and planning. No projects can be planned without making assumptions, and logging them means that they are consciously acknowledged and the impact of them (if they are proven to be untrue) can be managed through project change control processes.
- **Milestone log** (highly recommended) – it is good practice to define high-level milestones during project initiation and then to refine and expand these during planning. Once a baseline has been set, these become the set of milestones that are included in the project status report and are used to report and track actual progress against the PMP.
- **Risk log** (mandatory) – all projects are subject to the potential negative impacts of risks and these are typically collected together into the project risk log. This is also used to capture likelihood and impact analyses, risk management activities and overall risk status or ratings.
- **Issue log** (highly recommended) – this is used to record actions that are required in response to issues that arise. Risks that have actually occurred and assumptions that have

been proven untrue are considered issues and managed through this log. Either an *action log* or an *issue log* is mandatory. Preferably, use an issue log rather than an action log, as it encourages project team members to keep track of their own actions.

- **Action log** (highly recommended) – this is used to record all major actions that have been assigned to project team members. The log records the successful (or not) executions of these actions, often on a weekly basis.
- **Decision log** (highly recommended) – this is used to record major decisions which are made that impact the project, especially those made by the project sponsor or steering committee. This log is particularly useful instead of minutes from steering committee meetings, as it is much easier to find the actual decisions that have been made in a log rather than searching back through meeting minutes which have been written in MS Word.
- **Change log** (mandatory) – this log is critical and should be used on all projects. It records all change requests that relate to a project and the decisions made in terms of accepting or rejecting them. Any change requests that are accepted must be included in the scope of the project for it to be considered complete. It is important to record all change requests, even those which have been rejected, as it is common for similar or identical change requests to be submitted more than once. They also provide valuable information on the weak areas of project planning and execution.
- **Lessons learned log** (highly recommended) – this log captures lessons learned by the project team during the planning and delivery of the project. It is good practice to capture these as they are revealed, rather than waiting until the closure of the project, as more detail is remembered. All major positive and negative learnings should be captured so they can be shared with future projects in order to enhance the chances of successful delivery.

Determining the project methodology and approach

The basic project management lifecycle included in the PMBOK® Guide has four phases: initiation, planning, execution and closure. Each of the phases also consists of a set of processes which form a process group, as well as the monitoring and controlling process group. Figure 3.4 shows the standard project lifecycle from PMBOK® Guide.

FIGURE 3.4 PROJECT LIFECYCLE: FOUR PHASES AND FIVE PROCESS GROUPS

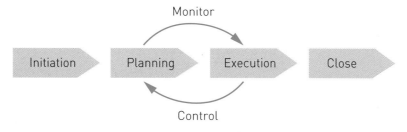

This following section of the chapter contains more advanced project management techniques which require experience and critical thinking skills, or at least consultation with experts in the project management office.

REAL-WORLD EXPERIENCE

ADDITIONAL PROCESS GROUPS

I have a different preference and by default I always adapt the PMBOK® Guide project lifecycle to contain six process groups. I maintain the four basic phases, but add the following two process groups: monitoring and controlling and directing and managing, as per Figure 3.5. This slightly modified version shows the true importance of the directing and managing activities, as well as the monitoring and controlling activities.

FIGURE 3.5 PROJECT LIFECYCLE: FOUR PHASES AND SIX PROCESS GROUPS

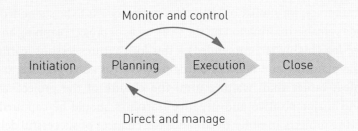

Source: Project Management Institute, *A guide to the Project Management Body of Knowledge*, (PMBOK® Guide), p. 50. Project Management Institute, Inc 2013. Copyright and all rights reserved. Material from this publication has been reproduced with the permission of PMI.

REAL-WORLD EXPERIENCE

PROJECT APPROACH AND METHODOLOGY ADAPTATIONS

Over the years I have further modified the PMBOK® Guide project lifecycle to suit the particular needs of different organisations and different projects. Figure 3.6 shows one such recent adaptation I have made to the standard lifecycle.

FIGURE 3.6 PROJECT LIFECYCLE: FIVE PHASES AND SEVEN PROCESS GROUPS

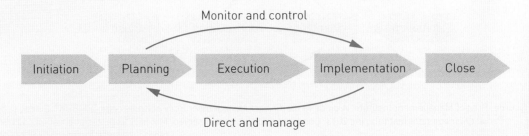

Source: Project Management Institute, *A guide to the Project Management Body of Knowledge*, (PMBOK® Guide), p. 50. Project Management Institute, Inc 2013. Copyright and all rights reserved. Material from this publication has been reproduced with the permission of PMI.

I have used this basic project lifecycle for small, non-complex projects so as to ensure that the right amount of critical discipline is applied without overloading the project with an unnecessary administrative burden. It is one that I have applied in many large organisations to ensure that the project managers pay more attention to the implementation and change management activities related to business projects. This suits any project that is implementing major change in an existing business, including business process improvement and business restructuring, as well as software upgrades and new systems implementations.

The legal project lifecycle was developed during my time with a major commercial law firm and is designed for application to most legal matters and transactions, with the exception of litigation (see Figure 3.7 below). It uses standard legal terminology and was designed to encourage better project management practices among legal teams in order to improve the delivery on client expectations around cost and timeframes.

FIGURE 3.7 PROJECT LIFECYCLE: THREE PHASES AND FIVE PROCESS GROUPS

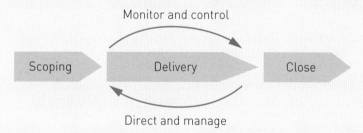

The next section illustrates different combinations of lifecycles that are commonly used for project delivery.

Combining different project lifecycles

Many project managers do not appreciate the importance of selecting and synthesising different project management approaches to develop a customised lifecycle that will ensure the best chances of success for each project in every context. Many will follow one particular methodology as it is often the first one they learnt, even when it is obviously not applicable to the specifics of their current project. The following diagrams show common combinations that can be used to satisfy the requirements of many projects.

PROCESS IMPROVEMENT PROJECTS

These projects can benefit from the application of standard process improvement approaches, such as Six Sigma. Many Six Sigma practitioners believe that the process provides a project management framework.

REAL–WORLD EXPERIENCE

PROCESS IMPROVEMENT AND PROJECT MANAGEMENT

As a previously certified black belt, I find that Six Sigma approaches are great for process improvement but do not contain sufficient discipline for project management. I like to combine the standard PMBOK® Guide project lifecycle with the Six Sigma process improvement steps of DMAIC – define, measure, analyse, improve and control (see Figure 3.8).

FIGURE 3.8 PROCESS IMPROVEMENT PROJECT LIFECYCLE

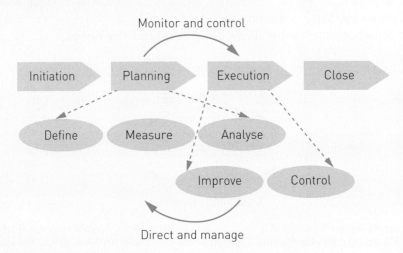

Source: Project Management Institute, *A guide to the Project Management Body of Knowledge*, (PMBOK® Guide), p. 50. Project Management Institute, Inc 2013. Copyright and all rights reserved. Material from this publication has been reproduced with the permission of PMI.

SOFTWARE DEVELOPMENT PROJECTS

Many projects involve some form of software development or systems upgrade; sometimes this is the primary purpose of the project, while at other times it is a subordinate outcome of a broader project. The following lifecycle has been used many times to successfully implement projects with software components. Figure 3.9 shows the expansion of the execution phase to include the phases of the standard software development lifecycle. This approach is particularly effective when managing teams of IT professionals with indirect reporting lines to the project manager.

Figure 3.10 shows how you can also incorporate an Agile software development approach into an overall project lifecycle. Figure 3.11 shows how you can combine the concepts of waterfall and Agile into the same project delivery approach. Waterfall is the more traditional approach for software development and is also traditionally used for many other forms of projects. It works it ways through each project phases one after the other with no consideration for how value can be delivered more quickly via in smaller stages. Many IT departments and vendors are now using Agile techniques to develop IT solutions, often combined with Waterfall in a hybrid. The hybrid approach is now often being seen in non IT projects as well.

FIGURE 3.9 SOFTWARE DEVELOPMENT PROJECT LIFECYCLE

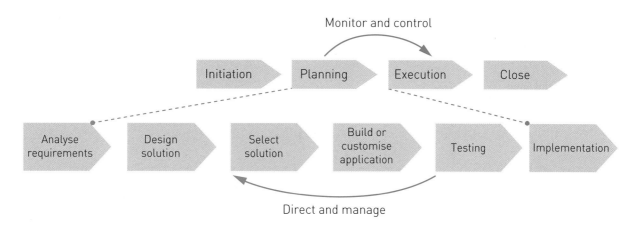

Source: Project Management Institute, *A guide to the Project Management Body of Knowledge*, (PMBOK® Guide), p. 50. Project Management Institute, Inc 2013. Copyright and all rights reserved. Material from this publication has been reproduced with the permission of PMI.

FIGURE 3.10 AGILE SOFTWARE DEVELOPMENT LIFECYCLE

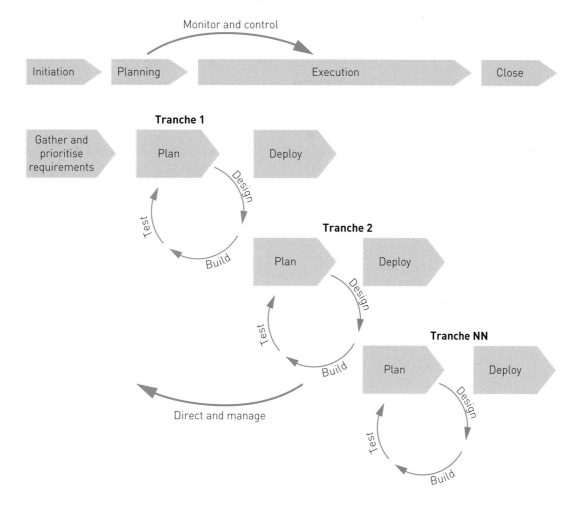

FIGURE 3.11 COMPARING WATERFALL AND AGILE LIFECYCLES

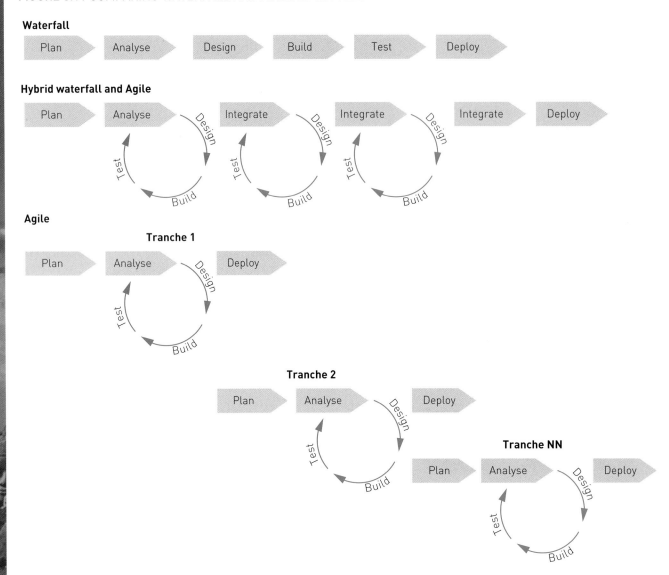

CONSTRUCTION PROJECTS

The construction industry does not use the standard PMBOK® Guide project lifecycle as there is a preference for the use of industry-specific terminology for the phase names. Figure 3.12 overlays common construction phase names onto the PMBOK® Guide lifecycle.

FIGURE 3.12 CONSTRUCTION PROJECT LIFECYCLE

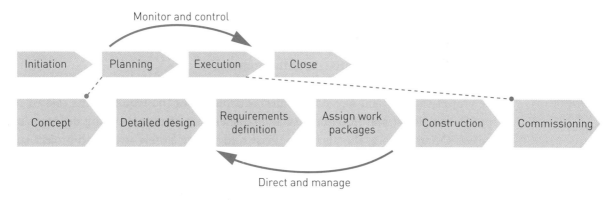

Source: Project Management Institute, *A guide to the Project Management Body of Knowledge*, (PMBOK® Guide), p. 50. Project Management Institute, Inc 2013. Copyright and all rights reserved. Material from this publication has been reproduced with the permission of PMI.

RESEARCH AND REFLECTION ACTIVITY

PROJECT METHODOLOGIES

There are many different project methodologies available to the project manager. There are various standards which have been adopted by various countries; for example, PMBOK® Guide in the US and Prince2 in the UK, as well as ITIL for the management of information technology operational processes.

Conduct some online research and answer the following questions.

1 What are the main differences between PMBOK® Guide and Prince2?
2 Can you see Prince2 being particularly useful for certain project types or industries?
3 What are the origins of Agile software development?
4 Can Agile be applied as a generic project methodology for any type of project?
5 What are the origins of Lean Manufacturing and Six Sigma?
6 Are there project methodologies or specific tools which can be applied to specific problems?
7 What is the relationship between ITIL and Prince2? How are they different from each other?

Related processes from the PMBOK® Guide

As mentioned earlier in this chapter, more than half of the project management processes identified in the PMBOK® Guide are contained within the planning process group. The critical process which is '4.2 Develop the project management plan' has been examined here in detail. There are many contributing processes which are examined further in the respective chapters on each key knowledge area. They are summarised below.

Project scoping processes

See PMBOK®
Guide Chapter 5
Project scope
management

5.1   ***Plan scope management (planning):*** The process of creating a scope management plan that provides guidance and direction as to how the project scope will be defined, validated and controlled throughout the project.

5.2   ***Collect requirements (planning):*** The process of defining and documenting the needs of the project sponsor and key stakeholders. Encompasses the requirements related to the specific functional and non-functional characteristics of outputs being delivered by the project. Occurs during the planning phase and is very closely related to project success measures, because if the end products do not meet the requirements then it is highly unlikely the project sponsor will sign off on the completion of the project.

5.3   ***Define scope (planning):*** The process of developing a detailed description of the project and the end products, or outputs, of the project. A detailed scope statement is critical to project success and good practice dictates that the detailed scope is signed off by the project sponsor, as well as key stakeholders.

5.4   ***Create work breakdown structure (WBS) (planning):*** The process of subdividing project deliverables and project work into smaller, more manageable components. The WBS defines all the work to be undertaken by the project team in order to achieve the project objectives and create the required deliverables. It enables the assignment of tasks to resources and forms the basis for the development of the project schedule.

More detail is provided in Chapter 7.

Project time processes

See PMBOK®
Guide Chapter 6
Project time
management

6.1   ***Plan schedule management (planning):*** The process for establishing the policies and procedures that will be used to plan, manage and control the project schedule. The schedule management plan provides guidance and direction as to how the project schedule will be managed.

6.2   ***Define activities (planning):*** The process of identifying the specific actions to be performed to produce the project deliverables. The actions must relate back to a deliverable from the WBS. If an activity doesn't relate to a project deliverable then it is either unnecessary or something has been omitted from the WBS. It is closely linked to '5.4 Create WBS'. Many project managers use the terms *activities* and *tasks* interchangeably when in reality tasks break activities down into smaller units of work.

REAL-WORLD EXPERIENCE

ACTIVITY DURATIONS

I do not recommend breaking down activities into durations of less than one day or more than a week.

6.3 ***Sequence activities (planning):*** The process of identifying and documenting relationships between the project activities. These are not to be confused with project dependencies which impact the project on a macro scale. Rather, they relate to the interdependencies between activities or tasks and these are best managed by the use of project scheduling software.

6.4 ***Estimate activity resources (planning):*** The process of estimating the types and quantities of material, people, equipment or supplies required to perform each activity. It is closely linked to '9.1 Develop human resource management plan' and '9.2 Acquire project team' and the project procurement management processes.

6.5 ***Estimate activity durations (planning):*** The process of approximating the number of work periods needed to complete individual activities with estimated resources. Work periods may be hours, days, weeks, months and so on and different resources will exhibit differing productivity levels.

6.6 ***Develop schedule (planning):*** The process of analysing activity sequences, durations, resource requirements and schedule constraints to create the project schedule. This is best completed with the aid of project scheduling software such as MS Project.
More detail is provided in Chapter 8.

Project cost processes

7.1 ***Plan cost management (planning):*** The process for establishing the policies and procedures that will be used to plan, manage and control costs for the project. The cost management plan provides guidance and direction as to how project costs will be managed.

7.2 ***Estimate costs (planning):*** The process for developing an estimate of costs to complete all activities required to finish the project. These estimates are a prediction based on the information known at any point in time and the assumptions that have been made for planning purposes.

See PMBOK®
Guide Chapter 7
Project cost
management

7.3 ***Determine budget (planning):*** The process for aggregating the costs of individual activities to form the overall budget for the project. An important component of this process is the establishment of the budget baseline for the project, against which all actual progress and variations will be reported. More detail is provided in Chapter 9.

Project quality processes

8.1 ***Plan quality management (planning):*** The process for identifying the quality requirements and quality standards applicable to a project and documenting how these requirements will be achieved for each deliverable. This also includes the identification of the quality assurance and quality control techniques that will be used to check that each deliverable has met the required quality expectations.
More detail is provided in Chapter 10.

See PMBOK®
Guide Chapter 8
Project quality
management

Human resource processes

See PMBOK®
Guide Chapter 9
Project human
resource
management

9.1 ***Plan human resource management (planning):*** The process for creating a project human resource plan by identifying project roles, responsibilities, required skills and reporting relationships. Other components may also include training needs, team building strategies, reward and recognition programs and performance management processes, as well as workplace health and safety procedures.
More detail is provided in Chapter 11.

Communication processes

See PMBOK®
Guide Chapter 10
Project
communication
management

10.1 ***Plan communications management (planning):*** The process for determining the project stakeholder information needs and for developing tailored communication approaches to meet those needs. Other components can include defining the communication needs within the project team.
More detail is provided in Chapter 12.

Risk management processes

See PMBOK®
Guide Chapter 11
Project risk
management

11.1 ***Plan risk management (planning):*** The process for defining how to conduct risk management activities for a project. This involves determining the risk management framework, including concepts such as the risk breakdown structure, likelihood and impact, and risk management approaches. Excellent international standards exist for risk management and many organisations have incorporated these into their own organisational processes.

11.2 ***Identify risks (planning):*** The process for identifying the risks that may impact the project. It is useful to have a broad group of key stakeholders, project team members and internal experts participate in the risk identification session. Good practice dictates that as far as possible all major risks should be identified during the planning phase, although this is an ongoing process as often risks are unpredictable and new risks become obvious during execution.

11.3 ***Perform qualitative risk analysis (planning):*** The process for prioritising risks for further analysis or mitigating actions by assessing a combination of the likelihood and impact of each risk. Project success is improved if the major, or high-priority risks, are minimised or avoided.

11.4 ***Perform quantitative risk analysis (planning):*** The process for numerically analysing the impact of the high-priority risks. This is often done in terms of the cost and time impacts on the project if each risk occurred. These can then be added together to contribute to the assignment of contingency for the project.

11.5 ***Plan risk responses (planning):*** The process for developing risk management strategies that will reduce the impact of major risks on the project objectives and success criteria.

Risks can be accepted, transferred, mitigated or avoided, and the specific actions selected should be in line with the priority and potential impact of the risk. The concept of the risk owner is applied to ensure that one person is accountable for enacting any risk management plans that may be required.

More detail is provided in Chapter 13.

Procurement processes

12.1   ***Plan procurement management (planning):*** The process for identifying the procurement requirements for a project. This involves identifying all resources and equipment that must be purchased and utilised in order to complete the project, as well as specifying the procurement approach and selection criteria. It considers potential suppliers and the contractual arrangements that may be required to manage these external parties to achieve the project objectives.

More detail is provided in Chapter 14.

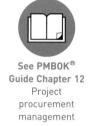

See PMBOK®
Guide Chapter 12
Project
procurement
management

Stakeholder processes

13.2   ***Plan stakeholder management (planning):*** The process of developing stakeholder management strategies that are tailored to the specific needs of groups and individuals who are impacted by, or interested in, the project. It is important to consider their possible impact on project success and also their relative importance.

More detail is provided in Chapter 15.

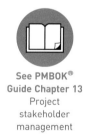

See PMBOK®
Guide Chapter 13
Project
stakeholder
management

CHAPTER SUMMARY

»   Project planning is the primary function of the project manager in the early phases of the project management lifecycle.

»   The project planning process groups contain all the activities required to develop plans for all 10 key knowledge areas. These processes develop the PMP and other related project deliverables that will be used to manage the execution of the project.

»   More than half of the processes contained within the PMBOK® Guide fall into the project planning process group.

»   The PMP is the most important deliverable produced out of the project planning phase. It defines and documents the actions necessary to prepare and integrate all subsidiary plans for all key knowledge areas of project management.

» Good practice dictates that the PMP is baselined at the end of the planning phase, particularly in the areas of scope, cost and time. It is progressively updated during project execution via the perform integrated change control process.

» The relationship between the PMP and scope, time and cost is slightly different to the other key knowledge areas of communication, risk, human resources, quality and procurement.

» There are no stand-alone scope, time or cost planning processes, as they are all contained within the develop PMP process, while the other key knowledge areas have separate processes for planning that are defined in their respective process groups.

» There are many templates available for the PMP, but generally these do not cover the contents in sufficient detail to enable the novice project manager to complete a comprehensive PMP without the aid of previously developed examples.

» PMPs often include support documents called subsidiary management plans. This is common for large projects where different project professionals are responsible for the planning and delivery of specific key knowledge areas such as risk, quality and procurement.

» The most common subsidiary plans are: communications management plan, procurement management plan, quality management plan, risk management plan and the requirements management plan.

» Other documentation is also often set apart from the PMP and these supplementary deliverables include: project budget spreadsheet, project control logs, risk log and procurement contracts.

» It is recommended that links are provided to all subsidiary plans, supplementary deliverables and relevant internal and external standards and procedures in the PMP.

» Some project managers establish project control logs during project initiation. If not, then they must be set up in the project planning phase as they form the backbone of the monitoring and controlling processes.

» It is important to select the best project management approach and methodology to ensure success for each different project. It can be necessary to modify and adapt the PMBOK® Guide project lifecycle to suit the particular needs of different organisations and different projects.

REVISION QUESTIONS

See detailed mapping grid for performance criteria covered

1   What functions are covered in the project planning phase?
2   Who has the primary responsibility for project planning?
3   What are the common contents of a PMP?
4   What are some of the common subsidiary plans?
5   When is the project baseline established?
6   What are the three expected project baselines?
7   What are the main project planning processes that cover scope, time and cost?
8   What processes are covered in quality planning activities?
9   What processes are covered in human resource planning activities?
10 What processes are covered in communication planning activities?
11 What processes are covered in the risk planning activities?
12 What processes are covered in procurement planning activities?
13 What common project control logs are established during the planning phase?

DISCUSSION QUESTIONS

See detailed mapping grid for performance criteria covered

1   Why do PMPs sometimes incorporate all 10 key knowledge areas and why do they sometimes split these into subsidiary plans?
2   What are the benefits of subsidiary plans for quality, risk and procurement?
3   How can project managers ensure that they are adhering to all the expected cost management processes?
4   What is the difference between quality assurance and quality control?
5   Why is the quality component of project planning often done poorly and what can be done to improve this?
6   What is the purpose of project control logs and why are they useful for concepts such as assumptions and decisions?
7   What is the purpose of the project baseline and when should it be established?
8   How do project managers determine the project methodology and approach that will provide the best possible framework for success?
9   Is it more important to exactly follow a prescribed methodology or to tailor the methodology to the needs to each project?
10 What are the pros and cons of assigning specialised key knowledge areas, such as quality and procurement, to professionals in these disciplines?

ONLINE RESOURCES

Visit the online companion website at http://www.cengagebrain.com to link to important additional resources, including templates, real-world case studies, revision quizzes and additional study material.

FURTHER READING AND REFERENCES

Dobie, C. (2007). *A handbook of project management: A complete guide for beginners to professionals*. Sydney: Allen and Unwin.

Hartley, S. (2008). *Project management: Principles, processes and practice* (2nd ed.). Sydney: Pearson Education.

Kerzner, H. (2007). *Project management: A systems approach to planning, scheduling, and controlling* (9th ed.). Brisbane: John Wiley & Sons.

Kloppenborg, T. J. (2012). *Contemporary project management* (2nd ed.). Melbourne: Cengage Learning.

Mulcahy, R. (2006). *PM crash course – Real-world project management tools & techniques*. Minnetonka, MN: RMC Publications.

Portny S. E., Mantel, S. J., Meredith, J. R., . . . Sutton, M. M. (2008). *Project management – Planning, scheduling and controlling projects*. Brisbane: Wiley.

Project Management Institute (PMI). (2013). *A guide to the Project Management Body of Knowledge* (PMBOK® Guide) (5th ed.). Newtown Square, PA: author.

Schwable, K. (2014). *Information technology project management* (revised 7th ed.). Brooks/Cole, a part of Cengage Learning.

Verzuh, E. (2005). *The fast forward MBA in project management*. Brisbane: John Wiley & Sons.

Project execution

LEARNING OBJECTIVES   IN THIS CHAPTER YOU WILL:

1 become familiar with the processes and activities performed when executing a project

2 appreciate the major roles and leadership behaviours of the project manager during the execution phase

3 understand the responsibilities of the project manager when directing and managing a project

4 appreciate the importance of acquiring the right team members for the project team

5 learn about specific tools and techniques to improve team member selection

6 understand the importance of flexibility when managing individual team members and the project team as a whole

7 learn about leadership and team formation models that will help you to more effectively manage project teams

8 appreciate the difference between planning for quality and performing quality assurance activities

9 appreciate the difference between planning procurements and conducting procurements

10 consider the importance of defining processes for collecting project performance data so that it can be distributed

11 understand the activities involved in executing the communications plan

12 develop an appreciation of the complexities of managing stakeholder expectations

13 learn about key skills that will assist in the identification, anticipation and management of stakeholder expectations.

Context

The project execution process group involves directing and managing the project team and resources in order to perform the activities that complete the deliverables required to deliver the project scope. This critical coordination effort ensures that the project is undertaken in accordance with the project management plan (PMP).

Many inexperienced project managers and project sponsors underestimate the importance of the execution phase of the project lifecycle, tending to concentrate their efforts on the planning phase in the naive belief that all you need is a detailed plan in order to successfully execute a project. The executing process group is one of the least populated in the PMBOK® Guide as this is where the specific activities and unique deliverables of the project are fulfilled. The project manager needs to define these deliverables and activities according to the detailed scope and requirements of the project and then ensure they are delivered. It is where the real magic of project management happens.

It is common for changes to occur during project execution which require replanning and re-baselining of the project. This is where the process of integrated change control becomes extremely important and it is one of the critical related processes from project integration management. The only thing you can know for certain once you have completed the planning and moved into project execution is that the project will deviate from the plan. It is the project manager's role during execution to keep the project on track by:

- responding to and resolving issues as they arise
- enacting risk action plans for risks that have occurred
- acquiring the project team
- directing and managing project team members
- managing stakeholder expectations
- managing and implementing change requests
- distributing information about project performance
- conducting procurement activities
- managing vendor relationships.

PMBOK® Guide processes for project execution

The majority of the processes in this group relate to the management of the project team members and stakeholders. It used to be thought that project managers just needed to be proficient at the technical aspects of project management, but research into the primary causes of project failure indicate that the two most common reasons for failure are incorrect, or inadequate, resourcing coupled with a lack of understanding and management of stakeholder expectations.

The PMBOK® Guide processes for project execution are:

4.3   Direct and manage project work

8.2   Perform quality assurance

9.2   Acquire project team

See PMBOK®
Guide Table 3-1
Project
management
process groups
and knowledge
area mapping

9.3   Develop project team
9.4   Manage project team
10.2   Manage communications
12.2   Conduct procurements
13.3   Manage stakeholder engagement.

Please see Chapter 11 (pages 276-81) for information about acquiring the project team and techniques for selecting members.

RESEARCH AND REFLECTION ACTIVITY

HUMAN RESOURCE MANAGEMENT

Review your organisation's recruitment policies and processes.

- Do they include supporting tools for the recruitment process?
- Does your HR department provide assistance with recruitment and candidate selection?
- Are there any competencies or standard position descriptions available for project management roles?

There are many excellent websites and resources available to support project managers in selection and hiring activities. Undertake online research into the following topics:

- targeted selection
- interviewing and selection
- behavioural testing
- aptitude testing
- best practices in reference checking
- best practices in recruitment.

Directing and managing the project

Directing and managing project execution is the process of leading the project team in the performance of the work that has been defined in the PMP in order to achieve the project objectives. This significant process is comprised of supplementary processes and these are discussed below.

People and project leadership skills

According to the PMBOK® Guide, project managers require specific interpersonal skills in order to successfully lead projects. These are:

- leadership
- team building

- motivation
- communication
- influencing
- decision making
- political and cultural awareness
- negotiation
- trust building
- conflict management
- coaching.

MANAGING TEAM MEMBERS

There are many techniques and frameworks that exist to support project managers in the following areas.

REAL-WORLD EXPERIENCE

SITUATIONAL LEADERSHIP®

My preferred people leadership model is Situational Leadership®, which was developed by Dr Paul Hersey and Ken Blanchard in the 1970s. This could be because it was the very first people leadership model that I was taught as a young project leader in the 1980s. I have personally found it very reliable and adaptable over the last 25 years, so for me it has stood the test of time and practical application for many hundreds of team members.

Hersey and Blanchard's Situational Leadership theory states that instead of using just one style, the most successful leaders adapt their leadership style based on the maturity, or capability, of each team member and the specific nature of the task they will be executing. In brief, they exercise emotional intelligence to select the leadership style that will get the job done most successfully.

LEADERSHIP STYLES

According to Hersey and Blanchard, there are four main leadership styles:
- **Directing (S1)**: Leaders tell their people exactly what to do, and how to do it. The communication tends to be mostly from the leader to the team member and detailed instructions are provided, as well as regular progress reviews.
- **Coaching (S2)**: Leaders still provide information and direction, but there's more communication with the team member. Leaders 'sell' their message to get the individual on board and engaged with the task.

- **Supporting (S3)**: Leaders focus more on the relationship and less on the provision of specific instructions or detailed direction. The leader works with the team member and allows them to contribute to how the task will be undertaken.
- **Delegating (S4)**: Leaders pass most of the responsibility to the team member, while maintaining oversight of progress.

The telling and selling styles are focused on getting the task done. The participating and delegating styles are more concerned with developing the abilities of team members. They are all valid and effective in different situations and most leaders will have a specific preference for one style over the others. With this in mind, the most successful people leaders will consciously choose the most effective leadership style for each situation.

MATURITY OR DEVELOPMENT LEVELS

According to Hersey and Blanchard, the other major factor which contributes to the selection of the leadership style is the maturity or development level of the team member. It is a good idea to expand upon this to include the capability or competency of the individual.

The four levels are:

- **Development level 1 – low capability and low commitment (D1)**: Team members at this level of maturity are at the bottom level of the scale. They lack the knowledge, skills or confidence to work on their own, and they often need to be pushed to take the task on. This level is low ability and low confidence.
- **Development level 2 – medium commitment with limited capability (D2)**: These team members might be willing to work on the task, but they still don't have all the skills to do it successfully. This level is low ability and medium to high confidence.
- **Development level 3 – medium commitment with higher capability (D3)**: These team members are ready and willing to help with the task. They have more skills than the D2 group, but they're still not confident in their abilities or are lacking critical experience for the task. This level is high to medium ability and low confidence.
- **Development level 4 – high commitment and high capability (D4)**: These team members are able to work on their own. They have high confidence and strong skills, and they're committed to the task. This level is high ability and high confidence.

It is critical to understand that maturity levels are specific to each combination of team member and specific task. A person might be generally skilled, confident and motivated in their job, but would still have a low maturity level when asked to perform a task requiring skills they don't possess.

Table 4.1 (see overleaf) is a slightly adapted version of the Hersey-Blanchard model and maps each leadership style to each maturity or development level.

TABLE 4.1 ADAPTED HERSEY-BLANCHARD LEADERSHIP MODEL

Development level	Most appropriate leadership style
Development 1 – low capability and low commitment (D1)	Directing (Situation 1)
Development 2 – medium commitment with limited capability (D2)	Coaching (Situation 2)
Development 3 – medium commitment with higher capability (D3)	Supporting (Situation 3)
Development 4 – high commitment and high capability (D4)	Delegating (Situation 4)

Figure 4.1 is a useful summary of the Hersey-Blanchard model which maps each leadership style to each maturity level.

FIGURE 4.1 THE HERSEY-BLANCHARD SITUATIONAL LEADERSHIP MODEL

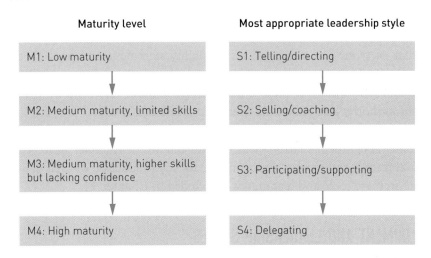

Developing the project team

Developing the project team is about enhancing the way the project team works together in order to deliver a successful project. Team work is a critical factor in project success and it is one of the primary responsibilities of the project manager during execution.

Some of the activities which improve team performance are listed below. Some experts believe that none of these happen spontaneously; they all need to be planned and managed by the project manager.

- Improving the skills and knowledge of project team members in order to increase productivity and the ability to complete project deliverables.
- Developing trust and collaboration within the team in order to raise morale, lower conflict and improve cooperation.
- Manage the risk of key human resources leaving during the project by encouraging cross-training, peer reviews and mentoring within the team.

CLARITY OF ROLES AND RESPONSIBILITIES

Conflict among project team members is common and can seriously impact productivity. One of the major sources of conflict arises from a lack of clarity over roles and responsibilities. This is relatively simple to address by ensuring that some of the following standard project management tools and techniques are applied:

- ensuring that everyone has a detailed responsibility statement and position description as this reduces confusion and tension
- developing and distributing a project team organisational chart showing reporting lines (and thereby authority levels) and the overall structure of the team
- assigning specific accountabilities and responsibilities for each deliverable via the use of a responsibility assignment matrix – this ensures that all deliverables have been assigned to an individual team member who is accountable for the production of their deliverable(s).
  More detail on these tools and techniques is included in Chapter 11.

TEAM DEVELOPMENT AND LEADERSHIP STYLES

In 1965, psychologist Bruce Tuckman came up with a model of team development which includes the following stages: forming, storming, norming and performing. This was the result of research that he conducted into high-performing teams. Then, in 1975, he added a final stage called adjourning or mourning. This specifically addressed the relatively new phenomenon of project teams which were temporarily formed to deliver a specific set of objectives and then disbanded once the objectives were met.

These stages are described in the Northern Sydney Institute (NSI) Online Certificate IV and Diploma of Project Management as follows:

- **Forming**: In this stage the team members meet each other and learn about the project and their individual roles and responsibilities. Team members tend to be polite and reserved. Some will be anxious while others are excited about being on the project. This is normally a short phase that lasts only a few weeks.
- **Storming**: The honeymoon is over and there is often tension and misunderstandings as the team members learn how to work together and test their understanding of the project objectives and approach. Some of the project work now starts and it is critical that team members remain open and considerate of each other as they move through misunderstandings. Otherwise destructive conflict can greatly impact productivity.
- **Norming**: In this stage team members start to work more collaboratively together and adjust their work habits, terminology and behaviours as the 'norms' for the team are established. Trust should be developing and productivity begins to rise. The norming phase and storming phase often overlap.
- **Performing**: Due to the transient nature of projects, some project teams never reach this level of high performance. In this stage the team operates as a cohesive unit and smoothly resolves issues resulting in very high productivity. More delegation will be possible and the team culture should be strong.
- **Adjourning (mourning)**: In the adjourning phase the project is completed and the team is disbanded. Breaking up a team can be traumatic for some team members, especially those that have developed strong interpersonal relationships and dislike change. The project manager needs to be sensitive to these issues and support people through the transition.

Using the Situational Leadership model, it is possible for the project manager to choose the most appropriate leadership style to lead the project team during each stage of team development and also to ensure the fastest possible transition through the phases. The two models are shown together in the following diagram.

FIGURE 4.2 TEAM FORMATION PHASES AND SITUATIONAL LEADERSHIP

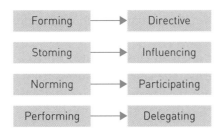

Adapted from Hersey and Blanchard's Situational Leadership model and Tuckman's Ladder of Team Development.

Just as with individual team members, the most successful project managers will adapt their leadership style to the specific phase of team development. These concepts are explained in further detail in Chapter 11.

REAL–WORLD EXPERIENCE

ADAPTING LEADERSHIP STYLES

The importance and relevance of the above model was reinforced for me a few years ago when I was the program director for the development of a major new superannuation product. Initially, we had a team of highly skilled business experts who had very little or non-existent project delivery experience. I immediately had to acquire (through internal and external recruitment) 10 additional professional project managers and many business and process analysts, and also organise the procurement of two major software packages including vendor delivery services. The storming phase was very rocky so I had to quickly move into a very directive style of leadership which was very much outside of my comfort zone. My personal preference is for the more collaborative and delegative leadership styles as I like to assemble the most highly skilled and experienced project team possible and then let them get on with it. I found myself in a situation where I had to be commanding and cut off any form of debate or refinement to the approach and objectives as this was the only way that we could make forward progress. I could have been gentler if we didn't have a fixed deadline for implementation which coincided with the delivery of new regulations into the industry. After a few months I could relax into a more participative style as the project managers established expected modes of behaviour and took more control of their various workstreams.

Collecting and distributing project performance information

The monitoring and controlling process group contains the processes to check the progress of the project against the actual plan. The performance data that is collected via these processes is then distributed by the process '10.2 Manage communications'. The main reason for collecting and distributing this information is to manage the expectations of the project sponsor and key project stakeholders via another process within the executing process group '13.3 Manage stakeholder engagement'. They are both closely related to '10.2 Plan communications' as well as '10.3 Control communications'. The latter is a process from the monitoring and controlling process group which reviews and reports on actual project performance and status. These are explained in more detail in Chapter 12. The basic principles, however, are included in this chapter to provide a complete view of the major activities which comprise the executing process group.

It is critical to establish expectations and processes for both the collection of performance data and the reporting of overall project status in the PMP. All relevant project performance information is then distributed to project stakeholders in accordance with the detailed communications plan, which includes preferences for timings of updates, specific content and areas of interest, preferred communication channels and so on.

Information distribution actually occurs throughout the entire project lifecycle but it is emphasised here in the executing phase as this is when the detailed communication plan is implemented, and there is a need to respond to unexpected requests for information. Some important skills required by the project manager to improve information distribution and communication include:

- meeting management techniques
- presentation skills
- facilitation skills
- active listening
- negotiation skills
- conflict resolution techniques
- decision making frameworks
- summarisation skills.

Managing stakeholder engagement

This is one of the most important and difficult roles for the project manager. Many projects fail due to a poor understanding, and hence poor management, of the expectations and requirements of key stakeholders. This process is about communicating and working with stakeholders (including the project sponsor) to meet their needs, manage their expectations and address specific issues as they occur. These are often difficult to predict as stakeholders can be subject to many undeclared forces and pressures from outside of the project. See Chapter 15 for more detail.

Managing expectations increases the likelihood of project success by helping stakeholders to understand the benefits and risks of a project, as well as the issues that arise along the way. In this way they can become active supporters of the project and can assist the project manager by further managing the expectations of other stakeholders.

It is also helpful to be able to anticipate the possible reactions of stakeholders to the project so that action can be taken to prevent potential negative impacts. This is one of the hardest skills to define and acquire, yet one of the most important skills for a project manager to possess.

Most of the key inputs into this process are produced during the earlier communications planning activities and include:

- the communications plan
- the stakeholder register
- stakeholder management strategies
- change management plans including schedules of communication, training and engagement activities.

The key skills required by the project manager to manage and anticipate stakeholder expectations are:

- intuition and judgement
- understanding of human behaviour and motivations
- political astuteness
- rapport building skills
- negotiation skills
- influencing skills
- problem solving skills
- active listening.

Kathy Schwable has developed an excellent matrix for managing stakeholder expectations (see Table 4.2).

TABLE 4.2 EXPECTATIONS MANAGEMENT MATRIX

Measure of success	Priority	Expectations	Guidelines
Scope	2	The scope clearly defines mandatory requirements and optional requirements.	Focus on meeting mandatory requirements before considering optional ones.
Time	1	There is no give in the project completion date. Every major deadline must be met, and the schedule is very realistic.	The project sponsor and program manager must be alerted if there are any issues that might affect meeting schedule goals.
Cost	3	This project is crucial to the organisation. If you can clearly justify the need for more funds, they can be made available.	There are strict rules for project expenditures and escalation procedures. Cost is very important, but it takes a back seat to meeting schedule and then scope goals.
Quality	6	Quality is important, and the expectation is that we follow our well-established processes for testing this system.	All new personnel are required to complete several in-house courses to make sure they understand our quality processes. All corporate quality standards must be followed.
Customer satisfaction	4	Our customer expects us to act professionally, answer questions in a timely manner and work collaboratively with them to get the project done.	All presentations and formal documents provided to the customer must be edited by a tech writer. Everyone should reply to customer requests within 24 hours.

(Continued)

Measure of success	Priority	Expectations	Guidelines
ROI projections	5	The business case for this project projected an ROI of 40% within two years of implementation.	Our finance department will work with the customer to measure the ROI. Meeting/exceeding this projection will help us bring in future business with this and other customers.

Source: From Schawble. *Information Technology Project Management* (with Microsoft Project 2010 60 Day Trial CD-ROM), 7th edition, © 2014 Brooks/Cole, a part of Cengage Learning, Inc. Reproduced by permission.

Performing quality assurance

All project quality assurance activities need to take place during execution and in many cases all of the quality control activities will be conducted as well, although the PMBOK® Guide considers quality control activities to be part of the monitoring and controlling process group. This process is closely related to '8.1 Plan quality management' which is explained in more detail in Chapter 10.

In reality, quality assurance and quality control activities are performed throughout the project as deliverables are executed and checked against requirements. Quality assurance activities are built into the development of each deliverable, whereas quality control activities are performed once a deliverable has been completed. It is much more cost and time effective to build quality into the production process rather than to check it at the end. There are many effective and very basic quality assurance tools and techniques that are often overlooked when developing the quality plan and these include:

- development methodologies
- work instructions and processes
- precedents and examples from previous projects
- interim reviews
- training and up-skilling
- selection of appropriately skilled team members
- statistical quality sampling techniques
- control charts
- benchmarking
- quality checklists.

Please see Chapter 10 (page 241) for a research and reflection activity on quality processes and standards.

Identification and implementation of change requests

This is a critical component of the execution phase that is overlooked by the PMBOK® Guide on the basis that change control is contained within the monitoring and controlling process group. As mentioned previously, the only thing that is certain once a project is being executed is that the project will not precisely follow the PMP.

Changes to the project baselines of scope, time and cost are identified during execution and need to be managed via '4.5 Perform integrated change control'. If they are approved then they must be implemented during the execution phases of the project. This involves the following project management activities:

- log change requests
- submit change requests for consideration
- communicate the outcomes of change request decisions to the project team and all impacted stakeholders
- direct the project team to undertake all approved change requests
- include change requests in the scope of work and quality activities
- update impacted project baselines for scope, time and cost
- check that change requests have been implemented via scope verification and quality control.

Figure 4.3 shows a basic change control process and a basic change implementation process. Change control is covered in more detail in Chapter 5.

FIGURE 4.3 CHANGE CONTROL AND IMPLEMENTATION PROCESSES – SIDE BY SIDE

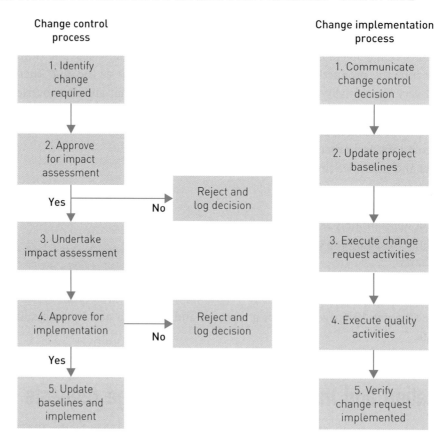

REAL-WORLD EXPERIENCE

WHY IS CHANGE CONTROL SO DIFFICULT TO IMPLEMENT?

I find it strange to observe that many project sponsors, managers and project teams are often reluctant to implement formal change control processes. In my experience, it is often due to a lack of understanding of the most common causes of project failure, coupled with a general reluctance on both sides to have difficult conversations.

Change control is an integral part of the project management processes of many industries, especially the construction industry where discussions of variations are common and processes are normally clearly laid out in contracts. This is largely driven by the prevalence of fixed price engagements in the industry which drives the need for additional project control and scope control disciplines.

Nevertheless, change requests or variations are still the cause of much conflict on projects where the client or project sponsor will argue that the item was always part of the project scope, while the project manager will argue that it is a change request. This proves my argument for detailed requirements and scoping documentation, as the more detailed these are, the less conflict creeps in.

Conducting procurement activities

Procurement activities are conducted during the execution phase in line with the procurement plan which is developed in the planning phase via the '10.1 Plan procurement management' process. This process starts at the point where bids are being received from suppliers for items that need to be procured. Tender documentation, supplier briefing materials, requirements and selection criteria have all been developed during planning.

Figure 4.4 shows basic processes for the planning of procurements. Project procurement management is covered in more detail in Chapter 14.

FIGURE 4.4 PLAN AND CONDUCT PROCUREMENT PROCESSES – SIDE BY SIDE

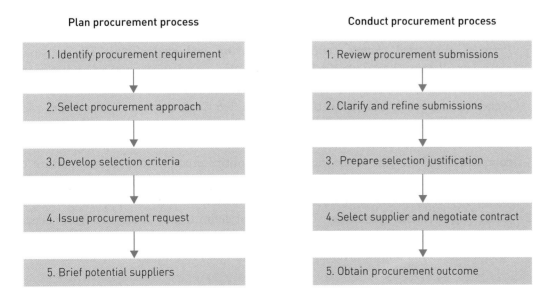

Plan procurement process	Conduct procurement process
1. Identify procurement requirement	1. Review procurement submissions
2. Select procurement approach	2. Clarify and refine submissions
3. Develop selection criteria	3. Prepare selection justification
4. Issue procurement request	4. Select supplier and negotiate contract
5. Brief potential suppliers	5. Obtain procurement outcome

These can seem like simple processes but for major procurements they can be very complex and time consuming.

Related processes from the PMBOK® Guide

4.3 ***Direct and manage project work (execution)***: The process of performing the work defined in the PMP in order to achieve the project's objectives. The project manager directs the execution of the planned activities, sometimes with the assistance of a project management team for larger projects. The PMBOK® Guide includes this process within the execution phase but there is merit in thinking of it as a separate process group having equal importance to monitoring and controlling.

4.4 ***Monitor and control project work (execution)***: The process of tracking, reviewing and regulating the progress made towards the objectives defined in the PMP. The project manager is specifically responsible for the monitoring and control of project work, sometimes with the assistance of a project management team or project management office for larger projects. Monitoring is an aspect of project management performed throughout the project, but it becomes more critical during the execution phase. It is closely linked to '5.6 Control scope', '6.7 Control schedule', '7.4 Control costs', '8.3 Quality control', '10.3 Control communications' and '11.6 Control risks'.

4.5 ***Perform integrated change control (monitoring and controlling)***: The process of reviewing all change requests, including approving or rejecting changes and managing the flow-on, impacts on all project deliverables and all components of the PMP. All requested changes should be identified through '5.6 Control scope'. The activities within this process are critical to managing stakeholder expectations and to ensuring the highest chance of project success. They occur from project inception through to completion and are part of the monitor and control process group. It is important that only approved changes be incorporated into the project, as it is surprisingly common to see unapproved changes being inadvertently undertaken.

5.2 ***Collect requirements (planning)***: The process of defining and documenting the needs of the project sponsor and key stakeholders. Encompasses the requirements related to the specific functional and non-functional characteristics of outputs being delivered by the project. Occurs during the planning phase and is very closely related to project success measures, because if the end products do not meet the requirements then it is highly unlikely the project sponsor will sign off on the completion of the project.

5.3 **Define scope (planning)**: The process of developing a detailed description of the project and the end products, or outputs, of the project. A detailed scope statement is critical to project success and good practice dictates that the detailed scope is signed off by the project sponsor, as well as key stakeholders.

5.4 **Create work breakdown structure (WBS) (planning)**: The process of subdividing project deliverables and project work into smaller, more manageable components. The WBS defines all the work to be undertaken by the project team in order to achieve the project objectives and create the required deliverables. It enables the assignment of tasks to resources and forms the basis for the development of the project schedule.

6.1 **Plan schedule management (planning)**: The process for establishing the policies and procedures that will be used to plan, manage and control the project schedule. The schedule management plan provides guidance and direction as to how the project schedule will be managed.

6.4 **Estimate activity resources (planning)**: The process of estimating the types and quantities of material, people, equipment or supplies required to perform each activity. It is closely linked to '9.1 Plan human resource management' and '9.2 Acquire project team' and the project procurement management processes.

6.6 **Develop schedule (planning)**: The process of analysing activity sequences, durations, resource requirements and schedule constraints to create the project schedule. This is best completed with the aid of project scheduling software such as MS Project.

8.1 **Plan quality management (planning)**: The process for identifying the quality requirements and quality standards applicable to a project and documenting how these requirements will be achieved for each deliverable. This also includes the identification of the quality assurance and quality control techniques that will be used to check that each deliverable has met the required quality expectations.

8.3 **Control quality (monitoring and controlling)**: The processes conducted to ensure that each deliverable meets all requirements and specifications. Quality control is performed as each deliverable or related set of deliverables are completed and often involves testing and inspection. It is closely related to '5.5 Validate scope'.

9.1 **Plan human resource management (planning)**: The process for creating a project human resource plan by identifying project roles, responsibilities, required skills and reporting relationships. Other components may also include training needs, team building strategies, reward and recognition programs and performance management processes, as well as workplace health and safety procedures.

10.1 **Plan communications management (planning)**: The process for determining the project stakeholder information needs and for developing tailored communication approaches to meet those needs. Other components can include defining the communication needs within the project team.

10.2   ***Manage communications (planning)***: The process of collecting and distributing project performance and status information. This involves the periodic collection of actual performance data and comparing this against the planned baselines of the project. This enables the reporting of performance as well as reforecasting the future performance of the project.

11.5   ***Plan risk responses (planning)***: The process for developing risk management strategies that will reduce the impact of major risks on the project objectives and success criteria. Risks can be accepted, transferred, mitigated or avoided, and the specific actions selected should be in line with the priority and potential impact of the risk. The concept of the risk owner is applied to ensure that one person is accountable for enacting any risk management plans that may be required.

12.1   ***Plan procurement management (planning)***: The process for identifying the procurement requirements for a project. This involves identifying all resources and equipment that must be purchased and utilised in order to complete the project, as well as specifying the procurement approach and selection criteria. It considers potential suppliers and the contractual arrangements that may be required to manage these external parties to achieve the project objectives.

13.2   ***Plan stakeholder management (execution)***: The process of developing management strategies to engage stakeholders throughout the project lifecycle in order to satisfy their needs and improve the chances of project success.

CHAPTER SUMMARY

»   Project execution is about completing the specific deliverables that are required to meet the scope and objectives of the project.
»   The majority of the processes in this group relate to the management of the project team members and stakeholders.
»   The two most common reasons for project failure are incorrect, or inadequate, resourcing coupled with a lack of understanding and management of stakeholder expectations.
»   Project managers need to be adept at leading the project team and managing the expectations of stakeholders, including the project sponsor.
»   If there is a formal approval gate between the initiation and execution phases, then the first action taken by the project manager in the execution phase is to acquire the project team; it would be wasteful of monetary resources to start project team members before the project has been approved to proceed.
»   In practice, a common method of accelerating project delivery timeframes is to overlap the initiation and execution phases and to acquire the project team as early as possible. This is a sound strategy if the project is mandatory and no formal approval is required between initiation and execution.

» Primary techniques for team member selection include: position descriptions, behavioural testing, targeted selection, reference checks, background checks and aptitude testing.

» Project managers need to adapt their leadership styles to get the best out of individual team members and the project team as a whole.

» Situational Leadership is a simple and easily applied model for managing individuals who have differing levels of capability and maturity.

» Situational Leadership can be successfully combined with the team formation stages of forming, storming, norming and performing to ensure that the best leadership style is adopted to accelerate transition and productivity.

» A major reason for collecting and distributing project performance information is to manage the expectations of the project sponsor and key project stakeholders.

» It is critical to establish expectations and processes for both the collection of performance data and the reporting of overall project status in the PMP.

» Some of the key people skills required by the project manager to manage and anticipate stakeholder expectations are: intuition and judgement, rapport building and influencing skills, negotiation skills and active listening.

» All project quality assurance activities need to take place during execution and in many cases all of the quality control activities will be conducted as well.

» Quality assurance activities are built into the development of each deliverable, whereas quality control activities are performed once a deliverable has been completed.

» Changes to the project baselines of scope, time and cost that are identified during execution need to be implemented.

» Change requests may arise from many different factors and events, including: risks that occur, planning assumptions that are untrue, costing assumptions that are untrue and additions or adjustments to scope.

» Procurement activities are conducted during the execution phase in line with the procurement plan which is developed in the planning phase.

REVISION QUESTIONS

1   What functions are covered in the project execution phase?
2   Who is responsible for managing and directing the project?
3   What skills are required by the project manager during this phase?
4   What tools and techniques can the project manager use to select the best possible project team?
5   What tools and techniques can be used to develop the project team?
6   What are the four main leadership styles of the Situational Leadership model?
7   What are the four development or maturity levels of the Situational Leadership model?
8   What are the stages of Tuckman's model of team development?
9   What specific activities are involved in the collection and distribution of project performance information?
10   How do project managers manage the expectations of stakeholders?
11   What activities are involved with performing quality assurance?
12   How do project managers identify and implement change requests?
13   What is the purpose of change control processes?
14   What activities are involved with conducting procurements?

See detailed mapping grid for performance criteria covered

See detailed mapping grid for performance criteria covered

DISCUSSION QUESTIONS

1   Why is the execution phase often overlooked when the detailed project plans are being prepared?

2   Why is it important to acquire the best possible project team and what techniques can project managers use to improve team member selection?

3   Why are project managers not always in control of the team members assigned to their projects?

4   What activities are involved in successful targeted selection techniques for team member selection?

5   How can the Situational Leadership model be applied to improve both individual and project team performance?

6   Why is it important to focus on quality assurance activities in preference to quality control activities?

7   Why is resistance often encountered when project managers introduce formal change control processes?

8   Why is it recommended that change control processes have two stages of approval: (1) prior to the investigation of impacts; and (2) after the investigation of impacts?

9   What are the advantages of conducting procurement activities as part of the planning phase rather than in the execution phases?

10 What disadvantages are there if procurement activities are undertaken too early?

ONLINE RESOURCES

Visit the online companion website at http://www.cengagebrain.com to link to important additional resources, including templates, real-world case studies, revision quizzes and additional study material.

FURTHER READINGS AND REFERENCES

Clarke, N., & Howell, R. (2009). *Emotional intelligence and projects*. Newtown Square, PA: Project Management Institute.

Dobie, C. (2007). *A handbook of project management: A complete guide for beginners to professionals*. Sydney: Allen and Unwin.

Flannes, S., & Levin, G. (2005). *Essential people skills for project managers*. Vienna, VA: Management Concepts.

Hartley, S. (2008). *Project management: Principles, processes and practice* (2nd ed.). Sydney: Pearson Education.

Kerzner, H. (2007). *Project management: A systems approach to planning, scheduling, and controlling* (9th ed.). Brisbane: John Wiley & Sons.

Kloppenborg, T. J. (2012). *Contemporary project management* (2nd ed.). Melbourne: Cengage Learning.

Mulcahy, R. (2006). *PM crash course – Real-world project management tools & techniques.*. Minnetonka, MN: RMC Publications.

Portny S. E., Mantel, S. J., Meredith, J. R., . . . Sutton, M. M. (2008). *Project management – Planning, scheduling and controlling projects.* Brisbane: Wiley.

Project Management Institute (PMI). (2013). *A guide to the Project Management Body of Knowledge* (PMBOK® Guide) (5th ed.). Newtown Square, PA: author.

Schwable, K. (2014). *Information technology project management* (revised 7th ed.). Brooks/Cole, a part of Cengage Learning.

The Ken Blanchard Companies. (2001). Situational Leadership II: The article. Item # 13526 (V020101). Accessed 19 July 2013, http://moodle.unitec.ac.nz/pluginfile.php/250852/mod_resource/content/2/ Blanchard%20Situational%20Leadership%20II.pdf.

Verzuh, E. (2005). *The fast forward MBA in project management.* Brisbane: John Wiley & Sons.

5

Project monitoring and controlling

Context

The purpose of the monitoring and controlling process group is to regularly observe and measure project performance so that variances are identified. It consists of the processes involved in tracking and reviewing the progress and performance of the project against the project management plan (PMP). It also involves the critically important processes of identifying areas of change on the project and managing these changes back into the project for delivery.

Some of the critical activities performed are:

- controlling changes to the project and preventing the inadvertent inclusion of changes
- recommending preventative actions to avoid future problems
- monitoring progress against the project baselines of scope, time and cost
- reviewing risks to determine if they have occurred
- ensuring that all quality control activities have been completed and that resulting defects are resolved.

PMBOK® Guide processes for monitoring and controlling

The processes in this group relate to the measurement and management of project performance in accordance with the PMP. The PMBOK® Guide processes for monitoring and controlling are:

4.4	Monitor and control project work
4.5	Perform integrated change control
5.5	Validate scope
5.6	Control scope
6.7	Control schedule
7.4	Control costs
8.3	Quality control
10.3	Control communications
11.6	Control risks
12.3	Control procurements
13.4	Control stakeholder engagement.

See PMBOK®
Guide Table 3-1
Project
management
process groups
and knowledge
area mapping

Monitor and control project work

The process to monitor and control project work is part of the Project Integration Management key knowledge area and it is concerned with tracking, reviewing and regulating the progress made towards the objectives defined in the PMP. The project manager is responsible for the monitoring and control of project work, sometimes with the assistance of a project management team or project management office for larger projects. Monitoring is an aspect of project management performed throughout the project, but it becomes more critical during the execution phase. It is closely linked to '5.6 Control scope', '6.7 Control schedule', '7.4 Control costs', '8.3 Control quality', '10.3 Control communications' and '11.6 Control risks'.

Continuous monitoring reveals the health of the project and areas requiring special attention. This activity, when combined with directing and managing, can easily keep a project manager fully occupied during the execution phase.

The monitor and control process group is concerned with:

- comparing actual performance against the PMP
- assessing performance to determine corrective and preventative actions
- identifying new risks and monitoring existing risks
- identifying new issues and monitoring existing issues
- maintaining accurate and up-to-date progress and status information
- providing information for status reports
- the tracking and reforecasting of progress
- providing reforecasts of cost and timelines
- monitoring implementation of approved change requests.

Source: The Northern Sydney Institute, Part of TAFE NSW.

Monitoring involves the collection, measurement and distribution of project performance information, as illustrated in Figure 5.1. Controlling involves assessing actual progress against planned progress in order to take action to bring the project back on track.

FIGURE 5.1 COLLECTING, MEASURING AND DISTRIBUTING PROJECT PERFORMANCE DATA

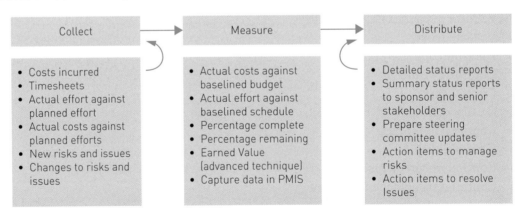

Source: The Northern Sydney Institute, Part of TAFE NSW.

The major outputs are:

- change requests
- updates to project schedule management plan
- updates to project cost management plan
- updates to quality management plan
- changes to scope baseline
- changes to cost baseline

- changes to schedule baseline
- reforecasts
- performance and status reports
- updates to risk and issue logs.
  More detail on this process is included in Chapter 16.

Perform integrated change control

The performance of integrated change control is the process of reviewing all change requests that have been identified by the monitoring and controlling of project work (as explained above). This also includes approving or rejecting changes and managing the flow-on impacts on all project deliverables and all components of the PMP. Integrated change control occurs from project inception all the way through to project completion.

All requested changes should be identified through the '4.4 Monitor and control project work' and '5.6 Control scope' processes.

The following change activities are often undertaken:
- influencing stakeholders and the project team to ensure only approved changes are implemented
- reviewing, analysing and approving change requests quickly
- understanding the complete impacts of the approved changes and managing their implementation
- maintaining the integrity of project baselines for scope, time and cost
- coordinating changes across the entire project.

According to the NSI Online Certificate IV and Diploma of Project Management, the project manager has the primary responsibility for controlling scope and managing changes, although the project sponsor should review and approve or reject all change requests. It is dangerous for the project manager to take on accountability for this decision making; this should be avoided.

It is important that everyone on the project team, as well as the project sponsor and key stakeholders, understand the change control process and be vigilant in identifying potential scope changes for review, rather than simply incorporating them into the project scope by accident. This phenomenon is prevalent on projects and can directly lead to project failure in terms of timelines and budgets. It is known as scope creep and is explained further in Chapter 7.

PROJECT MANAGEMENT MASTERY

TIPS FOR STRONG CHANGE CONTROL

- All change requests must be documented.
- Do not automatically approve all change requests.

- Assessing the impact of change requests needs to include all aspects of the project and all key knowledge areas, not just time and cost.
- Keep a log of all change requests and the associated impacts and approve/reject decision.
- Whenever a change request is approved, automatically seek approval for new baselines for time, cost and scope.
- The later a change is addressed, the greater the impact to time, cost and risk.

Source: The Northern Sydney Institute, Part of TAFE NSW.

REAL-WORLD EXPERIENCE

CHANGE CONTROL PROCESS FLOWCHARTS

My recommended basic change control process is shown in Figure 5.2.

FIGURE 5.2 CHANGE CONTROL PROCESS

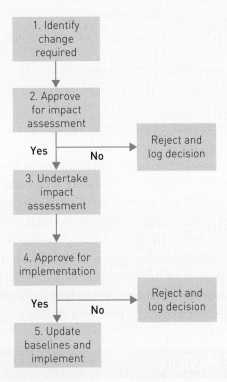

I believe project practitioners often fail to understand the importance of integrated change control. So I have developed a detailed process model of integrated change control (see Figure 5.3) and I recommend that this model be applied to larger, more complex projects. It is best to introduce and embed the basic change control process first and then move on to this more sophisticated model once the inevitable resistance has been reduced.

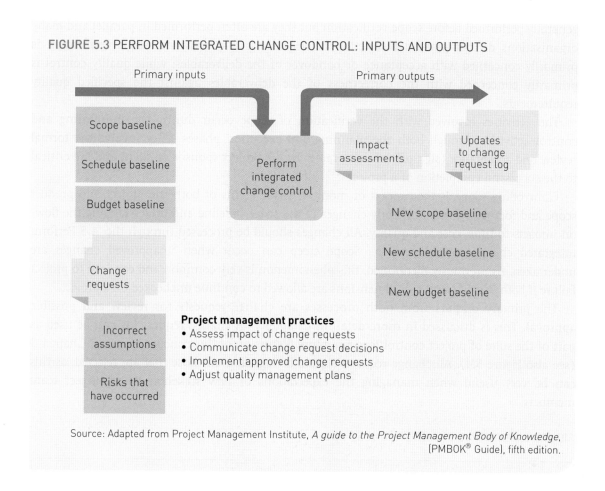

FIGURE 5.3 PERFORM INTEGRATED CHANGE CONTROL: INPUTS AND OUTPUTS

Source: Adapted from Project Management Institute, *A guide to the Project Management Body of Knowledge*, (PMBOK® Guide), fifth edition.

Causes of change on projects

Change requests may arise from many different factors and events. The following list is by no means exhaustive but it does cover some lesser known events which can lead to change requests:

- risks that occur that require specific mitigating actions
- planning assumptions that are untrue and will impact one of the project baselines – scope, time or cost
- costing assumptions that are untrue
- additions or adjustments to scope.

Validating and controlling scope

These two processes are intimately linked and tend to occur simultaneously, and in addition the validate scope process is also closely related to '8.3 Control quality'. Quality control is generally performed before scope verification but they are often performed in parallel and many organisations do not make a distinction between these two activities. Scope verification is primarily concerned with acceptance or handover of the deliverables, while quality control is primarily concerned with the correctness of the deliverables against the specified quality requirements.

The activities involved with the verification of scope occur during the monitoring and control activities through both the planning and execution phases. They involve the formal review and acceptance (sign off) of deliverables by the project sponsor or client and are critical to the successful completion of a project.

Controlling scope is the process of monitoring the status of both the project and product scope and focuses on managing any changes to the scope baseline and understanding the flow-on impacts to time, cost and quality. All changes should be processed through the '4.5 Perform integrated change control process'. Scope creep can occur when unapproved changes are undertaken. As previously mentioned, this phenomenon is very common and can lead to project failure if both the time and cost dimensions are allowed to continue unchecked on a project.

The primary outputs from both processes are change requests for review and possible approval. This is discussed in more detail in Chapter 7. A change request log can be used as part of the suite of project control logs and more discussion of this concept occurs in Chapter 3 (see also Figure 5.4). All change requests should be logged, even those that are rejected, as this can be very useful when managing the expectations of new stakeholders or project team members.

FIGURE 5.4 EXAMPLE CHANGE REQUEST LOG

Change request log template available online

Change request log				
Date submitted	Description	Impact	Approver	Date approved

Controlling the project schedule

This is the process of monitoring the status of the project in order to update and manage any changes to the baseline project schedule. It includes:

- determining the current status of the project schedule
- influencing the factors that create the schedule changes
- determining that the project schedule has changed
- managing actual changes as they occur, either by reworking the schedule or by raising a change request for consideration.

In order to control the schedule, project managers need to gather performance data for the activities in the project schedule, input this data into the schedule and then analyse the impacts on the project timeframe and critical path. Good practice dictates that the following data is entered into the GANTT chart on a weekly basis:

- actual start date of any activity commenced in the last week
- revised start dates and end dates for activities that were to commence in the last week but have been delayed
- actual end date of any activity completed in the last week
- revised end dates for activities that were due for completion in the last week but have been delayed
- estimated percentage completes on all activities that are underway.

This data is best obtained from project team members who are accountable for executing the activities contributing to their specifically assigned deliverables. This can be done via time recording mechanisms or during weekly project status meetings.

Fast tracking and crashing the project schedule

Once the data has been entered into the project schedule, the important project management tasks of analysing the impacts and working on the schedule commence. Project managers will need to revise the interrelationships between tasks in order to compensate for activities which are not completely following the schedule baseline. This is a process known as fast tracking and it involves running activities in parallel that would normally have been done sequentially.

If fast tracking doesn't bring the project back on schedule then the project manager will need to try another technique known as crashing the schedule. This involves adding more resources to activities and it only works when an activity can be effectively undertaken by more than one resource, thereby shortening the duration of the activity.

Fast tracking does not result in increased cost but it does increase the risk, as activities that were originally intended to be performed sequentially are now performed in parallel. Crashing the schedule always results in increased risk and increased cost as additional resources are added on top of the original project team allocation. With both techniques there is a greater probability of miscommunication and potential rework.

REAL-WORLD EXPERIENCE

FAST TRACKING DOESN'T ALWAYS WORK

The ability to fast track the schedule implies that some of the finish-to-start relationships between activities are discretionary. This is not always the case as there are some activities that must absolutely finish before the next activity can start. A car washing example (which I must credit to David A. Zimmer, PMP) illustrates this perfectly and in simple terms that anyone can understand. We wash the car, dry the car and then wax the car. It makes no sense to dry the car before we wash it. And certainly waxing the car first only grinds the dirt into the paint rather than protecting it.

The activities in car washing naturally fall into a finish-to-start relationship. Of course, we could overlap the activities. In other words, we could start drying the car before we are finished washing it, but we do risk water overspray causing additional necessary drying. The overlapping of activities still follows the definition of a finish-to-start relationship because the one spot being dried must be washed and rinsed first.

REAL–WORLD EXPERIENCE

NEITHER DOES CRASHING THE SCHEDULE

Another easily accessible example best explains a circumstance where crashing an activity is not possible. There is a joke that while it takes one woman nine months to have a baby, it is not possible to get nine women to have a baby in one month. Think about it for a moment. The moral to the story is that sometimes adding more resources to an activity doesn't shorten the duration.

Controlling the project budget

Cost control involves monitoring expenditure on the project and managing changes to the cost baseline. The primary activities that are undertaken during this process are:
- reviewing of invoices and expenses
- updating the project budget with actuals
- revising the forecasted total budget
- monitoring variances from the cost baseline
- identifying change requests that will impact the project budget.

Any changes that are identified that will impact the project budget need to be approved through '4.5 Perform integrated change control'.

Some of the factors that can cause variances to the cost baseline, and thereby generate the need for change requests, are:
- budgetary assumptions that are incorrect; for example, labour rates, exchange rates, etc.
- poor productivity where more effort is being expended than planned for particular activities

- poor planning where the time required to undertake activities was understated
- additional scope items
- loss of key resources.

The following data should be entered into the project budget tracking spreadsheet on a weekly basis:

- costs of invoices received for labour, goods and services
- accruals for costs which have been incurred but where invoices have not yet been received
- actual expenditure on activities
- revised forecasts of expenditure.

The primary techniques that can be used to monitor and control costs are earned value management, variance analysis and forecasting. These are discussed below.

Earned value management

PROJECT MANAGEMENT MASTERY

EARNED VALUE MANAGEMENT

Earned value management (EVM) is a concept that most project managers have heard of, but in Australia at least, very few have any real experience in its application. In my time as a project delivery professional I have only used it once when I was delivering projects for a major consulting firm. My understanding is that it is an almost mandatory technique for project managers practising in the US, Canada and South America.

In brief, EVM is a technique that integrates the three key baselines of scope, time and cost; it measures the planned value, earned value and actual cost of each activity as it is being executed. It is the most accurate form of progress monitoring and also one of the most complex. In addition to an integrated baseline, it requires the extensive collection of work performance data for both cost and effort. EVM is discussed in more detail in Chapter 9.

The following standards for EVM are also very useful when first implementing the technique:

- Australian standard: AS 4817-2006 Project performance measurement using earned value management
- US standard: NDIA ANSI EIA 748A Earned value management standard
- NDIA ANSI EIA 748 Intent Guide: a companion to the above US standard
- PMI standard: *Practice standard for earned value management* (2nd ed.).

It is possible to use a simpler method of earned value calculation based on percentage completion estimates rather than actual effort data. This provides a lot of the benefits of the visual management that is gained from being able to graph project progress without the need for exhaustive performance data gathering. The same type of analysis can then be conducted to determine if the project is on, ahead of or behind the planned budget and schedule. These are determined by the cost performance index (CPI) and the schedule performance index (SPI) respectively.

Forecasting and variance analysis

REAL-WORLD EXPERIENCE

FORECASTING AND VARIANCE ANALYSIS

In my experience here in Australia, most project managers use more basic techniques to monitor and control the project budget. With vigilance, the budget can be controlled almost as well using the less formal practices of variance analysis and reforecasting. While these are less accurate, they also take less time and effort to perform and draw on standard practices from the accounting profession.

Forecasting is the technique of capturing cost data for activities from the bottom up and using experience gained from the work that has already been completed to estimate a revised cost forecast to complete each activity. These revised estimates can then be aggregated to determine the revised overall budget. Sometimes variances from the original planned budget can be one-offs and are able to be recovered to bring the project in on budget; at other times the variances are endemic and indicate that the project will be delivered either over or under budget.

Variance analysis looks more deeply at the root cause of positive or negative variances on activities (i.e. under- or over-budget amounts) to determine the impact they will have on the overall project budget. Sometimes corrective or preventative action can be taken to bring the estimated final cost back into line with the baselined budget. If not, then a change request needs to be generated and processed via '4.5 Perform integrated change control'.

Negative variances are considered to be variances which will take the project over the original budget estimate. Positive variances are typically variances that will bring the project in under the original budget. Interim positive variances are not always a sign of good project health as they can indicate that the project is behind schedule or that some scope elements have been omitted. Project managers need to carefully assess the root cause of any variance in order to determine the most appropriate response to bring the project back on track.

Performing quality control activities

All project quality control activities are considered to be part of the monitoring and controlling process group, no matter when they are executed. Many quality control activities are undertaken during the execution phase as each deliverable is completed, while others are conducted at the end just prior to project closure.

This process is closely related to '8.2 Perform quality assurance' which is explained in more detail in Chapter 10.

As mentioned in Chapter 4, quality assurance and quality control activities are performed throughout the project as deliverables are executed and checked against requirements. Quality assurance activities are built into the development of each deliverable, whereas quality control activities are performed once a deliverable has been completed. Quality assurance is designed to prevent defects, whereas quality control is designed to detect and rectify defects.

There are many effective and very basic quality control tools and techniques that are often overlooked when developing the quality plan and these include:

- quality standards
- quality metrics
- control charts
- quality checklists
- cause and effect diagrams for defects
- histograms of defect occurrence
- statistical sampling
- quality inspections.

The international standard – ISO 9001:2008 Quality management systems – is also very useful.

RESEARCH AND REFLECTION ACTIVITY

QUALITY MANAGEMENT POLICIES

Review any internal quality management policies and procedures that may exist in your organisation. Do they refer to any standards for quality management? If so, which ones? Search online for these and any other related quality standards you can find. Would any of these be useful as frameworks for managing quality on your projects?

As mentioned in Chapter 4, it is critical to establish expectations and processes for the collection of performance data and the reporting of overall project status in the PMP. Please see Chapter 12 (page 298) for an outline of all the project communication processes, such as reporting on project performance and creating project status reports.

A status reporting template is available online

Monitoring and controlling risks

This is the process of monitoring the risks that were determined during '11.2 Identify risks' to see if they have occurred or if the likelihood or impact has changed, and also to identify if any new risks have become apparent. Any risk that has occurred will require resolution via the execution of any risk management activities that have been predetermined for the risk during '11.5 Plan risk responses'. More detail on risk management processes can be found in Chapter 13.

Good practice dictates that the risks that have been captured in the risk log are reviewed on a weekly basis to determine:

- if project assumptions are still valid – any that are no longer valid need to be managed as risks to the project and will often result in a formal change request
- if a risk has changed in terms of its priority as calculated by combining an assessment of the likelihood and impact
- if a risk can be closed as it is no longer applicable due to the execution of risk management activities or a change in the project circumstances.

Any risk that has occurred should be copied into the project issue log and the specific risk management activities for that risk executed as a matter of urgency. Often this will involve a change request to be processed via '4.5 Perform integrated change control' due to the need for additional resources or time in order to execute risk response activities.

More detailed information on risk management is contained in Chapter 13 and also in many Australian and international standards.

The following standards for risk management are very useful:

- Australian standard: AS/NZS ISO 31000:2009 Risk management – Principles and guidelines
- HB 436:2004, Risk Management Guidelines Companion to AS/NZS 4360:2004
- US standard: Guide for applying the risk management framework to federal information systems: A security life cycle approach (NIST special publication 800-37, Revision 1)
- PMI standard: Practice standard for project risk management (2009).

Administering procurements

The administration of procurements is the combination of all the monitoring and controlling processes. The primary activities include:

- management of vendor relationships
- assessment of vendor performance against the terms of the procurement contract
- assessment of the goods and services delivered against the specific requirements in the procurement contract
- execution of project and organisational obligations as the purchaser
- monitoring and controlling of procurement related risks and execution of risk management actions if required

- initiation, review and approval of change requests related to procurement
- identification and review of defects for resolution
- management of financial obligations, such as purchase orders, invoice payment and cost tracking
- applying project management processes to procurement management for the project including directing and managing, performance reporting, quality control and change control
- identification and execution of modifications to procurement contracts if required due to changed circumstances
- reviewing the execution of contract terms and conditions
- execution of legal action if procurement contracts are breached.

The primary outputs of this process are change requests, defects and performance reports. The tools and techniques that exist to facilitate the administration and management of procurement activities are:

- change control processes as specified in each contract
- procurement and vendor performance reviews
- performance or status reporting
- independent inspections or audits as stipulated; for example, review by independent quality surveyors of construction progress
- administration of claims made under the contract terms and conditions
- detailed records management systems and processes for correspondence, invoices, specifications, change requests and claims.

More detail on procurement management activities is included in Chapter 14.

RESEARCH AND REFLECTION ACTIVITY

PROCUREMENT MANAGEMENT

There are many excellent websites containing information on procurement management. Search online to see if you can find useful manuals and procedures that you can use to enhance the procurement management activities of your organisation.

Monitoring stakeholder engagement

The controlling and monitoring of stakeholder engagement is a critical component of the monitoring and controlling process group. It involves managing stakeholder engagement via assessing the performance of the change management plans. These plans are collectively referred to as 'change management' and include:

- detailed communication schedules and activities
- detailed training schedules
- detailed engagement activities which are typically undertaken by direct line managers to cascade communication and to reinforce training outcomes.

Best practice for the monitoring of stakeholder engagement activities is to conduct regular surveys of impacted stakeholders to assess if their needs are being fulfilled and to seek feedback on additional requirements or gaps in the current approach. Some tips for effective surveys to assess stakeholder engagement are:

- retain anonymity but ensure that data is collected about the stakeholder group to which the respondent belongs
- use an online survey tool in preference to hardcopy forms
- keep surveys to five to seven questions
- keep the core questions consistent for each survey to be used as a benchmark from which to assess the effectiveness of change management activities
- allow for both quantitative and qualitative feedback
- seek commentary from participants on all questions
- analyse survey data to identify additional activities and to determine corrective action that may be required.

Stakeholder management activities are covered in more detail in Chapter 15.

RESEARCH AND REFLECTION ACTIVITY

STAKEHOLDER SURVEYS

Conduct online research into employee and stakeholder surveys that assess the effectiveness of change management activities and projects. There are many interesting online articles as well as different types of surveys, software, etc. that are useful resources when developing surveys to assess stakeholder engagement.

Related processes from the PMBOK® Guide

4.2 **Develop project management plan (planning)**: This is the process of defining and documenting the actions necessary to prepare and integrate all subsidiary plans for each of the other key knowledge areas of project management. The PMP is the primary deliverable from the planning phase. Good practice dictates that the PMP is baselined at the end of the planning phase, particularly in the areas of scope, cost and time. It is progressively added to during project execution via the perform integrated change control process.

The planning for all the key knowledge areas is normally performed at the same time as this process, or expanded upon shortly afterwards. All key knowledge areas have discrete processes for planning that are defined in their process groups.

This process is closely linked to '8.1 Plan quality management', '9.1 Plan human resource management', '10.1 Plan communications management', '11.1 Plan risk management' and '12.1 Plan procurement management'.

4.3 ***Direct and manage project work (execution):*** The process of performing the work defined in the PMP in order to achieve the project's objectives. The project manager directs the execution of the planned activities, sometimes with the assistance of a project management team for larger projects. The PMBOK® Guide includes this process within the execution phase but there is merit in thinking of it as a separate process group having equal importance to monitoring and controlling.

5.1 ***Plan scope management (planning):*** The process of creating a scope management plan that provides guidance and direction as to how the project scope will be defined, validated and controlled throughout the project.

5.3 ***Define scope (planning):*** The process of developing a detailed description of the project and the end products, or outputs, of the project. A detailed scope statement is critical to project success and good practice dictates that the detailed scope is signed off by the project sponsor, as well as key stakeholders.

6.1 ***Plan schedule management (planning):*** The process for establishing the policies and procedures that will be used to plan, manage and control the project schedule. The schedule management plan provides guidance and direction as to how the project schedule will be managed.

6.6 ***Develop schedule (planning):*** The process of analysing activity sequences, durations, resource requirements and schedule constraints to create the project schedule. This is best completed with the aid of project scheduling software such as MS Project.

7.1 ***Plan cost management (planning):*** The process for establishing the policies and procedures that will be used to plan, manage and control costs for the project. The cost management plan provides guidance and direction as to how project costs will be managed.

7.3 ***Determine budget (planning):*** The process for aggregating the costs of individual activities to form the overall budget for the project. An important component of this process is the establishment of the budget baseline for the project, against which all actual progress and variations will be reported.

8.1 ***Plan quality management (planning):*** The process for identifying the quality requirements and quality standards applicable to a project and documenting how these requirements will be achieved for each deliverable. This also includes the identification of the quality assurance and quality control techniques that will be used to check that each deliverable has met the required quality expectations.

10.1 ***Plan communications management (planning)*:** The process for determining the project stakeholder information needs and for developing tailored communication approaches to meet those needs. Other components can include defining the communication needs within the project team.

10.3 ***Control communications (monitoring and controlling)*:** The process of collecting and distributing project performance and status information. This involves the periodic collection of actual performance data and comparing this against the planned baselines of the project. This enables the reporting of performance as well as reforecasting the future performance of the project.

11.2 ***Identify risks (planning)***: The process for identifying the risks that may impact the project. It is useful to have a broad group of key stakeholders, project team members and internal experts participate in the risk identification session. Good practice dictates that as far as possible all major risks should be identified during the planning phase, although this is an ongoing process as often risks are unpredictable and new risks become obvious during execution.

11.5 ***Plan risk responses (planning)***: The process for developing risk management strategies that will reduce the impact of major risks on the project objectives and success criteria. Risks can be accepted, transferred, mitigated or avoided, and the specific actions selected should be in line with the priority and potential impact of the risk. The concept of the risk owner is applied to ensure that one person is accountable for enacting any risk management plans that may be required.

12.1 ***Plan procurement management (planning)***: The process for identifying the procurement requirements for a project. This involves identifying all resources and equipment that must be purchased and utilised in order to complete the project, as well as specifying the procurement approach and selection criteria. It considers potential suppliers and the contractual arrangements that may be required to manage these external parties to achieve the project objectives.

13.1 ***Identify stakeholders (initiation)***: The process for identifying the people, groups and organisations that are interested in, or impacted by, the project. They could in turn affect the outcomes of the project depending on their relative power. Their interests and influence are critical to project success.

CHAPTER SUMMARY

» The project manager is responsible for the monitoring and control of project work, sometimes with the assistance of a project management team or project management office for larger projects.

» Monitoring is an aspect of project management performed throughout the project, but it becomes more critical during the execution phase.

» The project manager has the primary responsibility for controlling scope and managing changes via '4.5 Perform integrated change control'. However, the project sponsor should review and approve or reject all change requests.

» Strong integrated change control processes contribute to the success of projects by providing the project manager with a framework from which to control change to scope, time and cost.

» Once the actual performance data has been entered into the project schedule the important project management tasks of analysing the impacts and working on the schedule commence. Two primary techniques exist for bringing a project schedule back under control – fast tracking and crashing.

» The primary activities that are undertaken to control the project budget are: reviewing of invoices and expenses, updating the project budget with actuals, revising the forecasted total budget, monitoring variances from the cost baseline and identifying change requests that will impact the project budget.

» Three key techniques exist for assessing project financial performance: earned value management, reforecasting and variance analysis.

» Earned value management (EVM) is a technique that integrates the three key baselines of scope, time and cost by measuring the planned value, earned value and actual cost of each activity as it is being executed. It is the most accurate form of progress monitoring and also one of the most complex.

» Many quality control activities are undertaken during the execution phase as each deliverable is completed, while others are conducted just prior to project closure.

» The project performance reporting process is often referred to as status reporting. It involves periodically collecting and analysing actual project performance data against the baselines of scope, cost and time in order to communicate project progress. The major reason for status reporting is to manage the expectations of the project sponsor and key project stakeholders.

» It is critical to establish expectations and processes for both the collection of performance data and the reporting of overall project status in the PMP.

» The project status report is often the only deliverable that many stakeholders will see from a project. Therefore, it also fulfils the purpose of promoting the project. If it is poorly formatted, difficult to understand or contains spelling and grammatical errors, then many stakeholders will unfairly assume that the project is sloppy and poorly run. It is critical to ensure that it is well formatted, clear and accurate.

» Any risk that has occurred will require resolution via the execution of risk management activities that have been predetermined for the risk during '11.5 Plan risk responses'. Good practice dictates that the risks that have been captured in the risk log are reviewed on a weekly basis.

» Excellent Australian and international standards are available in the areas of risk management, earned value management and quality management.

» The administration of procurements requires the combination of all the monitoring and controlling processes for the project.

REVISION QUESTIONS

1   What functions are covered in the monitoring and controlling process group?
2   Who is responsible for monitoring and controlling the project?
3   What phases of the project lifecycle involve monitoring and controlling?
4   What tools and techniques are used to control the project scope?
5   Which aspects of the project baselines are included in integrated change control?
6   What tools and techniques are used to control the project schedule?
7   What is fast tracking and when can it be used?
8   What is crashing the schedule and when can it be used?
9   What tools and techniques are used to control the project budget?
10 What are the typical contents of a project status report?
11 What is earned value management (EVM)?
12 What quality control activities are typically performed during monitoring and controlling?
13 What risk management activities are typically performed during monitoring and controlling?

See detailed mapping grid for performance criteria covered

See detailed mapping grid for performance criteria covered

DISCUSSION QUESTIONS

1   What is the difference between '5.6 Control project scope' and '4.5 Perform integrated change control'?
2   Why is it often difficult to collect all the required project performance data?
3   What is the difference between monitoring and controlling a project and producing a project status report?
4   Why are the project baselines critical to the successful reporting of project performance?
5   How can scope creep be avoided on projects?
6   How is EVM used to track project performance?
7   Why is EVM rarely used in Australia?
8   How are risks monitored and controlled?
9   What specific actions are required if a risk comes to fruition?
10 What is the difference between quality assurance and quality control?
11 What is the difference between verifying scope and performing quality control activities?

ONLINE RESOURCES

Visit the online companion website at http://www.cengagebrain.com to link to important additional resources, including templates, real-world case studies, revision quizzes and additional study material.

FURTHER READINGS AND REFERENCES

Dobie, C. (2007). *A handbook of project management: A complete guide for beginners to professionals.* Sydney: Allen and Unwin.

Hartley, S. (2008). *Project management: Principles, processes and practice* (2nd ed.). Sydney: Pearson Education.

Kerzner, H. (2007). *Project management: A systems approach to planning, scheduling, and controlling* (9th ed.). Brisbane: John Wiley & Sons.

Kloppenborg, T. J. (2012). *Contemporary project management* (2nd ed.). Melbourne: Cengage Learning.

Mulcahy, R. (2006). *PM crash course – Real-world project management tools & techniques.* Minnetonka, MN: RMC Publications.

Portny S. E., Mantel, S. J., Meredith, J. R., ... Sutton, M. M. (2008). *Project management – Planning, scheduling and controlling projects.* Brisbane: Wiley.

Project Management Institute (PMI). (2013). *A guide to the Project Management Body of Knowledge* (PMBOK® Guide) (5th ed.). Newtown Square, PA: author.

Schwable, K. (2014). *Information technology project management* (revised 7th ed.). Brooks/Cole, a part of Cengage Learning.

Tan, H. C., Anumba, C., Carrillo, P., ... Udeaja, C. (2010). *Capture and reuse of project knowledge in construction.* Chichester, UK: Wiley-Blackwell.

Verzuh, E. (2005). *The fast forward MBA in project management.* Brisbane: John Wiley & Sons.

Project closure

LEARNING OBJECTIVES

IN THIS CHAPTER YOU WILL:

1   become familiar with the processes and activities performed to close a phase or an entire project

2   understand the difference between closing a phase and closing a project

3   describe possible scenarios for project closure

4   revisit the concepts of project success criteria and understand how these are important to project closure

5   examine different approaches to gathering feedback from stakeholders

6   appreciate the benefits of identifying, analysing and sharing lessons learned

7   consider approaches for transitioning a project to 'business as usual' or on-going operations

8   understand the concept of benefits realisation and who should take ownership for the delivery of benefits.

Context

Project closure is the process of finalising all activities across all of the process groups and key knowledge areas to formally close a phase or a project. The current version of the PMBOK® Guide provides little detail in this area and will be substantially supplemented in this chapter with good practices from real-world experience. For example, most project management practitioners consider the post-implementation review to be the primary deliverable from the project closure phase, yet this document is not mentioned in the PMBOK® Guide.

Post-implementation reviews are strongly recommended at the end of a project to identify lessons learned that will assist the success of future projects

PMBOK® Guide and best practice processes for project closure

The PMBOK® Guide has only two processes identified for project closure:
  4.6   Close project or phase
  12.4   Close procurements.
    Best practice dictates that we also consider the following additional processes:
- gather stakeholder feedback
- identify and share lessons learned
- develop the post-implementation review
- develop the project transition plan
- perform accounting closure
- update estimating tools
- conduct project team performance reviews
- benefits realisation.

Closing the project or phase
What is project success?

No matter the size or complexity of a project, it is good practice to reflect on the effectiveness of a project once it has finished and to measure success against well-defined criteria. Comparison against the initial success criteria helps to determine whether the project has achieved the expected outcomes. Comparison against the baselines set at the end of the planning phase helps to determine the level of adherence to the documented plan, and comparison against the planned approaches to each of the key knowledge areas helps to determine the level of adherence to methodologies and standards.

Recapping from Chapter 2, project success occurs when the:
- expectations of the project sponsor or client are met
- agreed project objectives have been met
- business outcomes have been realised
- timeframe and budget have been delivered
- quality and scope requirements have been delivered.

Why review a project phase?

There are three main reasons why you would conduct a review at the end of a project phase, rather than waiting until the completion of the project:

1 the project is large and complex
2 to ensure the greatest likelihood of project success
3 to assess approval for the next phase.

It is necessary to measure the success of the project against well-defined criteria captured in the success criteria. These help to determine whether the project is on track to achieve the desired outcomes and deliver on stakeholder expectations. Undertaking a review at the end of a phase can help to determine if the project is likely to achieve the success criteria. If not, then action plans can be put in place and adjustments made to the remaining phases of the project. This is particularly important for large, complex projects and those of long duration.

Some methodologies include an approval process that requires a formal gate at the end of each phase. The project is evaluated up to that point to determine if it is on track and formal permission is required before it can progress to the next phase.

There is a related reason to review project at any time other than closure, and that is when an evaluation is required to determine if the project should be cancelled. This form of review doesn't need to coincide with the end of a phase and can be conducted any time during the project lifecycle. It is typically called for when there is serious concern over the health of a project; it is often referred to as a project health check.

Project audits or health checks

A project audit, or project health check, is a special type of evaluation of a project that is carried out during the execution of the project, usually to determine if the project should be cancelled. For many long-established project management organisations, this is a regularly scheduled activity that is carried out by the project management office (PMO) every three to six months on all projects to ensure that they are achieving optimal results. For less mature organisations, it is a more ad-hoc evaluation that is called for when projects are experiencing signs of distress or are unlikely to meet the required outcomes and success criteria.

In Australia we tend to use the term *project health check*, whereas in the US the term is *project audit*. The process and contents are often very similar to those used to develop the post-implementation review. The same base template is used with minor adjustments depending on the project context and the primary purpose of the review. The main divergence is the inclusion of recommendations for rehabilitating the project in order to successfully deliver the required outcomes.

Post-implementation reviews

According to the New South Wales Treasury:

> The post-implementation review (PIR) process collects and utilises knowledge learned throughout a project to optimise the delivery and outputs of future projects. A PIR can be used on projects ranging from the design and construction of buildings to the development of an asset strategy or an asset register ... it is a process, a tool and a means of collecting and communicating information and can be used to evaluate all stages in the asset (or project) life cycle.

Source: New South Wales Treasury, 2004, p. 1.

The post-implementation review (PIR) is the last activity in the project closure phase of the project lifecycle and represents the formal closure of the project. The primary purpose is to capture and distribute lessons learned, as well as key metrics that can be used to improve the outcomes of future projects.

Figure 6.1 shows a generic process for the development and completion of a PIR.

Purpose of the post-implementation review

A PIR assesses the performance of the project in the following areas:
- objectives and success measures
- project sponsor and stakeholder expectations
- agreed and baselined scope, including approved change requests
- agreed and baselined project schedule
- agreed and baselined project budget
- agreed project management methodology and processes
- conformance to the overarching project management plan (PMP).

Other key outcomes include the recognition of project achievements and acknowledgement of the contributions of the project manager and project sponsor, as well as the project team and stakeholders.

A PIR can also be used to:
- identify techniques and approaches that worked well so steps can be devised to ensure that they are used again on future projects or incorporated into work in progress
- identify techniques and approaches that didn't work well so steps can be devised to ensure that these are done differently next time.

FIGURE 6.1 POST-IMPLEMENTATION REVIEW PROCESS PERSPECTIVE

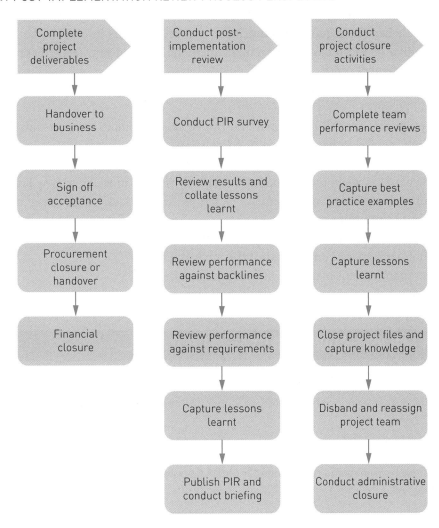

Benefits of post-implementation reviews

The benefits of the PIR are:
- the capture and sharing of good practices and example deliverables that can be reused to improve the delivery of future projects
- the capture of metrics for cost and time that can be used to accelerate planning for future projects
- the symbolic closure of the project for the team which assists with transition to new roles
- increased morale and performance for the project manager through continuous improvement of their knowledge of project methodology, tools and data
- it often results in the creation of new templates and tools, as well as the improvement of existing project management resources

- improved business performance resulting from improved project performance
- improved decision making with respect to project investments and prioritisation.

Some of these benefits require a commitment over several years in order to be realised. The primary custodian of the project management methodology and knowledge base is normally the project management office.

Despite these obvious benefits, PIRs are rarely performed. The primary reasons for not performing a PIR are:

- the perception that the PIR is optional and can be skipped due to time pressures, which are usually more intense as the project nears completion
- a lack of planning and provisioning for the time and cost of performing the PIR
- scheduling conflicts when project managers urgently need to move on to new projects
- weak project knowledge management practices and a lack of a sense of a project management community
- cultural issues where any suggestion of lessons learned or improvements will be unfairly seen as poor performance on the part of the project manager
- low project management maturity within the organisation
- an unwillingness to expose project members to criticism.

RESEARCH AND REFLECTION ACTIVITY

POST-IMPLEMENTATION REVIEW

Consider projects that you have been involved with, either as a team member or project manager.
- Was a PIR conducted?
- Who completed the PIR?
- What assessment criteria were used?
- How were the learnings and recommendations distributed?
- Was it effective?

PROJECT MANAGEMENT MASTERY

BENEFITS REALISATION

Some organisations attempt to use the PIR process as a means of assessing if a project has delivered on business benefits. It is good practice for the responsibility for benefits realisation to be assigned to the eventual owner of the project outcomes, who is also often the project sponsor. It is poor practice to assign this responsibility to the project manager as it is rare that benefits are achieved immediately; they generally flow in over many months or years after the project has been completed.

Project managers have the responsibility to deliver the project outcomes and requirements which in turn should provide the conditions for the achievement of the business benefits. It is only in rare circumstances that they should be held accountable for achieving the business benefits; for example, if they are also the project sponsor or business owner, or where the benefits are achieved in one single instalment immediately upon completion of the project.

Many project management methodologies provide a template for benefits realisation. I recommend that this process is undertaken by the business owner at an appropriate time after the completion of the project and then repeated regularly to track if the benefits are being realised over time. It is most useful when there is an original business case against which the benefits can be assessed. The PMO often ensures this assessment process is undertaken, as the project manager has usually moved on to other projects.

Benefits realisation ensures that value is being delivered via projects. Most large corporations achieve their strategic business outcomes through the delivery of projects, or use projects to provide their source of revenue. It is a shame that this critical process is rarely performed, as it makes it difficult to assess the value obtained from project portfolios.

Project knowledge management

Project knowledge management is a collection of techniques and processes that ensures knowledge from past projects is captured, shared and reused. The benefits of effective project knowledge management are:
- reduced project execution risk
- increased likelihood of successful delivery
- accelerated project scoping and planning
- increased accuracy and completeness in project scoping and planning.

PROJECT MANAGEMENT MASTERY

PROJECT KNOWLEDGE MANAGEMENT

Project knowledge management is an important asset to organisations, as evidenced by the well-established field of knowledge management. Knowledge management is about capturing and sharing knowledge to improve organisational performance and it is the key to success for professional services firms. Law firms develop precedents as a means of capturing, distributing and reusing knowledge; consulting firms have sophisticated knowledge management frameworks to leverage knowledge across clients and engagements. Knowledge management underpins the value of the services that these firms sell.

Project knowledge management is the field of applying knowledge management principles and processes within a project management environment and it is the key to ensuring the successful delivery of projects. The success or failure of projects is dependent on the willingness of project practitioners to create project knowledge and to share it with others. It is critical that the lessons learned, and other useful project knowledge, are captured and effectively shared within the project management community of practice. The project manager will generally require the assistance of the PMO in this process. Figure 6.2 outlines the project knowledge management framework.

FIGURE 6.2 PROJECT KNOWLEDGE MANAGEMENT FRAMEWORK

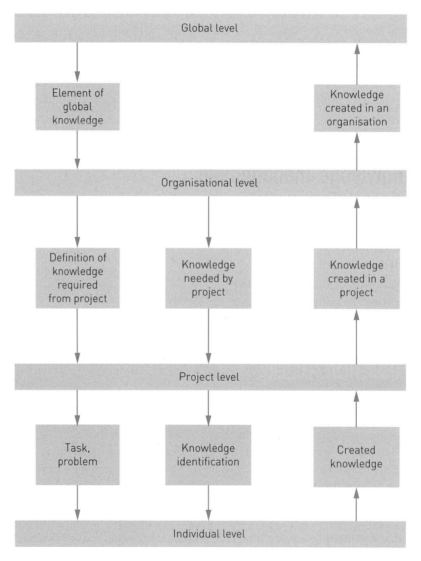

Source: *Project Management Journal* by Stanishaw Gasik, John Wiley and Sons, © 2011 Project Management Institute. Licensed through CCC Rightslink.

REAL-WORLD EXPERIENCE

TASMANIAN GOVERNMENT PROJECT REVIEW AND CLOSURE GUIDELINES

The Tasmanian Government has a comprehensive project management methodology available at http://www.egovernment.tas.gov.au/project_management. It provides templates for various types of project and phase reviews; these are outlined in Table 6.1.

TABLE 6.1 PROJECT CLOSURE GUIDELINES

Title	Best suits	Purpose
Project review and evaluation report	Large or complex projects	A useful tool to assist a project sponsor and/or steering committee to: » determine if the appropriate project management framework has been selected and appropriately applied thereby enabling any deficiencies to be remedied » validate a decision to 'stop' the project » make an informed decision about closing the project and capturing the lessons learned.
Project review and closure report	Small projects Large or complex projects	Excellent tool for capturing lessons from small projects and formally closing the project. If a detailed review is not being undertaken, then this is an ideal way to capture the lessons learned from the project and formally close the project.
Project phase review report	Large or complex projects (phases)	A useful tool to assist the project sponsor and/or steering committee to: » determine if the appropriate project management framework has been selected and appropriately applied thereby enabling any deficiencies to be remedied » validate a decision to 'stop' the project » make an informed decision about closing the project and capturing the lessons learned.
Project closure report	Large or complex projects	A tool to assist a project sponsor and/or steering committee to 'tidy up' any loose ends and formally close the project. It may follow on from a project phase review report or a project review and evaluation report.

Source: © The Crown of Tasmania (Australia).

These different reviews are designed to cater for the needs of differently sized projects. I recommend undertaking phase completion reviews at the end of each phase for large, complex projects. The Tasmanian Government's methodology indicates that these are used to obtain approval to move on to the next phase or to determine whether or not a project should be stopped before completion. They also provide a separate post-implementation review template, known as a project review and closure report, that is highly recommended as it allows the capturing of lessons learned.

Who should review a project?

Any form of project review, whether it is a PIR, project audit or health check, should ideally be performed by an independent third party. The likely candidates include:

- a representative from the PMO
- another project manager from within the organisation
- an external project management expert or consultant.

Unfortunately, for the same reasons that PIRs are rarely done, it is often the project manager who must undertake the PIR. In order to achieve benefits from the lessons learned and recommendations, it is critical to remain as objective as possible. Some of the following tools and techniques will assist in the production of the PIR and in maintaining independence.

PROJECT MANAGEMENT MASTERY

FINANCIAL SERVICES PRODUCT DEVELOPMENT

I was the program director for the development of a new superannuation product for the wealth management division of one of Australia's largest banks, part of the Westpac group of companies. It was a ground breaking, first of its kind, online retail superannuation product. The project was extremely intense and complex as it was the first time in 10 years that this division had undertaken product development and we had fixed deadlines due to the upcoming introduction of new regulations. The culture of the organisation was very resistant to the use of formal project management techniques and senior staff were not used to being held accountable for delivery.

Key characteristics of the project were the 12-month timeframe, fixed end date, a team of 250 full-time resources and another 200 part-time contributors, two external vendors, software package implementation, software integration with existing systems and new software development. The project successfully delivered the outcomes within the required timeframe, but not the benefits of the business case as these would take months and years to be realised. A major change request due to delays with the software development by an external, offshore vendor was successfully incorporated into the final delivery.

Given the strategic nature of the project, a comprehensive independent post-implementation review was undertaken by an external consultant. In summary, it concluded that the project was a success and that the project management techniques had contributed to that success. It found that myself and the core project management team were capable and skilled professionals, but also concluded that the immaturity of the organisation and the selection of an untried external vendor for software development had created several major obstacles along the way. The sponsor and senior IT stakeholders were found to have made a poor choice in the software development vendor and approach.

It is interesting to note that the project sponsor met with the consultant to discuss the draft version of the report and requested that more negative commentary be included about the perceived poor performance of myself, as the program director, and the core project management team. The consultant refused to do this as the request was inconsistent with the findings of the PIR.

Post-implementation review tools and techniques

TEMPLATES

Using a specific template for the post-implementation review is the simplest and most effective way to ensure that all required elements of project performance are being evaluated.

RESEARCH AND REFLECTION ACTIVITY

POST-IMPLEMENTATION REVIEWS

Conduct online research to find processes and templates for post-implementation reviews. Check to see if there is any common content between the various templates that you find.

You can also refer to the Tasmanian Government's website (see page 119) for examples of templates for different types of reviews.

CHECKLISTS

Pro-forma checklists ensure that all project closure activities are completed and that all aspects of the PIR have been assessed. They can be developed to facilitate the PIR and also for the purposes of approval prior to handover to operations, sometimes known as project transition.

SURVEYS

Surveys are one of the most common tools used to gather data and feedback for the evaluation of the project against objectives and they are included in the PIR report. It is common to have standard survey questions provided as part of a methodology. Online survey tools, such as Survey Monkey, often have higher response rates than hardcopy surveys as they are faster to complete. They also facilitate easier data analysis and reporting.

These surveys should be tailored for both the intended audience and the specific context of each project. In particular, the survey which is sent to the project sponsor and senior stakeholders will receive more relevant responses if it is short, focused on the achievement of outcomes and avoids the extensive use of project management language. Surveys for project team members can be more comprehensive and are often based on the key knowledge areas from the PMBOK® Guide.

INTERVIEWS

The most effective, albeit time consuming, approach to gathering data is to conduct structured interviews with key stakeholders which arc typically focused on the assessment criteria that would be included in data gathering surveys. Interviews can be most effective when an independent review has been commissioned and they would normally be reserved for key stakeholders such as the project sponsor and project manager.

WORKSHOPS

Workshops can be effective for many activities associated with PIRs, including:
- gathering data from the project team
- determining lessons learned and recommendations
- debrief of the PIR and formal closure of the project
- communication of results to key stakeholders.

Workshops need to be carefully planned and facilitated with clear ground rules otherwise they can degenerate into non-productive sessions which serve only to erode morale.

INSPECTION

There are three different types of inspection recommended:
1 deliverable reviews
2 process reviews
3 baseline reviews.

In each case, the review or inspection needs to review the actual outcomes against the planned outcomes. The baseline reviews are particularly important and need to be conducted against the three formal baselines for scope, time and cost.

PROJECT MANAGEMENT MASTERY

REFLECTING CHANGE TO BASELINES

Many inexperienced project managers or reviewers will often conduct the inspection of the actual and planned baselines against the original baselines that were set at the end of the planning phase. This approach almost always guarantees a negative result as projects are subject to many change requests, or variations, during the execution phase, and in some cases during planning or even initiation. Best practice dictates that the review of baselines is conducted against the last approved baselines, not the original baselines. This allows for the incorporation of approved changes as part of a holistic review process.

Why do projects close early?

There are many reasons why projects close early. These include:
- **Mutual decision**: agreement is obtained to close the project with the project sponsor, project manager and key stakeholders. This can occur whether the project is successful or not, and sometimes prior to the planned end of the project.
- **Loss of support**: due to reprioritisation of the overall project portfolio or simply a lack of on-going support due to political issues or environmental changes within the organisation; e.g. budget cuts, competitor activity, change of sponsor, mergers, etc.
- **Business as usual**: sometimes activities require initial execution as a project but are then incorporated into ongoing business-as-usual activities as people's priorities and roles are adjusted; this can occur part way through a project or at the end of the planned project delivery.
- **Project integration**: due to replanning or reprioritisation of the project portfolio so that it makes sense to change the scope of existing projects and merge them.

In these cases, it is recommended that some form of project review is undertaken to capture lessons learned and formally close the project.

REAL-WORLD EXPERIENCE

ONLINE BANKING SYSTEM

I was the program director of a BPAY and internet banking project for a mid-tier financial services organisation just before they were taken over by one of the major banks. The objectives of the project were to implement BPAY and to develop internet banking in two discrete phases. These phases were overlapping and completed by the same core team of business analysts, subject matter experts and developers. Not long after the BPAY components were successfully implemented, the entire team began to focus on finalising and going live with internet banking.

The internet banking system we were working on was state of the art. It was completely integrated into the core banking package and designed from a user-centric position. It had many features and functions that would put it well in front of the online banking solutions of the major banks. Six weeks before go-live I was confronted with the takeover and asked to meet with the bank in question's head of ecommerce. She made it clear that the approach to integrating the two companies was to use her company's IT systems. There was no room to challenge this approach and our customers would eventually be ported over to the bank's existing online banking system. This bank was the first to provide online banking in Australia and their system offered limited functionality and was less than intuitive. I was asked to consider the best approach to completing the current development. After a week I met with the bank's head of ecommerce again and much to her surprise I recommended that we immediately terminate our internet banking project for the following reasons:

- the solution was going to be redundant
- it could not easily be integrated into the bank's older system
- it would have been an extremely poor experience for customers to go live with an advanced internet banking system only to be ported over to the old fashioned and clunky one within six months.

I further recommended that we should automatically sign up all of our customers to the bank's internet banking service as part of the customer transition process. In this way they could see the takeover as a positive event that resulted in additional services; customers never had to know that we had a much better solution just weeks away from going live. The user design and advanced functions of our system were then used to form the basis of a substantial upgrade and overhaul of the bank's internet banking service.

The project team were devastated by the news and found it hard to cease working even though it was obviously the best outcome for customers. We gave them all a few days paid leave so they could have a long weekend and then come back to the work with a new scope.

RESEARCH AND REFLECTION ACTIVITY

FINISHING PROJECTS

- Can projects be completed if they haven't been completed 'successfully'?
- Can a project be closed if it is not yet finished?
- How do you determine that a project is finished?
- What does a completed project look like?
- What does success and failure look like?

Closing procurements

This is a collection of activities which, according to the PMBOK® Guide, relate to the closing of procurements that were undertaken in the project. The PMBOK® Guide places much emphasis on **closing procurements**, yet ignores many other important processes that should be included in project closure. Not all projects need to undertake procurement activities; the following table summarises the various types of projects and common procurement requirements.

TABLE 6.2 CLOSING PROCUREMENTS

Project	Typical procurement scope and activities	Procurement closure activities
Process improvement (Lean Six Sigma)	» Many process improvement projects using the Lean Six Sigma approach require absolutely no procurement. » The primary focus is on reducing defects, improving customer satisfaction and reducing time to delivery of products or services.	» Not applicable. » Final timesheets and accrual of costs for final invoices which may not have been presented. » Termination of personal services contracts.
Software package acquisition and installation	» These normally require a formal request for a tender and selection process. » The contract may include both the software licence and installation services.	» Finalisation of contracts for installation services based on complete provision of the services. » Handover of the ongoing software contract to a systems owner who manages ongoing licence and support payments.
Office building construction	» Major procurement activities for design and construction services, equipment and materials. » Many **work packages** awarded to subcontractors using formal tender processes.	» Complex procurement closure activities to finalise those procurement activities that conclude with the handover of the building and to initiate defect repair periods. » Potential disputed procurement items requiring mediation or legal processes. » Formal handover to building manager and tenants for ongoing maintenance.

Developing the project transition plan

Project transition plans are useful when formal handover of the project deliverables, outcomes or assets is required to a business owner. Often this is the project sponsor, but not always. They are also useful if there are any residual activities that have not been completed by the project and can reasonably be handed over to the business owner for finalisation. There are many more templates online for project transition plans than for post-implementation reviews which supports observations that the transition plan is undertaken much more often than a PIR.

The content of a project transition plan often includes:

- transition activities
- transition schedule
- roles and responsibilities
- contract details
- maintenance processes
- defect resolution processes.

Performing accounting closure

Performing accounting closure is a critical process. There are many common activities that are required as part of finalising the project budget which are completely overlooked by the PMBOK® Guide. These include:

- reconciliation of paid and outstanding invoices so that accruals can be made for any remaining committed but unpaid costs at the time of project closure
- assessment of budget performance to determine the final positive or negative variance against the approved budget
- establishment of the benefits tracking process for any financial benefits to be reported by the business owner going forward
- project cost centre closure to prevent additional costs from being attributed to the project after the finalisation of remaining invoices. Unfortunately it is relatively common for incorrect charges to flow into project cost centres once the project is finished. This could be due to invoice coding errors, incorrect timesheet entries and, occasionally, fraud.

Updating estimating tools

It is best practice at the end of a project to capture project metrics to enhance and accelerate the planning and estimation of future projects with similar features. This is particularly important in the construction industry which relies heavily on industry published estimating tables, as well as internal metrics, to profitably deliver projects under fixed price, or guaranteed maximum price, arrangements.

The most common metrics to be captured into estimating tools are those which relate to cost and time. It often requires a high level of project management maturity and a strong PMO to harvest and reuse this form of data.

Conducting project team performance reviews

This is a critical and often overlooked activity which captures the performance of project team members at the end of the project. It is particularly important to undertake a performance assessment for permanent employees in order to help them move on to other engagements and also to contribute to their annual performance review.

Most organisations have formal annual performance review cycles and project completion often doesn't coincide with these cycles. It is important that performance reviews are undertaken at the completion of each project so that the information is captured while it is fresh and relevant. Performance should be measured against the project-related responsibilities and objectives of each individual.

Forward thinking project managers will also assist project team members to find new roles via their own contacts and the provision of references. It is in the best interests of project managers to maintain good relationships with effective project team members as they will find it easier to form project teams in the future. Effective team members can also provide informal positive endorsements to other potential resources.

RESEARCH AND REFLECTION ACTIVITY

PERFORMANCE REVIEWS

Investigate your organisation's internal performance management process and cycle.

How would you work within this framework to provide formal performance assessments at the end of each project?

How would you ensure that each project-based performance review was included in the overall annual performance assessment process?

Related processes from the PMBOK® Guide

4.5   *Perform integrated change control (monitoring and controlling)*: The process of reviewing all change requests, including approving or rejecting changes and managing the flow-on impacts to all project deliverables and all components of the PMP. All requested changes should be identified through '5.6 Control scope'. The activities within this process are critical to managing stakeholder expectations and to ensuring the highest chance of project success. They occur from project inception through to completion and are part of the monitor and control process group. It is important that only approved changes be incorporated into the project, as it is surprisingly common to see unapproved changes being inadvertently undertaken.

8.3 ***Control quality (monitoring and controlling)***: The processes conducted to ensure that each deliverable meets all requirements and specifications. Quality control is performed as each deliverable or related set of deliverables is completed and often involves testing and inspection. It is closely related to '5.5 Validate scope'. It ensures that each project deliverable has been delivered according to the requirements and is fit for purpose. Projects with strong quality assurance and quality control processes often deliver more successfully. The outcomes of quality control activities feed directly into the post-implementation review and any remaining non-critical defects are often handed over as part of the transition.

- ***Monitoring and controlling process group***: there is at least one process in each of the key knowledge areas, with the exception of Project Human Resource Management, that relates to the monitoring and controlling of a project. These all work together to ensure that projects are kept on track and they deliver the required outcomes to the required level of quality. There is a relationship between all the monitoring and control processes and project closure.

CHAPTER SUMMARY

» Most project management practitioners consider the PIR to be the primary deliverable from the project closure phase.

» PIRs assess the relative success or failure of a project based on the objectives and baselines for scope, time and cost.

» The primary benefit of the PIR is the increased morale and performance of the project manager through continuous improvement of their project methodology, knowledge base, tools and data.

» There are many reasons why PIRs are not conducted. The most common are a lack of planning for the time and cost of the PIR at the beginning of the project and urgency around moving the project team on to new assignments.

» Ideally PIRs are conducted by an experienced, senior and independent project management practitioner.

» Benefits realisation is often incorrectly assigned to the project manager but it should generally be the on-going responsibility of the business owner or project sponsor. It should not be included in the PIR unless benefits are achieved immediately upon completion of the project.

» Project knowledge management involves the capture and sharing of the lessons learned, and other useful project knowledge within the project management community of practice.

» Feedback and data are often collected from the project manager, project sponsor, project team and key stakeholders. Different tools and techniques can be used including surveys, interviews and workshops.

» Projects can be closed prior to completion due to a variety of factors, including a change in business priorities or a prediction that the project is unlikely to deliver the expected outcomes.

» The transition of projects to ongoing operations or business as usual is often guided by the project transition plan. This deliverable is more common than the PIR.

» The closure of procurement activities is emphasised by the PMBOK® Guide but can be virtually non-existent for some types of projects; for example, a process improvement project utilising the Lean Six Sigma approach.

» Account closure for a project includes the finalisation of outstanding invoices, accruals for committed and unpaid expenses and the closure of project cost centres to prevent incorrect costs being posted to the project after finalisation.

» Performance assessments should be conducted for all permanent project team members at the end of each project and then included in their annual performance assessment.

» Project closure is closely related to '4.5 Perform integrated change control', '8.3 Control quality' and the monitoring and controlling processes in the PMBOK® Guide.

REVISION QUESTIONS

1 What functions are covered in the closure phase?
2 What activities are performed when closing a project budget?
3 What activities are performed when closing project procurements?
4 What is the purpose of a PIR?
5 What are the typical contents of a PIR?
6 What measures are used to determine if a project has been successful?
7 What tools and techniques can be used to conduct a PIR?
8 What is project knowledge management?
9 Who should conduct project team performance reviews at the end of a project?
10 What role do the project baselines play in the closure of projects?

See detailed mapping grid in the preliminary pages for performance criteria covered

DISCUSSION QUESTIONS

1 What are the benefits of conducting a PIR?
2 Why are formal PIRs rarely conducted?
3 How can the lessons learned from PIRs be harnessed and shared with other project managers?
4 Who should be responsible for benefits realisation and why is this responsibility sometimes incorrectly assigned?
5 What are the advantages and disadvantages of conducting formal surveys as part of a PIR?
6 Why are project team performance reviews recommended at the end of each project?

See detailed mapping grid for performance criteria covered

ONLINE RESOURCES

Visit the online companion website at http://www.cengagebrain.com to link to important additional resources, including templates, real-world case studies, revision quizzes and additional study material.

FURTHER READINGS AND REFERENCES

Clarke, N., & Howell, R. (2009). *Emotional intelligence and projects.* Newtown Square, PA: Project Management Institute.

Dobie, C. (2007). *A handbook of project management: A complete guide for beginners to professionals.* Sydney: Allen and Unwin.

Flannes, S., & Levin, G. (2005). *Essential people skills for project managers.* Vienna, VA: Management Concepts.

Gasik, S. (2011). A model of project knowledge management. *Project Management Journal, 42*(3), pp. 23–44.

Hartley, S. (2008). *Project management: Principles, processes and practice* (2nd ed.). Sydney: Pearson Education.

Kerzner, H. (2007). *Project management: A systems approach to planning, scheduling, and controlling* (9th ed.). Brisbane: John Wiley & Sons.

Kloppenborg, T. J. (2012). *Contemporary project management* (2nd ed.). Melbourne: Cengage Learning.

Mulcahy, R. (2006). *PM crash course – Real-world project management tools & techniques.* Minnetonka, MN: RMC Publications.

New South Wales Treasury. (2004). *Post-implementation review guidelines.* Sydney: author.

Portny S. E., Mantel, S. J., Meredith, J. R., ... Sutton, M. M. (2008). *Project management – Planning, scheduling and controlling projects.* Brisbane: Wiley.

Project Management Institute (PMI). (2013). *A guide to the Project Management Body of Knowledge* (PMBOK® Guide) (5th ed.). Newtown Square, PA: author.

Schwable, K. (2014). *Information technology project management* (revised 7th ed.). Brooks/Cole, a part of Cengage Learning.

Tan, H. C., Anumba, C., Carrillo, P., ... Udeaja, C. (2010). *Capture and reuse of project knowledge in construction.* Chichester, UK: Wiley-Blackwell.

Tasmanian Government. (2011). Project management. http://www.egovernment.tas.gov.au/project_management.

Tasmanian Government, Dept of Premier and Cabinet. (2008). Project review and evaluation report: Template and guide, version 1.2, April. Tasmania: author.

Verzuh, E. (2005). *The fast forward MBA in project management.* Brisbane: John Wiley & Sons.

Project management key knowledge areas

PART OVERVIEW

Part 2 of this text aligns with the 10 key knowledge areas within the PMBOK® Guide. There is one chapter for each key knowledge area and each chapter highlights the applicable tools and techniques with a particular emphasis on those commonly used in the real world. Part 2 also maps out the relationships with the competencies for the Certificate IV and Diploma of Project Management.

Note that the 10th key knowledge area was added in the last edition of the PMBOK® Guide which was released in January 2013.

FIGURE 0.2 KEY KNOWLEDGE AREAS

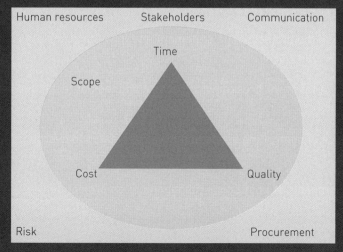

7

Project scope management

Context

Project scope management includes the processes that ensure the project executes all the work required in order to deliver the project outcomes. When talking about scope, it is preferable to concentrate on the tangible deliverables, such as a new product, new system, new building or new road.

The intangible objectives, such as improved employee satisfaction, lower road tolls, etc., fall within the domain of project integration management. And, as mentioned in Chapter 2, it is important that these intangible objectives are clearly measurable and realistic. If they are included in a business case, then it is recommended that they become the responsibility of the project sponsor who can ensure that they are achieved after the project is completed and the project manager has been reassigned.

Project scope is the 'what' and the project objectives are the 'why'.

Project scope definition is one of the most important and yet surprisingly difficult aspects of project management. There is a natural tension between taking the time to identify all the deliverables included in scope and starting on the actual delivery. However, if major deliverables are omitted then it can be difficult to include them later without compromising the original timeline, budget or quality.

Once the project scope is defined and agreed with the project sponsor, the activity of controlling scope becomes one of the major challenges for the project manager.

See PMBOK®
Guide Figure 5-2
Project scope
management:
inputs, tools and
techniques, and
outputs

PMBOK® Guide processes for project scope management

According to the PMBOK® Guide, the major processes associated with project scope management are:

5.1   Plan scope management
5.2   Collect requirements
5.3   Define scope
5.4   Create work breakdown structure (WBS)
5.5   Validate scope
5.6   Control scope.

See PMBOK®
Guide Figure 5
Project scope
management

5.1   ***Plan scope management (planning)***: The process of creating a scope management plan that provides guidance and direction as to how the project scope will be defined, validated and controlled throughout the project.

5.2   ***Collect requirements (planning)***: The process of defining and documenting the needs of the project sponsor and key stakeholders. Encompasses the requirements related to the specific functional and non-functional characteristics of outputs being delivered by the project. Occurs during the planning phase and is very closely related to project success measures, because if the end products do not meet the requirements then it is highly unlikely the project sponsor will sign off on the completion of the project.

5.3   ***Define scope (planning)***: The process of developing a detailed description of the project and the end products, or outputs, of the project. A detailed scope statement is critical to

FIGURE 7.1 PROJECT SCOPE MANAGEMENT: A PROCESS PERSPECTIVE

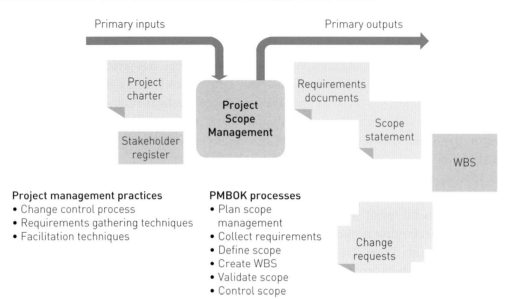

Source: Adapted from Project Management Institute, *A guide to the Project Management Body of Knowledge*, (PMBOK® Guide), fifth edition.

project success and good practice dictates that the detailed scope is signed off by the project sponsor, as well as key stakeholders.

5.4   ***Create work breakdown structure (WBS) (planning)***: The process of subdividing project deliverables and project work into smaller, more manageable components. The WBS defines all the work to be undertaken by the project team in order to achieve the project objectives and create the required deliverables. It enables the assignment of tasks to resources and forms the basis for the development of the project schedule.

5.5   ***Validate scope (monitoring and controlling)***: The process of formal review and acceptance (sign off) of completed project deliverables by the project sponsor and key stakeholders. Closely linked to '8.3 Control quality' and also to the successful completion of the project.

5.6   ***Control scope (monitoring and controlling)***: The process of monitoring the status of both the project and product scope. It focuses on managing any changes to the scope baseline and understanding the flow-on impacts on time, cost and quality via the related process of '4.5 Perform integrated change control'.

REAL-WORLD EXPERIENCE

OFFICE DESIGN AND FIT-OUT

I have found that the order of the scope management processes varies depending on the type of project and the industry.

In the construction industry, where the majority of large projects are put out to tender, the typical sequence of events follows the process order as advocated by the PMBOK® Guide.

The detailed requirements are typically developed by the client in detail for inclusion in tender documentation. It is critical in this arrangement that the requirements are clearly detailed as they are used as selection criteria. Once selected, the construction company will then immediately clarify scope and scope management arrangements.

Sometimes the scope of the project being tendered can actually include assistance with the design, in which case the high-level scope is effectively set and the detailed design then undertaken. So collect requirements and define scope would be reversed.

FIGURE 7.2 OFFICE DESIGN AND FIT-OUT – SCOPE AND REQUIREMENTS

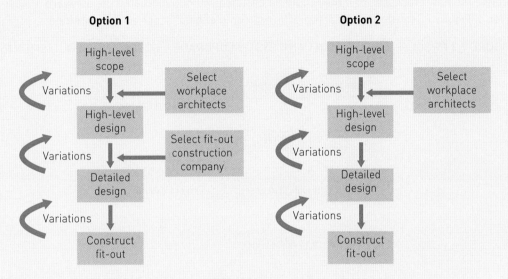

Let's take a specific example of a relocation of staff to new premises. In option 1 in Figure 7.2, one company is being engaged to support the client with detailed design of the new workplace and another company is being engaged to undertake the construction. From the perspective of the construction company, the requirements have already been collected and defined in detail before they develop and submit their tender response. Therefore the natural order to the project scope management processes is preserved.

In option 2, the client is looking for one consolidated bid where both the design and construction are undertaken by the same company. In this case, the scope is defined prior to the collection of requirements so the first two processes are reversed.

Based on my conversations with senior engineers, and also in class discussions, I have realised that the majority of tendered projects in the construction and engineering field follow the process order indicated in option 1.

I was recently the program director for a relocation project to move 1000 staff to a new building within the Sydney CBD. On this particular project we followed option 1 and then once the construction company was appointed we transferred the contract of the design company to sit under the contract of the construction company in order to reduce risk and simplify contract management. We no longer had a direct contract with the design company and the construction company took on the risk of managing their delivery.

REAL-WORLD EXPERIENCE

PROCESS IMPROVEMENT AND SYSTEM UPGRADE

This is a type of project that I have undertaken many times. Most recently, a project manager reporting to me undertook a project to improve the business processes for records management. The primary scope of the project was to determine if we could increase efficiency and internal service by revising our records management processes. It was also necessary to determine if we needed to upgrade our records management software package in order to achieve the new processes or if they could be changed without upgrading the software. Please refer to Figure 7.3 for the flow of activities in the completion of scope and requirements.

FIGURE 7.3 PROCESS IMPROVEMENT AND SYSTEM UPGRADE – SCOPE AND REQUIREMENTS

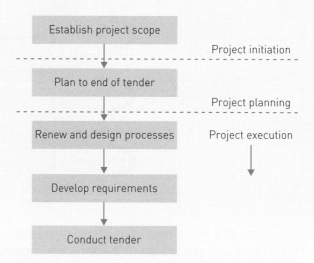

In this example, as with most similar projects I have encountered, the definition of scope happens well and truly before the collection of requirements. Indeed, the detailed documentation of requirements does not occur in the project planning phase; rather it is delayed until the first part of project execution. Otherwise the project initiation phase could potentially extend to half the duration of the overall project and therefore jeopardise overall support for the project.

PROJECT MANAGEMENT MASTERY

EXPERT ADVICE

These examples illustrate the importance of understanding the project context and environment in order to determine the specific approach to project delivery. Project managers need to be flexible and responsive to different contexts in order to be successful. If you doggedly design all your projects using the same framework, then you may be establishing a situation in which failure is the only possible outcome.

So, if you aren't sure about the best approach for a particular project, or you are entering a new industry, then seek advice from experts. This can be as simple as finding project managers in the new environment who have lots of experience and asking them to review your initial plans. Most of them will be flattered that you have sought them out for advice.

RESEARCH AND REFLECTION ACTIVITY

INDUSTRY APPROACH

Which approach best suits your industry and projects? Discuss this and work through the specific order of the scoping and requirements definition activities listed above.

Scope management planning

Planning for scope management involves the creation of a scope management plan that documents how the project scope will be defined, validated and controlled (PMI, 2013, p. 107). The scope management plan details procedures to control scope via scope change control and integrated change control, as well as instructions for the use of change logs and the completion of change requests or variations. It is important to understand the difference between project scope and product scope.

The PMBOK® Guide definitions are:

- product scope: the features and functions that characterise a product or service. It is often a subset of project scope.
- *project scope*: the work performed to deliver a product, service or outcome that is required to deliver the objectives of the project. It often includes a product (see 'product scope') that has to be delivered as part of the project.

The major inputs into the development of the scope management plan include subsidiary plans developed for other key knowledge areas, the project charter, policies and procedures and lessons learned from past projects.

Typical inclusions in the scope management plan are:

- processes and templates for developing a detailed scope statement
- guidelines and templates for the work breakdown structure (WBS)
- procedures to control scope and approve change requests
- processes for the acceptance and sign-off for completed deliverables.

The secondary output of this process is the requirements management plan which typically includes:

- processes for the planning and tracking of requirements
- requirements prioritisation and traceability processes
- criteria to be applied to determine if the requirements have been met.

Source: The Northern Sydney Institute, Part of TAFE NSW.

Collecting requirements

Collecting requirements involves defining and documenting the needs of stakeholders. It is important to document the specific characteristics of any products being delivered by the project. This aspect of scope is referred to as the product scope.

Sometimes there will also be specific processes involved in the creation of the end products. If this is the case, then they become a critical part of the requirements as they define *how* products are to be created.

REAL-WORLD EXPERIENCE

GREEN STAR

Green Star is a rating system for high-end office building construction and fit-out. More information can be obtained from the Green Building Council of Australia (http://www.gbca.org.au).

Organisations that wish to achieve a high rating for their office fit-outs must comply with many processes and frameworks. This impacts on the specification of requirements in many ways.

For example, when specifying and selecting loose furniture there must be a certain percentage of furniture which complies with environmental standards relating to the use of sustainable or recycled timber. This requires the manufacturer to show full chain of custody of the timber and to also obtain relevant certification. In turn, this process limits the furniture that may be selected for the fit-out and therefore impacts on both the specification and fulfilment of requirements in this aspect of the fit-out design.

So, a requirement to obtain a Green Star rating influences both the process of selecting the furniture and the end product itself.

According to the PMBOK® Guide, this process is undertaken during the planning phase, but as we have established earlier in this chapter, some projects will define the requirements at a high level during this process and then allow for a more detailed requirements definition process at the beginning of project execution.

There are many different types of requirements documentation that can be developed depending on the context of the project. The specific requirements that are necessary to clearly document the project outcomes are heavily influenced by, and often predetermined by, the nature of the end product, the industry, specific standards and the expectations or standards within the organisation.

Common requirements documentation are:

- business requirements
- functional requirements
- non-functional requirements
- quality requirements
- acceptance criteria
- design documentation
- construction drawings
- schematics and context diagrams.

Additional requirements can also be implied by, or revealed within, the project objectives, success measures, assumptions and constraints. It is important to review these as part of the requirements documentation processes to ensure that critical expectations of the project sponsor are taken into account and not overlooked.

REAL-WORLD EXPERIENCE

REQUIREMENTS, BUSINESS ANALYSIS AND SOFTWARE ENGINEERING

For many of the projects that I have delivered, the detailed documentation of the requirements has been the responsibility of a business analyst. This is a reflection of the context of my projects which have typically been delivered within major corporations and have involved new product development, process improvement and systems implementation. Business analysis is similar to project management in that it is both a set of tools and techniques and also a profession. Certification is possible via the International Institute of Business Analysis and industry standards/best practices are contained within the Business Analysis Body of Knowledge (BABoK).

The importance of detailed requirements

The collection and documentation of project requirements is often the most difficult process in this group. There is often tension coming from the project sponsor as they want to see execution and do not always appreciate the value of detailed requirements documentation. For them it is often obvious what is required and they can be both puzzled and surprised that the project team does not automatically understand what they want.

Sometimes the project team is inexperienced at the requirements gathering process and requirements collection can be a further problem if the team members are not subject matter experts in the particular field, or where the business analysis frameworks are weak, or worse, non-existent.

The cartoon in Figure 7.4 is a classic and has helped thousands, if not millions, of project managers, project sponsors and project teams understand both the importance of requirements and the potential implications of poor requirements.

FIGURE 7.4 PROJECT REQUIREMENTS

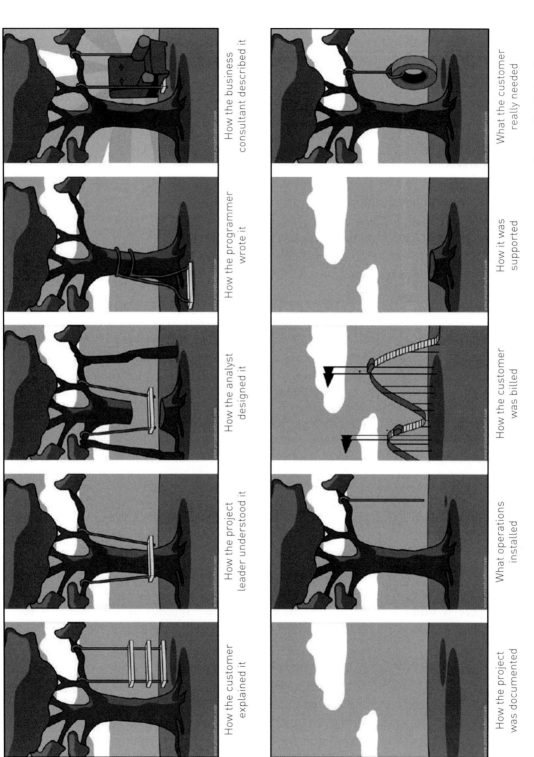

How the customer explained it

How the project leader understood it

How the analyst designed it

How the programmer wrote it

How the business consultant described it

How the project was documented

What operations installed

How the customer was billed

How it was supported

What the customer really needed

Source: The Project Cartoon.com

REQUIREMENTS DEFINITION PRACTICES AND TECHNIQUES

The Business Analysis Body of Knowledge (BABoK) and the Software Engineering Body of Knowledge (SWEBoK) have the most complete definition of requirements (see Table 7.1).

TABLE 7.1 BABoK AND SWEBoK REQUIREMENTS DEFINITIONS

BABoK requirements definition	SWEBoK requirements definition
A condition or capability needed by a stakeholder to solve a problem or achieve an objective.	A property which must be exhibited in order to solve some problem which is to be addressed by software.
A condition or capability that must be met or possessed by a solution to satisfy a contract, standard, specification or other formally imposed documents.	The requirements of particular software are typically a complex combination of requirements from different people at different levels of an organisation and from the environment in which the software will operate.
A documented representation of a condition of capability.	An essential property of all software requirements is that they be verifiable.

Source: *A Guide to the Business Analysis Body of Knowledge* (BABOK) Version 2.0, 2009; *Guide to the Software Engineering Body of Knowledge*, 2004 (SWEBOK).

PROJECT MANAGEMENT MASTERY

FUNCTIONAL REQUIREMENTS VERSUS NON-FUNCTIONAL REQUIREMENTS

Many definitions of requirements make a distinction between functional and non-functional requirements. This can be confusing for your project sponsor and key stakeholders as they often struggle to understand the difference and why it even matters. However, professional analysts and solution developers find the difference critical as it describes key criteria about the end product, which in turn influences how it is designed and delivered.

In short, functional requirements describe how the end result (product, system and building) needs to operate and what features it must possess; non-functional requirements describe how the client, user or occupant will experience the product, system or building.

The value of well-defined requirements

Requirements that are clear and detailed are advantageous and reduce the risk of not delivering on the expectations of the project sponsor. Well-defined requirements:
- increase the understanding between stakeholders
- reduce misunderstandings in communication and can decrease frustration and stress for all involved
- ensure solutions conform to business needs and are fit for purpose
- reduce costs via less need for rework and the potential to accelerate delivery
- increase the chance of end users accepting the product
- enable early error detection and reduce the costs of defect resolution
- enable faster reactions to changing business situations or changing requirements.

RESEARCH AND REFLECTION ACTIVITY

ANALOGOUS ESTIMATING

Search online for templates and examples of requirements documentation that are relevant to your industry. If you are working in business or IT projects you could use search terms such as 'business requirements', 'functional requirements', 'non-functional requirements', 'specification', etc.

I always start online when faced with the prospect of developing detailed requirements as it is often possible to find excellent examples for similar projects. I consider this to be good practice as there is no need to reinvent everything from scratch. This is a key project management practice known as analogous estimating.

I encourage all project managers to share past examples that are not considered to provide a competitive advantage. Be sure to comply with your organisation's confidentiality expectations.

Other requirements deliverables

The PMBOK® Guide details three primary requirements outputs or deliverables:

- requirements documentation
- requirements management plan
- requirements traceability matrix.

The requirements management plan is an advanced concept, often applied to large IT, defence and engineering projects. It provides details about processes and practices that will be implemented in order to plan, develop, track and report on the requirements development activities. It is especially important when a project is large enough to have a requirements workstream or subproject in this area.

The requirements traceability matrix is also an advanced concept. It links requirements to their origin in order to trace them through the project lifecycle. It is also most valuable when applied to large IT, defence and engineering projects. It helps to ensure that the final physical outputs from the project align to the original objectives and the detailed requirements. It can be especially beneficial by ensuring that all functional and non-functional requirements have been tested and delivered.

REAL-WORLD EXPERIENCE

SOFTWARE PROJECTS

I have found that the requirements management plan and requirements traceability matrix are often too complex or not required for many projects. This is dependent on both the size and context of the project. For example, small, low-risk software projects can be bogged down by too many formal processes around requirements which in turn can cause delays and additional costs. As such, these additional requirements deliverables and processes are not worth the effort.

Alternatively, the requirements management plan and requirements traceability matrix can yield significant benefits for large, complex software projects.

Defining scope
What is it?

Project scope is the work that must be performed by the project to deliver a product, service or result as per the specifications or requirements. As mentioned earlier, it is the 'what' that is expected to be delivered by the project. More specifically, it is:

- concerned with what is included in the project and what is excluded from the project
- determined at a high level during the project initiation phase and expanded on in the planning phase
- generally determined by the project sponsor, expanded on by the project manager and then reconfirmed with the project sponsor
- defined by the boundaries or range for the project including constraints, assumptions and dependencies
- related to the objectives, outcomes and requirements.

Project scope is defined at a high level during the early stages of the project and then progressively refined during the project as follows:

- assumptions are often applicable
- constraints will be applied
- pressures to expand
- changes need to be monitored
- key measures of success
- subject to trade-offs.

There is a somewhat iterative process involved in the definition of scope and the development of the project budget and the project schedule. Once the scope has been defined, this flows into time and cost estimation. Sometimes the initial time and cost estimates are too long or too high, therefore it is necessary to revisit the scope to see what can be reprioritised or removed.

Why is it important?

The definition of project scope is important as it:
- gives the project manager concrete goals
- ensures the objectives of the project sponsor are met
- provides the basis for expectation management, monitoring and reporting
- determines the baseline against which project success is measured.

Poor control over project scope is one of the most common reasons for project failure and projects that never seem to finish are normally suffering from a failure to control scope.

How do we define it?

Defining the scope involves developing a detailed description of the project and end products. According to the PMBOK® Guide, the primary output, or deliverable, of the scope definition process is the project scope statement. In practice, this particular deliverable is rarely produced for a project. It is rendered irrelevant by the project charter and the project requirements documentation.

It is critical to have a detailed statement of scope even if it is not contained within the deliverable known as the project scope statement, as a detailed definition of the scope is critical to project success. A project cannot be considered successful and complete until all the scope has been delivered.

REAL-WORLD EXPERIENCE

PROJECT CHARTER

While the project charter typically contains the high-level scope definition, the PMBOK® Guide refers to an additional scoping deliverable that is developed during project planning – the project scope statement. In practice, I have never developed one of these.

I prefer to expand upon the high-level scope in the project charter via the inclusion of a section that covers scope inclusions and scope exclusions. I then ensure that the detailed scope is clearly documented in some form of detailed requirements documentation. The typical suite of requirements documentation for my projects includes:
- business requirements
- business process models
- logical and physical context diagram
- technical requirements
- configuration specifications.

Naturally, the specific requirements deliverables depend on the nature and scope of the project.

RESEARCH AND REFLECTION ACTIVITY

SCOPE AND CHARTER

Search for the following online: 'project scope statement example' and 'project charter examples' and review the results. Discuss similarities between the examples of the scope statements and the project charter.

Do you think that these examples are sufficiently unique as to warrant two separate deliverables or can either the project scope statement or project charter be eliminated?

Creating the work breakdown structure

The work breakdown structure (WBS) is one of the most important project management deliverables and it should be a compulsory component of every project.

The WBS is a deliverable-oriented hierarchical breakdown of the work to be executed by the project team to accomplish the project objectives and create the required deliverables. It organises and defines the *total* scope of the project. If a deliverable does not appear in the WBS then it will not be executed by the project team.

The creation of the WBS involves processes to identify all the deliverables and subdivide the work to be undertaken by the project team. The WBS is initially created during the planning phase in the scope definition process. It is then refined as planning is undertaken in the related key knowledge areas of quality, risk and procurement.

The WBS forms the basis for the development of the project schedule. The deliverables identified in the WBS should all be included in the project schedule along with any activities necessary to execute the deliverable.

There are many different ways to structure the WBS. Many project managers start off using a phased approach and then move to a more workstream or discipline-based structure. The choice often relates to the structure of a typical project team within the project environment. If there are different project team members who will be responsible for certain areas or disciplines, then it is often most effective to have all their deliverables in the one section of the WBS so that their accountabilities are clear. They can then have their own discrete project schedule with clarity around their deliverables and activities, or their component of the project schedule can be self-contained but still within the overarching schedule.

The phased organisational approach is effective for smaller projects where the project manager is responsible for all deliverables and actively supervising the day-to-day duties of all members of the project team.

WBS hierarchies and inclusions

The WBS is made up of work packages from phases, deliverables and activities, down to tasks at the lowest level. A diagrammatic version of the WBS should only be taken to the deliverable level; anything beyond this level of detail is best captured in the tabular version of the WBS, which typically forms part of the project schedule and is used to generate the GANTT chart.

FIGURE 7.5 WBS POSSIBLE HIERARCHIES

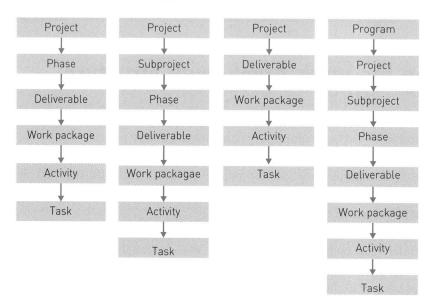

Source: The Northern Sydney Institute, Part of TAFE NSW.

The concept of work packages is not used very much in Australia, although it is commonplace in the US due to the dominance of the PMBOK® Guide as the project management standard. It is particularly useful to encapsulate work that will be tendered to external parties for execution and delivery. In this case, the work package represents the scope of work for the outsourced component(s) of a project.

ORGANISING BY PROJECT PHASE

When organising by phase it is really easy to identify the deliverables required in the initiation and planning phases as these are the outputs as prescribed in the PMBOK® Guide. Identifying and agreeing the deliverables for the execution phase can be more challenging as these are the unique outcomes for that particular project. The deliverables in the close phase need to be supplemented beyond those included in the PMBOK® Guide, as the PMBOK® Guide is surprisingly underpopulated in this phase.

FIGURE 7.6 WBS – PROJECT PHASE EXAMPLE

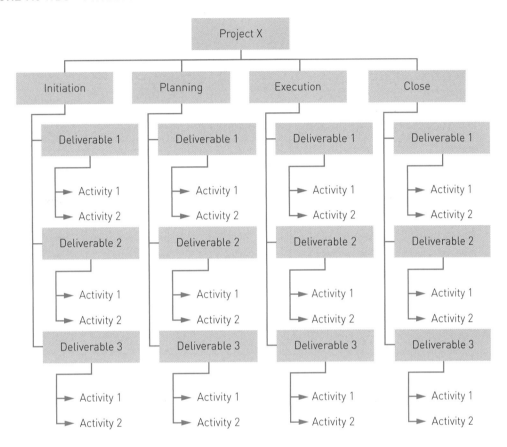

ORGANISING BY PROJECT DISCIPLINE

Many project managers who have initially adopted a project phase approach often convert to a project discipline approach, either part way through the planning phase or for their next project.

ORGANISING BY WORKSTREAM

This particular combination of using a project discipline approach within separate workstreams is the one that best fits larger projects that are undertaken by several project managers. This allows an overarching program-level structure which shows all the major projects broken down into their discipline-oriented workstreams.

FIGURE 7.7 WBS – PROJECT DISCIPLINE EXAMPLE

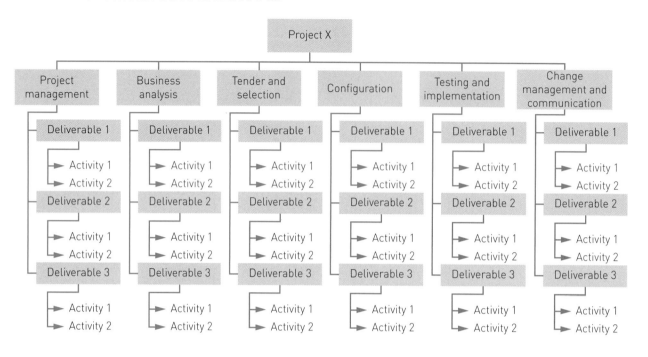

FIGURE 7.8 WBS – WORKSTREAM EXAMPLE

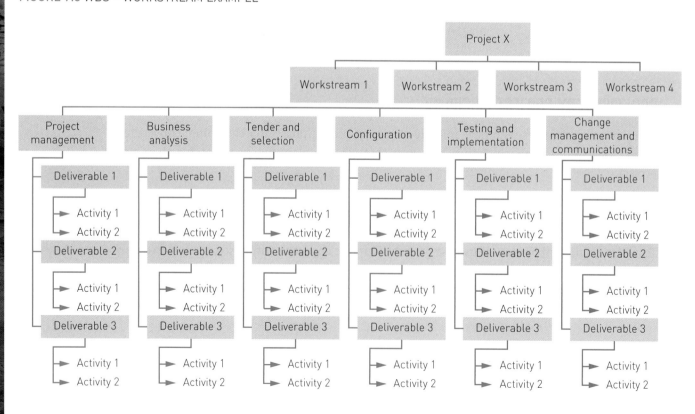

Relationship between the WBS and the project schedule

There is a fundamental relationship between the WBS and the project schedule (this is discussed further in Chapter 8). It is best practice to define the scope of a project using the WBS and then to take all the deliverables from the WBS and use them to populate the project schedule. The schedule will then be further refined during the planning phase with the addition of all the activities required to execute all the deliverables.

PROJECT MANAGEMENT MASTERY

ACTIVITIES VERSUS DELIVERABLES

My students and project managers often think I'm joking when I give them the advice that deliverables are nouns and activities are verbs and only nouns should appear in the WBS. This simple rule of thumb is essential to the creation of a best practice WBS but can be surprisingly difficult to follow.

As stated earlier, I believe that no project should ever be executed without a WBS. So, I have been astounded by the number of experienced project managers who have never consciously prepared one. Typically, they will dive straight into MS Project and start work on the project schedule without holistically defining the overall scope of the project via the WBS. This creates two risks for a project and these are outlined below.

- *Compromise scope verification*: as a high percentage of project sponsors go blank at the sight of a GANTT chart, the project manager loses the opportunity to review and verify the scope with the sponsor. I have found that most sponsors are better able to engage with the diagrammatic representation of the scope in the WBS. I have seen many sponsors quickly skim a WBS and identify a major flaw or gap in the scope, while they have completely switched off when presented with a GANTT chart.
- *Increased likelihood of omissions*: when project managers start completing the project schedule without reference to a WBS they will often plan some areas of the project in great detail and completely omit other deliverables. Then, during project execution, missed scope items will be identified and, as we know, adding to scope will have flow-on impacts on time, cost and/or quality. By not using a WBS, project managers are accepting a risk that they will almost certainly need to deal with change requests due to gaps in the scope.

When initially dealing with the WBS, many project managers will naturally gravitate towards the activities that are required to complete the project rather than the deliverables that make up the scope of the project. Project managers typically like planning and then, in turn, enjoy the action that comes from executing a good plan. So, we tend to be hardwired to think about activities rather than deliverables. Project delivery is greatly enhanced by taking a deliverables-based view as this makes it possible to ensure that no unnecessary activities are performed by the project team and therefore no time is wasted.

My philosophy is that if an activity doesn't relate to the execution of a physical deliverable then it is a waste of time and should not be undertaken.

I have found that it is helpful for project managers and project teams not to edit themselves too heavily when creating the initial draft of the WBS. I suggest either some initial brainstorming to generate as many activities as possible and to record these for later incorporation under the specific deliverables, or that blank paper is used to record all activities that come to mind while the deliverable-based WBS is being prepared. The project manager can then loop back to ensure that all activities naturally belong to a deliverable. This will often generate additional deliverables that have not been identified which improves the scope of the project. Or, it will clarify that particular activities are not required as they don't contribute to a deliverable. This is an example of a bottom-up technique (more on this later).

WBS templates
and examples

Several WBS templates and examples can be found on the companion website to this book.

WBS dictionary

In addition to the WBS, the PMBOK® Guide also identifies two other primary deliverables: (1) the WBS dictionary, and (2) the scope baseline. The scope baseline is a critical deliverable and is discussed in the next section.

The WBS dictionary is a document that contains detailed information about each item in the WBS. This level of detail is relevant in the higher-order items, such as subprojects, phases, disciplines and work packages, but can be a waste of effort for deliverables, activities and tasks. As such, it is acceptable practice to omit the WBS dictionary from the deliverables required as the definitions can easily be included in other relevant deliverables, as per Table 7.2.

TABLE 7.2 WBS DEFINITIONS

WBS item	Project deliverable containing the detailed definition
Project	Project charter Project management plan (PMP)
Subproject	Project charter PMP
Phase	PMP Project management methodology
Workstream	Workstream charter Workstream management plan
Work package	Statement of work Request for tender
Deliverable	Activities with the project schedule

Scope baseline

WHAT IS IT?

The scope baseline is one of three baselines that are set at the end of the project planning phase; the other two baselines are for project time and project cost. It is important to set these baselines as they are the benchmarks against which project progress and project success are measured. It is also surprisingly difficult to find an easy-to-understand and plain English definition of a baseline.

According to the PMBOK® Guide, the scope baseline is composed of the project scope statement, WBS and WBS dictionary. Another way of defining scope baseline for project managers follows.

The scope baseline is a combination of all the final scoping deliverables as at the end of the planning phase. The deliverables making up the scope baseline are:

- project scope statement as contained within the project charter and project management plan
- detailed requirements documentation in their various forms as applicable to the particular project
- detailed WBS.

WHY IS IT IMPORTANT?

Scope baseline is very important as it is used to measure progress towards project completion and to ensure that all the expected elements of the project scope are delivered as per specifications. The timing of the establishment of the scope baseline is critical. If it is set too early then the project manager may be judged against unrealistic and unreasonable performance benchmarks. If it is left too late then the project manager can rewrite history and ensure they delivered a successful project. Therefore, it is best practice to establish the baseline for scope, time and cost at the end of the planning phase.

WBS practices and techniques

The most common and useful practices and techniques for the creation of the WBS are:

- WBS standards and templates
- project knowledge management (past examples)
- decomposition
- brain storming.

WBS STANDARDS AND TEMPLATES

If your organisation or industry has standards for the development of the WBS then it is very important that you follow these. Standards are rare but many organisations will tend to have some form of template for the WBS. Refer back to previous content in this chapter for examples and templates.

RESEARCH AND REFLECTION ACTIVITY

WORK BREAKDOWN STRUCTURES

Undertake online research to see what standards and templates you can find for work breakdown structures. Hint: you should be able to find some very comprehensive ones from NASA and also the US Department of Defense.

Do you think you could incorporate some of these best practices into your project management practices or do you think they are too prescriptive? Can you see any benefits from having such comprehensive standards?

PROJECT KNOWLEDGE MANAGEMENT

The PMBOK® Guide refers to the use of data and deliverables from past projects as an 'analogous' technique. It is often associated with estimation techniques for project time and project cost, but can be a very powerful concept when applied to project scoping and in particular to the WBS. It can be as simple as using examples or precedents.

Using a WBS from a past and similar project is a good project management practice, especially in the area of knowledge management. Project knowledge management is a collection of techniques and processes that ensures knowledge from past projects is captured, shared and reused. The benefits of effective project knowledge management are:

- reduced project execution risk
- increased likelihood of successful delivery
- accelerated project scoping and planning
- increased accuracy and completeness in project scoping and planning.

RESEARCH AND REFLECTION ACTIVITY

REVERSE ENGINEERING WBS

Search online for standards and examples of work breakdown structures. Recall that a GANTT chart, or MS Project Schedule, is simply a detailed tabular extension of a WBS and as such you can use them to reverse engineer a WBS for a project from these deliverables. This technique is very handy if you have found a comprehensive GANTT chart for a project that is very similar to a project that you are about to initiate. Examples can be found at http://www.projectconnections.com and http://www.office.microsoft.com.

Standards for WBS development and notation can be found at http://www.everyspec.com. This website brings together freely available government standards across many fields, including project management.

DECOMPOSITION

There are two major decomposition approaches: top-down and bottom-up. Most project managers will have a natural preference for one over the other but both can be particularly useful and can easily be applied to the creation of the WBS and the verification of scope processes.

The *top-down* approach involves starting with the project phases and disciplines and then defining the major deliverables, subdeliverables, activities and tasks. The *bottom-up* approach involves starting at the activity or task level and then working backwards to associate these with a deliverable. These are simple techniques that most project managers will adopt unconsciously and therefore do not require any further explanation. Recall the earlier project management mastery section on activities versus deliverables (see p. 149); it includes a specific situation where the bottom-up approach can be very useful.

BRAIN STORMING

There are many brain storming techniques available and many of these can also be considered facilitation and creativity techniques. It is difficult to determine which of these techniques are the most popular and, therefore, which to showcase in this text. The preference for, and applicability of, specific brain storming techniques is determined by a combination of the project manager's preference, the culture of the organisation and the subculture of the project team.

Commonly favoured techniques and approaches include:

- structured brain storming
- facilitation
- mind mapping
- six hats thinking.

RESEARCH AND REFLECTION ACTIVITY

BRAIN STORMING TECHNIQUES

Undertake online research on the four categories listed above and any other brain storming techniques that appeal to you. Develop a list of tools and construct some tips on how to set up and execute them.

Many tools and techniques can be found at http://www.mindtools.com.

Now reflect on previous occasions where you may have used brain storming or facilitation techniques with groups or project teams. Recall specific occasions when the sessions went very well and other occasions where the choice of approach was uncomfortable or unsuitable for the situation. Discuss and consider alternative approaches that may have been more successful and what group or team characteristics may help you to select more applicable and effective techniques going forward.

Validating project scope

According to the PMBOK® Guide scope validation is the process of formally reviewing and accepting the completed project deliverables. There are a few problems with this definition and also with the location of this process in the process groups.

It is advisable to separate the sign-off of project scope from the verification of completed deliverables against the requirements. Hence, rename 'sign-off project scope' as a subprocess and undertake this at the end of the planning phase prior to moving into execution. Without this sign-off, it is very perilous to proceed to execution.

The project sponsor has the responsibility for signing off on the project scope. This can be challenging for them as they may wish to keep their options open and by signing off they are automatically reducing their flexibility as any changes post sign-off need to be managed by the control project scope process. The more experience the project sponsor has with projects then the easier it generally is to obtain sign-off. With inexperienced project sponsors, the project manager will need to use all the negotiation and influencing skills in their repertoire to convince the project sponsor to sign off.

REAL-WORLD EXPERIENCE

BUSINESS CONTINUITY MANAGEMENT

I once worked with two very senior project managers responsible for delivering the business continuity management framework for a legal services firm and they had a very unexpected encounter with the business owner when they requested formal sign-off in writing at the end of the project. They had already easily obtained sign-off from the project sponsor and the chief risk officer that the project had been successfully completed.

On a high they scheduled a meeting with the business owner, the facilities manager, who was to assume responsibility for the business continuity management processes going forward. They were very surprised when he pushed the folder full of handover documentation back across the desk and refused to sign it off. He was offended that they didn't trust his word and that he was expected to physically sign the handover documentation. Naturally the project managers were surprised.

In this case I believe there was a different motive underlying his refusal to sign off. There was a small list of residual action items that were being handed over from the project team to the business area for completion. This seemed to be the cause of the issue and he simply did not want to take responsibility for any of the project deliverables just in case there were problems for which he would be blamed in the future. In his view the entire scope of the project had not been completed.

This leaves scope verification to occur throughout the execution phase as part of the monitoring and controlling process group. The main techniques for verifying scope are deliverable testing to ensure the correct performance against functional requirements, and inspection to ensure non-functional requirements are also satisfied. This can be a source of confusion as these activities overlap with those contained within the Project Quality Management key knowledge area, most notably '8.2 Perform quality assurance' and '8.3 Control quality'. As mentioned in Chapter 5, quality control is generally performed before scope verification, but they are often performed in parallel and many organisations do not make a distinction between the two activities. The distinction, however, is that scope validation is primarily concerned with acceptance or handover of the deliverables, while quality control is primarily concerned with the correctness of the deliverables against the specified quality requirements.

The validate scope process should perhaps be more correctly renamed 'sign-off scope' or 'approve scope'.

Controlling project scope

This process is concerned with controlling changes to the project scope as contained within the scope baseline. This occurs during the monitoring and controlling activities through both the planning and execution phases and is closely related to another process which is critical to project success, '4.5 Perform integrated change control'. This is discussed further in Chapter 16.

Causes of scope change on projects

Changes are inevitable on projects and some project managers can create huge amounts of stress for themselves by ignoring this possibility or trying to deny requests for change. The point of change control is to consciously review and approve all positive or necessary changes and to review and reject all erroneous or unnecessary changes.

Sometimes the requirements for the project will change due to changes in the market or business conditions. But most often they will change due to a critical requirement being overlooked during scoping and planning and it will need to be incorporated in order to deliver the project objectives and to realise future benefits. It is easy to overlook critical requirements if there has been inadequate involvement from the project sponsor and key stakeholders during the requirements definition activities.

The goals of integrated change control, as explained further in Chapter 16, are to:

- influence the factors that cause scope changes
- ensure changes are processed according to procedures developed as part of integrated change control
- manage changes when they occur
- increase the chance of meeting the overall project objectives
- define and obtain approval for changes to the PMP and the baselines for scope, cost and time.

The project manager has the primary responsibility for controlling scope and managing changes, although the project sponsor should review and approve or reject all change requests. It is not recommended for the project manager to take on accountability for this decision making.

As first mentioned in Chapter 5, it is important that everyone on the project team, the project sponsor and key stakeholders understand the change control process and are vigilant in identifying potential scope changes for review, rather than simply incorporating them into the project scope by accident. This phenomenon is prevalent on projects and can directly lead to project failure in terms of timelines and budgets. It is known as *scope creep*.

Scope creep

Scope creep occurs when unapproved changes to scope are incorporated into the project without conscious thought. It is very common for projects to increase in scope by stealth and for these changes to not go through the formal scope or change control processes.

It seems inherent in human nature to want to get a little more and to give a little more than is agreed or expected. This is related to our need to belong and wanting to be accepted or liked. Another contributing factor is simply ignorance; inexperienced project sponsors and team members often do not understand the importance of scope management or the potentially detrimental flow-on impacts on project success due to a loss of control over the project.

Scope change control process

Change requests are referred to many times in the project scope processes and are primary outputs of the validate scope and control scope subprocesses. Good practice dictates that change requests are created to document any event which will impact on the project. This is typically a form (hardcopy or electronic) that allows a project stakeholder to request a change to any aspect of the project, but most commonly to scope. They will need to provide details of the requested change and a rationale. In reality, it is the project manager who most often enters and completes change requests as they have the most vested interest in a formal and well-managed change control process.

It is also worthwhile using a change request log as part of the suite of project control logs – more discussion of this concept is included in Chapter 5. All change requests should be logged, even those that are rejected, as this can be very useful when managing the expectations of new stakeholders or project team members.

A recommended change control process is outlined in Figure 5.2 on page 96.

Since there is always a natural resistance to formal processes, the change control process should be kept as simple and streamlined as possible. It is extremely important to have a two-step approval process, where a change request is initially approved to proceed to the impact-assessment step and then considered for a second time once the impact assessment has been completed.

Many change control processes omit the first approval step and this has unseen but inevitable negative impacts on the project. Any effort that is spent assessing the impact of a change request is diverting resources away from the already agreed project deliverables and scope. This will incrementally increase costs and extend the timeline, often without anyone noticing, such that it is a surprise to both the project manager and sponsor when the team informs them that they can't complete the project according to the original time and cost baselines. And project sponsors really dislike nasty surprises!

In practice, the initial approval or rejection step prior to assessing impacts will sift out many erroneous or misaligned change requests. Only those with real merit will progress to the impact assessment.

PROJECT MANAGEMENT MASTERY

TIPS FOR STRONG CHANGE CONTROL

- All change requests must be documented.
- Do not automatically approve all change requests.
- Assessing the impact of change requests needs to include all aspects of the project and all key knowledge areas, not just time and cost.
- Keep a log of all change requests and the associated impacts and approve/reject decisions.
- Whenever a change request is approved, automatically seek approval for new baselines for time, cost and scope.
- The later a change is addressed, the greater the impact on time, cost and risk.

Source: The Northern Sydney Institute, Part of TAFE NSW.

Project scope interrelationships

Scope is related to time, cost and quality. This relationship is often referred to as the 'triple constraint' which was discussed in Chapter 2 (see pages 19–20). Scope expansion and contraction have flow-on impacts on time, cost and quality, with trade-offs possible between all four relationships.

Related processes from the PMBOK® Guide

4.1 **Develop project charter (initiation)**: In practice, the high-level project scope is developed and documented during the initiation phase in the project charter. It forms the boundaries for subsequent scoping processes. Unfortunately, the PMBOK® Guide has the scope definition activities all occurring in the planning phase and is therefore out of sync with practice.

4.2 ***Develop project management plan (planning)***: During this process, the planning for all the key knowledge areas are often performed at the same time, or expanded upon shortly afterwards. In the PMBOK® Guide there are no stand-alone scope, time or cost planning processes as they are contained within the develop PMP process. The other key knowledge areas have discrete processes for planning that are defined in their process groups.

The scope management plan is an important output of this process and it is connected to the '5.3 Define scope' process. It is good practice to assemble the different scope definition and planning outputs into the one integrated document.

4.5 ***Perform integrated change control (monitoring and controlling)***: The process of reviewing all change requests, including approving or rejecting changes and managing the flow-on impacts to all project deliverables and all components of the PMP. All requested changes should be identified through '5.6 Control scope'. The activities within this process are critical to managing stakeholder expectations and to ensuring the highest chance of project success. This process is also closely related to '5.1 Plan scope management' which stipulates how the project scope is to be managed.

8.2 ***Perform quality assurance (execution)***: The process conducted during the execution of the project that ensures all deliverables perform as expected, they achieve specified quality requirements and they conform to any relevant standards. Quality assurance activities are included in the design and production of the deliverable. It is closely related to '5.5 Validate scope'.

8.3 ***Control quality (monitoring and controlling)***: The processes conducted to ensure that each deliverable meets all requirements and specifications. Quality control is performed as each deliverable or related set of deliverables are completed and often involves testing and inspection. It is closely related to '5.5 Validate scope'.

CHAPTER SUMMARY

» Project scope management includes processes for collection requirements, defining the scope, creating the WBS and verifying and controlling scope.

» The scope management plan includes processes and templates for developing the detailed scope statement and the WBS, as well as procedures for controlling scope, approving change requests and signing off on completed deliverables.

» The requirements management plan includes processes for the planning, tracking, prioritisation and traceability of requirements.

» Collecting requirements involves defining and documenting the needs of stakeholders. It is important to document the specific characteristics of any end products being delivered by the project. According to the PMBOK® Guide, this process is undertaken during the planning phase, but some projects will define the requirements at a high level during planning and then allow for a more detailed requirements definition process at the beginning of project execution.

» There are many different types of requirements documentation that can be developed according to the context of the project. The specific requirements are heavily influenced by, and often predetermined by, the nature of the end product, the industry, specific standards and the expectations or standards within the organisation.

» Defining the scope involves developing a detailed description of the project and end products. It is critical to have a detailed statement of scope as a project cannot be considered successful and complete until all the scope has been delivered.

» The detailed scope definition is contained in any and all of the following deliverables: project charter, project management plan, project scope statement and detailed requirements documentation.

» The WBS is a deliverable-oriented hierarchical breakdown of the work to be executed by the project team to accomplish the project objectives and create the required deliverables. It organises and defines the total scope of the project.

» It is good practice not to include activities in the WBS – the focus should be on including all deliverables. If an activity does not directly contribute to the creation of a physical deliverable then it is wasted effort.

» The creation of the WBS involves processes to identify all the deliverables and subdivide the work to be undertaken by the project team in order to achieve the project objectives and create the required deliverables. If a deliverable does not appear in the WBS, then it will not be executed by the project team.

» The WBS is initially created during the planning phase in the scope definition process. It is then refined as planning is undertaken in the related key knowledge areas of quality, risk and procurement. It is one of the most important project management deliverables and should be a compulsory component of every project.

» There is a fundamental relationship between the WBS and the project schedule. It is best practice to define the scope of a project using the WBS and then to take all the deliverables from the WBS and use them to populate the project schedule.

» The scope baseline is a combination of all the final scoping deliverables as at the end of the planning phase. The deliverables that make up the scope baseline include the project scope statement, as contained within the project charter and PMP, detailed requirements documentation and the detailed WBS.

» The scope baseline is one of three baselines that are set at the end of the project planning phase. The other two baselines are for project time and project cost. It is used to measure progress towards project completion and to ensure that all the expected elements of the project scope are delivered as per the specifications.

» The most commonly used practices and techniques for the creation of the WBS are: WBS standards and templates, project knowledge management and past examples, decomposition and brain storming.

» Change control is primarily the project manager's responsibility. Strong change control and a simple change control process are critical to project success. The process should include two approval or rejection steps, one prior to assessing impacts and one immediately after assessing impacts.

» Scope creep occurs when unapproved changes to scope are incorporated into the project without conscious thought. It is very common for projects to increase in scope by stealth and for these changes to not go through the formal scope or change control processes.

» Changes are inevitable on projects. The point of change control is to consciously review and approve all positive or necessary changes and to review and reject all erroneous or unnecessary changes.

» Poor control over project scope is one of the most common reasons for project failure; projects that never seem to finish are normally suffering from a failure to control scope.

» Project scope is closely related to time, cost and quality via a model known as the triple constraint. Trade-offs are possible between all of these elements. When scope increases or decreases there are flow-on impacts and interrelationships.

» Project scope processes are closely related to processes from other key knowledge areas: '4.1 Develop project charter', '4.2 Develop project management plan', '4.5 Perform integrated change control', '8.2 Perform quality assurance' and '8.3 Control quality'.

REVISION QUESTIONS

Revision questions are divided into two sections. The first covers Certificate IV understanding and the second covers Diploma-level understanding. Both sections are relevant to Diploma students and teachers, while only the first section is relevant to Certificate students and teachers.

Certificate IV of Project Management

BSBPMG409A performance criteria questions

These questions relate to the performance criteria stated in 'BSBPMG409A Apply project scope management techniques'.

1   What are the six project scope management process groups?
2   What is the purpose of the scope management plan?
3   What are the primary deliverables (or outputs) of the project scope management group of processes?
4   What are five of the common inclusions in a project scope statement?
5   What is the difference between project scope and product scope?
6   What is the difference between scope and requirements?
7   What deliverables can make up the project requirements documentation?
8   What does WBS stand for and when is it created (i.e. during which project scope management process)?
9   What other deliverables are produced by the create WBS process?
10   What is the scope baseline?
11   What are the other two critical project baselines?
12   What process is used to manage scope?
13   Which process manages variations to the scope baseline?
14   What is scope creep?

Diploma of Project Management

BSBPMG511A performance criteria questions

These questions relate to the performance criteria stated in 'BSBPMG511A Manage project scope'.

1   What is the difference between the project scope and the product scope?
2   What is the primary purpose of the requirements management plan?
3   What concepts are used to define project boundaries?
4   What is the difference between an assumption and a dependency?
5   Why is it critical to clearly document the in-scope and out-of-scope components of a project?
6   What are the primary project success criteria?
7   Why are project objectives or outcomes important?
8   What framework can be used to ensure that objectives are measurable?
9   How do you ensure that critical stakeholders have understood and approved the desired project outcomes?
10   What is normally included in the scope management plan?

11   What is a simple change control process? Draw a diagrammatic example.

12   Who normally approves change requests?

13   Why is it critical to ensure that the approval or rejection of change requests is clearly communicated to all project team members and key stakeholders?

14   Explain why change requests should *not* be automatically investigated for impacts?

DISCUSSION QUESTIONS

1   How would you organise the following WBS concepts into their hierarchical order from the highest to lowest: deliverable, phase, task, activity, work package and project?

2   What are the common inclusions for each deliverable in a WBS? Draw the column headings that you would use if organising the WBS in a table.

3   What are the relationships between the project scope statement, the project charter and the requirements documentation?

4   Why is it useful to document both scope inclusions and exclusions in the project scope statement and how do you determine what is out of scope?

5   Why is the verify scope process group important and how would you go about getting a project sponsor to sign off on the project scope? Have you encountered circumstances where the project sponsor doesn't wish to sign off on the scope? If so, why do you think this occurred?

6   Think of an example of a project where the collect requirements processes would be conducted before the define scope process group. What types of requirements documentation would be produced for this type of project?

7   Discuss the relationship between the perform integrated change control process group and the control scope process group. What are the primary outputs of these processes and which key project planning deliverables are impacted?

8   How can the project manager control changes to the scope baseline and prevent scope creep?

9   Detail the critical steps in the change control process. Why is it difficult to implement effective change control processes?

BSBPMG409A and BSBPMG511A performance criteria questions

ONLINE RESOURCES

Visit the online companion website at http://www.cengagebrain.com to link to important additional resources, including templates, real-world case studies, revision quizzes and additional study material.

FURTHER READINGS AND REFERENCES

Dobie, C. (2007). *A handbook of project management: A complete guide for beginners to professionals.* Sydney: Allen and Unwin.

Hartley, S. (2008). *Project management: Principles, processes and practice* (2nd ed.). Sydney: Pearson Education.

Kazemipoor, H., & Shirazi, F. (2012). A methodology for preventing and managing scope creep in projects (case study in Mapna, Iran). *Research Journal of International Studies, 23.*

Kerzner, H. (2007). *Project management: A systems approach to planning, scheduling, and controlling* (9th ed.). Brisbane: John Wiley & Sons.

Kloppenborg, T. J. (2012). *Contemporary project management* (2nd ed.). Melbourne: Cengage Learning.

National Aeronautics and Space Administration (NASA). (2010). Work breakdown structure (WBS) handbook (NASA/SP-2010-3404). Washington: author.

Portny S. E., Mantel, S. J., Meredith, J. R., ... Sutton, M. M. (2008). *Project management – Planning, scheduling and controlling projects.* Brisbane: Wiley.

Project Management Institute (PMI). (2013). *A guide to the Project Management Body of Knowledge* (PMBOK® Guide) (5th ed.). Newtown Square, PA. Chapter 5, pp. 105–140.

Schwable, K. (2014). *Information technology project management* (revised 7th ed.). Brooks/Cole, a part of Cengage Learning.

Project time management

Context

Project time management includes the processes to develop the project schedule and to manage the timely completion of the project. This covers all aspects of time and duration, from how long it takes to complete one activity right through to the timeframe for the entire project. All of the data related to managing the time dimension of a project is encapsulated in the project schedule. This critical deliverable comprises the planned dates for performing project activities, completing deliverables and meeting milestones. It is normally represented as a GANTT chart using MS Project or a similar project scheduling tool.

Time is one of the 'triple constraints' to project scope. It can be the least flexible out of the three primary factors which influence the scope of a project – quality, cost and time. The timeframe for a project is often imposed by the project sponsor based on business priorities, major dependencies or personal performance objectives, and these can bear no relation to the actual effort and direction required to complete all the project deliverables.

When the timeframe is fixed, then scope and quality will need to be sacrificed if additional effort is required due to invalid assumptions, missed deadlines or risks that have come to fruition. High-risk projects normally exceed original timeframes, sometimes by as much as 100 per cent.

See PMBOK®
Guide Figure 6-3
Project time
management:
inputs, tools and
techniques, and
outputs

PMBOK® Guide processes for project time management

See PMBOK®
Guide Figure 6
Project time
management

According to the PMBOK® Guide, the major processes associated with project time management are:

6.1   Plan schedule management
6.2   Define activities
6.3   Sequence activities
6.4   Estimate activity resources
6.5   Estimate activity durations
6.6   Develop schedule
6.7   Control schedule.

6.1   ***Plan schedule management (planning)***: The process for establishing the policies and procedures that will be used to plan, manage and control the project schedule. The schedule management plan provides guidance and direction as to how the project schedule will be managed.

6.2   ***Define activities (planning)***: The process of identifying the specific actions to be performed to produce the project deliverables. The actions must relate back to a deliverable from the work breakdown structure (WBS). If an activity doesn't relate to a project deliverable then it is either unnecessary or something has been omitted from the WBS. This process is closely linked to '5.4 Create WBS'. Many project managers use the terms *activities* and *tasks* interchangeably when in reality tasks break activities down into smaller units of work. It is good practice to not break down activities into durations of less than one day or more than a week.

FIGURE 8.1 PROJECT TIME MANAGEMENT – PROCESS PERSPECTIVE

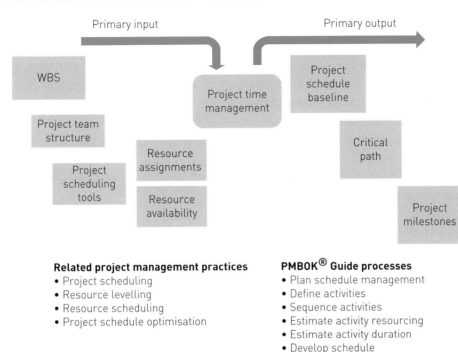

Source: Adapted from Project Management Institute, *A guide to the Project Management Body of Knowledge*, (PMBOK® Guide), fifth edition.

6.3 ***Sequence activities (planning)***: The process of identifying and documenting relationships between the project activities. These are not to be confused with project dependencies which impact the project on a macro scale. Rather, they relate to the interdependencies between activities or tasks and are best managed by the use of project scheduling software.

6.4 ***Estimate activity resources (planning)***: The process of estimating the types and quantities of material, people, equipment or supplies required to perform each activity. It is closely linked to '9.1 Plan human resource management' and '9.2 Acquire project team' and the project procurement management processes.

6.5 ***Estimate activity durations (planning)***: The process of approximating the number of work periods needed to complete individual activities with estimated resources. Work periods may be hours, days, weeks, months and so on and different resources will exhibit differing productivity levels.

6.6 ***Develop schedule (planning)***: The process of analysing activity sequences, durations, resource requirements and schedule constraints to create the project schedule. This is best completed with the aid of project scheduling software such as MS Project.

6.7 ***Control schedule (monitoring and controlling)***: The process of monitoring the status of the project to update project progress and manage changes to the schedule baseline. It is closely linked to '4.5 Perform integrated change control' and '10.2 Manage communications'. It is impossible to report on the progress of a project without first setting a baseline and then establishing processes and procedures for capturing work performance data along the way.

Planning schedule management

Planning for the management of project time involves the creation of a schedule management plan that documents how the project schedule will be developed during planning, as well as how the schedule will be managed during execution. The schedule management plan is a key component of the project management plan (PMP) as it determines how the schedule baseline will be developed and controlled.

The major inputs into the development of the schedule management plan include:

- scope baseline
- scheduling related information
- planning assumptions
- project charter
- resource availability and expertise
- schedule control tools and procedures
- scheduling templates
- change control procedures.

Typical inclusions in the schedule management plan are:

- scheduling methodology
- contingency guidelines
- guidelines on developing and managing the critical path
- units of time for measurement and capture
- project calendar – working days, working hours, freeze periods, etc.
- links to other key planning deliverables – e.g. WBS, scope baseline, etc.
- processes to capture time performance data
- processes for reporting the schedule status.

Source: The Northern Sydney Institute, Part of TAFE NSW.

Defining and sequencing activities

There are three definitions that are required in order to understand how to construct a schedule that is both complete and easy to maintain during execution.

- Deliverables are the physical outputs that your project must produce in order to meet the required outcomes. A good tip is to ensure that your deliverables are expressed as nouns (see also Chapter 7).
- Activities are the specific steps that need to be executed in order to produce a deliverable. These are expressed as verbs and should always be related to a deliverable. Orphaned activities can represent wasted effort and need to be avoided (see also Chapter 7). All activities should be linked to the production of a deliverable.

- **Tasks** are substeps under activities. It is usually not advisable to break down activities further into tasks, as this can create a burdensome effort to track their progress. Tasks are only useful when you have a project with a long duration and large-scale deliverables.

In the discussion of project scope management we focused primarily on identifying and defining deliverables. These are now broken down into the specific activities that need to be undertaken in order to produce each deliverable. Recapping from Chapter 7: deliverables are tangible outputs and are described using nouns, while activities represent the work to be performed and are typically expressed in a verb–noun format; e.g. review requirements, write communication plan, install equipment and so on.

Activities should relate to a specific deliverable within the WBS. If an activity doesn't relate to an agreed deliverable then it is wasting time or has revealed a deliverable that has been left out of the scope. Activities are generally identified by finding a WBS and project schedule from a previous similar project and adjusting these for your specific project context. This technique is known as analogous estimating. Another common approach is to break down the deliverables in the WBS into progressively smaller components (refer also to the section on decomposition in Chapter 7).

PROJECT MANAGEMENT MASTERY

ACCELERATE PROJECT SCHEDULING WITH ANALOGOUS AND PARAMETRIC ESTIMATING TECHNIQUES

It makes good sense to reuse and recycle, even when we are talking about developing project schedules rather than waste management. But it still surprises me how my project managers believe that they must develop their PMPs and project schedules completely from scratch with no reference to previous, similar projects. It is almost a badge of honour to specifically *not* reference projects from the past.

The first thing I do when scoping, structuring and scheduling a project is to check to see if there is an established project management methodology with prescribed templates that I need to use and to see if there is a collection of examples from past projects. The second thing that I do is to search for high-quality project management deliverables from past projects that I can modify, combine, tailor and reuse. This reduces both the execution risk of my project as I am using the collective experience of past project managers, and also greatly accelerates the completion of the initial WBS and project schedule.

Parametric techniques can also be used to accelerate, and improve the accuracy of, project scheduling. They involve the utilisation of metrics for standard activities and are very common in mature project management industries, such as construction and engineering.

RESEARCH AND REFLECTION ACTIVITY

Investigate within your organisation to see if there is a preferred project management methodology and associated knowledge bank of templates and examples that you can use to accelerate project planning.

Undertake online research to find project management templates and examples. There are many websites that have templates and examples for various types of projects; e.g. Microsoft for MS Project examples.

Now reflect upon your past practices. Have you derived benefits from the use of previous project management deliverables and examples? If not, do you feel that you could adopt this approach in the future? What are some of the benefits of using analogous techniques and past examples? What are some of the potential pitfalls and risks?

Decomposition

There are two major decomposition approaches: top-down and bottom-up. Most project managers will have a natural preference for one over the other but both can be particularly useful and can easily be applied to the creation of the WBS and the verification of scope processes.

The *top-down* approach involves starting with the project phases and disciplines and then defining the major deliverables, subdeliverables, activities and tasks. The *bottom-up* approach involves starting at the activity or task level and then working backwards to associate these with a deliverable. These are simple techniques that most project managers will adopt unconsciously and therefore do not require any further explanation. Recall the earlier project management mastery section on activities versus deliverables (see Chapter 7, p. 149); it includes a specific situation where the bottom-up approach can be very useful.

REAL–WORLD EXPERIENCE

HOW MUCH DETAIL IS TOO MUCH?

I have seen many novice project managers drown themselves and their projects in administrative effort by planning activities and tasks down to the hour. They do this when they are highly detail oriented and when they have the belief that the more detailed the schedule then the more control they will have over project execution. This can distract the project manager from the critical monitoring, controlling, directing and managing activities which keep the project on track during execution.

I have three primary rules that I apply when determining the level of detail that is required in a project schedule.

- *Linton's scheduling rule no. 1*: No activity is smaller than one day – even though a critical activity may take less than a day, I always use a day as my lowest estimating unit. This gives some contingency and is more reflective of real life where we are lucky to achieve true productivity rates of six to six and a half hours per day. This approach puzzles many project managers and they will often ask 'Why would I allow a day for an activity that will only take 30 minutes?' and my response is that even a 30-minute activity needs to take place on a particular day and it is mostly irrelevant in which 30 minutes it is completed, as long as it is completed on that day. This technique will also reduce the administrative overhead and allows for some give in your project schedule.
- *Linton's scheduling rule no. 2*: Make activities that take less than an hour a milestone. If the activity will take less than an hour and it is critical then I treat it as a milestone (an activity or event that is important and has zero duration). For example, the actual sign-off for a critical deliverable is likely to take only a few minutes once the person assigned to it sits down to do it. The effort that is expended on this activity is offset by the contingency that is built into rule no. 1.
- *Linton's scheduling rule no. 3*: No activity is longer than a week – even if something takes a month to accomplish, I will find a way to break it down into weekly chunks. This approach ensures that you can easily recover from an activity that is not completed on time, or at all. The longer the duration of an activity then the more difficult it is to recoup time lost on that activity if a project team member doesn't deliver. I find that a week is generally recoverable, unless of course the activity is on the critical path (more on this later). This means that if something slips then you can take corrective action to recoup a week, which is much easier than taking corrective action if a month has been lost.

Relationships between activities – precedence diagramming

The precedence diagramming method is one of the key techniques used to sequence activities in projects. It is a component of the critical path methodology that has become the industry standard and underpins the project management software that produces both GANTT and PERT charts. There are four different logical relationships between activities and these are outlined below.

1 **Finish-to-start (FS)**: The initiation of the successor activity depends on the completion of the predecessor activity. Translated, this means you can't start the second activity until the first one is finished. In a GANTT chart this is depicted as an arrow from the end of the first activity pointing to the start of the second activity. It is the most common type of logical relationship between activities.

2 **Finish-to-finish (FF)**: The completion of the successor activity depends on the completion of the predecessor activity. Translated, this means the first activity must end before the second activity can end. In a GANTT chart this is depicted as an arrow from the end of the first activity pointing to the end of the second activity and the end dates need to be the same.

3 **Start-to-start (SS)**: The initiation of the successor activity depends on the initiation of the predecessor activity. Translated, this means the first activity must start before the second activity can start. In a GANTT chart this is depicted as an arrow from the start of the first activity pointing to the start of the second activity.

4 **Start-to-finish (SF)**: The completion of the successor activity depends on the initiation of the predecessor activity. Translated, this means the second activity can't finish until the first activity starts. This relationship is extremely *rare* and not available in some project management software. In a GANTT chart this is depicted as an arrow from the start of the first activity pointing to the end of the second activity.

In order to produce a critical path in a project schedule, every activity (except the first and last) must be connected to at least one predecessor and one successor. There can be no doubt that the production of a project schedule and the connection of activity interdependencies is made much easier by the use of project scheduling software. This will be discussed later in the chapter.

Some scheduling software will only allow finish-to-start relationships, some will allow all relationships except start-to-finish, and some allow all four relationships.

REAL–WORLD EXPERIENCE

ACTIVITY RELATIONSHIP APPLICATION

I have been asked so often about the occurrence of each of the relationship types that I have settled on the following rule of thumb, based on my observations and experience in developing many project schedules.

TABLE 8.1 ACTIVITY RELATIONSHIP APPLICATION – RULE OF THUMB

finish-to-start	95%
start-to-start	2.5%
finish-to-finish	2.5%
start-to-finish	not applicable

RESEARCH AND REFLECTION ACTIVITY

ACTIVITY INTERRELATIONSHIPS

Search online for precedence diagramming and critical path method. You will find many examples of activity interrelationships, as well as exercises to help you understand the logical operators that link activities together to produce the critical path.

Are you able to find or come up with your own examples for each of the interrelationships, in particular the start-to-finish relationship?

Can you see that most start-to-finish relationships can simply be restated as finish-to-start relationships? Therefore, I would argue that the start-to-finish relationship is redundant. I have yet to use it in any project schedule that I have developed.

The importance of milestones

Milestones are events that generally mark the achievement of an important interim outcome that directly contributes to the finalisation of the project. They are typically shown in project schedules as activities or tasks that have no duration. It is good practice to have between seven and 10 major milestones for an entire project. Do not be tempted to populate the entire schedule with milestones as this will add unnecessary overhead. Here are some good examples of when to set a milestone:

- expected delivery date for external dependencies
- approval gates
- completion of project phases
- sign-off or approval of major deliverables.

Milestones are generally connected to predecessor and successor activities, but with some exceptions, particularly when the milestone denotes an external dependency or a major event that is outside of the project.

PROJECT MANAGEMENT MASTERY

MILESTONES AND STATUS REPORTING

It is very important to set all the milestones (from the commencement of execution to project closure) as soon as the baselines for scope, time and cost have all been agreed. These milestones then form the basis from which status reporting can be prepared and progress monitored. Significant deviation from the original milestones without formal approval of change requests indicates that the project is no longer on track and the status should be moved from green to amber or red depending on the severity of the delays and other compounding factors.

Estimating activity resources and durations

These two processes can be combined into one as they are intimately linked. The estimation of the duration of each activity is linked to the type and quantities of material, people and equipment supplied to perform each activity.

The process of approximating the number of work periods needed to complete activities involves estimating the work effort involved and the anticipated resources. Previous experience in the type of project and activities being estimated improves the accuracy of duration estimates. This is known as analogous estimating and is widely used to facilitate the development of the project schedule.

Different resources have differing productivity rates, motivation levels, external distractions, quality standards, skills and experience. These factors must be taken into account when the duration of activities is estimated. In the absence of a project team, assumptions need to be made by the project manager. This is best performed in conjunction with the resource definition and assignment activities from within the Project Human Resource Management key knowledge area – '9.1 Plan human resource management' and '9.2 Acquire project team'. The only difficulty with this approach is that most of the project team are not on board until the beginning of the execution phase. It is imperative that activity durations are reviewed once the project human resources are assigned.

The majority of the budget for most projects is spent on salaries. Therefore, the determination of the specific skill sets required and the time that each staff member is required is critical to determining both the schedule and the budget.

It would be wonderful if project managers were able to always choose the resources that are assigned to their projects. This would increase the chance of having the right number of people with the right skills assigned to deliver the project as successfully as possible. Unfortunately, as all experienced project managers know, the selection and allocation of project team members is often determined by factors outside of the project manager's control. These are outlined below.

- ***Availability of internal resources***: Sometimes the preferred internal subject matter expert is not available and an alternate resource without the optimal background may be assigned, or potentially an external resource will need to be sourced.

- ***Resource pools and resource calendars***: Some organisations will operate resource pools for project professionals that move from project to project. If these exist then it is important to tap into the overall process of resource allocation and availability to ensure that you have access to the right resources at the right time. This is also linked to resource calendars which may be held at a resource pool or individual resource level. It is useful to know of any planned commitments for resources before they are allocated to your project. For example, if someone has extended leave which has been approved and this falls within a critical period of your project then you may significantly increase the project execution risks if you allocate them to your project.

- ***Experience and productivity levels***: We have already established that different resources will have different productivity rates due to their previous experience, intrinsic motivation and so on. If resources are allocated to a project from a resource pool then the specific experience level may be outside of the project managers' control and this can have a negative impact on the duration of an activity. This issue also arises for non-human resources, although it is often less obvious. Some equipment will be less productive both at the beginning and end of its lifespan – as it gets older it may produce less or break down more often; when it is brand new it may take a while to work at optimal levels.

- **Organisational HR policies**: At various times in an organisation, the policies regarding the allocation of internal and external resources will change. There could be times when an organisation has decided that no external contractors are allowed and there is no internal source of the required expertise. There could be other times when internal resources are too busy and the only alternative is to source external resources that are unfamiliar with the organisations's products, processes, requirements and stakeholders.
- **Procuring human resources**: It is important to factor in the processes and timeframes for procurement of human resources that are not immediately available. The process timeframe for contractors is generally shorter than when recruiting additional permanent staff. If formal outsourcing is required then this will generally take longer, again due to formal tender processes. This all needs to be taken into account when estimating the activities and their durations.
- **Estimating and procuring non-human resources**: Many project managers forget that the estimation of resources is more than simply considering the human resources that are required. There are other resources such as office facilities, materials and equipment. If these are not readily available then the project manager may need to go through potentially lengthy processes for procurement. This may in turn delay the commencement of execution and also increase the need for resources to manage these activities.

  The major outputs of these activities are:
- activity resource requirements – captured in project management software or supplementary registers either in MS Word or Excel format
- resource breakdown structure – the hierarchical chart of resources required which is commonly depicted as the project organisation structure for human resources
- resource calendar – where resource commitments are captured to make them unavailable to other projects
- resource assignments – list the skills and experience of each resource along with the deliverables for which they will be accountable. This is a critical tool to ensure that you get the resources that best fit the requirements of the project and it is used during the related process '9.2 Acquire project team'.

Tips for creating realistic time estimates

Listed below are suggestions for creating the best possible time estimates.

1 **Verify all activity time estimates** with the resources that will be doing the work, or have them provide the initial estimates themselves. The major drawback with this is that the project manager is normally compelled to provide the project schedule well before the end of the planning phase, while the project team is normally assigned at the commencement of the execution phase.

2 **Estimate activity durations** without considering the preferred delivery dates or milestones, otherwise you could automatically introduce a bias (in that it is human nature to cut corners in order to meet deadlines). It is better to prepare estimates free from such

preconditions as you will achieve a much more accurate estimate, and this may generate the need for additional resources in order to meet imposed deadlines.

3 ***Ensure that all activities*** associated with the production of each deliverable are identified and estimated, including the review, rework, defect repair, quality assurance and quality control activities. These are often accidentally omitted in the early stages of schedule development.

4 ***Make sure that all time units are identical*** as misunderstandings around estimating units can cause major issues when combining estimates for activities into the overall project timeframe. People will have preferences for different estimating units. Make a selection and then ensure that everyone who is contributing to the estimates knows the unit that has been selected; e.g. hours, days, weeks, months, etc.

5 ***Most people tend to estimate optimistically***; i.e. many people will plan for eight productive hours per day when research shows that six to six and a half hours of genuine productivity is extremely high. Others will omit activities, such as review and rework, forget to plan for leave or overestimate the productivity impacts of inexperienced resources.

6 ***Some people tend to estimate pessimistically*** and will always pad out estimates, sometimes to extreme levels, such that schedules are unrealistically bloated by the inclusion of personal contingency. Pessimists seem to be the exception; most people tend to be natural optimists when preparing estimates. This creates more of an issue as this estimating bias is often a surprise to the project manager.

7 ***Make adjustments when using analogous estimating techniques*** as no matter how similar a past project, deliverable or activity is to the current circumstances, there will always be some differences in terms of the risk, complexity, project environment, specific resources, differing experience levels, etc. (Adapted from Kloppenborg, 2012, p. 181.)

REAL-WORLD EXPERIENCE

COUNTERING ESTIMATING BIASES

I have some relevant examples and recommendations to overcome the issues that can be created when people provide inaccurate estimates to the project manager.

Scenario 1 – Pressure prompted individual

I once had a developer working for me who, no matter how much I involved him in the establishment of the duration estimates for his work, would always let me down and deliver late. I was very unhappy with his performance so in preparation for the management of poor performance, I undertook analysis of his performance on specific tasks. I was lucky enough to have very detailed data available on the original duration and effort estimates and the actual duration and effort for each task as we were using an early forerunner of Primavera for all our scheduling and data capture. I was able to prove that he consistently took twice as long as the original estimate to complete activities even though he achieved the outcomes in the original effort estimate. This meant that he was not expending more effort than planned, but taking twice as long in terms of duration. When I sat down with him to discuss his poor performance and the ramifications for the overall team's performance on project delivery, this is what he had to say:

'Therese, I think that you always overestimate the duration of activities. If you think something will take two weeks then I know that it will only take me one week to complete, so I waste time for the first week and only get started on the task in the second week.'

He could not reconcile the data that I provided with his personal view that I always overestimated, even when I was able to show data that proved that he always delivered late. I realised that he was hardwired to only take action when he was close to a deadline or there was a genuine sense of urgency. There were two courses of action: (1) micromanage him by breaking down deliverables into daily tasks, which I felt was too time consuming; or (2) move him out of project delivery and into production support where every activity was pressure prompted. I was able to find an opportunity to move him into the production support area and he was much happier and far more successful. Myself and the remaining team members were also more successful and mush less stressed.

Scenario 2 – Leadership leading to unrealistic estimating

Recently I was teaching project management to all the managers and team leaders in an IT department that had a new chief information officer (CIO) due to the forced resignation of the old CIO because of poor performance and ill health. When it came time to discuss the provision of time estimates on projects they openly expressed their difficulties with providing accurate time estimates. Under the former CIO they had been forced to provide unrealistic time estimates that were based on the personal preferences of sponsors and the CIO, rather than being based on good practice estimating principles. Therefore, they always delivered all their projects late, regularly exceeding the original timeframe estimates by 100 per cent. In their language, 'it was better to get chewed out after the project was delivered' for late delivery than it was to face the temper of the CIO when they provided initial timeframes that were outside of his preferences. They were genuinely concerned about two issues: (1) that the new CIO didn't really mean it when she said that she wanted accurate timeframe estimates based on their skills and experience, rather than guesses; and (2) that the IT resources were now unable to provide realistic estimates due to years of preconditioning under the old CIO. I suggested that they employ my rule of thumb for activity estimating that I use when faced with optimistic estimating styles. I triple all initial estimates provided by staff for activities and over time reduce this to double, and eventually down to no compensation as they become more expert at realistic estimation and more conformable to the expectations.

Scenario 3 – Organisational culture leading to unrealistic estimating

When working on a big program at a major financial services organisation I noticed that the estimates that were made in the retail banking area were always too long; they regularly completed their deliverables much earlier than expected in the schedule and well under budget. This was not positive, as it meant that we had asked for more budget than was required – several small projects had been cancelled in order to provide the funding for the major program. When I discussed this with the workstream leader for that area of the program he confessed that in that part of the organisation project teams were rewarded for delivering under budget and ahead of the initial timeframe. This had driven behaviour that resulted in massive overestimation and the provision for large contingencies on each activity. This was very difficult to overcome and in the end it was necessary to bring the entire workstream together to review every duration estimate on every activity in order to remove contingency. This released over $4 million of funding back into the project pool for reallocation to, and the recommencement of, other projects.

Scenario 4 – Conflicting priorities leading to estimating difficulties

I observed interesting estimating biases with one team leader in another IT department. He was running a blended team that provided both production support services and also project resources. When asked about his team members' availability for projects he was adamant that they were available for 50 per cent of their time. Based on this estimate, his resources were allocated to projects and then these projects would run late as the resources from his team were never available for 50 per cent of their time; the best we were getting was up to 25 per cent of their time each week. When this issue was reviewed with him, due to the flow-on impact on project delivery, he admitted that he had underestimated the amount of production support work effort that was required and that this always had to take priority over the project work. When questioned further, he admitted that he had not meant that his people were available 50 per cent of their total time per week, but rather 50 per cent of whatever was left over each week after production support activities. This is an example of where people can use different estimating regimes. We implemented a new time tracking system via a very simple spreadsheet which captured the planned time for these resources on projects each week and then compared it with the estimate of the actual time the team members were able to provide to projects each week. This provided the basis for more accurate estimating going forward and also clearly highlighted delays on projects that resulted from underresourcing.

Best, likely and worst case estimating

The accuracy of activity duration estimates can be improved by considering contributing factors such as risk and the degree of uncertainty. Many project managers will adopt a three-point estimating technique designed to show the best, likely and worst case outcomes for duration. This can be applied to each activity (which may be overkill) or to the overall project timeframe. The concept has its origins in the program evaluation and review technique (PERT), which uses three estimates to define an approximate range for an activity's duration. It can also be used to determine ranges for activity costs, which is discussed further in Chapter 9.

Figure 8.2 shows the PERT equation and a worked example.

FIGURE 8.2 PERT ESTIMATING

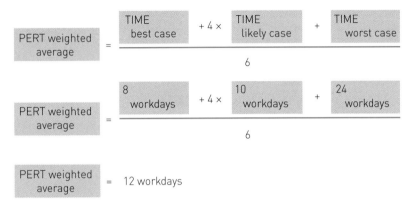

Source: The Northern Sydney Institute, Part of TAFE NSW.

PERT was created by a naval scientist, Frederick Taylor, in the 1950s and led to the development of network diagrams for projects, which in turn were used to calculate and plot the critical path in a GANTT chart (more on this later in the chapter). Figures 8.3 and 8.4 provide examples of project network diagrams using the PERT method.

FIGURE 8.3 NETWORK DIAGRAM EXAMPLE

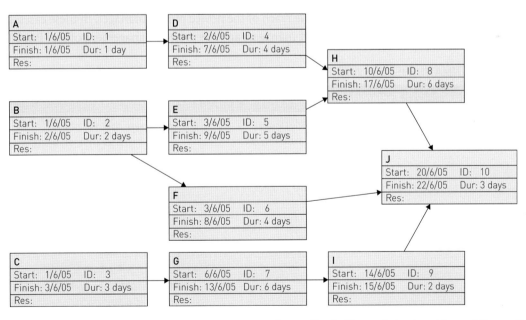

Source: Used with permission from Microsoft Corporation.

FIGURE 8.4 NETWORK DIAGRAM EXAMPLE

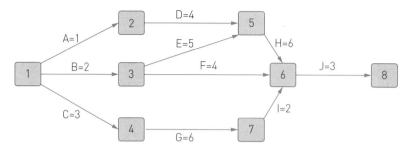

See PMBOK®
Guide Figure
6.5.2.4
Three-point
estimating

Note: Assume all duration are in days; A=1 means Activity A has a duration of one day.

Source: From Schwalbe. *Information Technology Project Management* (with Microsoft Project 2010 60 Day Trial CD-ROM). 7th edition, p. 244. © 2014 Brooks/Cole, a part of Cengage Learning, Inc. Reproduced by permission.

Common activity duration estimating issues

In order to get the most accurate estimate of the duration of an activity, it makes sense to ask the individual who will be doing the activity how long they think it will take. There are two major issues with this approach: (1) often at this stage of the project the project manager doesn't know which specific resources will be allocated, and (2) most people have some form of estimating bias.

Table 8.2 attempts to help project managers identify and respond to common activity duration estimating issues. Be aware that many of the possible solutions fall within the realms of project management mastery and will be beyond the reach of the novice project manager. In these cases, seek expert advice from more experienced project managers and the project management office (PMO).

TABLE 8.2 ESTIMATING ISSUES AND POSSIBLE SOLUTIONS

Estimating issue	Explanation	Possible solutions
Inexperience	When project managers are inexperienced they will almost always underestimate the duration of activities and therefore the duration of the entire project.	» Encourage the use of PERT analysis to assign best, likely and worst case estimates for major activities and the overall project, at least until the estimates can be verified when specific resources are assigned at the commencement of the execution phase. » Break down deliverables into detailed activities using a bottom-up approach. » Use analogous estimating techniques wherever possible by basing estimates and schedule development on previous projects with similar characteristics.

Estimating issue	Explanation	Possible solutions
		» Ensure that estimates are reviewed by more senior and experienced project managers or the PMO.
Omissions of review and rework	Many resources and project managers regularly forget to allow for review and rework as part of the estimating process for a deliverable.	» Ensure that the activities assigned to any deliverable take into account relevant review and rework activities. » Define and estimate all quality assurance and quality control activities for each deliverable. » Ask project resources who are contributing to duration estimates to ensure they have provided for appropriate review and rework activities.
Uncertainty	This is different to inexperience but can be mitigated using similar techniques. Some projects are genuinely unique; in these cases past experience and bottom-up estimating may be insufficient to accurately estimate duration.	» Use expert judgement to apply contingency across the overarching project schedule based on an estimate of the project's complexity, uniqueness and risk. » Encourage the use of PERT analysis to assign best, likely and worst case estimates for major activities and the overall project, at least until the estimates can be verified when specific resources are assigned at the commencement of the execution phase. » Break down deliverables into detailed activities using a bottom-up approach. » Ensure that estimates are reviewed by more senior and experienced project managers or the PMO.
Interdependencies	When complex interdependencies exist between activities it can be difficult to estimate duration, in particular when there are multiple predecessors for an activity.	» Use precedence diagramming techniques to undertake forward and backward pass analyses. » Use resource levelling to ensure that the critical path has been established without the overallocation of resources.

(*Continued*)

Estimating issue	Explanation	Possible solutions
Natural optimism	In practice, most people are naturally optimistic when estimating activity duration as they anticipate higher than feasible productivity rates and often overlook review and rework components.	» Apply a rule of thumb that is effective – initially triple all estimates provided by team members in order to counter the optimistic biases, then over time reduce this to double or to no compensation as the team become better at estimating all activities which contribute to final deliverable production. » Encourage the use of PERT analysis to assign best, likely and worst case estimates for major activities and the overall project, at least until the estimates can be verified when specific resources are assigned at the commencement of the execution phase. » Break down deliverables into detailed activities using a bottom-up approach. » Ensure that estimates are reviewed by more senior and experienced project managers or the PMO.

Developing the project schedule

The project schedule is seen by most project practitioners as the primary project management deliverable. The development of the schedule uses the results of all the preceding processes for project time management to establish the timeframe for a project. By completing the previous processes you have defined, sequenced and estimated the duration of all the activities which contribute to the production of all the deliverables which are within the scope of the project.

The initial draft project schedule is the result of the first attempt to combine all of the data that has been gathered to this point. The only thing for certain once you have developed the initial schedule is that it will require several waves of refinements before it can be baselined. The primary outputs of this process are the project schedule and the schedule baseline.

PROJECT MANAGEMENT MASTERY

THE SCHEDULE IS NOT THE PLAN

As first mentioned in Chapter 3, many inexperienced project managers and project sponsors refer to the project schedule as the project plan and believe that as long as you have a detailed schedule then you do not require a project management plan (PMP). This reflects a prevalent and naive view that if you have a detailed project schedule then you will be able to successfully manage and control the project. These practitioners will typically commence their project planning by opening an MS Project schedule and typing in all the activities they can think off and totally ignoring the other 10 key knowledge areas, most notably scope, risk and quality. No wonder so many projects are not successful.

Best practice in project schedule creation

Figure 8.5 shows the relationships between major outputs of the other project management processes and the project schedule. Below are 10 steps you should take when creating a project schedule.

FIGURE 8.5 CONSTRUCTING THE PROJECT SCHEDULE

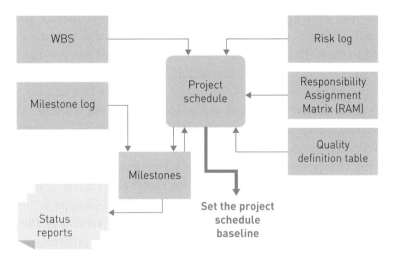

Step 1 – Create the draft project schedule by populating it with all the deliverables that have been defined in the WBS. Break these down into the activities that must be executed in order to complete each deliverable, including the assignment of interrelationships between the activities. Focusing on the scope definition prior to the development of the project schedule greatly reduces the likelihood of omitting major deliverables from the project. Refer also to Chapter 7.

Step 2 – *Ensure that your project schedule matches the phases and deliverables in your WBS*. This ensures consistency and avoids omissions, double-ups or other nasty surprises that will lead to change requests or variations.

Step 3 – *Break deliverables down into activities of no more than one week's duration and no less than one day*. A week-long activity that is off track is easier to recover than an activity that is a month long, especially when you find out on the last day that it is delayed. Even if an activity only takes an hour, it is a good idea not to plan to this level of detail (especially if you are using MS Project). The time and effort required to manage the performance data and changes to activities of less than a day is most often of little value; this project management effort can then be better directed towards weekly replanning and the resolution of issues that threaten to take the project off track. Refer to the scheduling rules earlier in this chapter.

Step 4 – *Consider the risk mitigation plans* that are required in order to reduce the impact of the major risks to the project and add these deliverables and activities into the schedule. Refer also to Chapter 13.

Step 5 – *Consider the quality activities that are required for the major project and product deliverables* and add these into the schedule. These are the quality assurance and quality control activities that ensure the deliverables are meeting requirements. This includes activities such as review, defect repair, testing, rework, sign-off, etc. Inexperienced project managers will often overlook the quality activities when estimating the duration of a deliverable and this in turn places the project timeframe in jeopardy. Refer also to Chapter 10.

Step 6 – *Consider the content of the responsibility assignment matrix (RAM)* and insert additional activities into the schedule along with the resources that have been assigned to these. Depending on the specific RAM that you are using, this can reveal additional activities, such as consultation with stakeholders, review, sign-off and the distribution of final deliverables. Refer also to Chapters 11 and 15.

Step 7 – *Identify major project milestones and include them in the schedule*. Also transfer them to the milestone log if you are using one. These milestones can become the basis for status reporting going forward and are also transferred to the project status report. They should not change throughout the life of the project unless a major change request has been approved. In this way it is possible to report on progress against an agreed set of milestones all the way through the project. Refer also to Chapter 5.

Step 8 – *Set the project schedule baseline by saving a specific version of the project schedule* that will be used as the benchmark to compare actual progress against the original plan. It is critical that this process is not undertaken too early as the project manager may then find themselves committed to an unrealistic delivery date. It is recommended that the schedule baseline is set at the very end of the planning phase and then reset only when a major change request has been approved. The process of negotiating to reset the schedule baseline is important. If major elements of the project change and the schedule baseline is not reset then once again the project manager may find themselves committed to an unrealistic delivery date.

Step 9 – *Define processes to capture performance data in the PMP*. This is a critical and often overlooked step. It is good practice to update the project schedule every week using performance data such as actual start dates, percentages complete, actual end dates and revised end dates. When actual data is entered into the schedule it will then need to be reviewed and adjusted in order to maintain the critical path and the original overall duration.

Step 10 – *Monitor and control the project schedule by entering the actual progress and revised end dates* of the activities in your schedule every week. This allows you to assess any impacts to the critical path and adjust the schedule accordingly by adding resources, reassigning activities, asking resources to multitask and running activities in parallel rather than sequentially (if this is possible given resource levels and task interdependencies).

Relationship between the WBS and the project schedule

There is a fundamental relationship between the WBS and the project schedule. It is best practice to define the scope of a project using the WBS and then to take all the deliverables from the WBS and use them to populate the project schedule. The schedule will then be further refined during the planning phase with the addition of all the activities required to execute all the deliverables.

PROJECT MANAGEMENT MASTERY

ACTIVITIES VERSUS DELIVERABLES

As stated in Chapter 7, I believe that the WBS is one of the foundation project planning tools and as such see it as mandatory. No project should ever be executed without one. So, I have been astounded by the number of experienced project managers who have never consciously prepared one. Typically, they will dive straight into MS Project and start work on the project schedule without holistically defining the overall scope of the project via the WBS. This creates two risks for a project:

- *Compromising of scope verification*: As a high percentage of project sponsors go blank at the sight of a GANTT chart, the project manager loses the opportunity to review and verify the scope with the sponsor. I have found that most sponsors are better able to engage with the diagrammatic representative of the scope in the WBS. I have seen many sponsors quickly skim a WBS and identify a major flaw or gap in the scope, while they have completely switched off when presented with a GANTT chart.
- *Increased likelihood of omissions*: When project managers start completing the project schedule without reference to a WBS they will often plan some areas of the project in great detail and completely omit other deliverables. Then, during project execution, missed scope items will be idenitifed and, as we know, adding to scope will have flow-on impacts on time, cost and/or quality. By not using a WBS, project managers are accepting the risk that they will almost certainly need to deal with change requests due to gaps in the scope.

Developing the GANTT chart and the critical path

The development of the GANTT chart and the critical path go hand in hand as it is virtually impossible to produce a critical path without first producing a project schedule in the form of a GANTT chart. Modern day project managers are spoilt as we have many different project scheduling tools and software to choose from. Back in the days of Henry Gantt, they needed to use pen and paper. Hopefully it was graph paper!

FIGURE 8.6 SAMPLE GANTT CHARTS

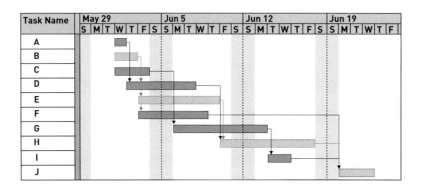

Source: Used with permission from Microsoft Corporation.

The purpose of developing a project schedule is to create a realistic representation of the time dimension of a project, so it:

1 forms the basis of monitoring the progress of the project against the original plan
2 provides clarity to project team members about the expectations for starting and completing their allocated deliverables and activities.

Let's look at some important definitions.

- **Project schedule**: a representation of the phases, deliverables and activities required in order to deliver the project scope. Note that it is incredibly difficult to find a comprehensive definition of a project schedule for the simple fact that everyone assumes that everyone knows what it means. Assumptions can be dangerous in the field of project management, so the expectations around the contents and use of the project schedule are set in the PMP. Most project managers will use software to create the project schedule as it allows for ease of adjustment and printing for reviews. Schedules can be as basic as a list of deliverables and activities in a table with start and end dates, all the way up to sophisticated models that combine the time dimension of the project with scope, cost and resourcing.
- **GANTT chart**: the most common tool used today for displaying project schedule information in the graphical form of a bar chart. It was developed by Henry Gantt in the early 1900s.
- **Critical path**: the combination of activities that generates the shortest duration of the project by finding the longest path through the project schedule based on the unique combination of activity interdependencies that have been stipulated in the schedule. It is the fundamental tool used by project managers to measure if a project is on schedule. If there is a delay to any activity on the critical path then the whole project will be delayed unless the interdependencies are broken and revised as part of regularly reworking the schedule.

PROJECT MANAGEMENT MASTERY

ESTABLISHING THE CRITICAL PATH

Many project managers struggle to find the critical path in their project schedules, despite the use of sophisticated project scheduling software. This can be due to the following:

1 The interdependencies between all tasks have not been established, leaving orphaned activities or groups of disconnected activities. To obtain a critical path, all activities except the first and last activities must connect to precursor and successor activities.
2 There may be a series of recurring tasks that have been used to depict regular project management processes, such as status reporting, or similarly for regular meetings such as project team or project steering committee meetings. These tend to interfere with the production of the critical path. This situation is easily solved in most scheduling software by selecting an option to determine 'multiple critical paths'.

- *Critical path method (CPM)*: this involves using project scheduling software to make a forward pass and a backward pass through the project schedule in order to validate the critical path and calculate the total float within a project schedule. The forward pass calculates the early finish dates for all activities; the backward pass calculates the late end dates for all activities. The results of these passes are then combined to provide the critical path and total float. The total float is the summation of the individual floats, or free floats, for each activity. These represent the amount of time an individual activity which is on the critical path can be delayed without impacting project duration.
- *Schedule baseline*: an approved version of the project schedule from which progress will be measured. Actual progress is compared against the baseline to determine if a project is on track. Good practice dictates that three baselines are established for a project at the end of the planning phase for scope, time and cost.

RESEARCH AND REFLECTION ACTIVITY

PROJECT SCHEDULES

Take some time to reflect on the different tools and techniques that can be used to develop the project schedule. Reflect also on how schedules are developed on your projects and those within your organisation. See if you can find some policies, standards or templates to assist with project scheduling. Look inside your organisation and do some online research also.

Refining the schedule

As established earlier, the initial schedule will normally require several passes over it to refine it before it can be locked in as the baseline for time. This section considers the more common methods for refining the schedule.

We have already discussed PERT and the CPM. There are many complex and mathematically based methods that can be employed. However, in my experience they yield little additional accuracy but generate a lot of additional stress and complexity for the project manager.

Generally, refining the draft schedule is about shortening the overall predicted duration of the project. The following are the two most useful schedule compression techniques. They are easy, practical and powerful and were first discussed in Chapter 5.

CRASHING THE SCHEDULE

This shortens duration without changing the scope by adding additional resources to activities which can be accomplished more quickly when more people are working on them, or additional equipment is supplied.

Unfortunately, the process of crashing the schedule doesn't always produce a viable result and often increases execution risk. As soon as you have multiple resources working on an activity, then there are inefficiencies and communication overheads to factor in. All this can result in more effort being required to complete the activity than if one resource was doing it all. This has flow-on, but less obvious, impacts on the cost of the project.

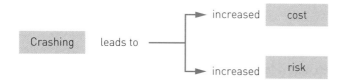

FAST TRACKING THE SCHEDULE

This shortens the duration without changing the scope by changing the interdependencies between activities so that activities or phases that are normally performed sequentially will be performed in parallel. This changes the relationships from finish-to-start to start-to-start or finish-to-finish. This may result in rework and increased execution risk and will only work to shorten the duration where activities can be legitimately overlapped to run in parallel. There may also be flow-on impacts in the form of additional cost, especially if any unanticipated rework is required.

This technique doesn't work for all activities. In some cases the finish-to-start interdependency is mandatory.

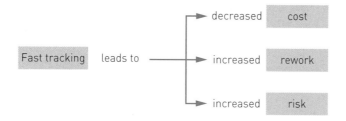

RESEARCH AND REFLECTION ACTIVITY

COMPRESSING SCHEDULES

Reflect on the two schedule compression methods above and see if you can come up with instances where each approach could definitely be applied, as well as instances where each approach would not work.

Controlling the project schedule

This process is concerned with monitoring the status of the project in order to update progress and manage any changes to the baseline project schedule. It occurs during the monitoring and controlling activities through both the planning and execution phases and is closely related to '4.5 Perform integrated change control' which is another process critical to project success.

The aims of this process are to determine the current status of the project schedule, influence and reduce the factors that create schedule changes, acknowledge that the schedule has changed and then manage those changes as they occur. The major inputs are the PMP, project schedule and performance data. The major outputs are change requests and the resulting updates to project baselines for time, cost and scope.

Monitoring the critical path

A vital responsibility of the project manager is to monitor the critical path. Any activity on the critical path that is delayed will automatically cause a delay to the overall project unless some form of mitigation action can be executed, such as crashing or fast tracking the schedule.

PROJECT MANAGEMENT MASTERY

WORKING WITH THE CRITICAL PATH

My mantra with respect to the critical path is '*to stay on track, project managers must make it their highest priority to resolve risks and issues which will delay critical path activities*'. If you are having difficulties establishing the critical path, then see the tips on ensuring you have the right preconditions for a critical path listed earlier in the chapter.

It is important to note that the critical path may change every time you work on the schedule and enter actual performance data. It is not a 'set and forget' feature of project management; the critical path is something that must be reviewed on a weekly basis.

Common issues leading to change requests

Table 8.3 outlines some of the major causes of variations in project time. If any of these arise, it is good practice to make these change requests as part of '4.5 Perform integrated change control'.

TABLE 8.3 CHANGE FACTORS LEADING TO CHANGE REQUESTS

Change factor	Explanation and understanding
Planning assumptions are untrue	Many assumptions need to be made in order to finalise the PMP and resulting baselines for scope, time and cost. When an assumption is untrue that relates to time, then approval for a change request and impact analysis of the flow-on effects should be sought.
Risk occurs	There is always a possibility that one of the documented risks will occur. Risks can often have an adverse impact on time as additional deliverables and activities may need to be added to the project schedule which could negatively impact the critical path.
Project scope change	Project scope changes due to omissions in the original scope are common and have flow-on impacts on both time and cost.
Pressure-prompted resources	As discussed earlier, if there is a severely pressure-prompted resource on your project team, this team member may struggle to complete activities on time as they tend to leave everything until the last minute. If the activities which are delayed are on the critical path and the delay cannot be recovered by working on the schedule, then a change request will be required. If this is not possible, then you can partially mitigate the risk by breaking down all the resource's activities into very small subtasks and providing closer supervision. However, it is recommended that, if possible, the resource be redeployed.
Multitasking	Issues with timely completion of activities can occur when resources are working on more than one project at a time or splitting their time across many activities within a single project. Multitasking is inherently inefficient and can cause delays due to the overhead of switching between activities, or when incorrect prioritisation is applied to the activities due to a lack of understanding of the critical path.
Undeclared priorities	This can be especially problematic when resources are being split across project activities and non-project work. Depending on the objectives and priorities of the resources, this situation can lead to the project manager not being aware of the other calls on the resource's time, and therefore they overallocate them to activities in the project schedule.
Estimating biases	This is covered in detail earlier in the chapter and covers a group of related tendencies that influence the ability of people to provide realistic duration estimates for activities.
Not reporting early completion	If expectations and communication channels are not clear, it is possible for resources to complete activities early but to not report on the early completion status. This could be due to ignorance or to a desire to slow down and relax.

(Continued)

Change factor	Explanation and understanding
Not reporting revised completion	This is the opposite issue to the one above and potentially creates larger impacts and delays to project schedules. People can be reluctant to communicate bad news and may not accurately report on reforecasted completion dates. It is common for activities to remain at 90 per cent complete for many reporting periods before they are finally declared as being drastically behind schedule. This can be partially addressed by creating an environment where early and accurate reporting is rewarded, even if it is bad news.

Tips for maintaining the project schedule

Here are some practical tips to help you develop and maintain a workable project schedule.

- **Monitor the project status and progress every week**. Enter the actual progress of the activities in your schedule every week.
- **Diligently control the project scope**. Once the actual performance data has been entered into the project schedule, the project manager will need to review the entire schedule for impacts to the critical path and changes to the interrelationships between tasks. Two common techniques to get a project back on track are crashing the schedule and fast tracking the schedule. These are explained earlier in the chapter.
- **Rebaseline the project schedule after any change requests are approved** and renegotiate the baseline project schedule whenever it changes due to external factors.
- **Closely monitor the critical path activities** by urgently resolving, or escalating any risks and issues.

REAL-WORLD EXPERIENCE

MONITORING STATUS

I like to have two meetings each week with my project teams – the first early in the week (preferably Tuesday morning) to review risks and issues and the second later in the week (preferably Friday morning) to review project status and progress on deliverables. At the status meeting later in the week, each team member needs to bring along their updated performance data for their assigned deliverables. As a bare minimum, I expect them to:

- indicate the *actual start date* for any activities that have commenced and explain any variances against the planned start date
- provide a *reforecast end date* for any activities that are underway and explain any variances against the planned end date, as well as actions to get things back on track or to compensate for delays

- indicate the *percentage complete* for any activities that are underway – this is not as accurate as timesheet data which can be used to calculate the earned value of each activity and deliverable, and ultimately the entire project
- present any potential *change requests* that may be required due to significant variations to scope, time and cost that cannot be recovered.

In my experience, the above disciplines are more than adequate to manage the schedule baseline closely. *Earned value* is another technique which is widely used in the US and is known to be significantly more accurate. The major drawback is that it requires considerably more performance data and it is not common practice in Australia.

The history of project scheduling

- **1900 to 1930s**: most people in the business world know that a GANTT chart is used as a key project scheduling tool and most believe that GANTT is an acronym, or abbreviation, for some form of fancy mathematical or scientific model. In fact, it is named after Henry Gantt (1861–1919) who is sometimes referred to as one of the founders of modern planning and control techniques. It was in the early 1900s that industrial forms of production were becoming more sophisticated and many academics at the time were developing methods to improve quality and reduce production time, while others were focused on establishing models to improve organisational and workforce performance. It was at this time that other concepts were emerging that led to the development of other project management tools including WBS and various approaches to resource scheduling. GANTT charts became popular on large construction projects in the 1930s.
- **1950s**: this period saw the beginning of modern project management techniques arising primarily from developments in the fields of engineering, construction and manufacturing. The profession was graduating from less formal methods, such as the GANTT chart (which started as a diagramming method and visual aid), and moving towards mathematically based models such as CPM and PERT. CPM was the result of a joint venture by DuPont Corporation and Remington Rand Corporation to develop improved techniques for managing plant maintenance projects. PERT was an outcome of work done by the consulting firm of Booz Allen Hamilton on the US Navy's submarine program. These two concepts combine to give us the modern day critical path.
- **1980s**: this period saw the commercialisation of the first computerised scheduling software with the first version of Primavera released in 1983, closely followed by the release of the first version of Microsoft Project in 1984. Project managers today couldn't imagine managing large and complex projects without the aid of scheduling tools and integrated project management information systems.

Project scheduling software

Detailed instructions on how to create and manage project schedules using one particular software package or another are beyond the scope of this book.

REAL-WORLD EXPERIENCE

STRENGTHS AND WEAKNESSES OF PROJECT SCHEDULING SOFTWARE

I have experience with four different project scheduling software packages: Primavera, MS Project, Clarity and Daptiv. I am happy to share my personal views on the relative strengths and weakness of each of these with one caveat – no one should use the information in Table 8.4 in place of a rigorous and independent selection process.

TABLE 8.4 STRENGTHS AND WEAKNESSES OF PROJECT SCHEDULING SOFTWARE

Primavera

Pros	Cons
» Highly sophisticated project management information system that enables the integrated management of scope, time and cost. » It also provides functionality for managing project resources via the allocation of activities and timesheeting. » Comprehensive support for integrated change control and status reporting. » Used by many large construction companies and major financial institutions to manage major projects.	» The highest price point for this type of software package. » Seen by many as too cumbersome for small, simple projects. » Often an alternative is provided for small projects, such as MS Project. » Requires extensive training in order to achieve competency with all functions. » Can have a complex upgrade path from one version to the next. » Can take a long time to configure and implement.

Clarity

Pros	Cons
» Comprehensive project management information system that enables the integrated management of scope, time and cost. » It also provides functionality for managing project resources via the allocation of activities and timesheeting. » Some support for integrated change control. » Comprehensive status reporting. » Approximately half the cost of Primavera, depending on licensing arrangements.	» Seen by many as too cumbersome for small, simple projects. » Requires moderate training in order to achieve competency with all functions. » Can take a long time to configure and implement.

Daptiv

Pros	Cons
» Basic project management information system that enables the integrated management of scope, time and cost. » It also provides functionality for managing project resources via the allocation of activities and timesheeting. » Good status reporting for projects and the portfolio. » Scheduling capability is similar to MS Project. » Approximately half the cost of Clarity, depending on licensing arrangements.	» Requires moderate levels of training in order to achieve competency with all functions. » No support for integrated change control. » Basic cost management functionality. » The scheduling interface is seen by many as clunky and unsophisticated. » Requires configuration to provide true portfolio functionality.

MS Project Server

Pros	Cons
» Depending on the number of users and the pricing model this can be one of the cheapest integrated scheduling software options. » Basic project scheduling functions provided by MS Project. » Provides additional functionality for the integrated management of the project portfolio. » Provides basic functionality that enables the integrated management of scope, time and cost. » It also provides functionality for managing project resources via the allocation of activities and timesheeting. » Comprehensive support for integrated change control and status reporting. » Used by many large construction organisations to manage project portfolios.	» Requires extensive configuration and sophisticated requirements in order to set up the overall functionality. » Requires technically competent internal technical administration staff. » Requires moderate levels of training.

MS Project

Pros	Cons
» Provides sophisticated functionality for managing the time dimension of projects. » Provides basic functionality for managing cost and human resources. » The cheapest solution. » By far the easiest to use; many people can create basic GANTT charts with minimal training. » An emerging standard. » Little to no upgrade path.	» Provides no integration across the project portfolio. » Normally requires supplementary schedules for cost and resource management due to lack of sophistication in these areas. » Basic cost and resource management functionality is cumbersome to use and doesn't support common scenarios. » Many inexperienced users will need to re-create their GANTT chart as they have not understood the underlying principles in GANTT chart production.

Related processes from the PMBOK® Guide

4.1 ***Develop project charter (initiation)***: In practice, the high-level project scope is developed and documented during the initiation phase in the project charter. It forms the boundaries for subsequent scoping processes. Unfortunately, the PMBOK® Guide has the scope definition activities all occurring in the planning phase and is therefore out of sync with practice.

4.2 ***Develop project management plan (planning)***: During this process, the planning for all the key knowledge areas is often performed at the same time, or expanded upon shortly afterwards. In the PMBOK® Guide there are no stand-alone scope, time or cost planning processes as they are contained within the develop PMP process. The other key knowledge areas have discrete processes for planning that are defined in their process groups. The project schedule is a critical output of this process.

4.5 ***Perform integrated change control (monitoring and controlling)***: The process of reviewing all change requests, including approving or rejecting changes and managing the flow-on impacts on all project deliverables and all components of the PMP. All requested changes should be identified through '5.6 Control scope'. The activities within this process are critical to managing stakeholder expectations and to ensuring the highest chance of project success. They occur from project inception through to completion and are part of the monitor and control process group. It is important that only approved changes be incorporated into the project, as it is surprisingly common to see unapproved changes being inadvertently undertaken.

5.1 ***Plan scope management (planning)***: The process of creating a scope management plan that provides guidance and direction as to how the project scope will be defined, validated and controlled throughout the project.

5.4 ***Create work breakdown structure (WBS) (planning)***: The process of subdividing project deliverables and project work into smaller, more manageable components. The WBS defines all the work to be undertaken by the project team in order to achieve the project objectives and create the required deliverables. It enables the assignment of tasks to resources and forms the basis for the development of the project schedule.

8.2 ***Perform quality assurance (execution)***: The process conducted during the execution of the project that ensures all deliverables perform as expected, they achieve specified quality requirements and they conform to any relevant standards. Quality assurance activities are included in the design and production of the deliverable. It is closely related to '5.5 Validate scope'.

8.3 ***Control quality (monitoring and controlling)***: The processes conducted to ensure that each deliverable meets all requirements and specifications. Quality control is performed as each deliverable or related set of deliverables is completed and often involves testing and inspection. It is closely related to '5.5 Validate scope'.

9.1 ***Plan human resource management (planning)***: The process for creating a project human resource plan by identifying project roles, responsibilities, required skills and reporting relationships. Other components may also include training needs, team building strategies, reward and recognition programs, and performance management processes, as well as workplace health and safety procedures.

9.2 ***Acquire project team (execution)***: The process of confirming human resource availability and selecting the team members necessary to complete the project activities. Project managers need to negotiate and influence in order to obtain the best team possible for the project, as they may not have direct control over resource selection due to industrial agreements, project sponsor preferences and internal HR policies. It is closely related to '6.4 Estimate activity resources' and '6.5 Estimate activity durations'.

10.3 ***Control communications (monitoring and controlling)***: The process of collecting and distributing project performance and status information. This involves the periodic collection of actual performance data and comparing this against the planned baselines of the project. This enables the reporting of performance as well as reforecasting the future performance of the project.

CHAPTER SUMMARY

» The schedule management plan defines how the schedule will be constructed and managed. It normally includes policies and procedures associated with time capture, developing the schedule and status reporting.

» Project timeframes are seen as one of the most difficult dimensions of project management and can cause conflict on projects when arbitrary deadlines are set that have no basis in reality.

» The development of the project schedule requires sophisticated processes to define, sequence, resource and estimate activities. It is seen by most project practitioners as the primary project management deliverable.

» Good practice dictates that activities in the schedule relate back to deliverables in the WBS and provide sufficient allowance for quality and risk management activities.

» Different resources will influence the duration of activities. It is important to allow for differing productivity rates and scheduling biases.

» The precedence diagramming method is one of the key techniques used to sequence activities in projects. It provides four logical operators to connect activities to each other: finish-to-start, start-to-start, finish-to-finish and start-to-finish. It is closely related to the production of the GANTT chart and the critical path.

» PERT uses three estimates to define an approximate range for an activity's duration and takes the weighted average of best case, likely case and worst case to generate a timeframe for an activity.

» Milestones are important events that generally mark the achievement of an important interim outcome that directly contributes to the finalisation of the project. They are typically shown in project schedules as activities or tasks that have no duration. It is good practice to establish milestones at the beginning of the project and report against these until completion.

» The GANTT chart is the most common tool used today for displaying project schedule information in the graphical form of a bar chart. It was developed by Henry Gantt in the early 1900s.

» The critical path is the combination of activities that generates the shortest duration of the project by finding the longest path through the project schedule based on the unique combination of activity interdependencies that have been stipulated in the schedule.

» The critical path and schedule must be monitored closely and worked on every week in order for the project to stay on track.

» It is possible to refine the project schedule using techniques such as fast tracking and crashing. The first will shorten duration if more resources are applied to reduce the duration of activities. The second will reduce the schedule if activities can be run in parallel. Both options increase risk.

» Controlling project time is one of the most difficult components of integrated change control.

» Many project managers do not fully understand the mathematical principles underpinning the development of the project schedule and this can lead to issues when using project scheduling software.

REVISION QUESTIONS

Revision questions are divided into two sections. The first covers Certificate IV understanding and the second covers Diploma-level understanding. Both sections are relevant to Diploma students and teachers, while only the first section is relevant to Certificate students and teachers.

Certificate IV of Project Management

BSBPMG410A performance criteria questions

These questions relate to the performance criteria stated in 'BSBPMG410A Apply project time management techniques'.

1   What is the purpose of the schedule management plan?
2   What are the project time management processes?
3   What is a finish-to-start relationship between activities?
4   What is a finish-to-finish logical relationship between activities?
5   What is a start-to-start logical relationship between activities?
6   What is analogous estimating?
7   What is parametric estimating?
8   What determines the duration of an activity?
9   What is a project schedule and how do GANTT charts contribute to this deliverable?
10   What is a project milestone?
11   What is an external dependency?
12   What is a schedule baseline?
13   What is the critical path?
14   How is actual progress compared against the baselined schedule?
15   How often is the project schedule updated and with what data?

Diploma of Project Management

BSBPMG512A performance criteria questions

These questions relate to the performance criteria stated in 'BSBPMG512A Manage project time'.

1   What are the major inclusions in the schedule management plan?
2   What are the benefits of having a schedule management plan?
3   How is the hierarchical work breakdown developed in scoping converted into the project schedule?
4   What factors determine the sequence of activities and task interdependencies?
5   What is the start-to-finish logical relationship between activities and why is it rarely used?
6   How is the critical path constructed and during which process group?

7   Why is the critical path important when monitoring progress against the baselined schedule?

8   When is the schedule baselined and what circumstances lead to a revised schedule baseline?

9   What are the analogous estimating and bottom-up estimating techniques?

10   What is critical for parametric estimating to be possible?

11   What are the primary outputs of the control schedule process group?

12   What tools and techniques are used to refine the project schedule?

13   What is the three-point estimating technique and what equation is used to determine the outputs of this technique?

14   How are variances to the project schedule identified and rectified?

DISCUSSION QUESTIONS

1   How is the project schedule different to the PMP?

2   What are the pros and cons of analogous estimating and bottom-up estimating?

3   Is three-point estimating most useful when estimating the duration of each activity or when estimating the total duration?

4   In what circumstances can a project schedule have more than one critical path?

5   Explain how you could use the fast tracking technique to reduce the critical path of a project. What are the main consequences of fast tracking?

6   Explain how you could use the crashing technique to reduce the critical path of a project. What are the main consequences of crashing?

7   What are the benefits and difficulties in using earned value analysis?

8   What are the possible impacts on cost and quality if the scope of the project is increased but the timeframe must remain the same?

BSBPMG410A and BSBPMG512A performance criteria questions

ONLINE RESOURCES

Visit the online companion website at http://www.cengagebrain.com to link to important additional resources, including templates, real-world case studies, revision quizzes and additional study material.

FURTHER READINGS AND REFERENCES

Dobie, C. (2007). *A handbook of project management: A complete guide for beginners to professionals.* Sydney: Allen and Unwin.

Hartley, S. (2008). *Project management: Principles, processes and practice* (2nd ed.). Sydney: Pearson Education.

Kerzner, H. (2007). *Project management: A systems approach to planning, scheduling, and controlling* (9th ed.). Brisbane: John Wiley & Sons.

Kloppenborg, T. J. (2012). *Contemporary project management* (2nd ed.). Melbourne: Cengage Learning.

Mulcahy, R. (2006). *PM crash course – Real-world project management tools & techniques.* Minnetonka, MN: RMC Publications.

Portny S. E., Mantel, S. J., Meredith, J. R., . . . Sutton, M. M. (2008). *Project management – Planning, scheduling and controlling projects*. Brisbane: Wiley.

Project Management Institute (PMI). (2013). *A guide to the Project Management Body of Knowledge* (PMBOK® Guide) (5th ed.). Newtown Square, PA. Chapter 6, pp. 141–192.

Schwable, K. (2014). *Information technology project management* (revised 7th ed.). Brooks/Cole, a part of Cengage Learning.

Verzuh, E. (2005). *The fast forward MBA in project management*. Brisbane: John Wiley & Sons.

Project cost management

IN THIS CHAPTER YOU WILL:

1 learn about the specific processes, tools and techniques and major deliverables related to the key knowledge area of Project Cost Management

2 become familiar with the identification, analysis and refinement of project costs to produce a project budget

3 understand how to use a project budget as the principle mechanism to control project costs

4 understand the importance of effective project budget management and the relationships with scope, cost and quality

5 examine the importance of the cost baseline and how this is used to measure and report on project status

6 learn how earned value and other techniques can be used to control project costs

7 learn how to estimate project costs and implement agreed cost management processes

8 appreciate how to identify and implement financial management processes and procedures

9 identify and select cost analysis methods and tools to identify cost variations, evaluate options and manage change requests

10 appreciate the importance of financial completion activities.

Context

Project cost management includes the processes to estimate and control the costs of a project so that it can be completed within the approved budget. This covers all the monetary resources that will be expended in order to execute the project. All of the data related to managing the cost dimension of a project is encapsulated in the project budget. This critical deliverable comprises the planned expenditure for performing project activities, completing deliverables and meeting milestones. It is normally represented as an MS Excel spreadsheet.

Cost is one of the triple constraints of quality, cost and time to project scope. It can be the most contentious of the three as the allocation of funds to one project is often done at the expense of other projects, especially if there is a fixed or limited project funding pool available.

When the project budget is fixed then scope and quality will need to be sacrificed if additional effort or monetary resources are required due to invalid assumptions, missed deadlines or risks that have come to fruition. High-risk projects normally exceed original cost estimates.

See PMBOK®
Guide Figure 7-2
Project cost
management:
inputs, tools and
techniques, and
outputs

See PMBOK®
Guide Chapter 7
Project cost
management

PMBOK® Guide processes for project cost management

According to the PMBOK® Guide, the major processes associated with project cost management are:

7.1   Plan cost management
7.2   Estimate costs
7.3   Determine budget
7.4   Control costs.

In addition to these processes, it is also important to perform financial closure activities and these will be examined later in the chapter.

7.1   ***Plan cost management (planning)***: The process for establishing the policies and procedures that will be used to plan, manage and control costs for the project. The cost management plan provides guidance and direction as to how project costs will be managed.

7.2   ***Estimate costs (planning)***: The process for developing an estimate of costs to complete all activities required to finish the project. These estimates are a prediction based on the information known at any point in time and the assumptions that have been made for planning purposes. The cost of an activity is a function of the effort required and the cost of the resource assigned to perform the activity. It is closely linked to '5.4 Create WBS'.

7.3   ***Determine budget (planning)***: The process for aggregating the costs of individual activities to form the overall budget for the project. An important component of this process is the establishment of the budget baseline for the project, against which all actual progress and variations will be reported. This process is greatly simplified by using spreadsheets or project management software.

7.4 *Control costs (monitoring and controlling)*: The process of monitoring the status of project expenditure. It involves updating the project budget with actuals, comparing performance against baseline and managing any changes. It is critical to monitor both the expenditure and the work performed for that expenditure. Any increase to the authorised budget can only be approved via '4.5 Perform integrated change control' and it is also closely linked to '10.3 Control communications'.

FIGURE 9.1 PROJECT COST MANAGEMENT – A PROCESS PERSPECTIVE

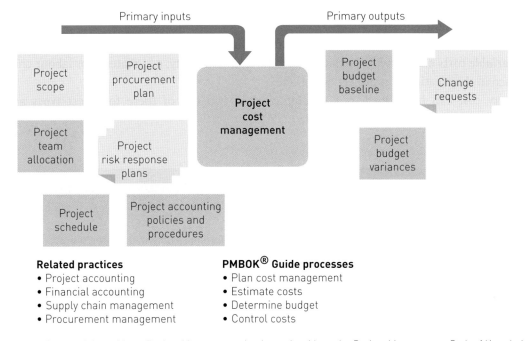

Source: Adapted from Project Management Institute, *A guide to the Project Management Body of Knowledge*, (PMBOK® Guide), fifth edition.

Cost management concepts

Project cost management is traditionally a weak area in many projects. Project managers must work to improve their ability to deliver projects within approved budgets and to correctly account for project expenses along the way. This requires the ability to prepare detailed budgets with clearly documented assumptions.

Project managers need to couple an overall understanding of cost management with a detailed understanding of organisational cost management policies and procedures. Most project sponsors and senior project stakeholders have a better understanding of financial terms than project terms

Project managers require a sophisticated understanding of cost management and accounting practices in order to prepare, track and monitor all cost elements associated with a project, and to manage the expectations of the project sponsor and stakeholders. It is critical that project managers understand the cost management policies and procedures within the organisation where they are executing the project, as these can differ vastly between organisations.

There are four basic types of cost that project managers need to keep in mind. These are direct, indirect, fixed and variable costs. They are defined below.

- **Direct costs** can be directly attributed to the product or project; e.g. material and labour costs (also known as tangible costs).
- **Indirect costs** cannot be directly attributed to the product or project, rather the costs are allocated or apportioned to the product or project based on some level of activity (also known as intangible costs). For example, overhead costs such as rent and insurance are considered indirect costs.
- **Fixed costs** do not vary with the level of production or activity; e.g. a lease on a building.
- **Variable costs** change with the level of production or activity; e.g. material or labour charges used in the creation of a project deliverable.

Every cost can be defined as a combination of two out of these four cost types as per Table 9.1.

TABLE 9.1 COST TYPES, DEFINITION AND EXAMPLES

Cost type	Definition and examples
fixed-direct	» These costs do not vary with production or activity levels and are directly related to the project. » Purchase of software package for implementation via the project. » Purchase of a crane for construction activities.
fixed-indirect	» These costs do not vary with production or activity levels and are indirectly related to the project. » Rental of premises that is apportioned and charged back to the project.
variable-direct	» These costs vary with production or activity levels and are directly related to the project. » Hourly contract labour costs. » Leasing of a crane for construction activities.
variable-indirect	» These costs vary with production or activity levels and are indirectly related to the project. » IT usage charges applied on a per head basis. » Public liability or workers compensation insurance charges.

Cost management terms and definitions

Just like in the discipline of project management, cost accounting uses specific accounting terms and concepts to consistently communicate meaning. Understanding these basic concepts is critical to the development and management of project budgets. Project managers will encounter the accounting terminology in Table 9.2 and will need to understand the definitions in order to discuss project accounting concepts with any credibility.

TABLE 9.2 COST MANAGEMENT TERMS AND DEFINITIONS

Term	Definition	Synonyms
Revenue	The income generated from the sale of goods or services, or any other use of capital or assets, associated with the main operations of an organisation before any costs or expenses are deducted.	Income Earnings Proceeds
Expense	Money spent, or costs incurred, in an organisation's efforts to generate revenue. Expenses may be in the form of actual cash payments (such as wages and salaries), a computed expired portion (depreciation) of an asset, or an amount taken out of earnings (such as bad debts).	Expenditure Cost Outlay
Profit	The surplus remaining after total costs are deducted from total revenue and the basis on which tax is computed and dividend is paid. It is the best known measure of success in an enterprise.	Income Earnings Proceeds
Lifecycle cost	The sum of all recurring and one-off costs over the full lifespan or a specified period of an asset, such as a piece of equipment, a building or a software system. It includes the purchase price, installation costs, operating costs, maintenance and upgrade costs, and remaining (residual or salvage) value at the end of ownership or its useful life.	Whole of life cost
Asset	Something that an entity has acquired or purchased which has monetary value. An asset can be: » something physical, such as cash, machinery, inventory, land and buildings » an enforceable claim against others, such as accounts receivable » a right, such as copyright, patent or trademark » an assumption, such as goodwill.	Tangible asset Intangible asset
Depreciation	The gradual conversion of the cost of a tangible capital asset or fixed asset into an operational expense (called depreciation expense) over the asset's estimated useful life.	Amortisation Writedown

(Continued)

Term	Definition	Synonyms
	The objectives of computing depreciation are to: » reflect the reduction in the book value of the asset due to obsolescence or wear and tear » spread a large expenditure (purchase price of the asset) proportionately over a fixed period to match revenue received from it » reduce an entity's taxable income by charging the amount of depreciation against the total income. Depreciation is computed at the end of an accounting period (usually a year), using a method best suited to the particular asset.	
Return on investment	The earning power of assets measured as the ratio of the net income (profit less depreciation) to the average capital employed (or equity capital) in a company or project. Expressed usually as a percentage, return on investment is a measure of profitability that indicates if a company is using its resources in an efficient manner.	Rate of return Yield
Payback period	The amount of time required to recover the costs outlaid on a project or the creation of an asset. It is the specific point in time (or in number of units sold) when revenue or monetary benefits exactly equals the total cost. This is the point of financial viability where loss ends and profit begins to accumulate.	Break even point
Sunk cost	Money already spent. Sunk costs are past costs that are irretrievable and, therefore, should be considered irrelevant to future decision making. Also refers to costs which have been incurred but not yet paid; i.e. committed costs.	Committed cost Embedded cost
Cash flow analysis	Defines the cash requirements for a project based on the rate at which monetary resources will be expended each period (normally monthly). This helps to manage the cash requirements for the company executing the project. Any cash inflows related to the project should also be considered.	Cash flow projection Cash flow forecast
Contingency	An amount of money or time that is added to an estimate to cover costs or timeframes that are indeterminable at present. These are often calculated based on the risk, complexity or level of uncertainly for a project.	Reserves

Term	Definition	Synonyms
Capital expense	A cost associated with the acquisition or construction of an asset, such as buildings, machinery, equipment, vehicles and software systems. Often abbreviated to CAPEX.	CAPEX Capital cost
Operational expense	Recurring costs that are related to the operation of a business or asset. They are incurred in carrying out an organisation's day-to-day activities, but are not directly associated with production, activity levels or projects. Operating expenses include such things as payroll, sales commissions, employee benefits and pension contributions, travel, depreciation, rent, repairs and taxes. When referring to an asset they are generally related to the on-going support and maintenance of the asset.	OPEX Manufacturing expense Operational cost Overhead cost
Business case	A type of decision-making tool used to determine the effects a particular decision will have on profitability. A business case should show how the decision will alter cash flows over a period of time, and how costs and revenue will change. Specific attention is paid to internal rate of return (IRR), cash flow and payback period. A business case for a project involves making a comparative assessment of all the benefits anticipated from the project and all the costs of undertaking the project.	Cost-benefit analysis
Variance	A variance is a difference between the planned or budgeted cost and the actual or reforecasted costs. A favourable variance occurs when your actual costs are less than your budgeted or planned cost. An unfavourable variance is when actual costs are higher than planned.	Favourable variance Unfavourable variance
Project costing	This method of costing specifically tracks the costs associated with each project or each customer job. It assumes that every job or project is different and tracks all associated costs and income. It provides information on the relative profitability of each job or project.	Job costing
Activity-based costing (ABC)	ABC costing is used to analyse the costs of specific activities and allows for more detailed cost assignments.	ABC

(*Continued*)

Term	Definition	Synonyms
Cash accounting	An accounting method in which income is recorded when cash is received, and expenses are recorded when cash is paid out, regardless of when the commitments were incurred. Cash-basis accounting does not conform with the provisions of generally accepted accounting principles (GAAP) as it leaves a time gap between recording the cause of an action (sale or purchase) and its result (payment or receipt of money). It is, however, simpler than accrual-basis accounting and quite suitable for small organisations that transact business mainly in cash.	Cash-basis accounting
Accrual accounting	A system of accounting based on the accrual principal, under which revenue is recognised (recorded) when earned, and expenses are recognised when incurred. Totals of revenues and expenses are shown in the financial statements (prepared at the end of an accounting period), whether or not cash was received or paid out in that period. Accrual-basis accounting conforms with generally accepted accounting methods (GAAP) in preparing financial statements for external users, and is employed by most companies.	Accrual-basis accounting

Adapted from Sources: Australian Accounting Standards Board terms and definitions, http://www.aasb.gov.au/Pronounce-ments/Glossary-of-defined-terms.aspx; Boyd, K. (2013). Cost accounting for dummies. New Jersey: John Wiley & Sons, Inc.

Project prioritisation and budget allocation processes

In many large organisations there is an allocated annual budget which is set aside specifically for the execution of projects. Business units will typically need to compete for an allocation of these funds for their projects based on the overall priority of the projects. This priority is determined by a set of criteria including business benefits, return on investment, compliance, cost reduction, alignment to strategy and so on. Also, projects will often be categorised into some form of balanced scorecard evaluation such as mandatory maintenance, mandatory regulatory compliance, enhancement to client service, increased revenue or operational efficiency.

These processes are often run annually and then reviewed each quarter. Given the lead times for the overall prioritisation and approval mechanisms to take place, many projects will need to be submitted with no more than high-level estimated costs. Once the selected set of projects has been determined for the year, then the business units can commence planning and more detailed cost estimation. The next step is normally some type of approval of the specific project budget. Once projects commence it becomes critical that the cost performance is measured against the approved budget rather than the initial rough estimates.

Poor project cost estimating can have major negative consequences for others in the organisation, especially if the annual project funding pool is fixed. For example, if a high-priority project goes over budget then often other lower-priority projects will need to be cancelled. Or if a major project comes in under budget it can represent a missed opportunity as the unspent funds could have been used to execute another project which may not have otherwise been funded.

Cost management planning and procedures

The cost management plan establishes the criteria for planning, structuring, estimating, budgeting and controlling project costs. It is often overlooked on the assumption that all project team members understand and follow internal cost management policies and procedures. This can result in the inability to track specific cost categories or actual costs against planned costs.

Ideally the cost management plan is established prior to performing the project cost management processes as it sets the expectations and procedures for how costs will be accounted for and managed on the project. Common inclusions in the cost management plan are:

- links to organisational cost management policies and procedures
- links to appropriate accounting standards and regulations
- cost management assumptions and standards
- cost tracking and performance procedures
- budget templates and reporting formats
- delegated authorities for cost management and approval decisions.

It is very important for the project manager to become familiar with the organisational cost management procedures as it can be a fatal flaw to assume that all major corporations apply the same accounting standards and techniques. The primary source of information and assistance in this area comes from the internal finance department and the project management office (PMO).

PROJECT MANAGEMENT MASTERY

ACCRUAL VERSUS CASH-BASIS ACCOUNTING

I recently had to create and introduce project accounting procedures into a major law firm as there were no disciplines being applied to the management of project budgets. One of the most surprising elements of this situation was that this major firm was undertaking formal accrual-based accounting for the financial statements on a monthly basis but had not applied any disciplines or formal techniques to the monitoring of project budgets. The budgets that had been tracked for major projects up until then had been done on a cash basis. This led to complexities and problems when reconciling expenditure for the end of year financial reporting obligations. A major project in excess of $80 million was being tracked on a cash basis and no accruals were being processed for any invoices. Large accruals had to be processed in the last period of the financial year in order to prepare valid financial accounts. This caused much rework and great confusion as the project manager had no notion of how to perform accrual-based accounting as they had never been asked to do this for previous periods.

It is considered best practice to track project expenditure on an accrual basis.

REAL-WORLD EXPERIENCE

DIFFERING PROJECT ACCOUNTING PRACTICES

Project asset depreciation

I encountered an interesting difference in project accounting procedures when I moved from a major telecommunications company to one of Australia's major banks. I was used to preparing budgets for projects that extended beyond the closure of the project for between three and five years. This practice is linked to the development of business cases for projects to assist with prioritisation, approvals and benefits tracking. It is standard practice under this type of regime to depreciate all assets which are procured for, or produced by, the project over their useful life as stipulated by the Australian Tax Office. This included software development, telephone networks, etc.

I was surprised to find that when I prepared project budgets for my new employer I was no longer required to include the depreciation schedules for major project assets as these were being expensed and no depreciation claimed. This was even more surprising in that the ATO stipulates that certain assets must be depreciated and not expensed. I am still not sure if the bank had a special ruling in order to do this, or if they were inadvertently breaching accounting regulations, or if someone in the finance department was taking the project budget data and independently preparing depreciation schedules for major project assets.

Research and development taxation credits

I have worked for most of Australia's major banking institutions and on several occasions I have been required to specifically track certain project cost categories in order to facilitate the claiming of taxation credits for research and development projects. This is challenging as it requires all members of the project team to capture time according to particular cost codes and if they get it wrong then millions of dollars in tax credits can be at stake. The time recording processes need to be established at the outset of the project and rigorously enforced. These projects are also more heavily monitored by internal finance departments and often the external auditors. More information can be obtained from the Australian Tax Office website (http://www.ato.gov.au) by searching for 'Research and development tax laws' and 'Research and development tax incentives'.

Estimating costs and determining the budget

In discussions on project scope management we focused primarily on identifying and defining deliverables. For project time management we focused on defining the activities required to execute the deliverables. When estimating project costs we need to focus on all the project deliverables and activities included in the work breakdown structure (WBS).

The primary inputs into the estimation of project costs are:
- WBS
- scope baseline
- project schedule
- project human resources
- risk register
- published commercial information
- cost accounting policies and procedures.

RESEARCH AND REFLECTION ACTIVITY

PROJECT ACCOUNTING PROCEDURES

Investigate within your organisation to see if there are formal project accounting procedures or templates that you need to follow when developing and tracking project budgets.

The PMO, finance department and other project managers are a good place to start.

What do you do if there are no existing project accounting policies or procedures?

Analogous estimating

Analogous cost estimating uses parameters such as scope, duration, complexity, similarity of end products and so on to identify similar past projects that can be used as the basis for estimating the costs of the current project. It is a holistic estimating technique that draws on the actual costs of previous, similar projects. It is the fastest way to develop a high-level cost estimate and can be relatively accurate providing that adjustments are made for differences to the current project.

This technique is particularly useful in the following circumstances:
- the development of high-level order of magnitude cost estimates in the initiation phase
- the submission of fixed-price quotes for tendered projects in industries doing many similar projects repeatedly, most notably construction and software installation
- to estimate a part of the project budget where a segment, or combination of specific deliverables, is consistent between different projects.

Bottom-up estimating

Unlike for project time management where there are two major approaches to decomposition, it is generally accepted that it makes sense to only apply the bottom-up estimating technique to project costings. This approach involves estimating the costs at the activity or task level and then working backwards to associate these with a deliverable. It is a good technique for the estimation of variable costs associated with each deliverable, such as labour rates, materials, etc.

Recall in Chapter 8 the discussion of the three rules for estimating the duration of an activity. These can also be relevant for cost estimating purposes where the cost is a function of the duration of the activity. Briefly recapping, Linton's scheduling rules are:

* *rule no. 1:* no activity is smaller than one day
* *rule no. 2:* create milestones for the activities that take less than an hour
* *rule no. 3:* no activity is longer than a week.

Parametric estimating

Parametric estimating uses historical data to estimate either the cost or duration of an activity based on specific parameters. This technique can increase the accuracy of cost estimates if the underlying model is sophisticated and suitable for the current project and conditions. And like analogous estimating, it can also be used very effectively on certain activities or a portion of a project even if it cannot be applied to the entire project.

There is a body of knowledge for cost estimating that has been developed by the International Cost Estimating and Analysis Association (ICEAA) and a handbook for parametric cost estimating that has been developed by the affiliated organisation International Society of Parametric Analysts (ISPA). These are:

* Cost Estimating Body of Knowledge (CEBOK), ICEAA, http://www.iceaaonline.org
* *Parametric estimating handbook*, ISPA, https://www.iceaaonline.org/documentation/files/ISPA_PEH_4th_ed_Final.pdf.

NASA has also developed a comprehensive cost estimating handbook which is easily found by a simple internet search.

RESEARCH AND REFLECTION ACTIVITY

INDUSTRY SPECIFIC STANDARDS

There are many standards, guidelines and estimating tables that have been developed by various government departments and industry organisations.

* Conduct online research to see if you can find any that specifically apply to your industry.
* Check if there are any estimating tables available to you within your organisation.

Best, likely and worst case estimating

As for project time management (discussed in Chapter 8), the accuracy of activity cost estimates can be improved by considering contributing factors such as risk and the degree of uncertainty. Many project managers will adopt a three-point estimating technique designed to show the best, likely and worst case outcomes for project costs. This can be applied to each activity (which may be overkill) or to the overall project. The concept has its origins in PERT, which uses three estimates to define an approximate range for an activity's cost. See Figures 8.2, 8.3 and 8.4 on pages 177–78 for examples of a PERT estimate and network diagrams.

See PMBOK®
Guide Section
7.2.2.5
Three-point
estimating

Project contingency assessment

A common technique for coping with uncertainly in cost estimates is to use contingency. Project contingency, or project reserves, is money that is set aside at the start of a project to be used if required to fund unforeseen additional costs. Contingency can be developed in five main ways:

- summing from the bottom up based on the requirements and uncertainty of each activity
- summing allowances made for the major risks that may occur and negatively impact the project
- summing allowances made for the major planning assumptions that will impact the project financially if they are found to be invalid
- developed for the project as a whole based on factors which are uncertain and may impact cost, such as risk, uncertainly, complexity, size, innovation, etc.
- developed for the project as a whole based on a percentage allocation that can be stipulated depending on the nature of the project and the phase in the project lifecycle; that is, it will often be reduced as each phase is completed and there is more certainty in the project plan.

The contingency amount will then often be expressed as part of the total project cost estimate by a statement of a ranged estimate. The money is typically only accessible via a formal approval process on a case-by-case basis. Sometimes this process will be embedded into '4.5 Perform integrated change control' and other times it will be a discrete approval process outlined in the cost management plan.

REAL-WORLD EXPERIENCE

OVERESTIMATING PROJECT BUDGET CONTINGENCY

In general, I am not in favour of having a formal contingency for a project as I believe that it leads to sloppy project planning and estimating. I have also experienced significant issues with obtaining project approvals for project budgets that are overinflated with contingency.

As the program director for a major product development, I had 10 project managers responsible for delivering different workstreams of the program. The overall program had a high-level estimate of around $30 million which had already been approved by the board. We were one of the organisation's highest-priority projects; nevertheless it would be difficult and time consuming to obtain approval for additional funding once the detailed planning had been undertaken for each workstream. After detailed planning, one of the many IT workstreams had increased the cost estimate by over 100 per cent. This just didn't seem right and after some very difficult and detailed cost review sessions it was revealed that each of the development team leaders had added contingency into their revised estimates.

They had done this in the misguided belief that it would be good for their performance reviews if they delivered their section of the project under budget (with a positive variance). This was completely misinformed as spending more funding on our project would have meant that other projects would need to be cancelled or could not commence as the overall project portfolio had a capped annual expenditure limit.

Myself, the PMO lead and the project manager needed to forensically review every line of the cost estimate and remove the contingency. We were able to settle on a revised estimate that was a little over 20 per cent above the original estimate and the workstream delivered within this amount.

Project contingency frameworks

There are several widely used frameworks for guiding project managers through the calculation of appropriate project cost contingency. I have included two that I have developed previously.

TABLE 9.3 PROJECT CONTINGENCY FRAMEWORKS

Project context	Risk level	Contingency factor
No financial risk. There are no significant risks which will impact the project costing; e.g. when the majority of the project is being delivered via a fixed-price contract and any residual activities will be performed by existing internal resources.	Zero	0%
Very low financial risk. Similar to above but there are financial risks associated with the components that are outside of the fixed-price contract.	Very low	10–15%
Low financial risk. Similar to above but there are financial risks associated with some part of the contract, as in the vendor is relatively new or there is some innovation involved with the major contracted deliverable.	Low	15–20%
Medium financial risk. There is generally less experience and predictability; e.g. a major time and materials contract, significant innovation or some project team members are inexperienced.	Medium	20–25%

Project context	Risk level	Contingency factor
High financial risk. The project team may be experienced in project delivery but there are high degrees of innovation and uncertainty; e.g. a new client, new project team members, new vendor relationships or new end products.	High	25–30%
Very high financial risk. The same as above but where financial penalties exist for late delivery; e.g. when delivering on a fixed-price contract with a high degree of uncertainty or where mandated delivery dates exist due to the introduction of new regulations.	Very high	30–50%

A contingency application method based on the level of accuracy (or rather inaccuracy) involved with project cost estimates at different stages in the project lifecycle can also be used. This is summarised in Figure 9.2 which is an example from Kloppenborg's *Contemporary project management*.

FIGURE 9.2 PROJECT COST ESTIMATE COMPARISONS

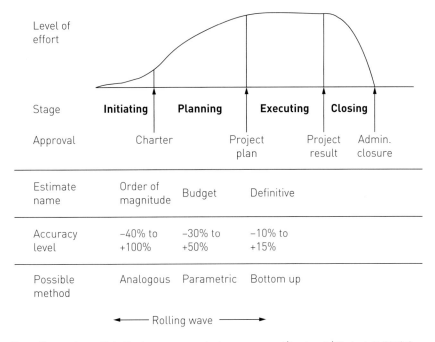

Source: From Kloppenborg, T. J. *Contemporary project management* (book only) 2nd ed. © 2012 Cengage Learning.

Project budget baseline and approvals

It is critical to set the project budget baseline at the end of the planning phase as it provides the basis for the monitoring of cost performance on the project. When actual progress commences and costs are expended this needs to be checked against the planned amounts in the budget baseline at the end of each accounting period, normally at least monthly.

The project budget baseline must be reset whenever the following events occur:

- the project budget is approved
- a change request that impacts the project budget is approved.

When the initial project budget baseline is set, the cash flow projections for the project will also normally be established so that under- or overexpenditure can be monitored for the entire project each accounting period, as well as within each expenditure area. Figures 9.3 and 9.4 show an example project budget for a fictitious IT project as well as the cash flow table for the project. As you can see it is common for specific cost categories to be used when preparing budgets and this needs to be consistent with the organisation's project accounting procedures.

FIGURE 9.3 PROJECT BUDGET SUMMARY

Surveyor Pro Project cost estimate created 5 October 2013

	# Units/hrs.	Cost/unit/hr. ($)	Subtotals ($)	WBS level 1 totals ($)	% of total
WBS items					
1. Project management				**306 000**	**20**
Project manager	960	100	96 000		
Project team members	1920	75	144 000		
Contractors (10% of software development and testing)			66 300		
2. Hardware				**76 000**	**5**
2.1 Handheld devices	100	600	60 000		
2.2 Servers	4	4 000	16 000		
3. Software				**614 000**	**40**
3.1 Licensed software	100	200	20 000		
3.2 Software development*			594 000		
4. Testing (10% of total hardware and software costs)			69 000	**69 000**	**5**
5. Training and support				**202 400**	**13**
Trainee cost	100	500	50 000		
Travel cost	12	700	8 400		
Project team members	1920	75	144 000		
6. Reserves (20% of total estimate)			253 540	**253 540**	**17**
Total project cost estimate				**1 521 240**	

*See software development estimate.

Source: From Schawlbe. *Information Technology Project Management* (with Microsoft Project 2010 60 Day Trial CD-ROM). 7th edition, p. 287. © 2014 Brooks/Cole, a part of Cengage Learning, Inc. Reproduced by permission.

FIGURE 9.4 PROJECT CASH FLOW

Surveyor Pro Project cost baseline created 10 October 2013

WBS items [$]	1	2	3	4	5	6	7	8	9	10	11	12	Totals
1. Project management													
Project manager	8 000	8 000	8 000	8 000	8 000	8 000	8 000	8 000	8 000	8 000	8 000	8 000	96 000
Project team members	12 000	12 000	12 000	12 000	12 000	12 000	12 000	12 000	12 000	12 000	12 000	12 000	144 000
Contractors		6 027	6 027	6 027	6 027	6 027	6 027	6 027	6 027	6 027	6 027	6 027	66 300
2. Hardware													
2.1 Handheld devices				30 000	30 000								60 000
2.2 Servers				8 000	8 000								16 000
3. Software													
3.1 Licensed software				10 000	10 000								20 000
3.2 Software development		60 000	60 000	80 000	127 000	127 000	90 000	50 000					594 000
4. Testing			6 000	8 000	12 000	15 000	15 000	13 000					69 000
5. Training and support													
Trainee cost									50 000				50 000
Travel cost									8 400				8 400
Project team members							24 000	24 000	24 000	24 000	24 000	24 000	144 000
6. Reserves				10 000	10 000	30 000	30 000	60 000	40 000	40 000	30 000	3 540	253 540
Totals	20 000	86 027	92 027	172 027	223 027	198 027	185 027	173 027	148 427	90 027	80 027	53 567	1 521 240

Source: From Schawlbe. *Information Technology Project Management* (with Microsoft Project 2010 60 Day Trial CD-ROM). 7th edition, p. 288. © 2014 Brooks/Cole, a part of Cengage Learning, Inc. Reproduced by permission.

Figure 9.5 shows the typical expenditure and funding pattern for a project. Most organisations will have staged approval processes for project budgets and the revised budget forecast will typically need to be reapproved at predefined gates. Also, from observation, most projects take longer to ramp up in the early stages and underspend against the early cash flow forecasts. They will then often accelerate and overspend against the later cash flow forecasts, even if the overall project is still delivered on budget.

FIGURE 9.5 TYPICAL EXPENDITURE AND FUNDING PATTERNS

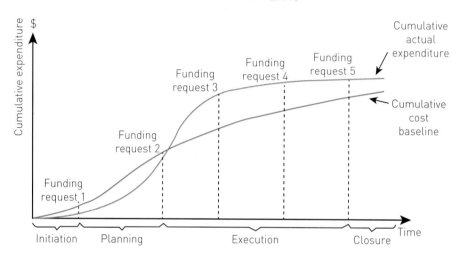

Source: The Northern Sydney Institute, Part of TAFE NSW.

Tips for creating realistic project budgets

Here are some suggestions for the creation of the best possible cost estimates. Much of this relates back to the tips for estimating activity timeframes, as accurate scoping and accurate time estimating together provide a solid basis for more accurate cost estimating.

- Verify all activity time and cost estimates with the resources that will be doing the work, or have them provide the initial estimates themselves.
- Estimate activity costs and durations without consideration for preferred delivery dates or order of magnitude budget estimates.
- Estimate both the variable and fixed costs for each activity.
- Include the direct and indirect costs for each activity, as well as the indirect costs that may be applied to the whole project.
- Ensure that all activities associated with the production of each deliverable are identified and estimated, including review, rework, defect repair, quality assurance and quality control activities.
- Make sure that all cost and time units are identical as misunderstandings around estimating units can cause major issues when combining estimates for activities into the overall project budget.
- Clearly document all budgeting assumptions which will impact the costs of activities, such as exchange rates, interest rates, productivity levels, charge-out rates, indirect cost allocation methods, etc.

- Compensate for the estimating biases of team members.
- Ensure that any contingency provisions are clearly identified and not absorbed into the estimate for each activity.
- Use parametric techniques to verify and double check activity cost estimates where relevant cost estimating tables exist.
- Make adjustments when using analogous estimating techniques, as no matter how similar a past project, deliverable or activity is to the current circumstances, there will always be some differences in terms of the risk, complexity, project environment, specific resources, differing experience levels, etc.
- Review project cost accounting policies and procedures with the PMO, finance department and other project managers to ensure that all sources of cost have been included. This is particularly important for indirect costs.

Project budgeting concepts

The development of the project budget is typically as simple as aggregating all the activity costs and allowing for any indirect costs that are independent of the activities.

There are typically five different types of cost estimates or project budgets which reflect the level of accuracy which increases with each phase of the project lifecycle.

1 ***Order of magnitude estimates***: these provide a rough, high-level estimate of the total project cost. They are normally established in the early stages of the project and are used for estimating purposes on the project charter. They are sometimes referred to as the preferred or predicted project cost as they are often set to align with the project sponsor's preference for the total cost of the project, or developed based on the gut feel and previous experience of the project manager. These are best expressed as a range as this will clearly indicate that they are still unrefined. The most common form of range is plus or minus:

    $10 000 +/− $500 – translates to a cost of between $9500 and $10 500

    $10 000 +/− 20% – translates to a cost of between $8000 and $12 000

2 ***Project budget estimate***: this estimate is typically used to set aside funding for a project as part of an organisation's project prioritisation and approval process. The order of magnitude estimate will be used initially, or perhaps an even less accurate estimate may have been provided earlier in order to meet decision-making timelines. Once planning has progressed to the point of having a project budget baseline, then this is normally confirmed against the approved budget and commitment to the project is then reaffirmed.

3 ***Definitive estimates***: these are often used for components of the project rather than the project as a whole. They drill down into one particular cost area or work package in more detail in order to make procurement decisions, or where the component requires independent cost validation.

4 ***Project budget baseline***: this is normally set at the end of the planning phase at the same time as the project scope and project time baselines are set. At this stage there is normally sufficient detail to create the project budget estimate, determine cash flow requirements and start tracking actual cost performance.

5   *Project budget reforecast*: this estimate occurs on a recurring basis once the project has moved into execution and at any point where the overall project budget is being reviewed. It provides an estimate of the revised budget for the project. Any amount that is indicated above the approved project budget baseline will need formal approval which should be sought as part of '4.5 Perform integrated change control', as major changes should be the result of a change request. Often there will be further budget approval processes over and above the change control process, especially if there is no contingency allowance or no mechanism to access the contingency without formal approval.

REAL-WORLD EXPERIENCE

INDIRECT COSTS IN PROJECT BUDGETS

It is common for projects to go over budget due to the allocation of unforeseen indirect costs to their project cost centre. These surprise cost items can include rent provisions, IT allowances, overhead distributions and so on. I have seen this circumstance occur several times to project managers who are new to different organisations. In one case, a project manager was asked to explain variances as the project was substantially over budget. He had a detailed project cost tracking spreadsheet where he was diligently recording all the invoices that had been submitted for his project. He was unable to reconcile the project costs being reported from the finance system with his spreadsheet and was convinced that there was an error, such as invoices and costs being incorrectly allocated to his project.

The PMO finally conducted a detailed review and found that the cause was the indirect costs that were apportioned to all projects on a per head basis to allow for corporate cost recovery. The impact on his project budget was relatively large as he had a large project team of internal resources who were not being charged to the project and a relatively small budget for other cost items. At this point it would be expected that a change request would be raised in order to seek approval for the additional funds required. Unfortunately, the organisation chose not to take this action. Rather, the project manager was asked to reduce the scope of the project so it could still be delivered in accordance with the original budget. This resulted in an approximately 50 per cent reduction of scope and significantly reduced the ability of the project to meet the business objectives. The impact was so major that the project was eventually cancelled.

Controlling the project budget

Cost control involves monitoring expenditure on the project and managing changes to the cost baseline. The primary activities that are undertaken during this process are:
- reviewing of invoices and expenses
- updating the project budget with actuals
- revising the forecasted total budget

- monitoring variances from the cost baseline
- identifying change requests that will impact the project budget.

Any changes identified that will impact on the project budget need to be approved via '4.5 Perform integrated change control'.

The following data should be entered into the project budget tracking spreadsheet on a weekly basis:

- costs of invoices received for labour, goods and services
- accruals for costs which have been incurred but where invoices have not yet been received
- actual expenditure on activities
- revised forecasts of expenditure.

The primary techniques that can be used to monitor and control costs are earned value management, variance analysis and forecasting.

Earned value management

PROJECT MANAGEMENT MASTERY

EARNED VALUE MANAGEMENT

Earned value management (EVM) is a concept that most project managers have heard of, but in Australia at least, very few have any real experience in its application. In my time as a project delivery professional I have only used it once when I was delivering projects for a major consulting firm. My understanding is that it is an almost mandatory technique for project managers practising in the United States, Canada and South America.

In brief, EVM is a technique that integrates the three key baselines of scope, time and cost; it measures the planned value, earned value and actual cost of each activity as it is being executed. It is the most accurate form of progress monitoring and also one of the most complex. In addition to an integrated baseline, it requires the extensive collection of work performance data for both cost and effort.

The following standards for EVM are also very useful when first implementing the technique:

- Australian standard: AS 4817-2006 Project performance measurement using earned value management
- US standard: NDIA ANSI EIA 748A Earned value management standard
- NDIA ANSI EIA 748 Intent Guide: a companion to the above US standard
- PMI standard: *Practice standard for earned value management* (2nd ed.).

It is possible to use a simpler method of earned value calculation based on percentage completion estimates rather than actual effort data. This provides a lot of the benefits of the visual management that are gained from being able to graph project progress without the need for exhaustive performance data gathering. The same type of analysis can then be conducted to determine if the project is on, ahead of, or behind the planned budget and schedule. These are determined by the cost performance index (CPI) and the schedule performance index (SPI) respectively.

Forecasting and variance analysis

REAL-WORLD EXPERIENCE

FORECASTING AND VARIANCE ANALYSIS

In my experience here in Australia, most project managers use more basic techniques than EVM to monitor and control the project budget. With vigilance, the budget can be controlled almost as well using the less formal practices of variance analysis and reforecasting. While these are less accurate, they also take less time and effort to perform and draw on standard practices from the accounting profession.

Forecasting is the technique of capturing cost data for activities from the bottom up and using experience gained from the work that has already been completed to estimate a revised cost forecast to complete each activity. These revised estimates can then be aggregated to determine the revised overall budget. Sometimes variances from the original planned budget can be one-offs and are able to be recovered to bring the project in on budget; at other times the variances are endemic and indicate that the project will be delivered either over- or underbudget.

Variance analysis looks more deeply at the root cause of positive or negative variances on activities (i.e. under- or overbudget amounts) to determine the impact they will have on the overall project budget. Sometimes corrective or preventative action can be taken to bring the estimated final cost back into line with the baselined budget. If not, then a change request needs to be generated and processed via '4.5 Perform integrated change control'.

Negative variances are considered to be variances which will take the project over the original budget estimate. Positive variances are typically variances that will bring the project in under the original budget. Interim positive variances are not always a sign of good project health as they can indicate that the project is behind schedule or that some scope elements have been omitted. Project managers need to carefully assess the root cause of any variance in order to determine the most appropriate response to bring the project back on track.

Figure 9.6 shows an example of the summary variances for an architecture firm that has many simultaneous projects. It depicts the variances in both effort and cost.

Some organisations use different terminology for positive and negative variances, preferring to call them *favourable* or *unfavourable variances*. This terminology allows for more clarity in the

FIGURE 9.6 EXAMPLE PROJECT COST VARIANCE REPORT

My Architect Company Pty Ltd
Budget forecast report

Project group name: live projects
Print date: 26/11/2013
Approved only: No
Budget period: All

Work name	Plan ($)		Work to date ($)		Estimate to complate ($)		Forecast ($)		Variance ($)	
	Plan effort	Plan cost	Actual effort	Actual cost	ETC effort	ETC cost	Forecast effort	Forecast cost	Variance effort	Variance cost
Active projects	1872.75	144 364.00	620.25	56 337.50	1517.25	114 254.00	2137.50	170 591.00	−264.75	−26 227.50
04-34 Bridge Point	283.75	20 635.00	163.75	15 115.00	243.75	17 355.00	407.50	32 470.00	−123.75	−11 835.00
04-23 Bond Rd	0.00	0.00	20.00	2 790.00	0.00	0.00	20.00	2 790.00	−20.00	2 790.00
04-04 36 Cranbury Ave	183.00	15 305.00	84.00	5 420.00	183.00	15 305.00	267.00	20 275.00	−84.00	−5 420.00
04-05 41 Gilby Rd, Tocting	249.20	24 715.00	66.00	4 360.00	249.20	24 715.00	315.20	29 075.00	−66.00	−4 360.00
04-06 41 Ox Lane, Harpenden	162.80	9 084.00	12.00	960.00	162.80	9 084.00	174.80	10 044.00	−12.00	−960.00
04-07 Sydney Art Gallery West	141.00	6 790.00	4.00	320.00	141.00	8 790.00	145.00	7 110.00	−4.00	−320.00
04-08 36 Lanrock Ave, Bondi	191.00	12 190.00	30.00	2 400.00	191.00	12 190.00	221.00	14 590.00	−30.00	−2 400.00
04-10 St Patricks Church	165.00	8 765.00	30.50	1 675.00	161.00	8 565.00	191.50	10 240.00	−26.50	−1 475.00
04-2 35 Francis St, Bondi	204.00	21 940.00	210.00	23 297.50	185.50	20 260.00	395.50	43 547.50	−191.50	−21 607.50
05- St Patricks Church	293.00	24 940.00	0.00	0.00	0.00	0.00	0.00	0.00	293.00	24 940.00

Source: From Schawlbe. *Information Technology Project Management* (with Microsoft Project 2010 60 Day Trial CD-ROM). 7th edition, © 2014 Brooks/Cole, a part of Cengage Learning, Inc. Reproduced by permission.

analysis and reporting of project budget variances. Favourable and unfavourable variances are concerned with whether a cost is over or under the baseline, as well as the specific impact of the variance. For example, some projects have both projected costs and projected revenue. In this case, if revenue numbers are more than what was budgeted then the variance is shown as favourable; if the revenue numbers are less than planned, then the variance is shown as unfavourable. However, if actual expenses are more than what was budgeted for then the variance is shown as unfavourable; if the expenses are more than was planned then the variance is shown as unfavourable.

There is specific formatting adopted by the accounting profession to allow for the different types of variance to be easily highlighted and interpreted in the financial reports. Unfavourable variances are reported as:

$$-\$999\ 999 \text{ or } -\$999\ 999 \text{ or } -\textbf{\$999\ 999}$$

$$(\$999\ 999), \text{ or } (\$999\ 999) \text{ or } \textbf{(\$999\ 999)}.$$

Common issues leading to change requests

The following table outlines some of the major causes of variations in project cost. Good practice is to create change requests as part of '4.5 Perform integrated change control'. Controlling project cost is a subcomponent of this process and is discussed in detail in Chapter 16.

TABLE 9.4 EXPLANATION OF CHANGE FACTORS

Change factor	Explanation and understanding
Planning assumptions are untrue	Many assumptions need to be made in order to finalise the PMP and resulting baselines for scope, time and cost. When an assumption is untrue then approval for a change request and impact analysis of the flow-on effects should be sought.
Budgetary assumptions are untrue	It is often necessary to document specific budgetary assumptions related to project costs, such as unit costs, labour rates, exchange rates, GST, etc. If a budgetary assumption is found to be untrue then approval for a change request should be sought.
Risks occurs	There is always a possibility that one of the documented risks will occur on a project. Risks can often have an adverse impact on cost as additional resources, deliverables and activities may need to be added into the project.

Change factor	Explanation and understanding
Project scope change	Project scope changes due to omissions in the original scope are common and have flow-on impacts on both time and cost.
Productivity rates are lower than planned	If the labour resources are less productive than planned then this will impact the duration of activities and have a flow-on impact on costs when the resources are being charged to the project.
Material consumption rates are higher than planned	If the assumed rate of material consumption is lower than the actual rate, then additional materials will be required which will impact the project budget. This could also occur if the wastage of materials is higher than expected.
Loss of key resources	When a project team or vendor loses key resources or experts then it can take some time to replace them. During this time the project will continue to move forward and consume costs even though some activities have not progressed. Also, once replaced, the new resource may not have the same level of expertise or productivity which will have a further impact.
Vendors go out of business	If a vendor of a major procurement goes out of business there can be massive impacts on time and cost. The project may need to find an alternate vendor and write off all costs incurred with the previous vendor, or even take on the specific activities themselves by hiring additional resources. In some cases the project organisation will bail out or even buy out the vendor in order to continue with the project.

Tips for tracking project costs

To stay on budget, project managers must:
- be knowledgeable about internal cost management policies
- understand all the cost elements of the project
- prepare a detailed budget and carefully document assumptions
- diligently control project scope
- re-baseline the project budget after any change requests are approved
- ensure accurate capture of actual costs
- closely monitor the critical path activities
- urgently resolve or escalate risks and issues on the critical path
- renegotiate the baseline project budget whenever it changes due to external factors
- manage stakeholder expectations closely
- evaluate performance against the agreed and re-baselined project budget.

Following are some practical tips to help you accurately track the project budget.

- ***Check all invoices carefully prior to authorisation***. Ensure that all invoices are correct and dispute any elements which are outside of scope or appear to be in error. It is okay to part-pay an invoice while a component of it is in dispute.
- ***Track and code your invoices yourself if possible***. It is preferable to have all invoices sent to the project manager for checking and coding (with the relevant project cost centre, activity codes, general ledger account, etc.) so as to ensure that invoices correctly hit the project cost centre.
- ***Check all cost allocations to the project cost centre***. Check any costs which have been allocated to the project cost centre outside of the invoice tracking processes. These could include indirect cost allocations made by finance, as well as costs incorrectly applied to the cost centre due to coding errors.
- ***Monitor the project status and progress every week***. Carefully tracking the overall progress of the project will assist in the management of the project budget.
- ***Make monthly accruals for major costs if invoices have not been received***. Ensure that accruals are made for major costs in the period in which they have been incurred even if the invoices have not yet been received.
- ***Reverse accruals at the beginning of the next period***. It is critical that accruals are reversed out at the beginning of the next period, or when the invoices are received you will have double counting issues that make it appear that the project has overspent.
- ***Review the project budget every month***. It is best if the overall project budget is reviewed at least monthly to ensure that all actual costs have been entered and all major cost categories reviewed. As a bare minimum, the following activities should be undertaken:
  - enter actual costs
  - estimate forecast to complete
  - calculate variances
  - explain variances
  - take mitigating actions if possible to bring costs back on track
  - initiate change requests if costs cannot be brought back into line with the project budget baseline
  - present any change requests that may be required due to significant variations to scope, time and cost that cannot be recovered.

  The above disciplines are more than adequate to closely manage the project budget baseline. Earned value is another technique which is widely used in the US and is known to be significantly more accurate. The major drawback is that it requires considerably more performance data and this is not common practice in Australia.
- ***Work the project schedule every week***. Once the actual performance data has been entered into the project schedule, the project manager will need to review the entire schedule for impacts on the critical path and changes to the interrelationships between tasks. This is critical where the cost of activities is directly related to duration. Specific techniques are discussed further in Chapter 8.

- ***Closely monitor the critical path activities*** by urgently resolving, or escalating, risks and issues that relate to activities on the critical path. This is covered in more detail in Chapter 8.
- ***Diligently control the project scope***. Inadvertent increases to project scope will impact both the schedule and the project budget. It is critical that the scope of the project is formally monitored and controlled. This is covered in more detail in Chapter 7.
- ***Re-baseline the project budget after any change requests are approved*** and renegotiate the baseline whenever it changes due to external factors.

Performing accounting closure

This is a critical process that is completely overlooked by the PMBOK® Guide. There are many common required activities that form part of finalising the project budget. They are outlined in the following list.

- Project cost centre closure to prevent additional costs from being attributed to the project after the finalisation of remaining invoices. Unfortunately it is relatively common for incorrect charges to flow into project cost centres once the project is finished. This could be due to invoice coding errors, incorrect timesheet entries and, occasionally, fraud.
- Reconciliation of paid and outstanding invoices so that accruals can be made for any remaining committed but unpaid costs at the time of project closure.
- Assessment of budget performance to determine the final positive or negative variance against the approved budget.
- Establishment of the benefits tracking process for any financial benefits to be reported by the business owner going forward.

Related processes from the PMBOK® Guide

4.2   ***Develop project management plan (planning)***: During this process, the planning for all the key knowledge areas are often performed at the same time, or expanded upon shortly afterwards. In the PMBOK® Guide there are no stand-alone scope, time or cost planning processes as they are contained within the develop PMP process. The other key knowledge areas have discrete processes for planning that are defined in their process groups. The project schedule is a critical output of this process.

4.5   ***Perform integrated change control (monitoring and controlling)***: The process of reviewing all change requests, including approving or rejecting changes and managing the flow-on impacts on all project deliverables and all components of the PMP. All requested changes should be identified through '5.6 Control scope'. The activities within this process are critical to managing stakeholder expectations and to ensuring the highest chance of project success. They occur from project inception through to completion and are part of the monitor and control process group. It is important that only approved changes be incorporated into the project, as it is surprisingly common to see unapproved changes being inadvertently undertaken.

5.1 ***Plan scope management (planning)***: The process of creating a scope management plan that provides guidance and direction as to how the project scope will be defined, validated and controlled throughout the project.

5.4 ***Create work breakdown structure (WBS) (planning)***: The process of subdividing project deliverables and project work into smaller, more manageable components. The WBS defines all the work to be undertaken by the project team in order to achieve the project objectives and create the required deliverables. It enables the assignment of tasks to resources and forms the basis for the development of the project schedule.

5.6 ***Control scope (monitoring and controlling)***: The process of monitoring the status of both the project and product scope. It focuses on managing any changes to the scope baseline and understanding the flow-on impacts on time, cost and quality via the related process '4.5 Perform integrated change control'.

6.4 ***Estimate activity resources (planning)***: The process of estimating the types and quantities of material, people, equipment or supplies required to perform each activity. It is closely linked to '9.1 Plan human resource management' and '9.2 Acquire project team' and the project procurement management processes.

6.5 ***Estimate activity durations (planning)***: The process of approximating the number of work periods needed to complete individual activities with estimated resources. Work periods may be hours, days, weeks, months and so on and different resources will exhibit differing productivity levels.

8.2 ***Perform quality assurance (execution)***: The process conducted during the execution of the project that ensures all deliverables perform as expected, they achieve specified quality requirements and they conform to any relevant standards. Quality assurance activities are included in the design and production of the deliverable. It is closely related to '5.5 Validate scope'.

8.3 ***Control quality (monitoring and controlling)***: The processes conducted to ensure that each deliverable meets all requirements and specifications. Quality control is performed as each deliverable or related set of deliverables is completed and often involves testing and inspection. It is closely related to '5.5 Validate scope'.

9.1 ***Plan human resource management (planning)***: The process for creating a project human resource plan by identifying project roles, responsibilities, required skills and reporting relationships. Other components may also include training needs, team building strategies, reward and recognition programs and performance management processes, as well as workplace health and safety procedures.

9.2 ***Acquire project team (execution)***: The process of confirming human resource availability and selecting the team members necessary to complete the project activities. Project managers need to negotiate and influence in order to obtain the best team possible for the project, as they may not have direct control over resource selection due to industrial agreements, project sponsor preferences and internal HR policies. It is closely related to '6.4 Estimate activity resources' and '6.5 Estimate activity durations'.

10.3 ***Control communications (monitoring and controlling)***: The process of collecting and distributing project performance and status information. This involves the periodic collection of actual performance data and comparing this against the planned baselines of the project. This enables the reporting of performance as well as reforecasting the future performance of the project.

11.5 ***Plan risk responses (planning)***: The process for developing risk management strategies that will reduce the impact of major risks on the project objectives and success criteria. Risks can be accepted, transferred, mitigated or avoided, and the specific actions selected should be in line with the priority and potential impact of the risk. The concept of the risk owner is applied to ensure that one person is accountable for enacting any risk management plans that may be required.

12.1 ***Plan procurement management (planning)***: The process for identifying the procurement requirements for a project. This involves identifying all resources and equipment that must be purchased and utilised in order to complete the project, as well as specifying the procurement approach and selection criteria. It considers potential suppliers and the contractual arrangements that may be required to manage these external parties to achieve the project objectives.

CHAPTER SUMMARY

» The cost management plan includes links to relevant policies, procedures, guidelines and templates for the management of cost on a project. It should always refer to the internal project accounting requirements.

» Project cost management processes include estimating costs and determining budget and control costs. This should be expanded to ensure that financial closure activities are also performed.

» There are many different types of project budget estimates and these normally become increasingly accurate as the project progresses through the lifecycle. These include rough order of magnitude estimates, budgetary estimates, definitive estimates and the project budget baseline.

» The techniques used to prepare budget estimates are analogous, bottom up and parametric. PERT techniques are also often used to develop best case, likely case and worst case estimates.

» A common technique for coping with uncertainly in cost estimates is to use contingency. Project contingency, or project reserves, is money that is set aside at the start of a project to be used if required to fund unforeseen additional costs.

» To manage the project budget, project managers must be knowledgeable about internal cost management and project accounting policies and processes.

» To prepare the detailed project budget it is necessary to understand all the cost elements of the project. It is critical to include both direct and indirect costs.

» In the preparation of the detailed project budget it is important to carefully document specific project budgeting assumptions.

» The project scope must be carefully controlled in order to ensure that the project remains on time and on budget. The project budget baseline should be updated after any change request is approved which will impact on the project budget.

» Project budget performance is evaluated against the agreed and re-baselined project budget and may contain either favourable or unfavourable variances.

» Earned value management and variance analysis are common techniques for monitoring and controlling the project budget.

REVISION QUESTIONS

Revision questions are divided into two sections. The first covers Certificate IV understanding and the second covers Diploma-level understanding. Both sections are relevant to Diploma students and teachers, while only the first section is relevant to Certificate students and teachers.

BSBPMG412A
performance
criteria questions

Certificate IV of Project Management

These questions relate to the performance criteria stated in 'BSBPMG412A Apply project cost management techniques'.

1   What are the project cost management processes?
2   What is earned value management?
3   What is variance analysis?
4   What is the difference between an order of magnitude estimate and project budget estimate?
5   What is contingency?
6   What is analogous estimating?
7   What is parametric estimating?
8   What determines the cost of an activity?
9   What sources of costs regularly occur on projects?
10   What is the difference between a fixed and variable cost?
11   What is the difference between a direct and indirect cost?
12   How is actual progress compared against the baselined project budget?
13   How often is the project budget updated and with what data?
14   What is the project budget forecast?
15   What can be done to prevent costs being attributed to a project once it has finished?

Diploma of Project Management

BSBPMG514A
performance
criteria questions

These questions relate to the performance criteria stated in 'BSBPMG514A Manage project cost'.

1   What are the common inclusions in the cost management plan?
2   What is the relationship between the duration and cost of activities?
3   Which organisational policies and standards are a critical input into the management of the project budget?
4   When is the project budget baselined and what circumstances lead to a revised schedule baseline?
5   What is the difference between cash accounting and accrual accounting?
6   What types of indirect costs are outside of the project manager's control and are often applied to project budgets?

7   Why are the costs that have been committed but not yet paid important when making decisions across the project portfolio?

8   What is the purpose of the project cash flow analysis?

9   What are the analogous estimating and bottom-up estimating techniques?

10   What is critical for parametric estimating to be possible?

11   What are the primary outputs of the control project costs process group?

12   What tools and techniques are used to refine the project budget?

13   What is the three-point estimating technique and what equation is used to determine the outputs of this technique?

14   How are variances to the project budget identified and rectified?

15   How is project budget variance analysis undertaken?

16   What is the difference between a positive and negative variance?

17   What activities are involved in the financial completion of a project?

DISCUSSION QUESTIONS

1   How is the project budget different from the project forecast?

2   Is it always good to come in under budget? In what circumstances might this be an undesirable outcome for a project?

3   How would you design a project funding gate approval process?

4   What are the pros and cons of estimating contingency for each budget item as opposed to estimating it for the entire project?

5   What is more important to the determination of project cost contingency – complexity or risk?

6   What are some of the difficulties in obtaining actual cost performance data on a timely basis?

7   What are the benefits and difficulties in using earned value analysis?

8   What are the possible impacts on time and quality if the scope of the project is increased but the budget must remain the same?

BSBPMG412A and
BSBPMG514A
performance
criteria questions

ONLINE RESOURCES

Visit the online companion website at http://www.cengagebrain.com to link to important additional resources, including templates, real-world case studies, revision quizzes and additional study material.

FURTHER READINGS AND REFERENCES

Boyd, K. (2013). *Cost accounting for dummies*. New Jersey: John Wiley & Sons, Inc.

Australian Accounting Standards Board Terms and Definitions, http://aasb.gov.au/Pronouncements/ Glossary-of-defined-terms.aspx

Australian standard – AS 4817-2006 Project Performance Measurement Using Earned Value Management.

Cost Estimating Body of Knowledge (CEBOK), ICEAA, http://www.iceaaonline.org

Clarke, N., & Howell, R. (2009). *Emotional intelligence and projects*. Newtown Square, PA: Project Management Institute.

ISPA. *Parametric estimating handbook*, https://www.iceaaonline.org/documentation/files/ISPA_PEH_4th_ed_Final.pdf.

Project Management Institute (PMI). (2013). *A guide to the Project Management Body of Knowledge* (PMBOK® Guide) (5th ed.). Newtown Square, PA. Chapter 7, pp. 193–226.

Schwable, K. (2014). *Information technology project management* (revised 7th ed.). Brooks/Cole, a part of Cengage Learning.

US standard – NDIA ANSI EIA 748A Earned Value Management Standard; NDIA ANSI EIA 748 Intent Guide – a companion to the above US standard.

Verzuh, E. (2005). *The fast forward MBA in project management*. Brisbane: John Wiley & Sons.

Project quality management

IN THIS CHAPTER YOU WILL:

1. learn about the specific processes, tools and techniques and major deliverables related to the key knowledge area of Project Quality Management

2. become familiar with the processes and standards for project quality management

3. be able to distinguish between quality assurance and quality control activities

4. understand the relationships with scope, cost and quality

5. understand the importance of project quality management for delivering products and services

6. define project quality management and understand how quality relates to various types of projects

7. describe quality management and its relationship to project management

8. describe the outputs of project quality management processes, including defects and change requests

9. learn about various quality frameworks, tools and techniques that can be selected and adapted for the specific requirements of each project

10. appreciate the background to the development of the quality frameworks that we have today.

Context

Project quality management includes the processes and activities to ensure that the quality requirements are delivered for the project and any deliverables or products that are executed.

The International Organization for Standardization (ISO) defines quality as 'the degree to which a set of inherent characteristics fulfils requirements' (ISO9000:2000). There are two primary considerations when assessing the delivery of quality:

1 *conformance to requirements* – the project's processes and products meet written specifications
2 *fitness for use* – a product can be used as intended in the design.

REAL-WORLD EXPERIENCE

CONFORMANCE AND FITNESS

Many people fail to understand the difference between 'conformance to requirements' and 'fitness for use'. Here is an example:

I need to buy a new car that can safely get me from Sydney to the Gold Coast. If this is my only requirement then I can buy any car on the market that can successfully make this journey. It would make sense to buy the cheapest car possible, as it would meet the 'fitness for use' criteria. Why then do I wait to buy the new Subaru Outback V6 turbo diesel? It is probably due to the fact that I had other non-stated requirements, such as wanting an all-wheel drive, a brand preference for Subaru and a high safety expectation. Buying the cheapest car would have met the 'fitness for use' criteria, but buying the Subaru meets my 'conformance to requirements' criteria.

Quality is one of the triple constraints to project scope which was discussed in Chapter 7. Unfortunately it is often the element that is the most easily sacrificed as compromises to the quality of the project outputs are often less visible than impacts to schedules or budgets. This is unfortunate as failure to meet the quality requirements is a common reason for project failure and can have serious negative results.

The quality of the end product of a project is critical; things can go drastically wrong if the end product does not meet the requirements; for example:

- people can die if machinery and medical equipment malfunctions
- people can lose their money if new banking systems don't work correctly
- space missions can fail if there are errors in project execution; take the *Challenger* space shuttle crash for example.

Source: The Northern Sydney Institute, Part of TAFE NSW.

**See PMBOK®
Guide Figure 8-3**
Project quality
management:
inputs, tools and
techniques, and
outputs

Important quality definitions

- **Quality**: the degree to which a set of inherent characteristics conform to the requirements and are fit for purpose.
- **Cost of quality**: total cost of all efforts related to quality throughout the project or product development lifecycle.
- **Quality audit**: the process of examining the quality system or quality management plan, often carried out by an internal or external quality auditor or an audit team. A key element in the ISO quality system.
- **Quality assurance**: quality activities (e.g. reviews, process checklists and quality audits) that are built into the processes used to create the product and deliverables – they can be performed by a manager, client or even a third-party reviewer.
- **Quality control**: quality activities (e.g. inspection and testing) performed at the completion of a product or deliverable; used to verify that deliverables meet the requirements and that they are complete and correct.

Quality control and quality assurance are important concepts, yet most project managers have only a vague understanding of the meanings of and differences between these terms. Quality assurance activities monitor and verify that the processes used to create the deliverables have been effective. Quality control activities monitor and verify that project deliverables meet defined quality standards.

```
Quality assurance  ⟷  During development

Quality control  ⟷  On completion
```

RESEARCH AND REFLECTION ACTIVITY

QUALITY ASSURANCE VERSUS QUALITY CONTROL

Consider the differences between quality assurance and quality control.

Come up with an example of a common process and prepare a detailed description of how quality assurance is built into the process and how quality control occurs at the end of the process.

Ensure that you have thought about all the different types of tools and techniques that could be used and include these details in your submission.

PMBOK® Guide processes for project quality management

See PMBOK®
Guide Chapter 8
Project quality
management

According to the PMBOK® Guide, the major processes associated with project quality management are:

8.1 Plan quality

8.2 Perform quality assurance

8.3 Control quality.

FIGURE 10.1 PROCESS QUALITY MANAGEMENT - A PROCESS PERSPECTIVE

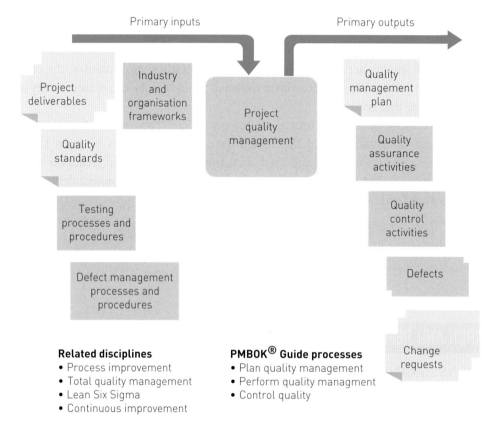

Source: Adapted from Project Management Institute, *A guide to the Project Management Body of Knowledge*, (PMBOK® Guide), fifth edition.

8.1 ***Plan quality management (planning)***: The process for identifying the quality requirements and quality standards applicable to a project and documenting how these requirements will be achieved for each deliverable. This also includes the identification of the quality assurance and quality control techniques that will be used to check that each deliverable has met the required quality expectations.

8.2 ***Perform quality assurance (execution)***: The process conducted during the execution of the project that ensures all deliverables perform as expected, they achieve specified quality requirements and they conform to any relevant standards. Quality assurance activities are included in the design and production of the deliverable. It is closely related to '5.5 Validate scope'.

8.3 ***Control quality (monitoring and controlling)***: The processes conducted to ensure that each deliverable meets all requirements and specifications. Quality control is performed as each deliverable or related set of deliverables is completed and often involves testing and inspection. It is closely related to '5.5 Validate scope'.

Developing the quality management plan

Quality planning involves identifying which quality standards are relevant to the project, product and deliverables and how these will be:

1 included in the design and build processes – quality assurance (QA)
2 checked for conformance on completion – quality control (QC).

Project managers are ultimately responsible for quality management on their projects, but many large organisations have internal quality departments that should be able to assist with the identification of relevant standards and methodologies, as well as internal policies and procedures.

To meet the quality requirements, project managers must:

- ensure that detailed requirements and specifications are documented and agreed upon with stakeholders
- understand the relevant quality standards for their industry and product
- understand and follow organisational quality methodologies, policies and procedures
- plan for quality assurance and quality control activities in detail
- detail the impacts of change requests on quality requirements and processes
- ensure that defects are repaired and monitored.

The quality management plan defines the acceptable level of quality for a project in terms of the deliverables, products and outcomes that are to be achieved. Ideally, it specifies the quality assurance and quality control activities and techniques that will be allied to each deliverable. Quality management activities ensure that the products are built to meet agreed standards and requirements, work processes are performed efficiently and as documented and defects are identified and corrected.

The quality management plan is often overlooked on the assumption that it is too difficult to put together and that the project team will just know what is expected in terms of quality. This can result in a failure to meet project, product and deliverable quality requirements, which can therefore lead to failure of the project or expensive rework and defect repair.

Common inclusions in the quality management plan are:

- links to organisational quality management policies and procedures
- links to specific quality standards that must be achieved
- quality assurance activities and techniques
- quality control activities and techniques
- quality roles and responsibilities

- detailed quality requirements
- defect tracking and repair processes.

Inputs into the development of the quality management plan are:

- scope baseline – scope statement and WBS
- cost baseline
- schedule baseline
- risk register
- government regulations
- standards – internal and external
- quality management system
- quality policies and procedures
- lessons learned from previous projects.

The primary output of the quality planning process is the quality management plan, but other related outputs include:

- quality metrics
- quality requirements
- quality standards
- quality checklists.

REAL-WORLD EXPERIENCE

SOFTWARE QUALITY PLAN

Stand-alone quality plans are common in the field of information technology. They are used extensively to plan the software testing processes that are required to ensure that software is delivered within defect tolerance levels. Most IT departments have comprehensive software testing methodologies which focus on quality control techniques but are often weak in the area of quality assurance.

In the field of software development, quality assurance techniques include:

- user-oriented design
- user-experience testing
- software development methodologies
- competency assessments of software developers
- requirements traceability
- peer reviews
- unit testing.

Quality control techniques include:

- functional testing
- integration testing
- user-acceptance testing.

Quality planning register

QUALITY PLANNING REGISTER

I find it very useful to organise the information into a table that I have devised called the quality planning register.

TABLE 10.1 QUALITY PLANNING REGISTER

Project deliverable	Quality assurance activities	Quality control activities	Quality requirements	Quality standards

It is critical to ensure that all activities are identified and planned in order to produce the project schedule. One of the most important, and often overlooked, sources of activities relates to the execution of quality assurance and quality control. Following are five simple steps to complete the quality planning register which can then be fed back into the project schedule. A failure to do this means resources will be overallocated to activities and the project delivery date will be in jeopardy from the completion of the first deliverable.

Step 1: **Define the QA activities for each deliverable**. Record them in the quality planning register and in the responsibility assignment matrix.

Step 2: **Define the QC activities for each deliverable**. Record them in the quality planning register and in the responsibility assignment matrix.

Step 3: **Specify any quality standards or performance measures** that must be met for each deliverable before it can be considered verified and complete.

Step 4: **Ensure the QA and QC activities are in the project schedule** as specific tasks associated with each deliverable. Make sure resources are allocated and that time has been allowed to execute these activities.

Step 5: **Make provision for revision and rework** due to defects that are identified during the QA and/or QC activities and in case the deliverable does not meet the required quality standards or performance measures. Allocate rework or defect repair activities as specific tasks that are associated with each deliverable. Ensure resources are allocated and that time has been allowed to execute these activities.

The following diagram repeated from chapter 8 (Figure 8.5) shows the relationships between the major outputs of other project management processes and the project schedule.

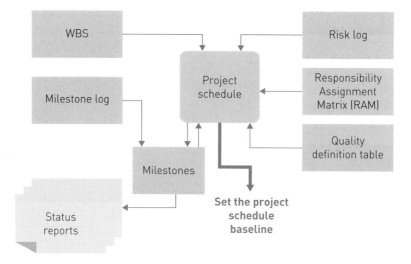

RESEARCH AND REFLECTION ACTIVITY

QUALITY PLANNING

Take some time to reflect on why many project managers neglect to produce a formal quality management plan.

Research the quality management system, policies and procedures that exist within your organisation. There are probably more available than you realise. Go to SAI Global at this link and search for quality standards: http://infostore.saiglobal.com/store/.

Consider these and determine the level of compliance with the policies and procedures that occurred in the projects you have experienced.

Arrive at three suggestions to improve both the management of project quality and the application of the related policies and procedures.

PROJECT MANAGEMENT MASTERY

PLANNING FOR CONTINUOUS IMPROVEMENT

The process improvement plan is an advanced technique that is rarely undertaken on projects, with the exception of large projects of long duration where there is time to learn along the way and to fold those learnings back into the plans for the execution of deliverables which have not yet commenced. The purpose of the process improvement plan is to document how the project team will analyse project and deliverable execution processes, to determine where improvements can be made and then implement these improvements.

Like a large part of project management methodology, process improvement is an iterative process that is performed throughout the project's lifetime.

This is sometimes done very formally at the end of each phase or interim review milestones; at other times it is done informally by the project manager and the project team by ensuring that they share lessons learned in order to improve the deliverable production processes going forward. If a process improvement leads to a revision of any of the project baselines – scope, time and cost – then it needs to be handled via '4.5 Perform integrated change control'.

Performing quality assurance

All project quality assurance activities need to take place during execution and in many cases all of the quality control activities will be conducted as well, although the PMBOK® Guide considers quality control activities to be part of the monitoring and controlling process group.

In reality, quality assurance and quality control activities are performed throughout the project as deliverables are executed and checked against requirements. Quality assurance activities are built into the development of each deliverable, whereas quality control activities are performed once a deliverable has been completed. It is much more cost and time effective to build quality into the production process rather than to check it at the end. There are many effective and very basic quality assurance tools and techniques that are often overlooked when developing the quality plan. These include:

- development methodologies
- work instructions and processes
- precedents and examples from previous projects
- interim reviews
- training and up-skilling
- selection of appropriately skilled team members
- statistical quality sampling techniques
- control charts
- benchmarking
- quality checklists.
  Inputs to perform quality assurance include:
- quality management plan
- process improvement plan (advanced technique)
- quality metrics
- work performance information
- status information
- quality control measurements.

Outputs of this process include:

- updates to quality standards
- change requests
- defect reports and defect register
- updates to quality management plan
- updates to schedule management plan
- updates to cost management plan
- quality audit and status reports
- updates to training plans
- updates to process documentation.

Performing quality control

As outlined in Chapter 5, all project quality control activities are considered to be part of the monitoring and controlling process group, no matter when they are executed. Many quality control activities are undertaken during the execution phase as each deliverable is completed and others are conducted at the end of execution just prior to project closure.

In reality, quality assurance and quality control activities are performed throughout the project as deliverables are executed and checked against requirements. Quality assurance activities are built into the development of each deliverable, whereas quality control activities are performed once a deliverable has been completed. Quality assurance is designed to prevent defects, whereas quality control is designed to detect and rectify defects.

There are many effective and very basic quality control tools and techniques that are often overlooked when developing the quality plan. These include:

- quality standards
- quality metrics
- control charts
- quality checklists
- cause and effect diagrams for defects
- histograms of defect occurrence
- statistical sampling
- quality inspections.
  Inputs to perform quality control include:
- quality management plans
- quality metrics
- quality checklists
- work performance information
- status information
- approved change requests
- products and deliverables for review and testing

- quality standards and policies
- defect reporting procedures.
  Outputs of this process include:
- quality control measurements
- new change requests
- validated change requests
- validated defect repairs
- validated and signed-off products and deliverables
- completed checklists
- lessons learned
- updates to quality management plan
- updates to process improvement management plan
- updates to quality standards.

Quality standards

Prior to preparing the quality management plan, project managers must seek out the quality standards relevant to:

- their industry
- the project
- the product.

RESEARCH AND REFLECTION ACTIVITY

QUALITY PROCESSES AND STANDARDS

Most large organisations will have extensive policies and procedures governing quality processes and standards. Review these and if they are found to be weak then review the quality frameworks that have been developed by various standards organisations and government departments. Specifically review the ISO 9000 series of standards.

Research both internal and external procurement frameworks and processes.

ISO quality standard

The International Organization for Standardization (ISO) is the world's largest developer and publisher of international standards. ISO is a network of the national standards institutes of 161 countries, one member per country, with a Central Secretariat in Geneva, Switzerland that coordinates the system.

ISO is a non-governmental organisation that forms a bridge between the public and private sectors. Many of its member institutes are part of the governmental structure of their countries, or are mandated by their government. Other members have their roots uniquely in the private sector, having been set up by national partnerships of industry associations.

ISO 9000 is a quality standard that:

- is a three-part, continuous cycle of planning, controlling and documenting quality in an organisation
- provides the minimum requirements needed for an organisation to meet its quality certification standards
- helps organisations around the world reduce costs and improve customer satisfaction.

The most commonly implemented family of quality standards is ISO 9001:2008 – Quality management systems – Requirements.

Standards Australia

Standards Australia is the nation's peak non-government standards organisation. It is charged by the Australian Government to meet Australia's need for contemporary, internationally aligned standards and related services.

The work of Standards Australia enhances the nation's economic efficiency and international competitiveness and contributes to community demand for a safe and sustainable environment. It leads and promotes a respected and unbiased standards development process that ensures all competing interests are heard, their points of view are considered and consensus is reached.

Standards are printed by their publishing company SAI Global, where you can purchase any ISO, AS (Australian Standard) or IEC (International Electrotechnical Commission) standards.

There are many common quality standards available that cover different industries:

- AS ISO 10006:2003 – Quality management system – guidelines for quality management in projects
- BCA 2008 and BCA 2009 – Building codes of Australia
- ISO 22000 – Food safety
- AS/NZS 4801:2001 – Occupational health and safety management
- ISO 14000/ 14001 – Environmental management standard
- ISO/IEC 15504 – Software process improvement and capability determination (SPICE)
- ISO/IEC 25000:2005 – Software product quality requirements and evaluation (SQuaRE).

Source: The Northern Sydney Institute, Part of TAFE NSW.

REAL-WORLD EXPERIENCE

STANDARDS FOR BUILDING AND CONSTRUCTION

Free guides to the standards applicable to different industries are available from SAI Global. One very handy guide for anyone managing construction projects is 'Guide to standards – building and construction'. Search at http://infostore.saiglobal.com.

Quality tools and techniques

There are many different quality tools and techniques (see below) and the selection of these is determined by:

- the type of product being delivered by the project
- organisational policies and procedures
- selected external standards.
- **Benchmarking**: Generates ideas for quality improvements by comparing specific project practices or product characteristics to those of other projects or products within or outside the performing organisation. Relates to lessons learned.
- **Cost-benefit analysis**: The primary benefits of meeting quality requirements are less rework, higher productivity, lower costs and increased stakeholder satisfaction. It compares the cost of the quality activity with the benefits.
- **Flowcharting and process analysis**: Graphical representation of a process that helps to identify potential quality problems; examination of process efficiency and failures.
- **Cost of quality**: Totals all costs incurred in quality assurance and quality control activities over the life of the project, product or deliverable. Includes cost of rework and defect rectification.
- **Control charts**: Statistical method used to determine if a project or production process is stable and has predictable performance. The upper and lower limits relate to the requirements.
- **Statistical sampling**: Examines a selection or sample group of outputs, products or deliverables for conformity to the requirements and quality standards.
- **Design of experiment**: Statistical method for identifying the factors that have the most influence over the quality of the end product; determines the accuracy of testing activities.
- **Inspection and checklists**: Examination of a deliverable or product to determine if it meets the documented quality standards and requirements.
- **Cause-and-effect diagrams**: Ishikawa or fishbone diagrams; they illustrate the linkages between quality problems and their potential causes.
- **Failure mode and effects analysis**: More comprehensive than cause-and-effect diagrams; involves determining *all* potential failures, the impacts of the failures and actions to both manage and prevent failures.
- **Histograms**: Bar chart used to document the frequency with which certain events (defects or failures) occur.
- **Pareto chart or Pareto diagrams**: Type of histogram that is ordered by frequency of occurrence. It shows the defects generated by the categories of the identified causes.
- **Run chart**: Similar to a control chart but doesn't display the upper and lower performance limits; shows total variation in a process over time to enable trend analysis.
- **Peer reviews**: Involves the review of a deliverable by another member of the project team or a suitably experienced expert.
- **System testing**: Used in the IT industry to formally test developed software to ensure that it meets the requirements. This is an extensive discipline and involves such concepts and

activities as unit testing, function testing, integration testing, regression testing and user-acceptance testing.

- **Project team selection**: This is a simple and yet often overlooked quality assurance technique which involves selecting the team members who have the most experience and qualifications to perform their assigned activities on the project.
- **Work practices**: Another important quality assurance tool that involves the specification of work practices (or methodologies, or processes) that must be used in order to execute activities and deliverables. This ensures that good practices are used.

Many useful templates for the above and additional quality tools and techniques can be accessed at iSixSigma (http://www.isixsigma.com/tools-templates/).

RESEARCH AND REFLECTION ACTIVITY

QUALITY TOOLS AND TECHNIQUES

Investigate within your organisation and industry and identify quality tools and techniques that are commonly used by other project managers. Start to develop a library of useful tools, examples and relevant standards that you can use for your projects going forward. Each industry will have different quality management approaches and requirements. Also undertake some online research to identify potential improvements in the area of quality.

- What are the most common tools you have found?
- Have your investigations revealed any weaknesses in quality management?

Business process modelling

The concepts of business process modelling, business process improvement and business process management underpin all of the recognised quality management methodologies. There are two main sources of standards in this area:

1 'Business process modelling notation' (BPMN 2.0) developed by the Object Management Group and available at their website (http://www.omg.org/spec/BPMN/2.0/). It has been widely adopted in a simplified form by most professional business and process analysts.

2 *Business process management common body of knowledge* (BPM CBoK) (2nd ed.) developed by the Association of Business Process Management Professionals and available from Amazon.com.

Quality management methodologies

Project quality management is compatible with many different quality management methodologies and frameworks such as Six Sigma, Lean Manufacturing, Total Quality Management and the ISO.

Quality management complements project management as both disciplines recognise the importance of:

- **Customer satisfaction**: defining requirements and managing expectations so that customer requirements are met.
- **Prevention over inspection**: quality should be built into the processes used to produce products and deliverables as the cost of preventing defects is less than the cost of fixing them at the end.
- **Continuous improvement**: learning from previous projects is built into future projects to ensure improvement; learnings can also be incorporated during project execution.

Six Sigma

Since the 1920s, the Greek symbol and the word 'sigma' has been used by statisticians, academics and engineers as a symbol for a unit of measurement in product quality variation. In mathematical terms, six sigma equates to 3.4 parts (or defects) per million.

In the mid-1980s, engineers at Motorola Inc. in the US, with the assistance of Joseph M. Juran, used 'Six Sigma' as the name for their in-house initiative for reducing defects in production processes. It has now become the most widely recognised and applied methodology for quality management in the business community. It also combines many of the concepts, tools and techniques of total quality management that were developed by Malcolm Baldrige (discussed later in the chapter).

Six Sigma has evolved and been adopted by many other leading organisations, perhaps most famously the GE Corporation and Dupont. According to Motorola University (Motorola's Six Sigma training and consultancy division), Six Sigma can be thought about at three different levels: (1) as a metric, (2) as a methodology and (3) as a management system.

1. **Six Sigma as a metric**: Six sigma equates to 3.4 defects per one million opportunities. It started as a target for defect reduction in manufacturing processes and has since been expanded and applied to service and other general business processes.
2. **Six Sigma as a methodology**: As Six Sigma has evolved, there has been less emphasis on the literal definition of 3.4 defects per million or on the counting of defects in products and processes. It has morphed into a business improvement methodology that focuses on:
   - understanding and managing customer requirements
   - aligning key business processes to achieve the requirements
   - applying rigorous data analysis to minimise variation in processes
   - driving rapid and sustainable improvement to business processes.
3. **Six Sigma as a management system**: When practised as a management system and adopted throughout an entire organisation, Six Sigma can be used to execute business strategy by:
   - aligning business strategy to the highest-priority improvement efforts
   - mobilising teams to undertake high-priority and high-impact projects
   - accelerating the achievement of improved business results
   - governing efforts to ensure improvements are maintained. (www.motorola.com).
     © Motorola Inc. All rights reserved.

The DMAIC model is the primary basis for all Six Sigma process improvement projects. It stands for – define, measure, analyse, improve and control.

FIGURE 10.2 DMAIC PROJECT LIFECYCLE

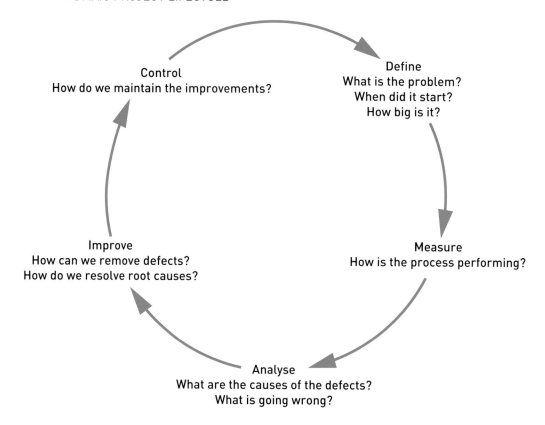

This is a very powerful approach to conducting a process improvement project and can be easily combined with the standard PMBOK® Guide project lifecycle as shown below.

FIGURE 10.3 PROCESS IMPROVEMENT PROJECT

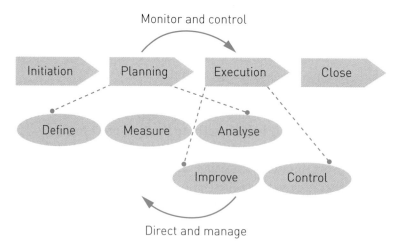

Source: Project Management Institute, *A guide to the Project Management Body of Knowledge*, (PMBOK® Guide), p. 50. Project Management Institute, Inc 2013. Copyright and all rights reserved. Material from this publication has been reproduced with the permission of PMI.

The training for Six Sigma is through a belt-based training system with certification provided by several major organisations, including the American Quality Society and the Australian Society for Quality. The belt levels are white belt, yellow belt, green belt, black belt and master black belt, similar to karate.

Lean Six Sigma

Lean Six Sigma is a process improvement framework that combines the concepts of Lean Manufacturing and Six Sigma. While Six Sigma primarily focuses on meeting customer expectations and reducing the amount of defect, Lean Six Sigma primarily focuses on removing waste from processes in order to reduce cycle or delivery times.

The seven kinds of waste that are reviewed are:
- transportation
- inventory
- motion
- waiting
- overproduction
- overprocessing
- defects.

The Lean Six Sigma concepts were first published by Michael George in 2002 in *Lean Six Sigma: Combining Six Sigma with Lean Speed*. Lean Six Sigma utilises the DMAIC phases similar to that of Six Sigma, with Sigma projects combining Lean's waste elimination focus with Six Sigma's quality characteristics.

Little's law is one of the key tools in Lean Six Sigma as it focuses on reducing work in progress (WIP) or inventory on the basis that minimising WIP increases the production rate. It provides an equation for relating lead time, WIP and average completion rate (ACR) for any process.

Search online for some extended project management mastery case studies involving improved project delivery.

Improved project delivery case study

ISO 9000 Quality management

There are many standards in the ISO 9000 suite but the most popular and widely adopted is ISO 9001:2008, which sets out the requirements of a quality management system. Other standards cover aspects such as definitions, quality audits and process improvements for the quality system. Many government departments in Australia have embraced the ISO 9000 quality standards and go so far as to stipulate that any organisation doing business with them must be ISO 9000 certified.

ISO 9001:2008 sets out the criteria for a quality management system and is the only standard in the suite where adherence can be certified. Certification within Australia can be obtained through the Australian Organisation of Quality. It is currently implemented in over one million companies and organisations in over 170 countries and, as such, must be the largest quality framework in use today.

The standard is based on a number of quality management principles including a strong customer focus, motivation and direct involvement by top management; the process management approach; and continual improvement. Using ISO 9001:2008 helps ensure that customers get consistent, good quality products and services, which in turn brings many business benefits. It is complementary to Six Sigma and can be used in conjunction with any quality improvement methodology.

History of quality

It is interesting to reflect on the work of leaders in the development of the modern quality management frameworks and thinking that we apply today. Most of the formal thinking and framework development commenced in the 1950s with a resurgence of interest in the 1980s and again now in the twenty-first century.

There are many prominent thought leaders who made significant contributions to the development of the field:

- W. Edwards Deming
- Joseph M. Juran, often referred to as the 'father of quality'
- Philip B. Crosby, sometimes referred to as the 'uncle of quality'
- Malcom Baldrige.

The Australian Organisation for Quality has three annual awards and these are named after international and national leaders in the field:

1 The *J.M. Juran Award* recognises persons who have contributed in an outstanding way to the application of effective quality management in Australia. Joseph M. Juran was deeply involved in management, and particularly the management of quality, before a lot of us knew what quality was. He became closely involved with the Australian Organisation for Quality (AOQ) back in AOQ's formative years in the late 1960s when it was known as the Australian Organisation for Quality Control. Dr Juran made several visits to Australia, running successful seminars under the banner of AOQC. Through this and other means he made an outstanding contribution to the development of AOQC and the stimulation of many Australian organisations to come to grips with what quality really means and how to achieve it.

2 The *Kevin Foley Award* recognises persons who have made a notable contribution to Australian quality practice through publication of a body of work (a minimum of 10 original items) on quality or related topics. This may include, but is not limited to, books, research articles, web-based material and training materials. Dr Kevin Foley is a prominent academic and leader in the Australian quality management arena.

3 The *Shilkin Award* recognises persons who have made a notable contribution to Australian quality practice through publication of an original paper on quality or related topics, to encouraging AOQ members' careers in quality, to developing their written communications skills and to disseminating their knowledge of quality technology for the benefit of others. Joe Shilkin was one of the pioneers of the Australian Organisation for Quality in Victoria.

Baldrige

Total quality management (TQM) is a management strategy that embeds awareness of quality in all organisational processes and became popular in the 1980s. TQM has been widely used in manufacturing as well as NASA space and science programs. It was initially developed by Malcom Baldrige. The primary principle is that prevention is a significantly more powerful technique for the achievement of quality than inspection and that quality can be embedded into all organisational processes.

Prominent US academics and government and business leaders worked together to distil Baldrige's work into seven criteria for performance excellence. These have since been used as the framework for assessment of the Malcolm Baldrige award which is bestowed annually by the US president.

TABLE 10.2 MALCOLM BALDRIGE NATIONAL QUALITY AWARD KEY AREAS AND SPECIFIC CRITERIA

Key area	Specific criteria
Leadership	» Senior leaders' personal actions. » Organisational governance system. » Fulfil responsibilities and support key communities.
Strategic planning	» Develop strategic objectives and action plans. » Deploy strategic objectives and action plans. » Measure progress.
Customer focus	» Engage customers. » Build customer-focused culture. » Listen to voice of customer and use the information to improve.
Measurement, analysis and knowledge management	» Select, gather, analyse, manage and improve data, information and knowledge assets. » Manage IT. » Review and use reviews for performance improvement.
Workforce focus	» Engage, manage and develop workforce » Assess workforce capability and capacity. » Build a workforce environment conducive to high performance.
Process management	» Design work systems. » Design, manage and improve key processes.
Results	» Performance and improvement in all six key areas. » Performance levels relative to competitors.

Source: adapted from Baldrige National Quality Program, 'Criteria for performance excellence', http://www.nist.gov/baldrige/publications/upload/2009_2010_Business_Nonprofit_Criteria.pdf

Juran

The key principle is: *It is much better to build quality into production than to check for it upon completion. This puts the emphasis on quality assurance over quality control.*

Juran is famous for developing the Pareto Principle in 1937; The Juran Trilogy™ is the foundation for the ISO 9000 suite of quality standards; and the 'breakthrough' concept is widely accredited as the start of Six Sigma. Indeed, Motorola, the company that first coined the name Six Sigma, was Juran's first client. The Juran Trilogy™ is a trademark of the Juran Institute, Inc.

FIGURE 10.4 JURAN'S QUALITY TRILOGY

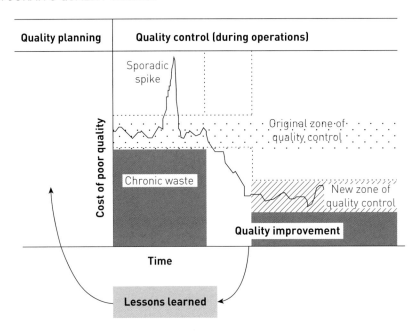

Source: Reproduced with permission of Juran Institute, Inc. www.juran.com.

Quality planning focuses on:
- identifying all customers and their needs
- developing requirements based on these needs
- developing processes to satisfy the requirements.

Quality control focuses on:

- identifying what to control
- defining measurement systems and standards
- identifying deviations or defects
- resolving defects.

Quality improvement focuses on:

- selection of process improvement projects
- proving the cause of problems and defects through data
- implementing solutions
- process management to maintain performance.

Deming

The key principle is: *Focusing on quality improvement will increase cost and increase customer satisfaction. Focusing on decreasing cost will decrease quality and decrease customer satisfaction.*

Deming is best known for the 'plan-do-check-act' cycle popularly named after him. He worked extensively with Japanese manufacturing companies from the 1950s and taught them how to improve design, product quality and testing through the application of statistical techniques. Many of these have been incorporated into Lean Six Sigma.

FIGURE 10.5 DEMING'S PLAN-DO-CHECK-ACT CYCLE

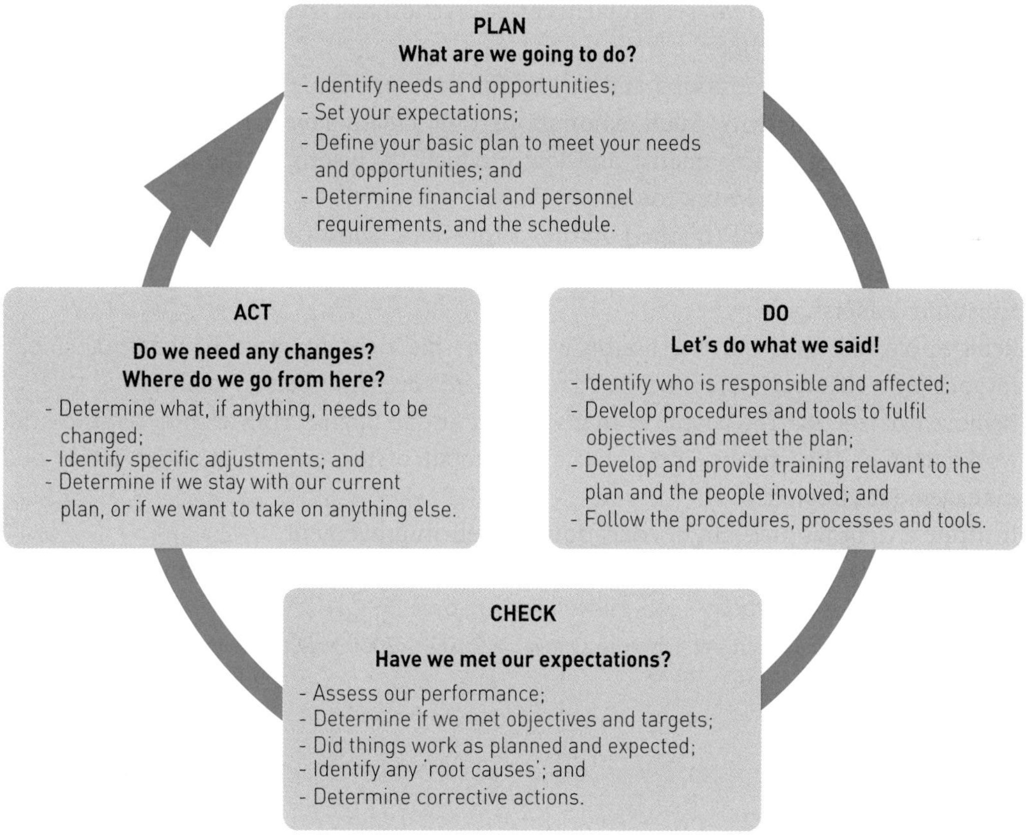

PLAN
What are we going to do?
- Identify needs and opportunities;
- Set your expectations;
- Define your basic plan to meet your needs and opportunities; and
- Determine financial and personnel requirements, and the schedule.

ACT
Do we need any changes?
Where do we go from here?
- Determine what, if anything, needs to be changed;
- Identify specific adjustments; and
- Determine if we stay with our current plan, or if we want to take on anything else.

DO
Let's do what we said!
- Identify who is responsible and affected;
- Develop procedures and tools to fulfil objectives and meet the plan;
- Develop and provide training relevant to the plan and the people involved; and
- Follow the procedures, processes and tools.

CHECK
Have we met our expectations?
- Assess our performance;
- Determine if we met objectives and targets;
- Did things work as planned and expected;
- Identify any 'root causes'; and
- Determine corrective actions.

Source: University of Texas Arlington, Environment, Health & Safety.

The following is an excerpt from Chapter 2 of *Out of the crisis* by W. Edwards Deming.

1 Create constancy of purpose toward improvement of product and service, with the aim to become competitive and to stay in business, and to provide jobs.

2 Adopt the new philosophy. We are in a new economic age. Western management must awaken to the challenge, must learn their responsibilities, and take on leadership for change.

3 Cease dependence on inspection to achieve quality. Eliminate the need for inspection on a mass basis by building quality into the product in the first place.

4 End the practice of awarding business on the basis of price tag. Instead, minimise total cost. Move toward a single supplier for any one item, on a long-term relationship of loyalty and trust.

5 Improve constantly and forever the system of production and service, to improve quality and productivity, and thus constantly decrease costs.

6 Institute training on the job.

7 Institute leadership. The aim of supervision should be to help people and machines and gadgets to do a better job. Supervision of management is in need of overhaul, as well as supervision of production workers.

8 Drive out fear, so that everyone may work effectively for the company.

9 Break down barriers between departments. People in research, design, sales and production must work as a team, to foresee problems of production and in use that may be encountered with the product or service.

10 Eliminate slogans, exhortations and targets for the work force asking for zero defects and new levels of productivity. Such exhortations only create adversarial relationships, as the bulk of the causes of low quality and low productivity belong to the system and thus lie beyond the power of the work force.

11 Eliminate work standards (quotas) on the factory floor. Substitute leadership.

12 Eliminate management by objective. Eliminate management by numbers, numerical goals. Substitute leadership.

13 Remove barriers that rob the hourly worker of his right to pride of workmanship. The responsibility of supervisors must be changed from sheer numbers to quality.

14 Remove barriers that rob people in management and in engineering of their right to pride of workmanship. This means, inter alia, abolishment of the annual or merit rating and of management by objective.

15 Institute a vigorous program of education and self-improvement.

16 Put everybody in the company to work to accomplish the transformation. The transformation is everybody's job. (www.deming.org)

Crosby

Phillip Crosby, former president of the American Society for Quality (ASQ), had a more practical approach to quality and did not subscribe to the strict statistical methods of many of his peers who were academics. His key principles are: if quality isn't ingrained in the organisation, it will never happen; and do it right the first time.

He developed Four Absolutes and 14 steps to achieving quality within an organisation.

Crosby's Four Absolutes of Quality Management are:

1 quality is defined as conformance to requirements, not as 'goodness' or 'elegance'
2 the system for causing quality is prevention, not appraisal
3 the performance standard must be zero defects
4 the measurement of quality is the price of non-conformance.

His 14 steps are outlined below.

1 Management commitment: Make it clear that management is committed to quality.
2 Quality improvement teams: Form quality improvement teams with senior representatives from each department.
3 Measure processes: Determine where current and potential quality problems lie.
4 Cost of quality: Evaluate the cost of quality and explain its use as a management tool.
5 Quality awareness: Raise the quality awareness and personal concern of all employees.
6 Correct problems: Take actions to correct problems identified through previous steps.
7 Monitor progress: Establish progress monitoring for the improvement process.
8 Train supervisors: Train supervisors to actively carry out their part of the quality improvement program.
9 Zero defects day: Hold a zero defects day to reaffirm management commitment.
10 Establish improvement goals: Encourage individuals to establish improvement goals for themselves and for their group.
11 Remove fear: Encourage employees to tell management about obstacles to improving quality.
12 Recognise: Recognise and appreciate those who participate.
13 Quality councils: Establish quality councils to communicate on a regular basis.
14 Repeat the cycle: Do it all over again to emphasise that the quality improvement process never ends.

Related processes from the PMBOK® Guide

4.2 **_Develop project management plan (planning)_**: This is the process of defining and documenting the actions necessary to prepare and integrate all subsidiary plans for each of the other key knowledge areas of project management. The PMP is the primary deliverable from the planning phase. Good practice dictates that the PMP is baselined at the end of the planning phase, particularly in the areas of scope, cost and time. It is progressively added to during project execution via the perform integrated change control process.

5.2 **_Collect requirements (planning)_**: The process of defining and documenting the needs of the project sponsor and key stakeholders. Encompasses the requirements related to the specific functional and non-functional characteristics of outputs being delivered by the project. Occurs during the planning phase and is very closely related to project success measures, because if the end products do not meet the requirements then it is highly unlikely the project sponsor will sign off on the completion of the project.

5.3 **Define scope (planning)**: The process of developing a detailed description of the project and the end products, or outputs, of the project. A detailed scope statement is critical to project success and good practice dictates that the detailed scope is signed off by the project sponsor, as well as key stakeholders.

6.2 **Define activities (planning)**: The process of identifying the specific actions to be performed to produce the project deliverables. The actions must relate back to a deliverable from the WBS. If an activity doesn't relate to a project deliverable then it is either unnecessary or something has been omitted from the WBS. It is closely linked to '5.3 Create WBS'. Many project managers use the terms *activities* and *tasks* interchangeably when in reality tasks break activities down into smaller units of work.

6.6 **Develop schedule (planning)**: The process of analysing activity sequences, durations, resource requirements and schedule constraints to create the project schedule. This is best completed with the aid of project scheduling software such as MS Project.

CHAPTER SUMMARY

» Project quality management consists of processes to plan, conduct and control quality activities in order to ensure the requirements of the project are met.
» Quality assurance focuses on building quality into the work practices that are used to execute a deliverable or end product of the project.
» Quality control focuses on ensuring that the quality requirements have been met at the end of the execution of a deliverable or end product.
» It is much more efficient to focus on building quality into the process rather than inspecting it at the end. Defects that are found during quality control are much more expensive to repair.
» Many tools and techniques exist to assist with quality management. One of the most common and widely used is business process modelling.
» Many quality methodologies exist. The most popular are Six Sigma and its variant Lean Six Sigma. These focus on improving quality based on the customer's requirements, reducing defects and reducing delivery timeframes.
» Many standards exist which define quality management. The most widely adopted and generic standard is ISO's 9000:2008. Other quality standards exist in each industry and project managers need to inform themselves about these in order to effectively complete project quality management activities.
» Many people contributed to the development of modern quality management frameworks, tools and techniques. Some prominent names include Juran, Crosby, Deming, Baldrige, Foley and Shilkin.
» Many useful templates and quality tools and techniques can be accessed at iSixSigma (http://www.isixsigma.com/tools-templates/).

REVISION QUESTIONS

Revision questions are divided into two sections. The first covers Certificate IV understanding and the second covers Diploma-level understanding. Both sections are relevant to Diploma students and teachers, while only the first section is relevant to Certificate students and teachers.

Certificate IV of Project Management

These questions relate to the performance criteria stated in 'BSBPMG411A Apply project quality management techniques'.

1   What are the project quality management processes?
2   What is the difference between quality assurance and quality control?
3   What are the typical contents of the quality management plan?
4   Where is information obtained to contribute to the quality requirements and criteria?
5   What primary tools and techniques exist in your industry for quality assurance?
6   What primary tools and techniques exist in your industry for quality control?
7   What is the purpose of the defects log?
8   Why is customer satisfaction important when setting the quality requirements?
9   What is the difference between prevention and inspection?
10   What is the meaning of continuous improvement?
11   What are the contents of the quality planning register?

BSBPMG411A
performance
criteria questions

Diploma of Project Management

These questions relate to the performance criteria stated in 'BSBPMG513A Manage project quality'.

1   What are the benefits of quality assurance over quality control?
2   Where can you obtain input into the quality management processes and standards for your industry and project?
3   What is the difference between conformance to requirements and fit for purpose?
4   What quality tools and techniques can be performed on project management deliverables such as the PMP and project schedule?
5   What is the difference between a defect and a change request?
6   What is the definition of total cost of quality? How is it estimated and tracked?
7   What is the impact of a defect that is found in the final stages of the execution phase?
8   What is the purpose of Six Sigma methodology?
9   Can Six Sigma concepts be applied to any project?
10   How can project processes be evaluated in order to implement continuous improvement?

BSBPMG513A
performance
criteria questions

DISCUSSION QUESTIONS

1   Is Six Sigma a project management methodology or a process improvement methodology?
2   Is software testing a part of project quality management?
3   How does finding appropriately skilled team members contribute to quality outcomes? Is this a part of quality assurance or quality control?
4   How can project processes be evaluated in order to implement continuous improvement?
5   Is continuous improvement possible on short projects?

BSBPMG411A and
BSBPMG513A
performance
criteria questions

6   What disagreements often occur related to defects and change requests?

7   How can disagreements over defects versus change requests be avoided?

8   What are the possible impacts on quality if the scope of the project is increased but the budget and timeframe must remain the same?

ONLINE RESOURCES

Visit the online companion website at http://www.cengagebrain.com to link to important additional resources, including templates, real-world case studies, revision quizzes and additional study material.

FURTHER READINGS AND REFERENCES

Business Process Modelling Notation (BPMN 2.0) developed by the Object Management Group. Accessed at http://www.omg.org/spec/BPMN/2.0

Business Process Management Common Body of Knowledge, 2nd edition, developed by the Association of Business Process Management Professionals.

Crosby, P. B. (1979). *Quality is free: The art of making quality certain.* Columbus, OH: McGraw-Hill Companies.

Deming, W. E. (2000). *Out of the crisis.* Cambridge, MA: MIT Press.

George, Michael. (2000). *Lean Six Sigma: Combining Six Sigma with Lean Speed.* New York: McGraw-Hill.

Kerzner, H. (2007). *Project management: A systems approach to planning, scheduling, and controlling* (9th ed.). Brisbane: John Wiley & Sons.

Kloppenborg, T. J. (2012). *Contemporary project management* (2nd ed.). Melbourne: Cengage Learning.

Mulcahy, R. (2006). *PM crash course – Real-world project management tools & techniques..* Minnetonka, MN: RMC Publications.

Project Management Institute (PMI). (2013). *A guide to the Project Management Body of Knowledge* (PMBOK® Guide) (5th ed.). Newtown Square, PA. Chapter 8, pp. 227–254.

Schwable, K. (2011). *Information technology project management* (revised 6th ed.). Melbourne: Cengage Learning.

Standards:
» ISO 9000:2008 - Quality management system, the most popular from the ISO 9000 suite of quality management standards
» AS ISO 10006:2003 – Quality management system – guidelines for quality management in projects
» BCA 2008 and BCA 2009 – Building codes of Australia
» ISO 22000 – Food safety
» AS/NZS 4801:2001 – Occupational health and safety management

» ISO 14000/ 14001 – Environmental management standard
» ISO/IEC 15504 – Software process improvement and capability determination (SPICE)
» ISO/IEC 25000:2005 – Software product quality requirements and evaluation (SQuaRE).

Tan, H. C., Anumba, C., Carrillo, P., . . . Udeaja, C. (2010). *Capture and reuse of project knowledge in construction.* Chichester, UK: Wiley-Blackwell.

Verzuh, E. (2005). *The fast forward MBA in project management.* Brisbane: John Wiley & Sons.

Project human resource management

Context

Project human resource management encompasses the processes that organise, manage and lead the project team. The project team is comprised of the people assigned to the specific roles that are required to execute the project and its deliverables. The composition of the project team changes during the different phases of the project and team members can be allocated under various arrangements, such as permanent, contract, outsourced, part-time and full-time.

The project management team is a concept applied to larger projects and is a subset of the project team that specifically assists the project manager with project planning and execution. The project management team may also have some responsibilities for directing and managing project team members who have been assigned to them.

There is often confusion between project stakeholders and project team members. The distinction is clear: project stakeholders are individuals or groups that are interested in, or may be impacted by, the outcomes of the project. Project team members are individuals who have been assigned specific accountability for the development and completion of assigned project deliverables.

Project managers use the processes and techniques of project human resource management to direct and manage the project team, whereas they use the processes and techniques of project stakeholder management to influence and manage stakeholders. Project communications management applies equally to both.

See PMBOK®
Guide Figure 9-2
Project human
resource
management:
inputs, tools and
techniques, and
outputs

PMBOK® Guide processes for project human resource management

The PMBOK® Guide processes for project human resource management are:
9.1   Plan human resource management
9.2   Acquire project team
9.3   Develop project team
9.4   Manage project team.

See PMBOK®
Guide Chapter 9
Project human
resource
management

9.1   *Plan human resource management (planning):* The process for creating a project human resource plan by identifying project roles, responsibilities, required skills and reporting relationships. Other components may include training needs, team building strategies, reward and recognition programs and performance management processes, as well as workplace health and safety procedures.

9.2   *Acquire project team (execution):* The process of confirming human resource availability and selecting the team members necessary to complete the project activities. Project managers need to negotiate and influence in order to obtain the best team possible for the project, as they may not have direct control over resource selection due to industrial agreements, project sponsor preferences and internal HR policies. It is closely related to '6.4 Estimate activity resources' and '6.5 Estimate activity durations'.

9.3 *Develop project team (execution):* The process for identifying skills development needs and improving competencies of the project team members. This also includes managing team member interaction and the overall team environment to enhance the performance and increase the probability of project success.

9.4 *Manage project team (execution):* The process for tracking team member performance, providing feedback, resolving issues and managing changes to improve team performance. This requires the skills of influencing team behaviour, managing conflict, resolving issues and managing team member performance appraisals.

FIGURE 11.1 PROJECT HUMAN RESOURCE MANAGEMENT – PROCESS PERSPECTIVE

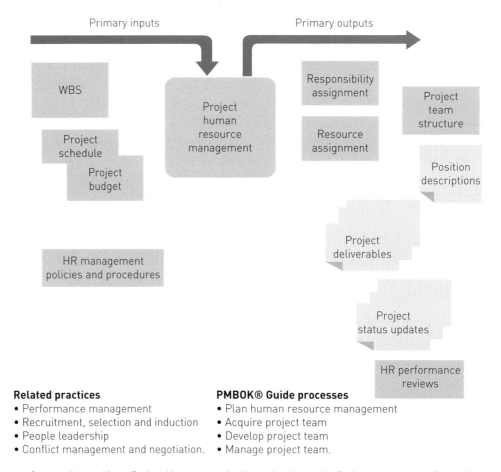

Related practices
- Performance management
- Recruitment, selection and induction
- People leadership
- Conflict management and negotiation.

PMBOK® Guide processes
- Plan human resource management
- Acquire project team
- Develop project team
- Manage project team.

Source: Adapted from Project Management Institute, *A guide to the Project Management Body of Knowledge*, (PMBOK® Guide), fifth edition.

Project managers are also people leaders

Project managers need to be people managers; it is not sufficient to be just good at managing scope, time, cost and quality. In order to improve the chances of successful delivery and achieving all the project objectives, project managers also require competencies in the areas of team selection and people management. Research into project failure often points to the importance of strong human resource management and effective communication as being the major factors that contribute to project success.

Some of the additional skills that project managers require in order to lead and manage the project team are discussed below (see PMI, 2013, pp. 513–19).

See PMBOK®
Guide Appendix X3
Interpersonal
skills

- *Leadership:* involves focusing the team on the delivery of the project objectives. It is the ability to get things done through others and involves the development of rapport, trust and respect. More detail on the Situational Leadership® model is included later in this chapter.
- *Team building:* involves helping a team of individuals to work together effectively. Projects face unique challenges in this area as teams are temporary and different groups are normally brought together for different projects based on their skills and availability. This means that project managers need to employ methods to accelerate team building in order to create high-performing teams on each project. More detail on the team formation cycle is included later in this chapter.
- *Motivation:* the overall success of a project depends on the project team's level of commitment, which in turn is dependent on its level of motivation. It is recommended that project objectives are assigned to project team members that are congruent with their values and will provide high levels of job satisfaction. The Situational Leadership model can assist with this.
- *Communication:* an area which has the greatest impact on project success or failure. Research into project failure has identified poor communication to be one of the major reasons that projects fail. Project managers need highly developed and flexible communication skills in order to lead the project team and to manage the expectations of stakeholders. Most importantly, project managers need to adapt their communication styles to meet the preferences of other parties. Communication processes and skills are covered extensively in Chapters 12 and 15.
- *Influencing:* can be defined as the ability to use interpersonal skills to encourage individuals to cooperate with others to achieve common goals and also to facilitate decision making in complex environments. The PMBOK® Guide recommends using the following methods to influence team members and stakeholders: lead by example and follow through with commitments, clarify how decisions will be made and adjust your interpersonal style for the characteristics of the audience.
- *Decision making:* is often challenging as stakeholders may not wish to be associated with an incorrect decision and project managers need to make many decisions on the basis of incomplete information or assumptions. Decision making processes are covered in Chapter 15.
- *Political and cultural awareness:* is critical due to the amount of organisational politics that is inherent in projects due to the differing expectations of the various project stakeholders. Many project managers seek to ignore or avoid internal politics and this often contributes to project failure. It is better to recognise that it is inevitable and employ leadership skills to create an environment of trust and cooperation. It is also a good idea to recognise the need for the careful use of power to break through road blocks and progress decision making.
- *Negotiation:* this skill is critical for project managers and is often combined with the application of influencing and decision-making skills in order to facilitate agreement between project team members or stakeholders who have differing points of view. This can often be challenging: decision-making processes are covered in Chapter 15.

- **Trust building:** this is a critical component of effective team leadership. When trust is compromised then relationships deteriorate, people disengage and collaboration breaks down. Trust provides the basis for cooperation and effective problem resolution. More detail is included in Chapter 15.
- **Conflict management:** when working as a project manager, there will be lots of opportunity to exercise conflict resolution skills. Most conflict occurs in the 'storming' phase and some level of conflict is to be expected. It can be positive if resolved well. Some tips for effective conflict management include remaining open by focusing on the issues and not the people and to concentrate on the present and not the past. Managing conflict is one of the most difficult challenges that project managers face and they need to draw on other interpersonal skills, as well as conflict resolution frameworks, in order to be successful. More detail on conflict management and resolution processes are covered later in this chapter.
- **Coaching:** this assists project team members to improve their competencies and skills and to achieve higher levels of team performance. Counselling is used in situations where the team member is already capable but does not want to undertake the required work effort. These concepts are covered later in this chapter in relation to the Situational Leadership model and performance management.

Human resource legislative frameworks

As soon as you are responsible for the management of people, you need be aware of, and comply with, all relevant human resource management (HRM) legal frameworks and organisational processes. In Australia there are various national, state, industry and organisation-specific regulations including:

- federal legislation
- federal regulations and guidelines
- state legislation
- state regulations and guidelines
- industry-specific regulations and guidelines
- organisational policies and procedures.

As a people manager you can be held personally liable for breaches of legislation, regulations, guidelines and organisational policies and procedures. Organisations seek to limit their liability and to reduce people management risks by transferring as much responsibility as possible to each person's direct manager. It is common knowledge that you can be convicted for not complying with HRM legislation and regulations.

Recent cases have set precedents for court action where organisational policies and procedures have also been incorrectly followed or ignored. If your organisation has documented HRM policies and procedures that are not being followed, then legal action can be taken against the organisation and people leaders who have not implemented the policies and procedures correctly.

Federal legislation

The Australian Government has passed a number of laws which aim to protect people from discrimination in public life and from breaches of their human rights, including the:

- *Workplace Gender Equality Act 2012*
- *Fair Work Act 2009*
- *Australian Human Rights Commission Act 1986*
- *Age Discrimination Act 2004*
- *Disability Discrimination Act 1992*
- *Racial Discrimination Act 1975*
- *Sex Discrimination Act 1984*
- *Privacy Act 1998.*

These are administered by the Australian Human Rights Commission which has the authority to investigate and conciliate complaints of discrimination and human rights breaches. More information can be found at http://www.humanrights.gov.au.

WORKPLACE GENDER EQUALITY ACT 2012

The Australian Government introduced legislation in March 2012 to retain and improve *The Equal Opportunity for Women in the Workplace Act 1999*. The objectives of the new *Workplace Gender Equality Act 2012* are to:

- promote and improve gender equality particularly with respect to remuneration
- support employers to remove barriers to the full and equal participation of women in the workforce
- promote the elimination of discrimination on the basis of gender in relation to family and caring responsibilities
- foster workplace consultation between employers and employees on issues concerning gender equality in employment and in the workplace
- improve the productivity and competitiveness of Australian business through the advancement of gender equality in employment and in the workplace.

Source: *Workplace Gender Equality Act 2012*. Commonwealth of Australia.

More information can be found at http://www.wgea.gov.au/.

FAIR WORK ACT 2009

On 1 July 2009, the Fair Work Commission (formerly Fair Work Australia) began operations as part of a new national workplace relations system underpinned by the *Fair Work Act 2009*.

Significant changes were made in areas such as:

- agreement making
- assistance for low-paid workers
- dismissals
- dispute resolution

- general protections
- good-faith bargaining
- industrial action – no formal start of bargaining
- minimum wage setting
- National Employment Standards.

More information can be found at http://www.fwc.gov.au and the Commonwealth Fair Work Ombudsman can provide information and advice about Australia's workplace rights and rules and the protection you have against harassment and discrimination.

COMMONWEALTH WORK HEALTH AND SAFETY ACT 2011

Work health and safety is primarily the role of the states and territories. However, the *Work Health and Safety Act 2011* regulates workplace health and safety (WHS) for all Australians. It aims to protect people from risks to their health or safety at work and promotes safe and healthy work environments. The Act was introduced as part of the 'harmonisation' package of federal, state and territory work health and safety legislations and commenced on 1 January 2012. It has been progressively adopted by the states and territories. States that have not yet adopted the new Act have their own state-based legislation. More information can be obtained at the websites of the various state-based workplace health and safety organisations and http://www.workplaceinfo.com.au.

The main objective of the Act is to provide for a balanced and nationally consistent framework to secure the health and safety of workers and workplaces by:

- protecting workers and other persons against harm to their health, safety and welfare through the elimination or minimisation of risks arising from work or from specified types of substances or plant
- providing for fair and effective workplace representation, consultation, cooperation and issue resolution in relation to work health and safety
- encouraging unions and employer organisations to take a constructive role in promoting improvements in work health and safety practices
- securing compliance with the Act through effective and appropriate compliance and enforcement measures
- providing a framework for continuous improvement and progressively higher standards of work health and safety, and maintaining and strengthening the national harmonisation of laws relating to work health and safety to facilitate a consistent national approach to work health and safety in this jurisdiction.

Source: © Commonwealth of Australia. The Work Health and Safety Act 2011.

Workplace violence, bullying and harassment

The definition of workplace bullying is 'the repeated less favourable treatment of a person by another or others in the workplace, which may be considered unreasonable and inappropriate workplace practice. It includes behaviour that intimidates, offends, degrades or humiliates a worker' (source: © Australian Human Rights Commission 2013).

Employers have a legal responsibility under various WHS and antidiscrimination laws to provide a safe workplace. An employer that allows bullying to occur in the workplace is not meeting this responsibility. In addition, a direct supervisor also has a duty to ensure the health, safety and welfare of all the employees who report to them. Employees can report incidents of bullying and harassment to the relevant state and territory work health and safety authority.

Bullying in the workplace can be difficult to clearly identify. The following examples have been taken from the fact sheet provided by the Australian Human Rights Commission which can be found at http://www.humanrights.gov.au/workplace-bullying-violence-harassment-and-bullying-fact-sheet. Bullying can be:

- repeated hurtful remarks or attacks, or making fun of your work or you as a person (including your family, sex, sexuality, gender identity, race or culture, education or economic background)
- sexual harassment, particularly unwelcome touching and sexually explicit comments and requests that make you uncomfortable
- excluding you or stopping you from working with people or taking part in activities that relate to your work
- playing mind games, ganging up on you, or other types of psychological harassment
- intimidation (making you feel less important and undervalued)
- giving you pointless tasks that have nothing to do with your job
- giving you impossible jobs that can't be done in the given time or with the resources provided
- deliberately changing your work hours or schedule to make it difficult for you
- deliberately holding back information you need to get your work done properly
- pushing, shoving, tripping or grabbing you in the workplace
- attacking or threatening you with equipment, knives, guns, clubs or any other type of object that can be turned into a weapon
- initiation or hazing – where you are made to do humiliating or inappropriate things in order to be accepted as part of the team.

Source: © Australian Human Rights Commission 2013.

Some practices in the workplace may not seem fair but do not constitute bullying. For example, an employer is allowed to transfer, demote, discipline, counsel, sever employment and/or retrench an employee as long as the employer is acting reasonably.

Human resource management planning

The human resource management plan identifies the number and types of human resources that will be required in order to successfully execute the project based on the defined scope, deliverables and objectives. It also establishes the processes by which the project team members will be managed. Common inclusions in the human resource management plan are:

- links to organisational human resource management policies and procedures
- links to appropriate competency frameworks
- links to appropriate legislation and regulations

- organisational and project-based structure charts
- responsibility assignment matrices
- position descriptions for project resources
- project governance structures and role statements for the project sponsor and other senior project stakeholders
- resource calendars – availability and project allocations
- staff induction plans
- staff training plans
- performance management processes and templates
- recognition and reward frameworks
- WHS plans
- WHS incident management procedures.

Ideally, the human resource management plan is established prior to acquiring the project team at the commencement of the execution phase. There may be a requirement for some less formal human resource (HR) planning prior to the engagement of the project manager (and potentially a small core team) to work on the initiation and planning phases.

The primary input into the development of the HR management plan for a project is the project management plan (PMP), in particular the specific resource assignment assumptions that were made when the activities were being scheduled as part of developing the project schedule.

There are many factors outside of the project manager's direct control which impact on and influence HR planning for a project. These include:

- organisational policies and procedures
- external competition for resources and scarce skills sets
- internal resource allocation and competition
- project prioritisation
- organisational culture and structure
- existing human resources
- labour market conditions
- industrial relations frameworks
- HR legislation and regulations
- competency frameworks.

Organisational policies and procedures

Most medium to large organisations have documented HRM policies and procedures. These must comply with relevant legislation and be followed by all people leaders in order to avoid legal action. The purpose of these more detailed policies and procedures is to protect workers' rights and safety, reduce the risk of legal action and assign some of the overall responsibility to people leaders.

Common examples of these policies and procedures include:

- equal employment opportunity
- work health and safety
- recruitment and termination
- people management
- performance management
- employee complaints.

There may be many other policies and procedures in addition to these examples. It is the responsibility of people leaders to locate and follow them. There are no excuses for ignorance.

RESEARCH AND REFLECTION ACTIVITY

HR POLICIES AND PROCEDURES

Investigate within your organisation to see where the policies and procedures related to HRM are stored and if all staff have access to them. What are the main areas covered? Were you made aware of them when you started?

Human resource practices and techniques

The most useful practices and techniques for the creation of the human resource management plan and the ongoing management of the project team are:

- organisational charts
- responsibility assignment matrices
- position descriptions.

ORGANISATIONAL CHARTS

Traditional hierarchical organisational charts can be very effective by showing team members where the project fits within the overall organisational structure and by depicting the structure and reporting lines for the project.

Even more useful are project organisational charts, which are sometimes also referred to as resource breakdown structures. These very quickly describe the size and structure of the project and reinforce the project reporting lines. It can be especially beneficial to also depict the project governance structure, including the project sponsor and steering committee, as well as any external sponsors and their managing bodies. Figures 11.2 and 11.3 depict simple and more complex examples of organisational charts. Figure 11.4 depicts an example of a complex project governance structure.

FIGURE 11.2 PROJECT ORGANISATION CHART – SMALL PROJECT

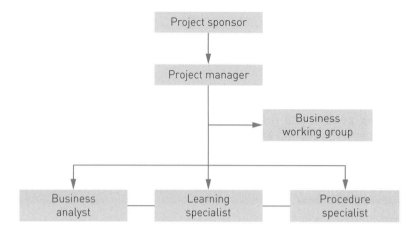

FIGURE 11.3 PROJECT ORGANISATION CHART – COMPLEX PROJECT

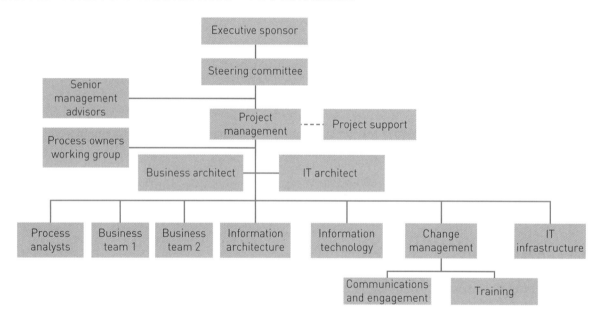

REAL-WORLD EXPERIENCE

COMPLEX INTERNAL PROJECT GOVERNANCE

In a project I completed for a not-for-profit organisation, it was critical for stakeholder engagement purposes to acknowledge the role of the business stakeholders in the project. This need was primarily driven by the lack of project management maturity within the organisation (the project was the first one ever undertaken within the administrative services side of the organisation). The scope was to improve business processes and systems support across the following areas: fund raising, client (donor) management, accounting and finance, and marketing. The lack of project delivery experience within the organisation and across the stakeholders (most of whom had been with the organisation for 10–20 years and had only ever worked within the not-for-profit sector) meant that there was a very real possibility of these subject matter experts leaving all the project-related decisions and the process design to the small team of external project contractors. Therefore, all key business stakeholders were allocated project-based roles that were included in the project organisation chart. This was designed to indicate the critical roles and time commitments that would be expected from them.

FIGURE 11.4 PROJECT ORGANISATION CHART – COMPLEX PROJECT GOVERNANCE

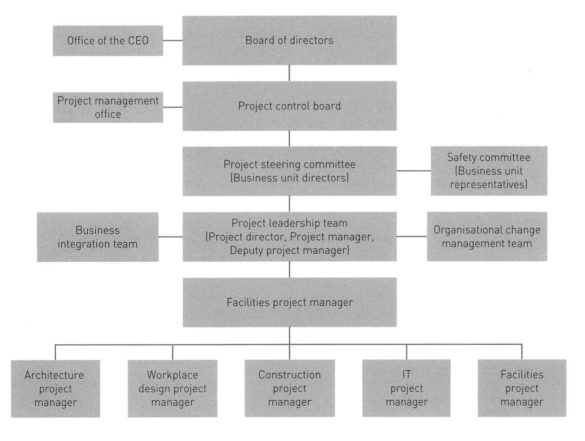

REAL–WORLD EXPERIENCE

COMPLEX INTERNAL AND EXTERNAL PROJECT STRUCTURE AND GOVERNANCE

Recently, I completed a major office relocation and fit-out project for a large commercial law firm. The project was complex and comprised both internal management committees and project teams, and external management committees and project teams from major external vendors and the prime contractor. This form of complex project structure is fairly common on large construction projects with major outsourcing arrangements in place. It is recommended that both sides of the project governance and project team structures are mapped out and understood by both sides. This will enable both sides to appreciate the processes for review and approval of major decisions so this can be factored into stakeholder management activities and sign-off timeframes.

RESPONSIBILITY ASSIGNMENT MATRIX (RAM)

The responsibility assignment matrix (RAM) is one of the most critical tools used to delegate the accountability for major project deliverables to various project team members.

It is a structured table that relates the project organisation chart to the work breakdown structure (WBS) to help ensure that all components of the project scope have been assigned to a project team or team member.

The benefits of using a RAM in project situations are:

- work assignments: delegates project work by assigning accountabilities to specific project team members or external resources
- conflict resolution: reduces team conflict by clarifying roles and responsibilities
- improved scheduling: ensures that additional activities that contribute to the development of deliverables are acknowledged and planned for
- complete scheduling: ensures that all project work is allocated
- streamlines approvals: it clearly assigns authority levels and roles for specific deliverables and activities
- workload analysis: can show when project resources are under- and overallocated
- stakeholder relationships: these can be improved by acknowledging stakeholders' roles in major deliverables and activities.

The original and most widely recognised form of the RAM is the RACI chart. It was probably developed by a consulting company at some point during the last century; the exact origins and inventor are unknown. However, some claim it was invented in the 1970s as part of a project management methodology called goal directed project management and subsequently published for the first time by Andersen, Grude and Haug.

Figure 11.5 is an example of a RACI as applied to some key project management deliverables.

FIGURE 11.5 RACI EXAMPLE

Deliverable/activity	Project sponsor	Project manager	Team member 1	Team member 2	Team member 3
Project charter	R	A	I	C	I
Communication plan	C	R, A	I	I	I
HR plan	I	R	A	C	C
Deliverable 1	I	R	I	C	A
Deliverable 2	C	R	C	A	I
Deliverable 3	I	C	R, A	C	C

R = Responsible, A = Accountable, C = Consult, I = Inform

Source: The Northern Sydney Institute, Part of TAFE NSW.

The different roles are defined below.

- *Responsible:* the person who has been assigned the obligation to undertake the activity or to execute the deliverable.
- *Accountable (often approver):* the person who is ultimately accountable for the completion of the task or activity according to the specifications or requirements. Often they are more senior than the person responsibile for executing the deliverable, and hence they have delegated the obligation or are the final approver of the activity or deliverable.

Many people find the distinction between the responsible and the accountable role to be extremely confusing and this can then be a source of conflict. Reputable thesauruses state that 'accountable' is a synonym for 'responsible' so no wonder there is confusion.

- *Consulted (often contribute):* those who contribute to the activity or deliverable, either by being consulted, by contributing expertise or assisting the person who has been assigned the responsibility.
- *Informed:* those who are kept informed on progress, or quite often only told once the activity or deliverable has been completed. There is no need to seek their input during the execution of the activity or completion of deliverable.

REAL-WORLD EXPERIENCE

IMPROVING THE RAM

Since first working for a major bank in the early 1990s, I have become accustomed to using a variant of the RACI known as the **RASIC**. This alternate version of a RAM has become a standard in the banking industry in Australia and I have also used it in large telecommunications and manufacturing companies.

The major advantage of the RASIC is that is reduces the conflict and confusion over the difference between the responsible and accountable roles by adjusting the definitions and introducing additional roles. These are outlined below.

- *Review*: people who check that the activity or deliverable has been undertaken according to the specifications or requirements. This is largely a quality assurance or quality control obligation. This is an additional role to those found on the RACI chart and it has been added to provide clarity and to acknowledge that very often certain individuals are required to review deliverables prior to them being submitted for final sign-off.
- *Accountable*: the person who is responsible for undertaking an assigned activity or to execute a deliverable. This is aligned to the definition of 'responsible' on the RACI chart.
- *Sign-off*: the person who has the final authority to sign off on an activity or deliverable as complete. This is aligned to the definition of 'accountable' in the RACI chart.
- *Informed*: those who are kept informed on progress, or quite often only told once the activity or deliverable has been completed. There is no need to seek their input during the execution of the activity or completion of the deliverable.
- *Consulted (often contribute)*: those who contribute to the activity or deliverable, either by being consulted, by contributing expertise or assisting the person who has been assigned the responsibility.

FIGURE 11.6 RASIC EXAMPLE

Deliverable/activity	Project sponsor	Project manager	Team member 1	Team member 2	Team member 3
Project charter	R, S	A	I	C	I
Communication plan	S	R	A	C	C
HR plan	I	S	R	A	C
Deliverable 1	I	R	I	C	A
Deliverable 2	C	R	C	A	I
Deliverable 3	I	R, S	A	C	C

R = Review, A = Accountable, S = Sign-off, I = Inform, C = Consult/contribute

Source: The Northern Sydney Institute, Part of TAFE NSW.

PROJECT MANAGEMENT MASTERY

BEST PRACTICES FOR THE RAM

The following rules will maximise the benefits derived from the RASIC.
- Linton's RAM rule no. 1: always choose the RASIC over the RACI chart for a RAM; it avoids the inevitable confusion and conflict that arises over the meaning of 'responsible' and 'accountable' in the RACI chart.

- Linton's RAM rule no. 2: use the RASIC to assign deliverables to team members and always populate the RASIC with the deliverables that have been identified in the WBS.
- Linton's RAM rule no. 3: ensure that only one person is accountable for each deliverable as this reduces conflict and confusion; other team members who will also work on the deliverable can be assigned the consult/contribute role.
- Linton's RAM rule no. 4: try to assign only one person to the sign-off role. In practice this can be difficult if many senior stakeholders are required to endorse a project.
- Linton's RAM rule no. 5: always assign the responsibilities for each deliverable in the following order, as this is the order in which the activities will be undertaken:
  » accountable
  » contribute
  » review
  » sign-off
  » informed.
- Linton's RAM rule no. 6: multiple team members can be assigned to 'review'.
- Linton's RAM rule no. 7: team members should only have one role for each deliverable.
- Linton's RAM rule no. 8: sometimes the same person can be assigned both the review and sign-off roles for a deliverable; this is particularly the case when there are flat organisational structures or on smaller projects.
- Linton's RAM rule no. 9: use the roles assigned for deliverables in the RASIC to expand on the activities that are included for each deliverable in the project schedule. This ensures that all quality assurance and quality control activities are captured for each deliverable and it will build a more robust project schedule with less surprise activities and fewer delays.

POSITION DESCRIPTION

Position descriptions document the detailed roles and responsibilities of each team member or position on the project. Project roles often have standard position descriptions and it is best to supplement these with a responsibility statement that has been tailored to the specific responsibilities for the project. These in turn form the basis for the team member's performance objectives and can be fed into the overall performance management framework.

Basic inclusions in a position description are:
- job title
- department
- reporting lines – up and down
- purpose
- team size
- budgetary authority
- other authority levels
- skills and experience
- qualifications.

Other common inclusions are:

- salary range
- type of employment – contract, permanent, fixed term
- detailed roles and responsibilities
- conditions and benefits
- organisation overview
- accountabilities
- key capabilities or competencies
- mandatory knowledge, skills and experience
- desirable knowledge, skills and experience
- policies and procedures to be followed.

Source: The Northern Sydney Institute, Part of TAFE NSW.

REAL-WORLD EXPERIENCE

CLARIFYING ROLES TO REDUCE CONFLICT

I was the Change Director for a major regulatory program in the financial services sector. The program team was assembled very quickly, and 12 months after all the other major banks had commenced their programs. As a result, people were taken on with little formal induction and no discussion of roles and responsibilities. We weren't even provided with the position descriptions that had been used in the recruitment processes.

I was faced with a team of extremely senior change managers who quickly needed to become productive and also work effectively with the team of recently recruited project managers. We had conflict on two levels – the first was simply due to the 'forming' and 'storming' processes for our team of change managers; and the second related to working with the team of project managers, many of whom had never worked on such a large program that required dedicated change managers. The project managers were very confused about the role of the change managers and we had some open conflict as a result. I prepared a presentation titled 'Working effectively together' which detailed the roles and responsibilities of both positions and how the positions were designed to work together. I then presented this to the combined teams and encouraged active discussions and questions to ensure that everyone was clear on the model. Over the next few weeks the teams began to operate more effectively together and we were able to deliver an incredibly successful implementation.

Common issues leading to change requests

There are key interrelationships between the resources that are assigned to project activities, the cost of the project and the size and composition of the project team. If the final project team is not consistent with the assumptions made during planning, then there will be flow-on impacts on the project schedule, the project budget and, potentially, project quality. There are also situations relating to project staffing that can arise during execution and these will have an impact on the outcomes of the project.

Table 11.1 outlines some of the major variations that relate to project resourcing. It is good practice to deal with these as change requests as part of '4.5 Perform integrated change control'.

TABLE 11.1 CHANGE FACTORS LEADING TO CHANGE REQUESTS

Change factor	Explanation and understanding
Insufficient resources are allocated	A critical assumption made during planning concerns the number of project team members. Team numbers directly impact the time and cost baselines. When fewer resources are assigned than assumed, then trade-offs will occur to scope and/or quality as there are less people available to execute deliverables. If no compromise can be made to scope or quality, then the timeframe is likely to be extended and the cost will likely be the same or a little higher.
Preassigned or identified resources are not available	It can be critical to project success to have a certain number of subject matter experts assigned due to the specialised nature of deliverables and outcomes. The non-availability of a planned expert can cause delays in commencement or cause it to be completely postponed. If internal experts are not available then it may be possible to obtain external expertise depending on organisational HR policies.
Less experienced resources are allocated	Project managers will usually specify resources with particular skills and experience levels in order to reduce project execution risk. However, these resources may not be available or may be too expensive for the project budget. This can have flow-on impacts on the timeframe of the project and the quality of deliverables.
Pressure prompted resources	A severely pressure prompted resource on your project team may struggle to complete activities on time as they tend to leave everything until the last minute. If the activities which are delayed are on the critical path, and the delay cannot be recovered by reworking the schedule, then a change request may be required. If the resource cannot be redeployed, then the risk can be partially mitigated by breaking down their activities into very small subtasks and providing closer supervision.
Resource scarcity increases resource costs	In times of high demand and strong economic conditions, many organisations will need to compete for scarce project resources and specialists, which can place upward pressure on project cost baselines.
Multitasking	Issues with timely completion of activities can occur when resources are working on more than one project at a time or splitting their time across many activities within a single project. Multitasking is inherently inefficient and can cause delays due to the overhead of switching between activities, or when incorrect prioritisation is applied to the activities due to a lack of understanding of the critical path.

(Continued)

Change factor	Explanation and understanding
Undeclared priorities	This can be especially problematic when resources are being split across project activities and non-project work. Depending on the objectives and priorities of the resources, this situation can lead to the project manager not being aware of the other calls on the resource's time, and therefore they overallocate them to activities in the project schedule.
Not reporting early completion	If expectations and communication channels are not clear, it is possible for resources to complete activities early but to not report on the early completion status. This could be due to ignorance or to a desire to slow down and relax.
Not reporting revised completion	This is the opposite issue to the one above and potentially creates larger impacts and delays to project schedules. People can be reluctant to communicate bad news and may not accurately report on reforecasted completion dates. It is common for activities to remain at 90 per cent complete for many reporting periods before they are finally declared as being drastically behind schedule. This can be partially addressed by creating an environment where early and accurate reporting is rewarded, even if it is bad news.

Acquiring the project team

The PMBOK® Guide implies that the first action taken by the project manager in the execution phase is to acquire the project team. This follows the theory that there is a formal approval gate between the completion of planning and the commencement of execution, so there is no logic to bringing on the project team until there is a firm expectation that the project will proceed. Indeed it would be wasteful of monetary resources to start project team members before they are required to commence work on execution activities.

REAL-WORLD EXPERIENCE

ACCELERATING PROJECT DELIVERY

In practice, waiting until formal approval has been given to proceed inevitably causes a delay between the two phases as it can take two to six weeks for the project team members to be selected and arrive. It is obviously faster if the team members are all being sourced internally and have been preassigned from a project pool of resources. This situation only occurs in project management organisations that are structured to deliver all work in projects. This organisational structure suits construction and software development organisations, but is not a common structure among most organisations.

Many organisations will seek to accelerate project delivery in several ways, such as by overlapping the planning and executing phases using a technique known as fast tracking which is explained in detail in Chapter 8. This is relatively low-risk if the project is high-priority and very unlikely to be stopped at the end of the planning phase, or where the project is mandatory and has been preapproved to proceed, which is common for regulatory projects. In these cases the project manager will begin to acquire the project team prior to the completion of planning so that the entire team is ready to get started as soon as the PMP has been approved. In some cases, the early team members can get started on the execution of near-term activities or deliverables with long lead times before planning is fully completed.

REAL-WORLD EXPERIENCE

SELECTING PROJECT TEAM MEMBERS

There is another fallacy held by many new project managers that relates to the acquisition of the project team. They are surprised to realise that they are not in control of the selection of their own project team members, as it is only logical that to increase the chances of project success then the project manager should have complete control over the people joining their project team. How else can they be held accountable for project delivery? There are many factors which can result in a less than perfect selection of project team members:

- lack of suitable internal candidates at a time when external candidates are not to be sourced
- scarcity of specific expertise due to undersupply in the project market
- project sponsor preferences for specific project team members
- poor definition of the specific skills and experience required in project team members
- poor definition of the project roles and responsibilities
- lack of understanding of the risks and serious impacts that the project team can have on project success.

In order to have the best possible chance of selecting and acquiring a strong project team with the right background to successfully deliver each project, the project manager needs to ensure that they have comprehensively identified the skills and expertise required for each project role via the related processes of '9.1 Plan human resource management' and '6.4 Estimate activity resources'. The most important output of these processes is a statement of roles and responsibilities for each position on the project team. It is also useful to supplement this with a detailed position description for each project role, as well as the behavioural characteristics that are required. In large organisations these can often be obtained from the project management office (PMO) or HR department. With this preparation completed, when a resource is being offered to the project manager and the resource does not meet the selection criteria then it is easier to explain the risk to project execution if the resource is assigned.

Recruitment and selection processes

Before the project manager commences the recruitment and selection processes, they should:
- determine the project scope
- define the WBS
- define the project team structure
- determine the vacancies
- develop detailed position descriptions
- understand organisational policies and procedures for recruitment
- check the preferred supplier list for recruitment agencies.

    The common steps in the recruitment and selection process are below.

    Step 1: identify the vacancy

    Step 2: review or create position description

    Step 3: obtain hiring approval if required

    Step 4: determine recruitment strategy:
    - resource pool
    - internal transfer or promotion
    - external market
    - advertising method
    - recruitment partner

    Step 5: prepare recruitment and selection materials
    - selection criteria
    - interview questions
    - reference questions
    - skills test
    - recruitment panel if required

    Step 6: review applicants and prepare short list
    - remember HR legislation and regulations

    Step 7: conduct interviews and selection activities

    Step 8: select preferred candidate and commence negotiations

    Step 9: execute employment contract

    Step 10: arrange appointment and organise induction process.

Source: The Northern Sydney Institute, Part of TAFE NSW.

RESEARCH AND REFLECTION ACTIVITY

INTERVIEWING PRACTICES

Refer back to the HR legislative frameworks section earlier in this chapter and consider examples of inappropriate questions you have been asked during interviewing and selection processes. Discuss with your friends to find more examples.

- Why do prospective employers ask inappropriate questions?
- How can you respond to inappropriate questions and still maintain the possibility of being offered the role?

REAL-WORLD EXPERIENCE

SELECTION TECHNIQUES

I have recruited many hundreds of project managers and project team members over the past 25 years and have come to rely on several highly respected selection techniques. These are:

- detailed position description
- targeted selection interviewing techniques
- reference checking
- behavioural testing and aptitude testing.

POSITION DESCRIPTION

A detailed position description based on specific competencies is the starting point for good recruitment and selection processes. There are excellent project management competency frameworks available which specify the competencies for project management roles at various levels of seniority and experience. The documented roles and responsibilities for each role on a project should be complemented by a comprehensive position description. Together they form the basis of the interviewing and reference checking questions.

TARGETED SELECTION

Targeted selection is a behavioural approach to conducting a job interview to improve recruitment decisions. It requires preparation and planning, with specific questions being developed to identify past behaviours that relate to the specific job requirements. The objective is to obtain job-related behaviour from a candidate's past history on the basis that past behaviour is the best predictor of future behaviour and it is also much more difficult to lie when asked to recount specific examples from the past.

REFERENCE CHECKS

Just as taking time to plan and structure the interview will yield more accurate results, it is also recommended that you take time to plan and structure the reference check as opposed to conducting an informal conversation. A structured reference check is a systematic evaluation of a candidate's past job performance, based on conversations with previous work colleagues and managers. It needs to be aligned to the experience, skills and behaviours required to perform successfully in the specific role. Good planning and a review with the HR department can also prevent the inadvertent asking of illegal or inappropriate questions.

COMPETENCY FRAMEWORKS

The Australian Institute of Project Management has a comprehensive set of competencies defined for project management roles at different levels; for example, project practitioner, project manager, project director and project executive. These can be downloaded at http://www.aipm.com.au.

BACKGROUND CHECKS

This tool is included for completeness as it is becoming increasing popular, and often mandatory, for independent background checks to be conducted to verify a candidate's past criminal, financial and educational records. There are many agencies and recruitment companies who can provide this service in accordance with government requirements.

BEHAVIOURAL TESTS

For critical, senior and long-term project roles it is good practice to conduct some form of behavioural test. Two successful, prominent behavioural tests include the Myers-Briggs Type Indicator (MBTI) and the Occupational Personality Questionnaire (OPQ). The MBTI assessment is designed to measure psychological preferences in how people perceive the world and make decisions. This in turn can predispose people to certain professions and preferences in the workplace. The OPQ gives organisations an understanding of how aspects of an individual's behavioural style will affect their performance at work.

APTITUDE TESTS

As above, for critical and long-term project roles it is good practice to have three aptitude tests conducted that cover verbal reasoning, numerical reasoning and inductive reasoning. I recommend using a reputable organisation to conduct these tests using standardised, online assessments. Many large organisations will subscribe to these services and the testing can often be arranged by the HR department.

HIRING PROJECT MANAGERS

Review your organisation's recruitment policies and procedures, or approach the HR department.
* Do the policies and procedures include supporting tools for the recruitment process?
* Does your HR department provide assistance with recruitment and candidate selection?
* Are there any competencies or standard position descriptions available for project management roles?

Conduct online research into the following topics to see if you can find additional resources to assist with recruitment and selection:
* project management competencies/competency frameworks
* behavioural questions for project managers
* sample targeted selection interview questions for project managers
* sample reference questions for project managers.

You should be able to find a wide range of useful tools and examples to improve your recruitment and selection processes going forward.

Developing the project team

Developing the project team is about enhancing the way the project team works together in order to deliver a successful project. Team work is a critical factor in project success and it is one of the primary responsibilities of the project manager during execution.

Some of the activities which improve team performance are listed below. I believe that none of these happen spontaneously; they all need to be planned and managed by the project manager:
* improving the skills and knowledge of project team members in order to increase productivity and the ability to complete project deliverables
* developing trust and collaboration within the team in order to raise morale, lower conflict and improve cooperation
* managing the risk of key human resources leaving during the project by encouraging cross-training, peer reviews and mentoring within the team.

See Chapter 4 pages 78–80 for team development and leadership styles, including a discussion of Tuckman's five stages of team development: forming, storming, norming, performing and adjourning/mourning.

Reducing team conflict

Conflict among project team members is common and can seriously impact productivity. One of the major sources of conflict arises from a lack of clarity over roles and responsibilities. This is relatively simple to address by ensuring that some of the following standard project management tools and techniques are applied:

- ensuring that everyone has a detailed responsibility statement and position description as this reduces confusion and tension
- developing and distributing a project team organisational chart showing reporting lines (and thereby authority levels) and the overall structure of the team
- assigning specific accountabilities and responsibilities for each deliverable via the use of a responsibility assignment matrix – this ensures that all deliverables have been assigned to an individual team member who is accountable for the production of their deliverable(s).

Other activities that can be undertaken by the project manager to reduce potential conflict within the team are:

- regularly review job descriptions to ensure they are up to date and reflect changes to responsibilities that may arise during execution
- seek input and agreement from team members on critical decisions
- build relationships with each of your direct reports by conducting regular one-on-one catch-ups to provide guidance, increase trust and increase influence
- conduct regular team meetings so that the team becomes accustomed to assisting each other on shared goals and to sharing expertise
- get regular status updates on accomplishments and progress, current risks and issues, plans for the upcoming period and areas requiring assistance
- conduct basic training and openly discuss the need for effective interpersonal communication, conflict management and resolution as well as delegation and decision making
- develop a team charter which includes rules and behaviours for working together
- develop approaches and procedures for major tasks based on team input and previous experience
- encourage feedback and input from team members on their individual tasks and team-based tasks
- prepare to acknowledge and act on good ideas
- communicate clearly the rationale behind suggestions that were not taken up
- consider an anonymous suggestion box in which employees can provide suggestions.

Source: The Northern Sydney Institute, Part of TAFE NSW.

Team development practices and techniques

PROJECT KICK-OFF MEETINGS

It is becoming increasingly common, once the bulk of a project team has been assembled, to conduct a team kick-off meeting that combines a briefing on the project objectives and approach and an opportunity for the team to get to know each other. Project kick-off meetings will typically have an agenda, such as:

1 introductions and background
2 confirmation of the high-level project scope
3 review of the project goals and objectives
4 outline of the team structure and project governance
5 outline of the major project deliverables
6 review of the proposed project delivery approach.

These meetings could also include a team building exercise, the development of a team charter or a workshop on risk identification and analysis. Kick-off meetings are highly recommended as they help push the team through the forming and storming phases and ensure that the team has a common understanding of the project goals and delivery approach.

TEAM CHARTER DEVELOPMENT

A team charter documents the expectations and behaviours that determine how the members of team are to work together. Ideally, it is developed by the team in the early stages of team development as it establishes the norms for team and individual behaviours, work quality, working practices and the processes to facilitate good working relationships.

Two other important benefits are that it provides focus and direction for the team and it manages expectations of senior project stakeholders in relation to team processes and objectives.

The team charter typically includes some or all of the following:

- overarching team goal and purpose
- team objectives
- behavioural guidelines and commitments
- conflict management and escalation processes.

Inputs into the development of the team charter typically include:

- project charter
- project scope statement
- project management plan
- organisational values
- organisational HRM policies and procedures.

The primary techniques for developing the team charter are:

- presenting the overarching characteristics of the project and providing an opportunity for team members to ask questions and clarify their understanding
- providing some form of facilitated activity in which team members consider the organisational values and what these will mean for their team in the execution of the assigned objectives
- developing these into statements about team behaviours and processes that the entire team is willing to adopt – these are often known as ground rules
- asking each team member to commit to the team charter, which often involves everyone signing the bottom of a poster-sized document that is displayed in the team's work area.

TEAM DEVELOPMENT ACTIVITIES

It is common practice to conduct a team building activity in order to accelerate the team through the forming and storming stages of the team development lifecycle. These are designed to build rapport and to create an appreciation of the different skills and preferences that exist within the project team.

It is considered best practice to hold an activity within the first few weeks to enable the team to get to know each other and then to hold regular activities or events along the way. It is important to take into account the composition of the team and the organisational environment when selecting the most appropriate team building activities. In the past it was common to organise team drinks after work, but this can disadvantage some team members who may have family commitments and not be able to stay after hours, or perhaps those whose religious beliefs require abstinence.

There are many team building exercises that can be purchased from learning organisations, such as the Australian Institute of Management, which are designed to illustrate the advantages of working in a team. Examples include Moon landings, lunar survival, desert survival, egg transportation and so on. An independent facilitator is required to supervise the execution of the activity so that all team members can participate fully.

MYERS-BRIGGS

The Myers-Briggs Type Indicator (MBTI)® is a widely used personality inventory (or test) which evaluates personality types and preferences. It is based on Jungian psychology and was developed by two sisters – Isabel Briggs-Myers and Katharine Briggs – in 1926. This instrument is covered in more detail in Chapter 12. Often a representative of the HR department is able to run a short MBTI exercise for the team and then debrief the different profiles of team members. This creates a level of understanding about different personality types, preferences and behaviours within the team and how these can contribute to team outcomes. It can be particularly useful to assist team members to identify introverts versus extraverts, detail-oriented versus concept-oriented individuals, and planful versus more flexible individuals.

DISC PROFILES

Along with the MBTI, conducting a DISC profile is a common rapport building tool for teams. The DISC model of behaviour was first proposed by William Mouton Marston in 1928. The belief is that normal human emotions lead to behavioural differences among groups of people and that understanding this can help people manage their experiences and relationships. The DISC profile instrument uses four dimensions of behaviour to identify preferences and strengths for team members – dominance, influence, steadiness and compliance. Similar to the MBTI, these styles can help team members appreciate and understand the different preferences and strengths of other team members.

RESEARCH AND REFLECTION ACTIVITY

UNDERSTANDING YOURSELF TO UNDERSTAND OTHERS

Search online or ask within your organisation for different personality and style tests that you can do on your own. Some simple tests which are consistent with the more extensive frameworks on which they are based are:

- personality and psychometric tests: http://www.psychometricinstitute.com.au/
- various; e.g. DISC, MBTI: http://www.123test.com/
- MBTI: http://www.16personalities.com/free-personality-test.

Also search for and review the following topics in order to increase your understanding of yourself, project team members and project stakeholders:

- effective team leadership
- effective communication skills
- improving team work
- reducing conflict in teams.

Rapport building activities

There are many simple and easy activities that can be used to build rapport. One of the simplest is 'two truths and a lie' and it proceeds as follows:

1 Ask each team member to think about some interesting skills they possess or interesting activities in which they have been involved.
2 Ask them to also consider plausible but untrue skills or activities that they can also share.
3 Get them to write these down privately – it is important not to share with the group at this stage.
4 Each team member takes a turn telling 'two truths and a lie' to the group and the group tries to decide which one is the lie.

REAL-WORLD EXPERIENCE

CREATIVE TEAM INTRODUCTIONS

Another interesting activity is to have the team split into pairs and conduct interviews with each other with the purpose of introducing the other person to the group. This alleviates anxiety in some team members who are uncomfortable introducing themselves to a team of strangers. Interesting questions can be added to the end of the introductions to help create rapport.

I have used this form of rapport building exercise very effectively in many different settings. Its major advantage is that it's quick and surprisingly effective at getting team members to discuss their interests and get to know each other. Most people are keen to introduce their partner in order to convey their special skills and experiences. My suggested questions for this exercise when used for a newly formed project team are:

- name
- last role or position
- skills and experience
- what they are excited about on the new project
- something interesting and unusual about them.

Other questions that can be substituted for the final questions include:
- Where was your last holiday?
- What are you planning for your next holiday?
- What would you do if you won $20 million?
- What are you most proud of – at work and/or outside of work?

INDIVIDUAL LEARNING AND DEVELOPMENT

One of the primary ways to enhance skills for project team members and to address skill gaps for current positions is to develop training and development plans for each team member. This is only really applicable in a team of permanent employees, or for those team members who are permanent employees. If contractors have been engaged then they should have the requisite skills and experience to perform the role without support from training and development activities.

Most people make the mistake of thinking that the only valuable learning and development activity are external training courses. Indeed, research shows that there are many learning and development activities that can be more effective and accelerate the acquisition of new skills, including:
- internal training sessions delivered by experts
- one-on-one coaching and skills transference
- self-study and research
- self-directed induction programs
- secondments to specialist areas or teams.

Directing and managing the project team

As first mentioned in Chapter 4, directing and managing project execution is the process of leading the project team in the performance of the work that has been defined in the project management plan in order to achieve the project objectives. There are many techniques and frameworks that exist to support the project manager in all of these areas.

Leading the project team

Hersey and Blanchard's Situational Leadership theory (see Chapter 4, pages 75–7) states that instead of using just one style, the most successful leaders adapt their leadership style based on the maturity, or capability, of each team member and the specific nature of the task they will be executing. In brief, they exercise emotional intelligence to select the leadership style that will get the job done most successfully.

LEADERSHIP STYLES

According to Hershey and Blanchard, the other major factor which contributes to the selection of the leadership style is the maturity or development level of the team member. It is a good idea to expand upon this to include the capability or competency of the individual.

The four levels are:

- **Development level 1 – low capability and low commitment (D1):** Team members at this level of maturity are at the bottom level of the scale. They lack the knowledge, skills or confidence to work on their own, and they often need to be pushed to take the task on. This level is low ability and low confidence.
- **Development level 2 – medium commitment with limited capability (D2):** These team members might be willing to work on the task, but they still don't have all the skills to do it successfully. This level is low ability and medium to high confidence.
- **Development level 3 – medium commitment with higher capability (D3):** These team members are ready and willing to help with the task. They have more skills than the D2 group, but they're still not confident in their abilities or are lacking critical experience for the task. This level is high to medium ability and low confidence.
- **Development level 4 – high commitment and high capability (D4):** These team members are able to work on their own. They have high confidence and strong skills, and they're committed to the task. This level is high ability and high confidence.

It is critical to understand that maturity levels are specific to each combination of team member and specific task. A person might be generally skilled, confident and motivated in their job, but would still have a low maturity level when asked to perform a task requiring skills they don't possess.

Table 11.2 is a slightly adapted version of the Hersey-Blanchard model and maps each leadership style to each maturity or development level.

TABLE 11.2 ADAPTED HERSEY-BLANCHARD LEADERSHIP MODEL

Development level	Most appropriate leadership style
Development 1 – low capability and low commitment (D1)	Directing (Situation 1)
Development 2 – medium commitment with limited capability (D2)	Coaching (Situation 2)
Development 3 – medium commitment with higher capability (D3)	Supporting (Situation 3)
Development 4 – high commitment and high capability (D4)	Delegating (Situation 4)

Figure 11.7 is a useful summary of the Hersey-Blanchard Leadership model.

FIGURE 11.7 HERSEY-BLANCHARD LEADERSHIP MODEL

Improving individual performance

There are two other excellent and simple models which can be used by project managers to improve the performance of individual team members: GROW and TIPS. These have been borrowed from the practice of coaching and can be used to allocate and gain commitment to project work, as well as to counsel team members on how to improve their performance. Both models rely on the use of specific questioning techniques by the leader, rather than on a 'telling' style.

The *GROW model* is most effective in a coaching situation where the team member has the required skills and attitude, or can quickly develop the required skills.

1 **Establish the Goal:** in conjunction with the team member you define and agree the goal or outcome to be achieved, which is normally a specific deliverable on the project. Useful questions to use at this stage include:
   - How will you know that you have achieved that goal?
   - How will you know the problem is solved?
   - Have you already taken any steps towards your goal?
   - Does this goal conflict with any other goals or objectives?

2 **Examine the current Reality:** ask the team member to describe their current situation in terms of their skills, concerns and tools they can use or support that may be available. This part of the conversation assists the team member to establish what methods they will use and how they will organise themselves (and call on others) in order to achieve the outcome. Useful questions to use at this stage include:
   - What is happening now?
   - What, who, when, how often?
   - What tools and techniques can you use?
   - Who else can contribute to the outcome?

3 **Explore the Options:** discuss the options that exist for the development of the deliverable or achievement of the goal. Help the team member to generate options and make suggestions if this is within your technical area of expertise. Useful questions to use at this stage include:
   - What else could you do?
   - What assistance would be useful?
   - What obstacles will detract from the achievement of the goal?
   - What could you do if obstacles and constraints were removed?
   - What are the advantages and disadvantages for each option?
   - What do you need to stop doing in order to achieve this goal?

4 **Establish the Will:** normally by working through these steps team members will feel confident that they can achieve the goal. If they are still lacking in confidence you can reconfirm your commitment to assisting them to be successful and get them to commit to taking specific action in order to complete the goal. Useful questions to use at this stage include:
   - What will you do next and by when?
   - What could stop you moving forward?
   - How will you overcome obstacles along the way?
   - How will you stay motivated?
   - When do we need to review progress? Daily, weekly, monthly?

Source: The GROW model, adapted from Center for Management & Organization Effectiveness.

The *TIPS model* is most effective in a counselling situation where the team member has the required skills but doesn't have the best attitude; perhaps they are resisting the overall approach or challenging the project objectives. The skills required and questions used are very similar to the GROW model with one key difference – the TIPS model is used when performance is not at the required level or the team member is not fully committed to the goal.

1 **Support:** this step is really applicable to both models and involves the preparation by the people leader or coach. It involves creating a rapport and adopting positive behaviours.

2 **Define the topic:** frame the specific topic or issue that you need to discuss and encourage the team member to participate in defining the current situation. To focus on the new outcomes, it is important that this is detailed, accurate and clearly understood.

3 **Establish the impact:** help the team member see the full picture and to gain awareness of the flow-on impacts if the situation cannot be changed or performance improved in order to achieve a previously agreed goal. This could be to their own performance rating, flow-on impacts on the goals of others, etc. It is important to create a sense of urgency or need to make a change in behaviours or outcomes.

4 **Develop a plan:** jointly develop creative solutions and a new course of action by exploring options and how constraints can be removed. Agree on the next steps and overall outcomes, including how progress will be reviewed along the way.

5 **Follow up and sustain:** regularly review progress, address obstacles and remove constraints to continue making progress towards the agreed goal.

Source: The TIPS model, adapted from Center for Management & Organization Effectiveness.

FIGURE 11.8 EMPLOYEE PERFORMANCE MANAGEMENT

Source: The Northern Sydney Institute, Part of TAFE NSW.

Related processes from the PMBOK® Guide

4.3 ***Direct and manage project work (execution):*** The process of performing the work defined in the PMP in order to achieve the project's objectives. The project manager directs the execution of the planned activities, sometimes with the assistance of a project management team for larger projects. The PMBOK® Guide includes this process within the execution phase but there is merit in thinking of it as a separate process group having equal importance to monitoring and controlling.

4.4 ***Monitor and control project work (monitoring and controlling):*** The process of tracking, reviewing and regulating the progress made towards the objectives defined in the PMP. The project manager is specifically responsible for the monitoring and control of project work, sometimes with the assistance of a project management team or project management office for larger projects. Monitoring is an aspect of project management performed throughout the project, but it becomes more critical during the execution phase. It is closely linked to '5.6 Control scope', '6.7 Control schedule', '7.4 Control costs', '8.3 Quality control', '10.3 Control communications' and '11.6 Control risks'.

4.5 ***Perform integrated change control (monitoring and controlling):*** The process of reviewing all change requests, including approving or rejecting changes and managing the flow-on impacts on all project deliverables and all components of the PMP. All requested changes should be identified through '5.6 Control scope'. The activities within this process are critical to managing stakeholder expectations and to ensuring the highest chance of project success. They occur from project inception through to completion and are part of the monitor and control process group. It is important that only approved changes be incorporated into the project, as it is surprisingly common to see unapproved changes being inadvertently undertaken.

6.4 ***Estimate activity resources (planning):*** The process of estimating the types and quantities of material, people, equipment or supplies required to perform each activity. It is closely linked to '9.1 Plan human resource management' and '9.2 Acquire project team' and the project procurement management processes.

6.5 ***Estimate activity durations (planning):*** The process of approximating the number of work periods needed to complete individual activities with estimated resources. Work periods may be hours, days, weeks, months and so on and different resources will exhibit differing productivity levels.

7.2 ***Estimate costs (planning):*** The process for developing an estimate of costs to complete all activities required to finish the project. These estimates are a prediction based on the information known at any point in time and the assumptions that have been made for planning purposes.

10.2 ***Manage communications (planning):*** The process of collecting and distributing project performance and status information. This involves the periodic collection of actual performance data and comparing this against the planned baselines of the project. This enables the reporting of performance as well as reforecasting the future performance of the project.

10.3 ***Control communications (monitoring and controlling):*** The process of collecting and distributing project performance and status information. This involves the periodic collection of actual performance data and comparing this against the planned baselines of the project. This enables the reporting of performance as well as reforecasting the future performance of the project.

11.2 ***Identify risks (planning):*** The process for identifying the risks that may impact the project. It is useful to have a broad group of key stakeholders, project team members and internal experts participate in the risk identification session. Good practice dictates that as far as possible all major risks should be identified during the planning phase, although this is an iterative process as often risks are unpredictable and new risks become obvious during execution.

CHAPTER SUMMARY

» Project managers are also people leaders and so they need to understand their obligations in terms of both HR legislation and internal organisational HRM policies and procedures.
» Key legislation and guidelines exist that relate to work health and safety, fair working conditions, antidiscrimination, bullying and harassment.
» Many people-related issues contribute to the need for change requests on projects.
» The major processes involved in project human resource management include acquiring the project team, developing the project team (and individuals) and managing the project team.
» The responsibility assignment matrix (RAM) is a critical tool used to manage the allocation of deliverables to team members. The RASIC is more complete and easier to understand than the traditional RACI style of RAM.
» Project structure charts assist team members in understanding their role within the context of the project, governance and the organisation.
» Position descriptions are very important in ensuring team members with the required skills and experience are selected. The selection of team members is an important contributing factor to project success.
» The bulk of project team members are not acquired until the commencement of the execution phase.
» In practice, a common method of accelerating project delivery timeframes is to overlap the initiation and execution phases and to acquire the project team as early as possible. This is a sound strategy if the project is mandatory and no formal approval is required between initiation and execution.
» Other techniques for team member selection include: behavioural testing, targeted selection, reference checking, background checking and aptitude testing.
» Tuckman's ladder of team development defines five stages of team development: forming, storming, norming, performing and adjourning/mourning. Project managers need to consider their leadership style during the different stages, and also the team development activities that assist the team through the first few stages.
» Most conflict on projects is experienced in the storming phase of team development and project managers can use different techniques to resolve and respond to this conflict.

» Project managers use different techniques to promote team work, including project kick-off meetings, team charter development, rapport building activities, individual learning and development plans.

» Some common frameworks which can be used to promote team work and build rapport include MBTI and DISC profiles.

» Project managers need to adapt their leadership styles to get the best out of individual team members and the project team as a whole.

» Situational Leadership® is a simple and easily applied model for managing individuals at different levels of capability and maturity.

» Situational Leadership® can be successfully combined with the team formation stages of forming, storming, norming and performing to ensure that the best leadership style is adopted to accelerate transition and productivity.

» Different coaching and counselling models, including GROW and TIPS, can be used for individual team members.

REVISION QUESTIONS

Revision questions are divided into two sections. The first covers Certificate IV understanding and the second covers Diploma-level understanding. Both sections are relevant to Diploma students and teachers, while only the first section is relevant to Certificate students and teachers.

Certificate IV of Project Management

These questions relate to the performance criteria stated in 'BSBPMG413A Apply project human resource management approaches'.

1   What key legislative frameworks exist to guide human resource management?
2   What are common human resource management policies and procedures?
3   When is the project team acquired?
4   What is a responsibility assignment matrix?
5   What are the common contents of a position description?
6   How are the skills required of the project resources determined?
7   What are the stages of team formation?
8   When do teams experience the most conflict?
9   What techniques can be used to improve team work?
10 How can human resource management issues contribute to change requests on projects?

BSBPMG413A
performance
criteria questions

Diploma of Project Management

These questions relate to the performance criteria stated in 'BSBPMG515A manage project human resources'.

1   What form of organisational charts are useful for project team members?
2   How do you determine the best structure for the project team and project governance?
3   What tools are used to ensure that the right resources are obtained for the project?
4   What impacts can be experienced if team members are assigned without the correct skills?
5   What techniques can be used to develop team members who do not have all the required skills and experience?
6   How can you ensure that new team members have the required skills, experience and behaviours?
7   How can you accelerate the creation of team work and rapport to improve team productivity?
8   How would you develop a team charter to improve team work and communication?

BSBPMG515A
performance
criteria questions

9   What human resource factors require remedial action and contribute to change requests on projects?

10 At what stages in the team formation cycle are different leadership styles best applied?

11 What are the primary functions of the responsibility assignment matrix?

BSBPMG413A and
BSBPMG515A
performance
criteria questions

DISCUSSION QUESTIONS

1   Why are so many project managers unaware of human resource management legislation and organisational policies and procedures?

2   What are the advantages of the RASIC over the RACI style of RAM?

3   How can you apply different leadership styles and approaches to get the best performance out of individual team members?

4   Do project managers also need to be great people leaders? Discuss your views.

5   What additional skills are important for project managers when leading a project team?

6   What are the primary causes of conflict on projects and what steps can be taken to reduce conflict in project teams?

ONLINE RESOURCES

Visit the online companion website at http://www.cengagebrain.com to link to important additional resources, including templates, real-world case studies, revision quizzes and additional study material.

FURTHER READINGS AND REFERENCES

Blanchard, K., Zigarmi, P., & Zigarmi, D. (1985). *Leadership and the one minute manager: Increasing effectiveness through situational leadership.* New York: William Morrow.

Bonebright, D. A. (2010). 40 years of storming: a historical review of Tuckman's model of small group development. *Human Resource Development International, 13*(1), pp. 111–20.

Brown, K., & Hyer, N. (2009). *Managing projects: A team-based approach.* Columbus, OH: Mcgraw-Hill.

Clarke, N., & Howell, R. (2009). *Emotional intelligence and projects.* Newtown Square, PA: Project Management Institute.

Covey, S. R. (2004). *The 7 habits of highly effective people: Powerful lessons in personal change.* London: Simon & Schuster.

Flannes, S., & Levin, G. (2005). *Essential people skills for project managers.* Vienna, VA: Management Concepts.

Landsberg, M. (2009). *The Tao of coaching.* London: Profile Books.

Project Management Institute (PMI). (2013). *A guide to the Project Management Body of Knowledge* (PMBOK® Guide) (5th ed.). Newtown Square, PA. Chapter 9, pp. 255–286.

Schwable, K. (2011). *Information technology project management* (revised 6th ed.). Melbourne: Cengage Learning.

Whitmore, J. (2009). *Coaching for performance: GROWing human potential and purpose – the principles and practice of coaching and leadership* (4th ed.). London: Nicholas Brealey Publishing.

Online references

Australian Institute of Project Management competency framework: http://www.aipm.com.au/AIPM/CERTIFICATION/COMPETENCY_STANDARDS/3G/P/pcspm.aspx?hkey=32ad63cc-73d1-4ba5-ae27-4a0a78ecbb86

Bullying and harassment: http://www.humanrights.gov.au/workplace-bullying-violence-harassment-and-bullying-fact-sheet

Fair Work Commission: http://www.fwc.gov.au

Federal antidiscrimination legislation: http://www.humanrights.gov.au/

The essentials of managing a project team: http://www.dummies.com/how-to/content/the-essentials-of-managing-a-project-team.html

Workplace Gender Equality Act: http://www.wgea.gov.au/

Workplace health and safety legislation: http://www.workplaceinfo.com.au/legislation/ohs/nsw-ohs-legislation

Project communications management

Context

Project communications management encompasses the processes required to ensure the timely and appropriate generation, collection, distribution, storage, retrieval and disposal of project information. Project managers spend the majority of their time communicating with team members, the project sponsor and other project stakeholders.

With the introduction of a new key knowledge area into the PMBOK® Guide – Project Stakeholder Management – it is now important to draw a clear distinction between project communications management and managing the expectations of project stakeholders.

This chapter focuses on the information distribution and communication requirements of the project team, project sponsor and senior stakeholders who are involved in project governance activities. The chapter on project stakeholder management (Chapter 15) will concentrate on the communication requirements of other project stakeholders and how to manage their expectations in order to improve the chances of project success. Project stakeholders are any person or organisation that is impacted by, or interested in, the outcomes of the project. They can be internal or external and can greatly affect the potential success of a project depending on their power and influence.

Effective communication enhances project success by creating understanding within the project team and also between diverse sets of project stakeholders. Poor project communication is one of the most common causes of project failure.

Common communication skills that increase the effectiveness of project managers, people leaders and individuals are:
- listening actively and effectively
- questioning to ensure better understanding
- educating to increase team knowledge and effectiveness
- fact-finding to identify and confirm information
- setting and managing expectations
- persuading someone to perform a desired action
- motivating to provide encouragement or reassurance
- coaching to improve performance and achieve desired results
- negotiating to achieve mutually acceptable agreements
- resolving conflict to prevent disruption
- summarising, recapping and agreeing next steps.

PMBOK® Guide processes for project communications management

The PMBOK® Guide processes for project communications management are:
10.1   Plan communications management
10.2   Manage communications
10.3   Control communications.

See PMBOK®
Guide Figure 10-2
Plan
communications
management:
inputs, tools and
techniques, and
outputs

FIGURE 12.1 PROJECT COMMUNICATIONS MANAGEMENT – A PROCESS PERSPECTIVE

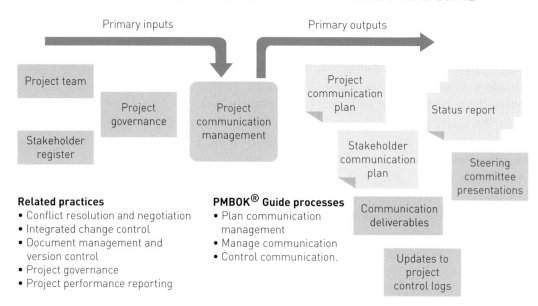

Source: Adapted from Project Management Institute, *A guide to the Project Management Body of Knowledge*, (PMBOK® Guide), fifth edition.

See PMBOK® Guide Chapter 10 Project communications management

10.1 ***Plan communications management (planning):*** The process for determining the project stakeholder information needs and developing tailored communication approaches to meet those needs. Other components can include defining the communication needs within the project team.

10.2 ***Manage communications (planning):*** The process of collecting and distributing project performance and status information. This involves the periodic collection of actual performance data and comparing this against the planned baselines of the project. This enables the reporting of performance as well as reforecasting the future performance of the project.

10.3 ***Control communications (monitoring and controlling):*** The process of collecting and distributing project performance and status information. This involves the periodic collection of actual performance data and comparing this against the planned baselines of the project. This enables the reporting of performance as well as reforecasting the future performance of the project.

Effective communication

Effective communication is the transferring and understanding of meaning. For communication to be effective, it is important to understand how the people you are interacting with have interpreted your message. It is not easy to ensure effective communication, as all parties convert information into meaning by using their senses, past experiences and through the application of other filters. Therefore, it is important to verify the receiver's understanding of your message and to verify your understanding of theirs.

Project managers need to choose the most effective communication styles and media for every piece of verbal or written communication they produce. The context and complexity of communication choices can be seen in Figure 12.2 which outlines the dimensions of communication.

FIGURE 12.2 COMMUNICATION DIMENSIONS

Source: The Northern Sydney Institute, Part of TAFE NSW.

Effective communication combines a set of skills, including non-verbal communication and active listening, with the ability to understand your own emotions and those of the people with whom you are communicating. Effective communication can be learned and practice will assist with the integration and application of different communication frameworks so that they become automatic and seamless.

Active listening

Active listening is a critical skill that underpins successful communication. It helps to ensure you have accurately understood the meaning and needs of project team members and project stakeholders. Naturally, it can only be effectively applied to verbal communication. The following tips can be learned and practised until they become second nature. Some relate to circumstances where you have direct visual interaction with the speaker, while others can only be used when you cannot see the speaker.

- ***Focus fully on the speaker:*** includes the actual words as well as non-verbal indicators, such as tone of voice and body language. If you are thinking of other tasks, or distracted by doing emails or responding to text messages, then you may miss something that is vital to your understanding of the message or situation. It can be difficult to remain focused on some speakers – you can try writing questions that you would like to ask them when they are finished, searching for underlying meaning and emotions, or repeating their words in your head to stay engaged.
- ***Take notes:*** this can assist with the understanding and recall of key messages or communications as it provides an alternative cognitive channel. It also conveys a sense of interest in what is being said.

- *Test your understanding:* this can be applied in both directions: you can test that you have correctly understood a message and also check that someone you are communicating with has correctly understood your message. It involves analysing the messages and repeating them using words that are similar to those used by the speaker, or by paraphrasing (converting the message into your own words).
- *Avoid interrupting or redirecting the conversation:* you can't concentrate on what someone's saying if you're forming what you're going to say next. Often, the speaker can read your facial expressions and know that you are not paying attention.
- *Neutralise emotions:* in particular, avoid seeming judgemental by adopting a positive or neutral attitude and body posture. In order to communicate effectively with someone, you don't have to like them or agree with their ideas, values or opinions. However, it is helpful to set aside judgement, withhold blame and avoid criticism in order to create rapport and to fully understand a message.
- *Show interest:* gestures and small verbal comments can be very powerful in conveying interest and attention without interrupting, such as nodding and smiling, as well as 'yes' or 'uh huh'.
- *Recap and summarise:* do this at the end of a conversation to ensure you have correctly understood the key messages. This technique also improves the action orientation of communication by reinforcing agreements and next steps.
- *Listening with questions in mind:* the following questions can be used to assist with the extraction of more interest and meaning out of presentations of verbal communication:
  - » What is the speaker saying?
  - » What does it mean?
  - » What point are they trying to make?
  - » How does it relate to previous messages?
  - » How can I use the information?
  - » Does it make sense?
  - » Am I getting the whole story?
  - » What outcomes are they trying to achieve?

Source: The Northern Sydney Institute, Part of TAFE NSW.

Non-verbal communication

When people communicate about things that are important to them, much of the meaning is conveyed in the non-verbal signals that accompany the message. Non-verbal communication is wordless communication and includes concepts such as:

- *body language:* posture, body movement, body position, muscle tension, breathing and heart rate
- *facial language:* eye contact, facial colour, expressions (smiling, frowning, etc.)
- *emotional language:* feelings about the interaction, the person doing the communicating and the topic
- *vocal language:* this is not the actual words that are being used but rather the pitch, tone, speed, complexity and meaning behind the words that have been chosen.

In a famous and often misunderstood study conducted in 1967, Mehrabian and Ferris found that the likeability of a presenter was determined by the following factors: 7 per cent content, 38 per cent vocal and 55 per cent non-verbal (Mehrabian & Ferris, 1967). The study related to likeability and rapport creation rather than the actual conveyance of correct understanding.

Developing the ability to understand and use non-verbal communication can help you to connect with others, convey accurate messages and build better relationships – which is particularly important when managing the expectations of project stakeholders.

Communication effectiveness and rapport can be greatly improved by ensuring that all non-verbal signals are congruent with the verbal content of the communication. You can improve non-verbal communication using the following methods.

- ***Matching non-verbal signals*** to the words and meaning you are conveying by ensuring they reinforce what is being said and do not contradict it. For example, there is little point trying to convince someone that you genuinely like them and value their contribution if you are smiling and nodding your head at the same time as having your arms crossed and your posture turned away from them.
- ***Adjust non-verbal signals for the context:*** communication is vastly improved by adjusting your tone of voice and complexity of language when addressing stakeholder groups at different levels of education and authority. This also applies to adjusting your choice of communication media or channel.
- ***Manage emotions and be aware of emotional responses*** in others. When emotions are running high, it impedes the effectiveness of communication. Practice being open and non-judgemental, focus on the content and not the person and share your emotions in a positive manner. Show empathy and understanding of the other person's viewpoint.
- ***Mirroring*** is a technique of matching your body positioning and other non-verbal communication factors to the audience. This improves your ability to create rapport and influence others.

Planning for project communications management

Now that there are two separate key knowledge areas in the PMBOK® Guide that deal with communications-related activities, it is important to make a distinction between the primary areas of emphasis of each. The focus of communications in this key knowledge area is on the processes and techniques required for the planning of communication activities that relate to the management of the project team, project sponsor and key stakeholders involved in project governance. The content of this section covers the following domains:

- project team – communication requirements and processes
- project sponsor – communication requirements and processes
- project stakeholders involved in governance – communication requirements and processes

- other project stakeholders – communication requirements only; stakeholder analysis activities and the development/delivery of stakeholder change management plans will be covered in Chapter 15.

Within this context, project communications planning covers processes for determining the information needs of the project team and all project stakeholders, but only those processes which relate to the execution of communication activities for the project team, project sponsor and those project stakeholders engaged in governance activities.

The primary output is a project communication plan that determines who needs what information, when they will need it, how it will be given to them and by whom. It is important to note that the information needs and communications mechanisms vary widely from project to project, and while many high-level processes, structures and communications approaches can be reused, often the content and emphasis of primary project communications deliverables will vary for each project sponsor.

The inputs to the project communication plan are:
- stakeholder register
- stakeholder analysis
- project governance structure
- project team structure
- communications standards
- document management policies and procedures
- lessons learned from past projects.

The contents of the project communication plan typically include:
- project team communications deliverables and processes
- project sponsor communications deliverables and processes
- project governance communications deliverables and processes
- resources allocated to communications activities, including time and cost
- escalation, approval and information flow processes
- project meeting schedule that lays out the frequency, purpose and attendees for planned project meetings
- project communication table
- links to relevant communications standards
- links to relevant documentation management policies and procedures
- templates for detailed weekly project status reports
- templates for monthly summary project status reports
- templates for steering committee presentations
- glossary of terms
- optional – stakeholder communications requirements which are implemented via the stakeholder management plan. It is recommended that these should now be developed and documented as part of the project stakeholder management processes.

Tools and techniques for planning communication

PROJECT COMMUNICATION TABLE

It is good practice to deliver many of the communications requirements for a project via the use of supplementary planning tables, registers or schedules. Table 12.1 is a basic communication planning table.

TABLE 12.1 PROJECT COMMUNICATION TABLE

Target audience	Communication needs	Communication deliverable	Responsible	Media or channel	Frequency
Project team	Why	What	Project manager	How	When
Project sponsor					
Project stakeholder 1					
Project stakeholder 2					
Vendor 1					
Vendor 2					
External stakeholder 1					
External stakeholder 2					

PROJECT MANAGEMENT MASTERY

Sample template is provided online

COMMUNICATION PLANNING TABLE

It is good practice to develop a communication planning table but there are traps that inexperienced project managers can fall into, such as:

- including only the communications needs of the project team and primary project stakeholders
- including only the communications needs of stakeholders with no direct involvement in project delivery
- focusing on the communication deliverables and then deciding who should receive them
- setting baselines for scope, time and cost prior to completing project communication planning – this places the project immediately behind as major deliverables and resource requirements have been omitted from the scope, time and cost planning processes.

It is best practice to consider and satisfy the communications needs of team members, stakeholders involved in project execution (including the project sponsor) and those involved in governance (the project steering committee), as well as stakeholders that are not directly involved in project execution but will be interested in, or impacted by, the project in some way. The completeness of communications planning is further enhanced by:

- identifying all stakeholders
- analysing and prioritising their communications needs
- considering the audience first and *not* the communication deliverable
- ensuring that all communications deliverables are included in the work breakdown structure (WBS) and project schedule
- providing sufficient time and resourcing to undertake communications activities
- being aware of any communications standards or approval processes that may be required when communicating with senior executives and major external stakeholders (such as regulators, unions and the government).

PROJECT MEETING SCHEDULE

A project meeting schedule can be extremely helpful in organising regular project-related updates and forums, as well as managing the expectations of stakeholders who are involved in project governance activities. Many senior stakeholders who are involved in project governance activities are also required to contribute as subject matter experts, provide their time for review and sign-off activities, and allocate resources to the project team. Table 12.2 depicts an example of a project meeting schedule.

TABLE 12.2 EXAMPLE PROJECT MEETING SCHEDULE

Project meeting	Frequency	Purpose and agenda	Attendees	Chairperson	Logistics
Project team meeting	Weekly	» Status updates » Risk » Issues	» Project manager » Project team » Project sponsor (optional)	Project manager	» Room booking » Teleconference or video conference arrangements » Project control log updates
Project steering committee meeting	Monthly	» Summary status updates » Decision making » Change requests	» Project sponsor » Executive sponsor » Senior stakeholders » PMO manager	Project sponsor or project manager	» Room booking » Presentation and prereading » Teleconference or video conference arrangements » Project control log updates
Project sponsor update	Weekly or fortnightly	» Issue resolution » Decision making	» Project sponsor » Project manager	One-on-one	» Project control log updates

REAL-WORLD EXPERIENCE

MANAGING PROJECT STAKEHOLDERS

I have only recently added the project meeting schedule to my practices in the project communications area. This is due to repeated issues regarding insufficient support and time allocation from senior project stakeholders who have project governance responsibilities. This is a beneficial tool even in organisations with high levels of project management maturity, as often the senior stakeholders have little experience with project requirements and have never participated on a steering committee before. Helping them to understand their role and also the time commitment that is required of them can greatly assist the smooth running of any project, especially as many senior stakeholders need to review and sign off on major project deliverables and make staff from their teams available to participate in the project as subject matter experts or as project team resources.

I first introduced the schedule when working for a major commercial law firm, as the project management maturity level was low and senior stakeholders, who were primarily partners in the firm, had no previous experience with project work. It was at this time that I also modified my standard version of the communication planning table to include a column for the physical communications deliverables which could then be woven back into the WBS and project schedule.

Project governance structures

Establishing the appropriate governance structure for a project is a critical activity, as it manages the communications needs of senior project stakeholders, including the project sponsor, and establishes the contributions that are required from these stakeholders in order to contribute to project success.

ROLE OF THE PROJECT SPONSOR

Despite the general acceptance of project sponsors getting involved in the management of projects, the actual role and responsibilities of project sponsors are often unclear and differ considerably within organisations and across industries. The appointment and selection of the right sponsor can have a huge impact on the success or failure of a project.

It is very important that the project sponsor is sufficiently senior in the organisation to provide support for the project. Experience with projects is a secondary consideration. The most successful approach appears to be when the project sponsor has a particular interest in the project outcomes and is self-appointed.

The role of the project sponsor includes:

- finding both monetary and people resources for the project
- setting the overall scope and objectives for the project
- approving the project plan, major deliverables and change requests
- being consulted on decisions by the project manager and ratifying decisions made by the project manager or project team
- making business-related decisions on behalf of the project
- making major decisions for the project that are outside of the project manager's authority
- assisting with the resolution of issues and management of risks
- supporting the project politically and clearing any road blocks.

ROLE OF THE STEERING COMMITTEE

For large projects, in addition to the project sponsor, there is generally some form of management body or committee that is assigned oversight and governance responsibility. The primary function of a steering committee is to take responsibility for the business issues associated with a project and to provide additional senior management support for the project sponsor and project manager. As with the role of the project sponsor, there is considerable variation in the responsibilities of steering committees within organisations and across industries.

The role of the steering committee includes:

- assessing the feasibility and business plan of a project prior to proceeding with planning or execution
- ensuring that funding and resources are supplied to the project based on its overall priority for the organisation
- supporting the project sponsor and project manager in the execution of the project
- ensuring the objectives, scope and requirements are consistent with the expectations of the stakeholder groups they represent
- providing guidance on project business issues and making business-related decisions that impact on the project
- assisting with the resolution of issues and management of risks
- supporting the project internally and clearing any road blocks
- assisting the project sponsor with change control processes and the approval of change requests
- responding to and reconciling conflict and differences of opinions at senior levels that may impact on the project
- managing any prioritisation conflicts.

STEERING COMMITTEE DELIVERABLES

The primary tools that are used to manage the steering committee are the:

- steering committee charter
- steering committee agenda
- steering committee update
- project control logs – decision, actions, change requests
- steering committee minutes.

Sample templates for the steering committee presentation and project control logs

The steering committee charter is the formalisation of the roles and responsibilities of the particular project steering committee as per the above list. It is important to discuss expectations with each steering committee member and then discuss all of their responsibilities at the inaugural meeting. This process should be repeated whenever a member of the committee is swapped or added.

The structure of the steering committee agenda and the contents of the update are very important when managing the expectations of this senior stakeholder group. The following list of contents can be used as a guide but will require adjustment based on the particular preferences and requirements of the organisation and the steering committee:

- key messages
- project status and summary performance metrics – time and costs
- major risks and issues requiring assistance
- scope management and change control – change requests for consideration
- major decisions required
- optional appendices with more detail can also be useful to refer to during the meeting and depend on how hands-on the steering committee is with the project:
  » project structure
  » detailed performance metrics
  » detail to support decisions
  » change control impact assessments
  » minutes and actions
  » decision log.

PROJECT MANAGEMENT MASTERY

STEERING COMMITTEE MINUTES

The management of the steering committee can be a difficult task that falls primarily to the project manager with support from the project sponsor. The most common output of the steering committee meetings are detailed minutes that record the discussions and decisions.

Steering committee minutes in MS Word format	
Advantages	Disadvantages
» Documents the discussion of the meeting » Documents the decisions made » Documents the actions assigned or progressed » Are the generally accepted output of important meetings	» Are a very time consuming administrative task that takes the project manager away from active management of the project » Are difficult for project administrative staff to prepare and position correctly » Often requires review and sign-off by the project sponsor prior to distribution, which delays required actions » Makes it difficult to trace back to when specific decisions were made

I have found a much more effective alternative to the formal meeting minutes and I have introduced this to the project management practices of many organisations over the years. In many cases, either the project manager or administrative staff should be able to capture the decisions and actions in the various logs during the actual meeting so they simply require refinement and review after the meeting.

REAL-WORLD EXPERIENCE

STEERING COMMITTEE MANAGEMENT

I now use the following process and outputs to manage the steering committee outcomes, and the outcomes of any major project-related forum:

- prepare summary status report – a consolidated monthly, rather than the individual weekly, review
- prepare steering committee presentation, in consultation with the project sponsor, and distribute several days prior to the meeting
- document major decisions in the project decision log including a detailed description, the date and the decision makers
- document steering committee actions in the project action log
- document change requests that have been processed (approved or rejected) in the change log
- distribute an email the day after the meeting and include links to the action and decision logs, as well as extracts in the body of the email from these logs with the additional items and updates included.

Project team meetings

Regular meetings with the project team, or with the project management team (depending on the size of the project), are a critical project communications activity as they play an important role in the directing, managing, monitoring and controlling of the project.

REAL–WORLD EXPERIENCE

PROJECT TEAM MEETING MANAGEMENT

I manage project team meetings in two ways. On large projects or programs I will meet twice each week with the project management team – this generally consists of myself, the project managers who report directly to me and sometimes the project sponsor. As I mentioned in Chapter 8, the first meeting of the week, generally on a Monday afternoon or Tuesday morning, is focused on the management and resolution of risks and issues, as well as the consideration of any change requests that may be required. The second meeting, generally Thursday afternoon or Friday morning, is focused on discussing status updates and progress, as well as uncovering additional issues that require resolution in order to stay on track.

For smaller projects I will combine these meetings into the one meeting and include the entire project team if it isn't too large. I still split the meeting into two parts – the first part concentrates on status and progress updates, while the second part covers the issues and risks.

I never issue any formal MS Word minutes from either of these meetings as I have a strong preference for the use of the different project control logs to capture decisions, allocate actions and record major project events such as change requests. As per my practice with steering committee meetings, I will issue an email the day after each meeting. This will have links to the updated logs and could include in the body of the email extracts of the recent activity in the logs.

Determining communication requirements

Understanding the communications requirements of the project team, project sponsor and key stakeholders involved in project governance is critical to the development of the project communications plan.

It is important to distinguish between the management processes used to manage the project team as opposed to the communication and stakeholder management processes used to manage stakeholders. Many people consider the project team to be a part of the stakeholders of the project, whereas it can be simpler to remove the team from the stakeholders and consider them a unique group led via the project human resource management processes that have been chosen by the project manager. Directing and managing the project team sits within the key knowledge area of Project Human Resource Management (see Chapter 11).

The stakeholders who have been identified and the stakeholder register are key inputs into the determination of the communications requirements and therefore the identification of the communications deliverables that must be produced. This process occurs during '13.1 Identify stakeholders' and '13.2 Plan stakeholder management'.

It is important to be flexible and to base communication planning on the needs and preferences of the stakeholders rather than what is convenient for the project team to provide. Further to this, project managers need to put aside their own communications preferences in order to undertake successful planning and management of project communication processes for the project team, project sponsor, steering committee and stakeholders. Too many project managers either place their preferences first and fail to recognise alternative preferences in others, or fail to allocate sufficient time to communications activities. This is one of the reasons that poor project communications has been clearly linked to project failure.

Tools and techniques to determine communication requirements

There are many tools that can help define communication requirements. Some of the simplest and most effective are:
- the Myers-Briggs Type Indicator (MBTI)
- learning preferences and styles
- consultation – ask the team members and stakeholders about their preferences
- lessons learned from past projects regarding communications that went well and communications that did not support project success
- project communications procedures – may be provided by the project management office, the internal communications department or a public relations department
- subject matter experts – change management, training and communication professionals may be part of the project team or specialist skills allocated from other internal departments to support the achievement of project outcomes.

MYERS-BRIGGS TYPE INDICATOR (MBTI)

Expanding on the discussion in Chapter 11, the MBTI is a useful instrument that helps us understand people's communication preference on four dimensions:
1 extraversion versus introversion – how we prefer to replenish our energy
2 sensing versus intuition – how we prefer to process information
3 thinking versus feeling – how we prefer to make decisions
4 judging versus perceiving – how we prefer to plan or manage our lifestyle.

FIGURE 12.3 MBTI – 4 DICHOTOMIES

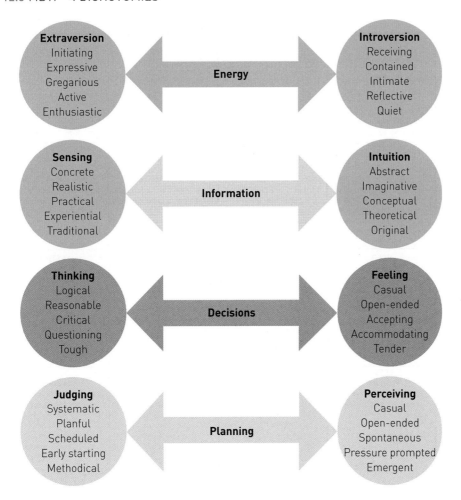

Individual preferences mean that stakeholders and project team members can be anywhere on each of the four continuums. The particular combination of each person's preferences determines the allocation of one of the 16 personality types (see Figure 12.4). Each of these types has different preferences for the way they interact with people, receive communications, assimilate information and approach the organisation of their work and lifestyle.

Table 12.3 brings together both observation and research to provide insights into the communication requirements generally attributed to the different dominant preferences. This knowledge contributes to both effective project communication planning and also to improved communication with project team members and stakeholders in general. This framework can be used to improve all forms of communication – written, verbal, reports and presentations – and also provides insights into how to support senior project stakeholders with complex decision making.

FIGURE 12.4 MBTI – 16 PERSONALITY TYPES

	Possible				
NF Valuing Manifesting universal values and valuing people	**ENFJ** **Teacher** Smooth talking charmers. Very inspiring and motivational. Often clergy. People leaders and persuaders. Great salespeople. Very relationship-orientated. Like to motivate groups.	**INFJ** **Counselor** Work is to inspire others to achieve great things. Great visionaries of human possibilities. Serious academics. Often professors or offer themselves to a religious order.	**INTJ** **Mastermind** If they say they are going to do something, they do it. Likely to be corporate leaders, scientists. Believe everything has room for improvement. Superior planners and visionaries of systems.	**ENTJ** **Field Marshall** Very leadership-orientated. Likely to be top executives, business persons. Big on reducing inefficiency, ineffectiveness. Take charge people. Can be overwhelming to less outgoing types.	**NT** Visioning Pulling people with ideas to an optimistic future
Personal	**ENFP** **Champion** Second only to ESFPs for fun. Want lives filled with excitement and romance. Very enthusiastic and creative. Often teachers, artists, writers. Great need for diversity and change.	**INFP** **Healer** Noble, aiding society. Different from ISFPs, they try to tackle long-term problems. Often psychologists or counsellors. Want to save the whales.	**INTP** **Architect** Deepest analysts of problems to be solved. Often physicists, scientists. Most aloof of types. Critical thinkers.	**ENTP** **Inventor** Want one exciting challenge after another. Love to problem solve. Good at analysis. Consider themselves full of ingenuity and ideas. Often involved in system analysis, design.	Logical
	ESFP **Performer** Number one in fun and enthusiasm. Always invite ESFPs to your party. The most generous of all types. Warm, friendly, vibrant people. Excellent customer service.	**ISFP** **Composer** Quietly harmonious with world. Very observing, benevolent. Inclined towards work with people in need. Work to solve problems of the immediate, such as homelessness, hunger.	**ISTP** **Operator** Ready to try anything once. Flushed with the rush of life. Seek excitement. A love of focus and the unity they offer. Inclined towards mechanical devices, can take apart and reassembly anything.	**ESTP** **Promoter** Excitement seekers. Never feel more alive than when taking risks. Great negotiators on the front end. Excellent promotional and entrepreneurial capabilities if someone else follows through.	
SF Relating Including and building trustworthiness	**ESFJ** **Provider** Hosts and hostesses. Graciousness of this type makes them excellent at entertaining, coordinating. May be teachers, nurses. Very conscious of appearances, should/shouldn'ts.	**ISFJ** **Protector** A high sense of duty. Upholders of family tradition. Often found in traditional helping professions including nursing, elementary education, etc.	**ISTJ** **Inspector** Doers of what should be done. Masters at completing practical details and adding finishing touches. Get-it-done people. Superb administrators. Duty bound and obligated, often in military.	**ESTJ** **Supervisor** Administrators, workers, pillars of strength in community. Loyal mothers, parents, employees. Often promoted to management positions. Dependable, consistent, straightfor-ward.	**ST** Directing Action from a strategic perspective
	Present				

Source: © Todd Atkins. http://batonrougecounseling.net. Reproduced with permission.

TABLE 12.3 COMMUNICATING WITH OTHERS

Communicating with extraverts 'Let's talk it over'	Communicating with introverts 'I need to think about this'
» Talk face to face » Discuss in groups and allow interaction » Express interest and enthusiasm » Prefer immediate responses and quick feedback » Process ideas by verbalising – 'think out loud' » Entertain socially while doing business	» Communicate in writing first » Like to have a detailed agenda, or purpose, prior to a discussion » Listen and allow time for responses » Provide information ahead of time » Allow time for reflection » Don't expect an immediate decision » Ensure valuable ideas are not overlooked » Don't require them to attend social functions to do business

Communicating with sensing types 'Just the facts please'	Communicating with intuitive types 'I can see it all now'
» Keep communication clear, explicit and practical » Don't use abstract language » Check that they are understanding the communication » Present practical and detailed plans » Back up summaries with detailed rationale and data » Present information sequentially » Emphasise immediate, tangible results » Be aware that they may be uncomfortable with change	» Give a big picture overview first » Emphasise concepts, ideas and innovation » Take a long term, future-oriented perspective » Be willing to brain storm outside-the-box ideas » Allow them to share their ideas and dreams » Provide facts and details only as necessary » Help link their ideas to a realistic plan
Communicating with thinking types 'Is this logical?'	**Communicating with feeling types** 'Will anyone be hurt?'
» Get straight to the point » Be calm, objective and demonstrate competence » Be concise, cogent and logical » Present pros and cons » Use logical, not emotional, arguments » Focus on tasks and objectives, not only people » Give frank feedback – not just positive comments » Criticisms and challenges are not meant personally	» Begin with areas of agreement » Connect first and challenge later » Create a warm and friendly atmosphere » Use personal anecdotes to create connections » Focus on people, not just on tasks and objectives » Acknowledge the validity of feelings and values » Avoid critiquing and evaluating while listening » Avoid competition – aim for mutual agreements and compromise
Communicating with judging types 'Just do something'	**Communicating with perceiving types** 'Let's wait and see'
» Be punctual » Be well organised with clear progression through the communication » Don't present too many options – prioritise » Be decisive, draw conclusions quickly » Expect a quick decision » Stick to schedules, milestones and deadlines » Provide clear expectations » Avoid last minute surprises or changes	» Present things in tentative, draft form » Describe situations rather than evaluate them » Let them draw the conclusions » Give them a number of options » Allow time for discussion and exploration » Don't force an immediate decision » Be open to new information and opportunities » Be aware that you will need to follow up » Confirm conclusions and agreements

Source: © The Institute of Actuaries of Australia *Effective Communication Using the MPTI*, Martin Mulcare and Leonie Tickle, presented at Insights Session 10 September 2009.

LEARNING PREFERENCES AND STYLES

Neil Fleming's VARK model is very popular and classifies a person's learning style and preferences. Fleming developed the testing instrument in 1987 in order to help people learn more about their individual learning preferences. The model also improves effective communication as we can better understand our audience's communication preferences.

The following is a practical adaptation of the VARK model based on experience and observation. The four VARK model preferences are:

1 *visual* – pictures, movies, diagrams
2 *auditory* – music, discussion, lectures
3 *reading and writing* – making lists, reading, note taking
4 *kinaesthetic* – movement, experiments, hand-on activities.

The most effective communication styles for visual learners are graphic displays such as charts, diagrams, illustrations, handouts, presentation and videos. People with this preference would rather see information presented in a visual form than a written form. It is possible to get them to read materials more effectively if they are presented in a visual manner and in conjunction with diagrams. It can be difficult to get them to focus on reading a very long document unless it is formatted to include lots of white space, tables and diagrams. Visual learners will often:

• need to see information in order to remember it
• pay close attention to body language
• have a strong sense of aesthetics
• visualise information in their mind to help them remember it.

The most effective communication styles for aural learners are all forms of verbal media – voice recordings, verbal presentations to accompany written materials, and being verbally briefed on a long document rather than reading it quietly on their own. They have a strong preference to hear information and to discuss the key points. Aural learners will often:

• prefer to listen rather than read
• remember information better if they read it out loud
• prefer to listen to a voice recording rather than review by reading.

The most effective communication styles for reading and writing learners involve displaying information in the form of words. Test-based communication materials are strongly preferred. This style is often omitted on the basis that it is covered by either the visual or aural preference. Reading and writing learners will often:

• learn new information by reading
• take lots of notes during presentations and meetings
• enjoy making lists, reading definitions and creating test-based presentations
• need a handout to accompany a verbal presentation.

The most effective communication style for kinaesthetic learners is to allow them to figure things out for themselves and be part of the experience. In the business world this approach can be challenging when timeframes are tight but it is possible to improve communication with these people by being active while you communicate. This could mean giving them something to fiddle with, walking with them, getting them to actively participate, or taking them out for a coffee. Kinaesthetic learners will often:

- enjoy performing tasks that involve directly manipulating objects and materials
- find it difficult to sit still for long periods of time
- be good at applied activities, such as cooking and sports
- doodle at the same time as listening.

Many people will be a combination of preferences and it is common for kinaesthetic learners to be combined with one of the other preferences; i.e. visual/kinaesthetic, aural/kinaesthetic and reading/kinaesthetic. Due to this combining of preferences and the need to communicate with a diverse group of team members and stakeholders at the same time, communication effectiveness can be vastly improved by considering all styles and preferences when developing presentations and written deliverables.

RESEARCH AND REFLECTION ACTIVITY

LEARNING PREFERENCES

Search online and find a questionnaire that determines your learning style.

1 Do the test – do you think it's accurate?
2 Consider interactions with family members and work colleagues – can you predict their learning styles?
3 Could you use some of the concepts from the VARK framework to improve communication outcomes with these people?

Managing communications

As mentioned at the beginning of the chapter, managing communications covers all the activities required to create, collect, distribute, store, retrieve and dispose of project information as per the processes and procedures laid out in the project communication plan. Some of the activities which are executed as part of project communications management are outlined below:

- ***Establishment and enforcement of project documentation management procedures***. This is a critical and complex set of project administrative activities which is often overlooked. It involves the set-up and maintenance of electronic and hardcopy project files for the classification and storage of deliverables, as well as the important (and often overlooked) concept of document naming conventions and version control.

- *Creation and distribution of communication deliverables as per the project communications management plan.* This is complex and time consuming and will often require the dedication of substantial portions of the project manager's time or a dedicated project communications resource.
- *Creation and distribution of project status reports and other work performance information.* This is another critical activity that is covered in more detail later in this chapter.
- *Communication and distribution of change control deliverables and outcomes for change requests that have been approved or rejected.* This involves ensuring that all affected project team members and stakeholders receive new versions of, and major updates to, requirements documentation and scope baselines, project schedules and project financials.
- *Management and distribution of communication with external parties*, such as external stakeholders (government bodies, partner organisations, regulators, unions, industry bodies, the media and general public) who are interested in, or impacted by, the project, as well as vendors who have been selected to fulfil procurement requirements.

Communication methods

There are three primary communication methods that can be used to share and distribute information to project teams and stakeholders.

1 *Interactive communications:* generally the most effective and involve multidirectional interaction between the communicating parties. It is the most efficient way to ensure a common understanding but may not always be feasible or indeed preferred by all stakeholders. Examples include meetings, phone calls, teleconferences, video conferences, instant messaging and so on.

2 *Push communications:* one-way communications that are sent to specific recipients who require the information or message. The information is distributed but this doesn't ensure that it was actually received or correctly understood. These can be more efficient as less time is required than for interactive methods, but less effective as correct meaning is not reviewed. Examples include emails, memos, letters, reports, faxes, voicemails, press releases, newsletters and blogs.

3 *Pull communications:* self-service style communications used for large volumes of information or to provide access to many unknown stakeholders. They are the most efficient in terms of time but the least effective in terms of establishing meaning. Recipients and interested parties access the communication content at their own discretion. Examples include intranet and internet websites, elearning, lessons-learned databases, newsletters, knowledge repositories and communication repositories.

The selection of the most appropriate communication method can greatly increase the effectiveness of communication activities for different stakeholder groups. It is useful to consider different communication methods in terms of the power and interests of different project stakeholders. Figure 12.5 is a stakeholder power and interest grid that shows the

FIGURE 12.5 STAKEHOLDERS AND COMMUNICATION METHODS

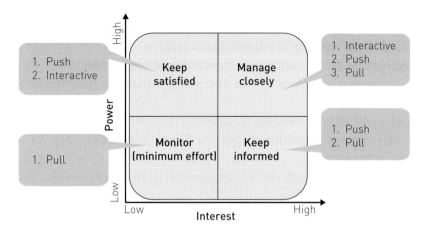

Source: Project Management Institute, *A guide to the Project Management Body of Knowledge*, (PMBOK® Guide), p. 397. Project Management Institute, Inc 2013. Copyright and all rights reserved. Material from this publication has been reproduced with the permission of PMI.

different communication methods that can be applied to stakeholder groups with different characteristics.

Consider stakeholders with the highest power and interest. They will have the biggest impact on the success of the project and their communication needs must be given priority. More time and effort can be spent on developing and reinforcing communications for this audience. Therefore, many of their communications will be interactive with push and pull mechanisms being used less frequently but still undertaken to cater for different preferences within this group.

The needs of stakeholders with the lowest power but high interest can often be adequately met by focusing on carefully constructed pull mechanisms and providing lots of information for them to select based on their areas of specific interest. This is efficient in terms of time allocation but can result in reactive communication measures when messages are incorrectly interpreted and escalated.

Communication channels and media

There are too many different communication channels and media to review them all. What is important is to use a variety of different channels and media while taking into consideration the culture of the organisation and the preferences of important stakeholder groups. The style and tone of the writing can range from informal to formal and from technically complex to plain English, and the channel, for example, can be from a podcast to a printed newsletter.

Below are some tips for selecting communication channels and media:
- Determine the detailed communication requirements of the major project stakeholders.
- Undertake detailed planning for project management communication activities and stakeholder management communication activities.

- Communicate according to the preferences of major stakeholders and not according to your own personal preferences.
- Cater for a wide variety of personalities and learning styles when creating communication deliverables and when selecting the distribution medium.
- Consider organisational communication standards and procedures.
- Focus the communication efforts on the stakeholders that can have the greatest influence on project success.
- Reinforce and repeat critical messages via different channels and media.
- Tailor the selection of communication mediums and technology to the technical sophistication of the audience.
- Tailor the language and complexity of the content to the backgrounds and needs of the audience.
- Consider communication deliverables and activities before finalising the project scope, time and cost baselines to ensure sufficient resourcing and funding is available to communicate effectively.
- Remember that poor project communications is one of the major factors contributing to project failure.

Barriers to effective communication

There are innumerable barriers to effective communication. Being aware of these when developing the project communication plan can improve communication outcomes. It is also important to reconsider them regularly and especially after less than effective communication outcomes occur. The barriers can be summarised into seven major categories which are discussed briefly below.

1 **Language barriers:** different languages, vocabularies, accents and dialects, as well as semantic gaps (words having similar pronunciation but multiple meanings, or different words with the same meaning). Difficulty can also be encountered with poorly expressed messages, incorrect interpretation, difficult technical terms and unqualified assumptions.

2 **Cultural barriers:** can create boundaries and separate people from each other in such a way as to prevent understanding. These include differing backgrounds, religious beliefs, cultural protocols, culturally specific body language and expressions.

3 **Individual barriers:** often expressed as individual prejudices and learned behaviours from previous experience. These include factors such as gender, age, religion, ethnic background, socioeconomic status, attractiveness, politics, education, etc. They are specific to an individual and can be very difficult to identify and to overcome.

4 **Organisational barriers:** are the result of the organisational culture, values, protocols, rules, regulations, accepted norms and behaviours and can include physical barriers such as team location, physical set-up of work stations, access to communication tools and working facilities.

5 ***Interpersonal barriers:*** are generally created by a lack of awareness of things such as non-verbal clues, body language, gestures, postures and eye contact. Other barriers involve a lack of empathy and inability to build rapport which can lead to a lack of trust.

6 ***Attitudinal barriers:*** often result from limitations in physical and mental ability, and differences in intellect, understanding and perceptions which can lead to a lack of trust and fear of consequences.

7 ***Channel barriers:*** often results from an inappropriate selection of communication channel and/or inappropriately structured messages; e.g. too long, no summary, no clear outcome and a lack of access. This affects the clarity, accuracy and effectiveness of the message.

Controlling communications

The notion of controlling project communication is relatively new and relates to the monitoring and controlling of communications throughout the project lifecycle to ensure the information needs of the project team and project stakeholders are met. It requires adjustments to the project communications plan as additional requirements for communication emerge or communication is undertaken with less than desired outcomes, perhaps requiring repetition or additional or supporting communications.

The primary inputs that are monitored to determine if adjustments to the communication deliverables and activities are required are:
- status of communication deliverables
- effectiveness of communication deliverables and messages
- cost and time allocations
- issues that can be resolved via more or different communication
- project performance data for inclusion in status reporting.

The major outputs of this process are communication activities associated with project status reports and change control.

Reporting on project performance

The project performance reporting process is often referred to as *status reporting*. It involves periodically collecting and analysing actual project performance data against the baselines of scope, cost and time in order to communicate project progress.

As mentioned in Chapter 4, it is critical to establish expectations and processes for both the collection of performance data and the reporting of overall project status in the PMP.

The major reason for status reporting is to manage the expectations of the project sponsor and key project stakeholders. They also help to keep the project team focussed on progress. Performance information such as actual time spent on activities, actual costs and re-forecasts are critical to the production of the status report.

REAL-WORLD EXPERIENCE

ESTABLISHING EXPECTATIONS

In my experience, project team members (including myself) will not willingly track their time on specific deliverables, nor enter timesheets, if they are not specifically required to do so.

Status reporting and establishing expectations

I vividly recall a conversation I had with an extremely experienced project manager who worked for me and who was also completing a Masters in Project Management. He was advocating that project status reports were unnecessary and a waste of time as no one read them and they took far too long to produce. In his opinion, the time that he needed to devote to the production of the status report could be put to better use in the production of deliverables for the project.

I explained to him that as a project management professional, I consider project status reports to be a valuable and mandatory deliverable and that he would suffer poor performance ratings while he worked for me if he didn't provide these each week. I further explained to him that the actual status report took around 15 minutes to physically produce and the half a day that he thought it took was actually the fulfilment of the vital project management responsibility called monitoring and controlling the project. I also promised that I would read his status report every week. Needless to say, he went on to produce status reports with no complaint from then on. And even though he no longer works for me, I know that he continues to do this and that he often uses my explanation to counter the grumbles that he receives from other project managers who are less than enthusiastic about producing status reports.

Project status reports normally contain some combination of the following information:
- project name and description
- project manager and project sponsor contact details
- status reporting period
- overall status indicator – often red, amber or green flags
- summary baseline information – planned budget and planned completion date
- milestone list with planned versus actual start dates, planned versus actual/forecast end dates and percentages completed
- major activities and deliverables completed last period
- major activities and deliverables due for completion next period
- current budget position – planned, actual to date, forecast at completion, variances
- explanation of any variance
- major risks or issues being managed
- new change requests raised and approved.

The project status report is often the only deliverable that many stakeholders will see from a project. Therefore, it also fulfils the purpose of promoting the project. If it is poorly formatted, difficult to understand or contains spelling or grammatical errors, then many stakeholders will unfairly assume that the project is sloppy and poorly run. It is critical to ensure that it is well formatted, clear and accurate.

It also helps to avoid the use of acronyms and abbreviations as these can be frustrating for casual readers who are not close enough to the project to remember the meaning of these from one reporting period to the next.

Another recommendation is to seriously consider the development of different status reports for different stakeholder groups. Good practice indicates that the project team and project sponsor will benefit from receipt of a detailed status report each week. Other project stakeholders, such as the steering committee, may only require a summary status report on a monthly basis.

One last tip is that the status report should include both good and bad news; for some reason many project managers are tempted to only include the bad news in their status reports. Ensure that all the positive achievements are clearly documented and reported.

Status reporting templates are available online

FIGURE 12.6 STATUS REPORT EXAMPLES

Source: © 2013 Microsoft.

Change control communication processes

Communication activities are critical to the success of the integrated change control processes for any project. The performance of integrated change control is the process of reviewing all change requests that have been identified by the monitoring and controlling of project work, as well as approving or rejecting changes and managing the flow-on impacts on all project deliverables and all components of the project management plan (PMP). If communication is not done effectively, then situations can result where approved change requests are not undertaken by all parties, which can dramatically affect project outcomes.

REAL-WORLD EXPERIENCE

THE IMPORTANCE OF DOCUMENT VERSION CONTROL AND COMMUNICATING CHANGE REQUESTS

The maintenance of strict version control and the distribution of the correct versions of detailed design specifications (part of scoping documentation) is extremely important in the construction industry. Can you imagine the chaos if different companies undertaking interrelated activities in the construction of a major building project had different versions of the detailed design specifications?

I have experienced many small-scale issues in the development and implementation of IT systems as a result of poor communication of change requests and poor version control requirements. But the most recent case involved an $80 million internal office fit-out. One critical objective of the project was to reduce hardcopy storage requirements for the firm by a minimum of 30 per cent in order to reduce demand for an additional floor and to reduce storage requirements. Aside from the obvious culling and electronic conversion activities that were planned, it was decided to convert all hardcopy files from upright A4 lever arch files to lateral A4 files. This meant that in the same floor space footprint, we could get an additional 25 per cent storage capacity out of the storage units, which would provide room for expansion in the future. About mid-way through the project, the storage reduction initiative was so successful that reductions of 50 per cent were now being predicted and it was decided to reduce the height of the storage units in-between the banks of desks to cater for three shelves of shelf lateral storage rather than three shelves of upright storage. This dropped the height of the cabinets by around 30 centimetres and improved sight lines and light distribution to the central areas on each floor. It had an added benefit of reducing the overall cost of the storage cabinets as well. The change request was submitted to the steering committee and approved and the detailed design specifications for the cabinets were duly updated by the interior architects. Unfortunately, when the cabinets were delivered they were as per the original specification as somehow the external manufacturer had not been informed of the change or was simply working off an incorrect version of the specifications.

The following communication activities are required to support the effective implementation of change control processes:

- ensuring that all project team members and project stakeholders involved in governance activities understand, and agree to follow, the change control process
- influencing stakeholders and the project team to ensure only approved changes are implemented
- communicating and coordinating the outcomes of change request analysis and approval or rejection decisions to all affected parties.

Related processes from the PMBOK® Guide

4.2 **Develop project management plan (planning):** This is the process of defining and documenting the actions necessary to prepare and integrate all subsidiary plans for each of the other key knowledge areas of project management. The PMP is the primary deliverable from the planning phase. Good practice dictates that the PMP is baselined at the end of the planning phase, particularly in the areas of scope, cost and time. It is progressively added to during project execution via the perform integrated change control process.

   The planning for all the key knowledge areas is normally performed at the same time as this process, or expanded upon shortly afterwards. All key knowledge areas have discrete processes for planning that are defined in their process groups.

   This process is closely linked to '8.1 Plan quality management', '9.1 Plan human resource management', '10.1 Plan communications management', '11.1 Plan risk management' and '12.1 Plan procurement management'.

4.3 **Direct and manage project work (execution):** The process of performing the work defined in the PMP in order to achieve the project's objectives. The project manager directs the execution of the planned activities, sometimes with the assistance of a project management team for larger projects. The PMBOK® Guide includes this process within the execution phase but there is merit in thinking of it as a separate process group having equal importance to monitoring and controlling.

4.4 **Monitor and control project work (monitoring and controlling):** The process of tracking, reviewing and regulating the progress made towards the objectives defined in the PMP. The project manager is specifically responsible for the monitoring and control of project work, sometimes with the assistance of a project management team or project management office for larger projects. Monitoring is an aspect of project management performed throughout the project, but it becomes more critical during the execution phase. It is closely linked to '5.6 Control scope', '6.7 Control schedule', '7.4 Control costs', '8.3 Quality control', '10.3 Control communications' and '11.6 Control risks'.

4.5 ***Perform integrated change control (monitoring and controlling):*** The process of reviewing all change requests, including approving or rejecting changes and managing the flow-on impacts on all project deliverables and all components of the PMP. All requested changes should be identified through '5.6 Control scope'. The activities within this process are critical to managing stakeholder expectations and to ensuring the highest chance of project success. They occur from project inception through to completion and are part of the monitor and control process group. It is important that only approved changes be incorporated into the project, as it is surprisingly common to see unapproved changes being inadvertently undertaken.

9.4 ***Manage project team (execution):*** The process for tracking team member performance, providing feedback, resolving issues and managing changes to improve team performance. This requires the skills of influencing team behaviour, managing conflict, resolving issues and managing team member performance appraisals.

13.1 ***Identify stakeholders (initiation):*** The process for identifying the people, groups and organisations that are interested in, or impacted by, the project. They could in turn affect the outcomes of the project depending on their relative power. Their interests and influence is critical to project success.

13.2 ***Plan stakeholder management (execution):*** The process of developing management strategies to engage stakeholders throughout the project lifecycle in order to satisfy their needs and improve the chances of project success.

13.3 ***Manage stakeholder engagement (execution):*** The process for communicating and working with stakeholders to meet their needs and manage their expectations. This includes change management activities such as training, communication and engagement.

CHAPTER SUMMARY

» Project communication focuses on the communication requirements of the project team, project sponsor and key stakeholders involved in project governance.

» Some of the primary activities performed include the establishment and enforcement of project documentation management procedures, creation and distribution of communication deliverables, creation and distribution of project status reports, communication and distribution of change control deliverables and outcomes, and management and distribution of communication with external parties.

» The communication and engagement requirements of other project stakeholders are analysed as part of the Project Stakeholder Management key knowledge area; their communication requirements are fulfilled via the project communication plan, but they may have other requirements in addition to this; e.g. training, change management and engagement activities.

» Effective communication enhances project success by creating understanding within the project team and also between diverse sets of project stakeholders. Poor project communication is one of the most common causes of project failure.

» Effective communication is the transferring and understanding of meaning. For communication to be effective, it is important to understand how the people you are interacting with have interpreted your message.

» Active listening is a critical skill that helps to ensure that you have accurately understood the meaning and needs of team members and stakeholders. The key components are focusing fully on the speaker, taking notes, testing your understanding, avoiding interrupting or redirecting the conversation, showing interest, recapping and summarising.

» There are three primary communication methods: push, pull and interactive. Interactive communication is always more effective but may not be possible given the location of the participants. It is also the most time consuming so it is mostly used for the primary stakeholders with the highest power and interest in the project.

» There are many barriers to effective communication. The most common are language, cultural, individual, organisational, interpersonal, attitudinal and channel barriers.

» The project performance reporting process is often referred to as status reporting. It involves periodically collecting and analysing actual project performance data against the baselines of scope, cost and time, in order to communicate project progress.

» Document management procedures and standards are a core component of project communications.

REVISION QUESTIONS

Revision questions are divided into two sections. The first covers Certificate IV understanding and the second covers Diploma-level understanding. Both sections are relevant to Diploma students and teachers, while only the first section is relevant to Certificate students and teachers.

Certificate IV of Project Management

These questions relate to the performance criteria stated in 'BSBPMG414A Apply project information management and communications techniques'.

1   What communication is required for project team members?
2   What is the project steering committee?
3   What is the project sponsor?
4   What are the components of the project communication plan?
5   What is a project status report?
6   What is the primary function of a status report?
7   How are project control logs used to support communication activities?
8   What primary communication methods are used to distribute communication?
9   How are communication activities monitored?

BSBPMG414A and
BSBPMG515A
performance
criteria questions

Diploma of Project Management

These questions relate to the performance criteria stated in 'BSBPMG516A Manage project information and communications'.

1   What is effective communication?
2   Why is communication so important to project success?
3   What are the components of the project communication plan?

BSBPMG516A
performance
criteria questions

4   What impact can project communication planning have on the scope, time and cost baselines?

5   How are project communication requirements different to stakeholder communication requirements?

6   What techniques can be used to determine communication requirements?

7   What communication methods are more appropriate for different project stakeholders?

8   What are project governance processes?

9   What is generally included in the steering committee update?

10   How are change requests communicated?

11   What techniques can be used to manage project deliverables and information?

12   What communication activities are required to support change control?

DISCUSSION QUESTIONS

BSBPMG414A and BSBPMG516A performance criteria questions

1   What is the difference between a project team member and a stakeholder?

2   Are the project sponsor and project steering committee stakeholders or project team members?

3   How can you ensure the communication requirements of the project team members and the stakeholders are met?

4   Why is communication such a major contributing factor to project success or failure?

5   Why are the roles of the project sponsor and steering committee rarely understood?

6   Is communication as important as scope, time and cost management? Consider both sides of this question.

7   How can communication barriers be factored into communication planning?

8   What determines the selection of the communication medium or channel?

ONLINE RESOURCES

Visit the online companion website at http://www.cengagebrain.com to link to important additional resources, including templates, real-world case studies, revision quizzes and additional study material.

FURTHER READING AND REFERENCES

Caltrans Office of Project Management Process Improvement. (2007). *Project communication handbook* (2nd ed.). Sacramento, CA: author.

Clarke, N., & Howell, R. (2009). *Emotional intelligence and projects.* Newtown Square, PA: Project Management Institute.

Dunning, D. (1999). *Introduction to type and communication.* Mountain View, CA: CPP.

Flannes, S., & Levin, G. (2005). *Essential people skills for project managers.* Vienna, VA: Management Concepts.

Jha, S. (2010). *The project manager's communication toolkit.* Boca Raton, FL: CRC Press.

Mehrabian, A., & Ferris, R. (1967). Inference of attitudes from non-verbal communication in two channels. *The Journal of Counselling Psychology, 31*, pp. 248–52.

Muller, R., &Turner, R. J. (2004). Communication and cooperation on projects between the project owner as principal and the project manager as agent. *European Management Journal, 21*(3), pp. 327–36.

Project Management Institute (PMI). (2013). *A guide to the Project Management Body of Knowledge* (PMBOK® Guide) (5th ed.). Newtown Square, PA. Chapter 10, pp. 297–308.

Project risk management

IN THIS CHAPTER YOU WILL:

1 learn about the specific processes, tools and techniques and major deliverables related to the key knowledge area of Project Risk Management

2 become familiar with the processes for project risk management and the creation of the risk register and risk action plans

3 understand the importance of identifying project risks and analysing them for their potential negative impacts

4 learn about different approaches to analysing risks including qualitative and quantitative approaches

5 learn about different approaches to treating and managing risks to reduce their impact

6 appreciate different risk rating tools and how beneficial these are to the prioritisation of risks for treatment

7 understand key concepts such as likelihood and impact, probability and consequences

8 understand the activities required to monitor and control project risks.

Context

The PMBOK® Guide defines a project risk as 'an uncertain event or condition that, if it occurs, will have a positive or negative effect on a project's objectives' (PMI, 2013, p. 559).

The risk management profession likes to think of the concept of positive risk, in that uncertain events may have either a positive or negative influence on a project. Most people automatically associate risk with negative outcomes. For example, one definition of risk is:

1 exposure to the chance of injury or loss, and
2 insurance –
    a the hazard or chance of loss
    b the degree of probability of such loss
    c the amount that the insurance company may lose.

Source: http://www.dictionary.com.

Risks can generally be defined and predicted at the beginning of a project and project risk management will decrease the probability of risks occurring, as well as any possible negative impacts on the project.

Risks that occur during a project can seriously impact time, cost, scope and quality. So the more thorough project managers identify, analyse and plan risk responses then the more chance there is of project success.

Characteristics of project risk

It is important for the project manager to clearly understand the characteristics of project risk, which can be summarised as:

- project risk is always in the future
- risks are uncertain events or conditions; if they occur they will have an impact (usually negative) on at least one project objective – scope, time, cost or quality
- good practice dictates that *all* assumptions documented in any of the planning processes are automatically placed into the risk log to enable effective monitoring and control
- project risk has its origins in the uncertainty present in all projects
- a project risk that has occurred can also be treated as an issue
- known risks are those that have been identified and analysed during project planning
- unknown risks may also occur during the project and for which no risk planning has been conducted
- for high-risk, large and complex projects a contingency is often added to cover responses to unexpected risks if they occur
- project sponsors, project managers and organisations will have different appetites for risk; these needs are to be taken into account when determining the contingency.

**See PMBOK®
Guide Figure 11-2**
Plan project risk
management:
inputs, tools and
techniques, and
outputs

**See PMBOK®
Guide Chapter 11**
Project risk
management

PMBOK® Guide processes for project risk management

The PMBOK® Guide processes for project risk management are:

11.1   Plan risk management

11.2   Identify risks

11.3   Perform qualitative risk analysis

11.4   Perform quantitative risk analysis

11.5   Plan risk responses

11.6   Control risks.

The following standards for risk management are very useful:

- Australian standard: AS/NZS ISO 31000:2009 Risk management – Principles and guidelines
- HB 436:2004 – Risk management guidelines companion to AS/NZS 4360:2004. Unfortunately, this has not been updated for the new standard which was issued in 2008. But it is still 100 per cent relevant today.
- US standard – Guide for applying the risk management framework to federal information systems: A security life cycle approach (NIST Special Publication 800-37, Revision 1)
- PMI standard – Practice standard for project risk management (2009).

FIGURE 13.1 PROJECT RISK MANAGEMENT – A PROCESS PERSPECTIVE

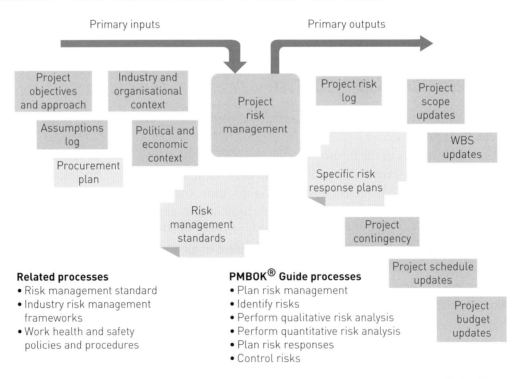

Source: Adapted from Project Management Institute, *A guide to the Project Management Body of Knowledge*, (PMBOK® Guide), fifth edition.

11.1   ***Plan risk management (planning):*** The process for defining how to conduct risk management activities for a project. This involves determining the risk management framework, including concepts such as the risk breakdown structure, likelihood and impact, and risk management approaches. Excellent international standards exist for risk management and many organisations have incorporated these into their own organisational processes.

11.2   ***Identify risks (planning):*** The process for identifying the risks that may impact the project. It is useful to have a broad group of key stakeholders, project team members and internal experts participate in the risk identification session. Good practice dictates that as far as possible all major risks should be identified during the planning phase, although this is an iterative process as often risks are unpredictable and new risks become obvious during execution.

11.3   ***Perform qualitative risk analysis (planning):*** The process for prioritising risks for further analysis or mitigating actions by assessing a combination of the likelihood and impact of each risk. Project success is improved if the major, or high-priority risks, are minimised or avoided.

11.4   ***Perform quantitative risk analysis (planning):*** The process for numerically analysing the impact of the high-priority risks. This is often done in terms of the cost and time impacts on the project if each risk occurred. These can then be added together to contribute to the assignment of contingency for the project.

11.5   ***Plan risk responses (planning):*** The process for developing risk management strategies that will reduce the impact of major risks on the project objectives and success criteria. Risks can be accepted, transferred, mitigated or avoided, and the specific actions selected should be in line with the priority and potential impact of the risk. The concept of the risk owner is applied to ensure that one person is accountable for enacting any risk management plans that may be required.

11.6   ***Control risks (monitoring and controlling):*** The process of monitoring the risks that have been determined during '11.2 Identify risks' to see if they have occurred, or if the likelihood and/or impact has changed. Any new risks can also be identified. Any risk that has occurred will require resolution via the execution of risk management activities that have been predetermined for the risk during '11.5 Plan risk responses'.

RESEARCH AND REFLECTION ACTIVITY

RISK MANAGEMENT STANDARDS

Take some time to locate the risk management policies and procedures of your organisation. Also review the Australian risk management standards and the companion handbook.

Are there specific standards, tools and templates that your organisation provides to assist project managers to plan for and identify risks?

Compare your organisation's risk management policies with the suggestions in the standard. How can they be improved?

Risk management roles and responsibilities

Both the project manager and the project sponsor have important roles to play in the management of risks. One of the primary responsibilities of a project manager is to monitor and control the project. This means they need to review the progress and status of the project regularly and make adjustments to ensure the project stays on track – risks and issues that occur during the project are the main reasons for slippage.

To reduce the impact of project risks, the project manager must:

- undertake an overall project risk assessment
- identify, monitor and control risks
- identify, monitor and control issues.

It is vital that:

- risks are identified during planning and monitored during execution
- risk response plans need to be ready for immediate implementation
- issues are logged, reviewed and resolved regularly
- risks and issues on critical path activities require urgent action as they can have the greatest impact on the project timeline
- the impacts of major risks and issues are communicated to the project sponsor and senior stakeholders in advance of them occurring.

The project sponsor and senior stakeholders also have key roles when it comes to project risks. They need to:

- participate in risk identification
- participate in risk management planning
- assist in both risk and issue resolution.

Unfortunately, they don't always realise that they need to contribute and the burden can often unfairly fall onto the project manager. One solution is to clearly define the expectations that the project has in regard to the project sponsor and senior stakeholders, including the steering committee if there is one.

REAL-WORLD EXPERIENCE

RISK APPETITE

When I was the Program Director for BT Super for Life I conducted weekly risks and issues meetings with all my project managers and the project management office (PMO). We reviewed the risk log to determine if any risks had occurred or changed materially, and discussed progress on any issue resolution. This was a very complex and high-risk program due to the following circumstances:

- there was a fixed timeframe due to regulatory changes
- this was the first new product developed by the organisation in over 10 years
- integration was required across more than 40 systems at BT and Westpac

- new leading edge software was being developed for online access to superannuation
- the software developers were using an Agile approach within a traditional waterfall IT shop and these two styles of software development do not always integrate successfully
- the software developers were offshore in India which created communication difficulties and delays
- two new back-end system platforms were being procured and implemented that had never been integrated before
- new back office support departments were being created
- this was the pilot for a new offshoring arrangement involving India for selected servicing processes
- the program manager was new to the organisation and all the project managers were recently hired contractors.

There were many high-priority risks and also many active issues. The project managers and myself were working positively through each review and were focused on actions that would reduce the impact of the risks. It was only a month or so into the program and the project sponsor was in a meeting. He was very dedicated to the program and (at least in the beginning) was in the habit of attending all project status meetings and all project risk and issue meetings. This meeting was generally a positive session, but towards the end of the meeting the project sponsor stood up in frustration and slammed his palms down on the table while admonishing all of us to be more positive. He then stormed out the meeting, much to the surprise of the group. My team of project management professionals were stunned by this outburst and resolved the issue by suggesting to the sponsor that he not attend these meetings in the future. He wanted me to cancel them but I explained that they were a critical component of monitoring and controlling the project and without them I would not be able to successfully deliver the program. He reluctantly agreed and continued to attend the status meetings each week but not the risk and issue meetings.

I learned that many project sponsors wish to avoid the concept of negative risk and that this will be dependent on their overall understanding of project management practices as well as their personal risk appetite.

Overall project risk assessment

PROJECT MANAGEMENT MASTERY

OVERALL PROJECT RISK ASSESSMENT

Detailed risk planning enhances the overall chances of project success and increases the visibility of the degree and types of risk inherent in a specific project.

Table 13.1 contains sample risk management questions that can be used to determine the overall risk rating of a project based on common characteristics. This is often useful during project initiation and also as an input into deciding the overarching contingency based on complexity and risk.

Project risk assessment template

TABLE 13.1 PROJECT RISK ASSESSMENT

	Characteristics	Low impact	Medium impact	High impact
Project scope				
A1	The scope of the project is ...	Well defined and understood	Somewhat defined, but subject to change	Poorly defined and/or likely to change
A2	All cooperating agencies and organisations are ...	Identified and committed	Identified and not committed	Unknown
A3.	Historical information, lessons learned and similar past projects are ...	Extensive	Limited	Not available
A4.	Environmental constraints ...	Not applicable	Environmental assessment	Environmental impact statement
Project schedule				
B1.	Are the project's major milestones ...	Flexible – may be established by the project team	Firm – pre-established	Fixed – pre-established by a specific commitment or legal requirement and beyond the team's control
B2.	The total estimated effort hours are ...	Less than 2000	Between 2000 and 5000	Greater than 5000
B3.	Project duration is estimated at ...	Less than two years	Two to four years	Greater than four years
Project budget				
C1.	The project budget is based upon ...	Top-down estimating based on the WBS and analogous or parametric estimating techniques	Top-down estimating based on the WBS	Informal methods or techniques
C2.	This type of project ...	Is undertaken regularly by the organisation and is almost predictable in terms of cost	Has been done at least once before or estimating data exists from similar external projects	Has never been done by the organisation before
Management support				
D1.	The project sponsor is ...	Identified, committed and experienced in project management techniques	Identified, committed and inexperienced in project management techniques	Not identified and not committed

	Characteristics	Low impact	Medium impact	High impact
D2.	The project is . . .	Aligned to organisational strategy and is considered a high priority	Aligned to organisational strategy and is considered a medium priority	Not aligned to organisational strategy or is considered a low priority
Project human resources				
E1.	The project manager's experience and training is . . .	Recent success in managing projects similar to this one	Recent success in managing a project not similar to this one or trained and no actual experience	No recent experience or project management training
E2.	The project team is . . .	Experienced in use of project management tools and techniques	Trained in the use of project management tools and techniques but has little or no practical experience	Has no formal training or practical experience in the use of project management tools and techniques
E3.	The project team is . . .	Located together	Located within the same city but at different buildings	Dispersed at multiple sites within the country and/or partially offshore
Other business or organisational impacts				
F1.	Processes, procedures and policies require . . .	Little or no change	Occasional to frequent changes	Substantial change
F2.	The number of functional areas the project will affect are . . .	1–4	4–6	6 or more
Technology				
G1.	The technology being utilised consists of . . .	Mature (existing design software, hardware, languages, databases or tools)	Emerging (but some past experience with design, software, hardware, etc.)	Leading edge (new design software, hardware, languages, databases or tools)
G2.	The technical requirements for this project are . . .	Similar to others already installed	Upgrades to existing software or new and simple	New and complex
Vendor engagement				
H1.	Vendors are required and committed to the project . . .	No vendors are required	One to two vendors are required and there is past experience working with them on similar deliverables	More than two vendors are required and/or there is no experience working with some of the vendors

Source: US Department of Transportation. (2013). *Risk and opportunity management plan* (revised July 23). Lakewood: CO: Central Federal Lands Highway Division, pp. 1–3

Developing the risk management plan

As mentioned in Chapter 3, the risk management plan documents the processes, tools and procedures that will be used to manage and control risks that may have a negative impact on a project. It typically includes:

- risk identification and categorisation processes
- risk likelihood and impact assessment processes
- risk management approaches
- a specific risk plan for high-priority risks
- risk monitoring and controlling processes
- relevant risk standards and methodologies
- a template and processes for compiling the project risk register or risk log
- a template and processes for developing and recording risk response plans or risk action plans for specific, high-priority risks
- overall project risk assessment.

Basic risk log template

It is common practice to present the information for each risk in the form of a table. These can be quite lengthy for large or complex projects and this is why they are often developed as a subsidiary plan, rather than being included in the main body of the PMP.

FIGURE 13.2 BASIC RISK LOG

Risk ID	Risk category	Risk description	Risk owner	Likelihood	Impact	Risk rating	Management /mitigation strategies	Residual likelihood	Residual impact	Residual rating	Status	Priority
❶	❷	❸	❹	❺	❻	❼	❽	❾	❿	⓫	⓬	⓭

❶
- Can be as simple as a number
- May relate to the risk category
- Used as a unique identifier
- May be an internal standard

❷
- Can be taken from industry frameworks
- Can be set at internal standards
- May need to be developed/tailored
- Ensures identification of all risks
- Assists with monitoring and control

❸
- Plain English explanation of the risk
- One to two sentences in length
- Ensures common understanding

❹
- A specific person or role
- Ensures clear ownership of the risk
- Responsible for monitoring and control

❺
- Probability of the risk occurring
- Typically defined in a risk rating matrix
- Has both a number scale and definition
- Requires judgement and prediction
- More accurate if can leverage lessons learnt

❻
- Consequences of the risk occurring
- Impacts one or more project objectives
- Includes scope, time, cost and quality
- Has both a number scale and definition
- Requires judgement and prediction
- More accurate if can leverage lesson learnt

❼
- Combines likelihood and impact
- Normally multiplied together
- Enables overall prioritisation of risks

❽
- **Avoid** – remove entirely
- **Mitigate** – reduce likelihood or impact
- **Accept** – normally for LOW risks
- **Transfer** – to another party; e.g., contract or outsource

❾
- Probability of risk occurring after management or mitigation actions

❿
- Impact of risk occurring after management or mitigation actions

⓫
- Revised risk rating
- Most important for risk monitoring

⓬
- Typically RED, GREEN, AMBER

⓭
- Typically HIGH, MEDIUM, LOW

Source: The Northern Sydney Institute, Part of TAFE NSW.

Inputs into the development of the risk management plan are:

- project scope statement
- project planning assumptions
- project budgeting assumptions
- cost management plan
- schedule management plan
- communications management plan
- enterprise environmental factors
- organisational process assets, such as:
  - » risk management standards
  - » risk management policies and procedures
  - » risk categories and definitions
  - » standard templates
  - » lessons learned from previous projects
- stakeholder registers.

Identifying risks

Risk identification is the process of determining which risks may affect the project and documenting their characteristics. While it is best practice to identify as many risks as possible during the planning phase, the process is in fact iterative and continues all the way through to project closure as new risks may evolve or become known during project execution.

The more comprehensive the risk identification process and risk mitigation activities then the greater the chance of project success. It is important to approach risk identification as a positive activity; the more risks that can be predicted and managed then the lower the likelihood of negative impacts on the project that will erode project outcomes.

It is recommended that a broad range of stakeholders participate in risk identification activities. These can include:

- project manager
- project team members
- project sponsor
- key stakeholders
- risk management experts
- PMO representatives
- subject matter experts
- other project managers
- internal clients
- external clients (on occasion).

There is a vast array of inputs into the risk identification process, including:

- risk management plan
- activity cost estimates
- activity duration estimates
- scope baseline
- stakeholder register
- cost management plan
- schedule management plan
- quality management plan
- project documents such as:
  - » assumptions log
  - » work performance reports
  - » requirements
- enterprise environmental factors:
  - » research and publications
  - » external risk management standards
  - » checklists and benchmarks
  - » industry studies
  - » risk attitudes
- organisational process assets such as:
  - » project files
  - » risk management templates
  - » lessons learned
  - » standard risk categories.

Risk breakdown structure

One of the most important risk identification techniques is to start with standard risk categories. These are normally contained in a risk breakdown structure (RBS) and help to ensure that all aspects of risk on a project are considered. Standard risk categories can be difficult to find and it is recommended to start with the key knowledge areas from the PMBOK® Guide, as well as any applicable industry frameworks.

The PMBOK® Guide has a standard risk breakdown structure that is a useful starting point. Figure 13.3 contains an example risk breakdown structure that has been adapted slightly from the PMBOK® Guide's standard risk breakdown structure.

The risk breakdown structure lists the categories and subcategories within which risks may arise for a typical project. Different risk breakdown structures will be appropriate for different types of projects, different organisations and different industries. The example in Figure 13.3 provides a good starting framework.

FIGURE 13.3 EXAMPLE RISK BREAKDOWN STRUCTURE

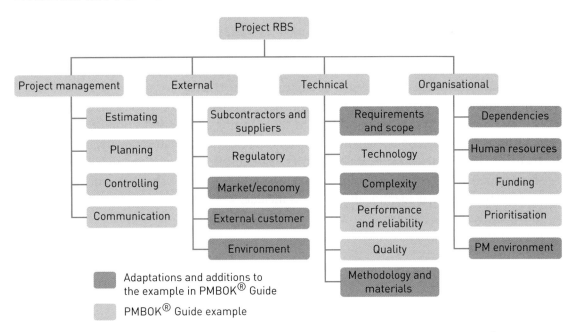

Source: Project Management Institute, *A guide to the Project Management Body of Knowledge*, (PMBOK® Guide), p. 280.
Project Management Institute, Inc 2010. Copyright and all rights reserved. Material from this publication has been
reproduced with the permission of PMI.

RESEARCH AND REFLECTION ACTIVITY

RISK CATEGORIES

See if there is a list of preferred risk categories or perhaps a risk breakdown structure within your
organisation. The PMO is a good starting point. If nothing exists to guide risk identification then
investigate risk categories that may exist within your industry, perhaps starting with industry
professional bodies.

Reflect on why it is often difficult to obtain standard risk categories and also on what can be
done to improve risk identification within your organisation and industry.

Other risk identification tools and techniques

This next section covers other common tools and techniques that can be used to improve the
identification of risks on projects.

- **Risk checklists and questionnaires:** many organisations and certain industries have
standard risk checklists and questionnaires that assist with the identification of the overall
risk on a project, as well as the specific risks that may be applicable.
- **Assumptions analysis:** any assumptions that have been documented during the planning
processes need to be analysed and included in the risk log. If any assumption does not prove

to be true there will be impacts on project objectives; therefore, the risk of assumptions proving untrue must be evaluated.

- **SWOT analysis:** a standard approach used to identify risks and opportunities during business planning and marketing activities which can also be applied to risk identification. It involves analysing an organisation's strengths, weaknesses, opportunities and threats. Weaknesses and threats may need to be captured in the risk log.
- **Expert judgement:** many organisations will have specialised risk management teams that can provide expert assistance to projects in the planning and identification of risks. In very risky projects, it may also be helpful to consult external subject matter experts.
- **Industry risk frameworks:** some industries, particularly construction and defence, have standard risk frameworks which are extremely helpful to project risk management.

The outputs of the risk identification process include:

- initial entries in the risk log
- list of identified risks
- potential risk owners
- lists of potential responses.

Figure 13.4 illustrates the columns which are typically completed in the risk log as a result of the risk identification process.

FIGURE 13.4 INCLUSIONS IN THE RISK LOG DURING RISK IDENTIFICATION

Source: The Northern Sydney Institute, Part of TAFE NSW.

The project manager is normally charged with the task of organising the risk identification and analysis sessions, as well as populating the risk log. As a result, many stakeholders can incorrectly assume that the project manager has complete responsibility for all project risks. It is good practice to ensure that the most appropriate stakeholder is assigned to own each risk. The best person to own a risk is the person who can undertake and control risk mitigation actions.

Risk analysis and prioritisation

There are two forms of risk analysis – qualitative risk analysis and quantitative risk analysis. Qualitative risk analysis considers the likelihood and consequences of risks in order to determine their priority based on the extent of the negative impact they may have on the project. Quantitative risk analysis involves estimating the measurable impact of a risk on project objectives, specifically cost, time, scope and quality.

Qualitative risk analysis is the most common type of analysis as it can be astonishingly accurate and requires less effort than quantitative risk analysis. Best practice requires that both analysis activities are undertaken and this will often occur concurrently, although qualitative risk analysis is often skipped altogether. A decision to skip qualitative risk analysis in itself can represent a substantial risk to the project, especially for large, complex projects where the organisation is inexperienced.

Qualitative risk analysis

The primary purpose of qualitative risk analysis is to determine the relative priority of all the project-related risks so that limited project resources can be focused on reducing the highest-priority risks. It is critical to establish definitions of the levels of probability and impact so as to provide a framework for the analysis and to reduce bias in the assessment.

The reduction of bias in this form of informal analysis comes from establishing criteria and definitions for the *likelihood* and *consequences* of each risk, but first it is important to understand that people commonly use these terms interchangeably.

> Likelihood = Probability

> Consequences = Impact

Likelihood represents the expected probability that a risk may occur, and consequences represent the possible impact of the risk on project outcomes if it does occur. There are two common scales for likelihood and consequences – a two-point rating scale versus a five-point rating scale. See Figures 13.5 and 13.6 overleaf.

The basic matrix in Figure 13.5 provides a two-point rating scale and can be used for most small, simple projects, or for those that are inherently very low risk. Sometimes using the more comprehensive five-point rating scale seen in Figure 13.6 can overburden a small, simple project with administration.

Figure 13.6 is an adapted version of the standard risk likelihood and consequences scales depicted in the *Risk management companion – handbook HB4360*. It is often necessary to adapt standard risk-rating scales to the boundaries and context of each particular project.

FIGURE 13.5 BASIC RISK ANALYSIS MATRIX

Low risk	Green	Business as usual	Acceptence
Medium risk	Amber	Heightened action	Monitor closely
High risk	Red	Immediate action	Mitigate or avoid

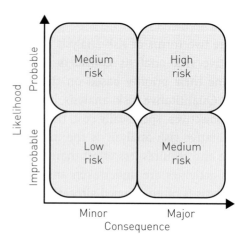

Source: Reproduced with permission from SAI Global under License 1311-c049.

FIGURE 13.6 STANDARD RISK LIKELIHOOD AND CONSEQUENCES SCALE

Likelihood scale

Rating	Definition	Scale
Almost certain	Will definitely occur or will occur on an annual cycle	5
Likely	Similiar events have been experienced several times during the project	4
Possible	May occur once during the project	3
Unlikely	Occurs from time to time	2
Rare	Occurrence is possible but highly unlikely	1

Consequences scale

Rating	Definition	Scale
Severe	Most objectives cannot be met	5
Major	Some important objectives cannot be met	4
Moderate	Some objectives impacted but may still be met	3
Minor	Minor effects that can be remedied	2
Negligible	Almost no impact on objectives	1

Source: Reproduced with permission from SAI Global under License 1311-c049.

This risk rating matrix shown in Figure 13.7 is fairly standard and is used to combine the effects of the consequences and likelihood ratings into an overall assessment of risk priority. The risks with the highest ratings have the potential to greatly impact project outcomes so more time and effort is directed towards the risk reduction activities for these risks. Risks with very low priority ratings will often be accepted, which means that no risk treatment activities are undertaken.

FIGURE 13.7 STANDARD RISK RATING MATRIX

Rating	Severe	Major	Moderate	Minor	Negligble
Almost Certain	Red 25	Red 20	Red 15	Amber 10	Green 5
Likely	Red 20	Red 16	Amber 12	Amber 8	Green 4
Possible	Red 15	Amber 12	Amber 9	Green 6	Green 3
Unlikely	Amber 10	Amber 8	Green 6	Green 4	Green 2
Rare	Green 5	Green 4	Green 3	Green 2	Green 1

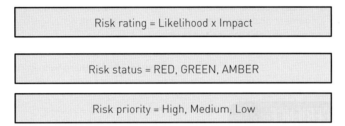

Risk rating = Likelihood x Impact

Risk status = RED, GREEN, AMBER

Risk priority = High, Medium, Low

Source: Reproduced with permission from SAI Global under License 1311-c049.

The inputs into qualitative risk analysis include:
- draft risk log
- risk management plan
- project scope statement
- organisational process assets:
  » risk management standards
  » risk management policies and procedures
  » risk categories and definitions
  » standard templates
  » lessons learned from previous projects
  » risk databases and checklists.

The outputs include:
- risk log updates
- likelihood and impacts
- prioritised list of project risks
- risks requiring response in near term
- risks requiring additional analysis and response planning
- risks grouped by categories
- root cause analysis
- watch lists of low-priority risks.

Figure 13.8 shows the columns of the risk register or risk log that are normally populated as a result of performing quantitative risk analysis.

FIGURE 13.8 INCLUSIONS IN RISK LOG DURING RISK ANALYSIS

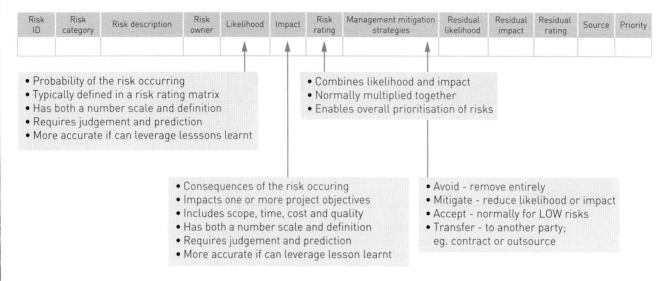

Risk ID	Risk category	Risk description	Risk owner	Likelihood	Impact	Risk rating	Management mitigation strategies	Residual likelihood	Residual impact	Residual rating	Source	Priority

- Probability of the risk occurring
- Typically defined in a risk rating matrix
- Has both a number scale and definition
- Requires judgement and prediction
- More accurate if can leverage lesssons learnt

- Combines likelihood and impact
- Normally multiplied together
- Enables overall prioritisation of risks

- Consequences of the risk occuring
- Impacts one or more project objectives
- Includes scope, time, cost and quality
- Has both a number scale and definition
- Requires judgement and prediction
- More accurate if can leverage lesson learnt

- Avoid - remove entirely
- Mitigate - reduce likelihood or impact
- Accept - normally for LOW risks
- Transfer - to another party; eg. contract or outsource

Source: The Northern Sydney Institute, Part of TAFE NSW.

REAL-WORLD EXPERIENCE

RISK IDENTIFICATION AND ANALYSIS WORKSHOP

In practice, many project managers will conduct a workshop with the project team, project sponsor, key stakeholders and subject matter experts in order to quickly identify and perform qualitative risk analysis. Figure 13.9 shows the toolkit and approach that I personally use when conducting a risk workshop for a project.

Reference to the complete risk workshop toolkit is available on the companion website

FIGURE 13.9 RISK WORKSHOP TOOLKIT

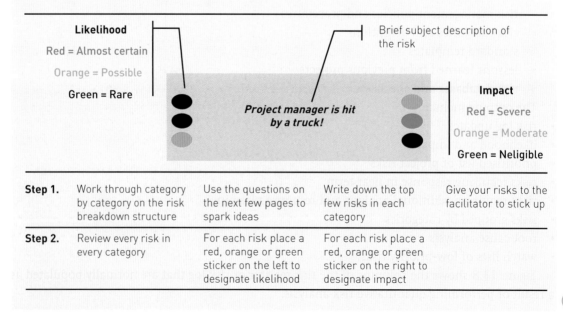

Step 1.	Work through category by category on the risk breakdown structure	Use the questions on the next few pages to spark ideas	Write down the top few risks in each category	Give your risks to the facilitator to stick up
Step 2.	Review every risk in every category	For each risk place a red, orange or green sticker on the left to designate likelihood	For each risk place a red, orange or green sticker on the right to designate impact	

I use brain storming techniques to identify the risks and then to conduct a quick analysis of the likelihood and consequences. This is extremely beneficial as it accelerates the completion of the project risk log and helps to engage the core team that is working on the project as well as critical stakeholders. The suggested steps are:

1 allow at least two hours for the workshop
2 set the framework for the session by sharing the risk breakdown structure, likelihood and consequences scales, and the risk rating matrix
3 have the risk breakdown structure highly visible and specific categories placed around the room
4 ask everyone to brain storm as many project risks as they can on large sticky notes
5 ask participants to organise their project risks under the relevant risk breakdown structure category and to de-duplicate them as they go
6 once the de-duplicated set of project risks has been established, hand out green, orange and red sticky dots to all participants
7 ask participants to place dots on either side of each project risk to indicate the likelihood (on the left-hand side) and the consequences (on the right-hand side).

After the workshop the project manager uses the sticky notes to populate the risk log and the average colour of the sticky notes to complete the likelihood and consequences columns.

Quantitative risk analysis

REAL-WORLD EXPERIENCE

ANALYSIS OF QUANTIFIABLE RISK IMPACTS

In practice, quantitative risk analysis is often omitted depending on the organisation's risk appetite and maturity of the project and risk management processes. It is typically only applied to risks with high priorities, as assessed during qualitative risk analysis, as these have the biggest potential impact on the project.

Estimates are often made, based on past experience, of the impact that a high-priority risk may have on scope, time, cost and quality. These are typically captured in specific risk response plans that can be executed if the risk does come to fruition.

The inputs to the quantitative risk analysis process include:
- draft risk register
- risk management plan
- cost management plan
- schedule management plan

- organisational process assets, such as:
  - » risk management standards
  - » risk management policies and procedures
  - » risk categories and definitions
  - » standard templates
  - » lessons learned from previous projects
  - » risk databases and checklists.

  The outputs of this process include:
- risk log updates
- probabilistic analysis of the project
- probability of achieving cost and time objectives
- prioritised list of quantified risks
- trends in risk analysis results.

QUANTITATIVE RISK ANALYSIS TOOLS AND TECHNIQUES

Most of the tools and techniques used in this process are more rigorous than those of qualitative analysis and are based on mathematical principles. This contributes to their lack of application.

- **Interviews and expert judgement:** these techniques are normally done together and draw on the experience of experts as well as previously captured historical data to quantify the impacts of risks on project objectives. Often three-point data is gathered on pessimistic, likely and optimistic outcomes as they will impact the project budget, timeframe, etc. This technique quantifies an estimate of the cost and time impact required to manage or treat the risk should it occur.
- **Modelling and simulation:** uses a model of the project to simulate the outcomes of the project, including the impact of uncertain events such as risks. For cost risk analysis the simulation uses cost estimates. Similarly, for schedule risk analysis the simulation uses the schedule network diagram and duration estimates. This category covers a range of advanced techniques that require extensive data on past and similar projects, a high degree of statistical expertise and statistical software. Iterative simulations are typically performed using the Monte Carlo technique.
- **Expected monetary value analysis:** this is another advanced technique that is rarely used except for defence and scientific projects, such as space exploration. It specifically examines the impacts on project cost due to uncertain risk events and is normally used in conjunction with decision tree analysis.
- **Decision tree diagrams:** these can be used in conjunction with modelling and simulation and expected monetary value analysis, or can be prepared in a more informal manner. They enable the analysis of the cumulative impacts of decisions to take different paths through a project.

See PMBOK®
Guide Figure 11-16
Decision tree
diagram

PROJECT MANAGEMENT MASTERY

CALCULATING RISK VALUES AND CONTINGENCY

For high-risk, large and complex projects, a contingency is often added to cover responses to unexpected risks. In project management terms, contingency is defined as an amount of money or time that is added to an estimate to cover costs or timeframes that are indeterminable at present. These are often calculated based on the risk, complexity or level of uncertainty for a project.

This is a fairly simple qualitative analysis technique and is very useful in the determination of an appropriate project budget contingency. The steps are:

1 identify and prioritise project risks
2 select the risks with the most material impacts
3 estimate the cost to rectify the risk if it occurs
4 multiply the rectification cost for all high-priority risks by the likelihood of each risk occurring – it is critical that this is done in terms of a percentage.

This gives you a contingency value for each risk and the specific formula is:

risk contingency value = probability of the risk occurring × rectification cost of the risk

These individual risk contingency values can then be added together to give a good estimate of the budgetary contingency to be applied to the project using the following formula:

project budget contingency = sum of all risk contingency values

The same approach and formulae will also work when applied to the schedule impact of rectifying risks and will provide the following project schedule contingency:

risk contingency timeframe = probability of the risk occurring × rectification timeframe for the risk

project schedule contingency = sum of all risk contingency timeframes

Planning responses to specific risks

After all the project risks have been identified and analysed, the project manager and project sponsor need to determine how each risk will be managed. It also needs to be determined which risks will undergo specific risk response, or action, planning and which will not. It is typical to focus risk response planning on risks that fall into the high and upper end of the medium priority as per the selected risk-rating matrix. This rule of thumb can be flexible depending on the specific risk guidelines of the organisation and the personal risk appetite of the project manager and project sponsor.

Developing specific risk action plans involves the identification of options and the selection of actions to reduce the threat and impact of the risks. It includes the identification and assignment of one person to be the risk owner, as well as the selection of the best management or mitigation actions. These are normally determined by the risk owner (in conjunction with the project manager) who are also responsible for monitoring and controlling any risks that are assigned to them. Planned risk responses must be appropriate to the significance of the risk and be cost effective.

There are four standard approaches to risk response planning, as shown below.

Negative risks or threats	Positive risks or opportunities
1. Avoid 2. Transfer 3. Mitigate 4. Accept	1. Exploit 2. Share 3. Enhance 4. Accept

Risk avoidance

Risk avoidance involves removing a specific threat by eliminating the causes of the risk. This often involves changing the PMP to eliminate or bypass the risk entirely. This often requires extreme replanning or the inclusions of significant additional activities and deliverables. This approach is typically reserved for the highest-priority risks that are likely to have the largest detrimental impacts on project objectives.

REAL-WORLD EXPERIENCE ....

IT PROJECT RISKS

For example, there are constant technological breakthroughs and new versions of software products that project teams could use in the execution of major IT projects. Often, though, the risks associated with using an unfamiliar or leading edge tool can pose a major threat to project success. This explains why many IT projects specifically choose not to use the latest advancements in software development tools and technology. This is especially true if delivery dates are fixed.

Risk transference

Risk transference involves shifting some or all of the ownership of a risk to a third party and therefore also transferring the negative impact. It doesn't mean that the risk has been eliminated; it simply means that someone else is responsible for managing the consequences and likelihood.

Transferring a risk often involves some form of contractual arrangement between the organisation executing the project and the organisation taking on the risk management responsibility.

REAL–WORLD EXPERIENCE

IT PROJECT RISKS

Let's go back to our previous example of an IT project. Many IT projects will choose to outsource software development activities to third parties who specialise in the required software development tools. While this definitely transfers the software development risk, it creates other risks that must be managed by the project; for example, the risk that the third party may go out of business, the risk of unclear requirements leading to the delivery of software that is not 'fit for purpose', or that the third party's ethical and business practices do not align with those of the project or executing organisation.

REAL–WORLD EXPERIENCE

CONTRACTS IN THE CONSTRUCTION INDUSTRY

In the modern practice of project management, many components of projects are delivered by third parties under some form of contractual arrangement. In the construction industry in particular, the organisation commissioning the project will often seek to completely transfer risk by establishing fixed-price contracts with specialist construction companies. With fixed-price contracts, the vendor organisation is assuming all of the price risk. This means that they will have applied a generous amount of contingency before agreeing to the fixed price.

One of my recent experiences in managing an $80 million design and fit-out program entailed a guaranteed maximum-price contract with Lend Lease. Under this arrangement, once the guaranteed maximum price was set at the end of the detailed design phase (the indicative maximum price had been provided on the completion of earlier phases including concept and high-level design), this became the baseline for the ongoing performance of the contract. This was an excellent way to transfer risk to a third party and for that third party to also reduce their risk in assuming the responsibility. Under a guaranteed maximum price arrangement the two parties share any upside if the project is delivered below the guaranteed maximum price.

Risk mitigation

Risk mitigation strategies cover any actions that are taken in order to reduce the impacts of any risk. Mitigation activities can reduce the likelihood of a risk, the consequences of a risk, or both.

Taking early action to try to reduce the impacts of a risk is generally more effective than trying to rectify the situation once a risk has occurred. This is especially true for risks with medium- to high-risk priority ratings. Recall a principle from the chapter on project quality management – it is much cheaper and easier to repair a defect the earlier it is detected. This same principle applies to risk mitigation – the earlier a risk is treated, the less negative impact it will have.

REAL-WORLD EXPERIENCE

HUMAN RESOURCE RISKS

I have found that there is a common risk related to key subject matter experts that occurs on most projects. When there are certain key staff who are the only ones within an organisation to possess particular knowledge it can be a significant risk to rely on their skills and experience. The risk is that the key resource will leave and therefore the project is delayed while an appropriately skilled alternative resource is found. There are two approaches that I have successfully used to reduce the impact of this event:

1 the key team member is placed on a retention bonus that is only payable if they remain to the end of the project

2 secure an understudy who works closely with the key team member in order to absorb their skills and to reduce the impact if the key person decides to leave the project early.

In the above scenario, it can be difficult to obtain approval for either of the two risk mitigation approaches I suggested. In this case, there is often no choice but to accept the risk and then plan for the impacts if the key team member leaves the project prior to completion. It is still possible to plan the responses to a risk even if the decision is to simply accept the risk. Responses that I recommend in this situation are to secure an alternate expert from a consulting organisation at a premium or to look in the international and national market for an alternate expert who can be secured at a premium. The outcome of accepting this form of risk with no response planning would be a substantial delay to the project, depending on the specific expertise that is no longer available and the stage of project execution.

Risk acceptance

This risk response strategy involves passively accepting that the risk may occur and choosing not to mitigate or respond to it in any way. Risk acceptance is generally only recommended when the risks have a low-risk priority rating; that is, they are either extremely unlikely to occur or there is minimal negative impact if they do occur.

For these risks it would be wasteful of scarce project resources to undertake any form of risk management activity. It is critical, however, that these risks are included within the scope of risk monitoring activities in case the risk should increase in priority.

Risk response planning outputs and residual risk

The primary outputs of risk response planning are:

- risk register updates to include residual risk ratings
- risk owner assignments
- risk response plans or risk action plans documented for high-priority risks
- risk-related contract decisions and negotiations
- project schedule updates to include additional risk management deliverables and activities
- project budget updates to include the cost of additional activities, deliverables and risk contingency
- procurement management plan update to include risk transference requirements
- human resource assignment if additional team members are required to execute risk responses
- WBS to include additional risk-related deliverables.

PROJECT MANAGEMENT MASTERY

RESIDUAL RISK

The following is an extract from an article on inherent risk versus residual risk. The full text can be found at http://www.protecht.com.au.

Consider the following: You are hiring a car for a colleague and are considering whether to take out additional insurance to reduce the $3000 excess to $500. When considering the cost/benefit of this you need to consider the extent to which 'accident risk' is reduced against the cost of the insurance.

This requires an assessment of the degree to which 'accident risk' is reduced by the additional insurance.

Let's assume the following:

	Likelihood (L)	Consequence (C)	L×C
Inherent risk	1%	$3000	$30
Effect of insurance		($2500)	
Residual risk	1%	$500	$5
Reduction in risk			$25

If the insurance costs less than $25 we might consider it worthwhile.

As insurance is a remedial control; we have only reduced the consequence. However, is there an impact on likelihood that we have not considered? Consider how the hirer may drive the car when we do not take out the additional insurance – probably more like they drive their own car! This contrasts as to how they might drive the car if we take out the additional

There is a risk action plan template available on the companion website

assurance – like a hire car! This change of behaviour by the driver on the basis that there is now a financial safety net if things go wrong may lead to an increase in the likelihood.

Let's reassess our risk:

	Likelihood (L)	Consequence (C)	L×C
Inherent risk	1%	$3000	$30
Effect of insurance		($2500)	
Residual risk	9%	$500	$45
Increase in risk			$15

In this analysis, the increase in the likelihood from 1 per cent to 9 per cent more than offsets the reduction in consequence and the residual risk is now higher than inherent risk.

This example may be extreme in order to illustrate that it is possible for residual risk to be higher than inherent risk. However, the underlying question is simple: Can certain remedial controls lead to a change in behaviour that leads to an increase in likelihood of risk events and ultimately an overall higher cost to the organisation?

Source: An article written by David Tattam, Director and Founder of Protecht Pty Ltd. Protecht is a risk management training, advisory, services and software company. The full text version of the article 'Can residual risk be higher than inherent risk?' can be viewed at: http://www.protecht.eu/resources/articles/can-residual-risk-be-higher-than-inherent-risk.

FIGURE 13.10 INCLUSIONS IN RISK REGISTER AFTER RISK RESPONSE PLANNING

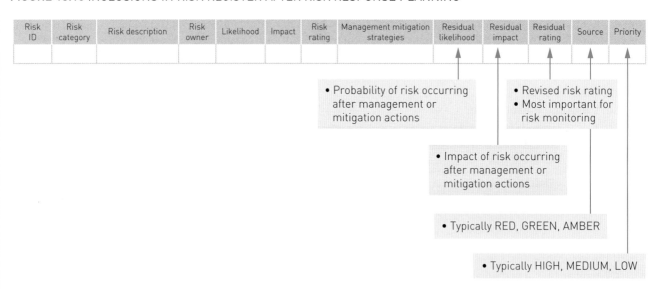

Source: The Northern Sydney Institute, Part of TAFE NSW.

Monitoring and controlling risks

This is the process of monitoring the risks that were determined during '11.2 Identify risks' to see if they have occurred or if the likelihood or impact has changed, and also to identify if any new risks have become apparent. Any risk that has occurred will require resolution via the execution of any risk management activities that have been predetermined for the risk during '11.5 Plan risk responses'.

Good practice dictates that the risks that have been captured in the risk log are reviewed on a weekly basis to determine:

- if project assumptions are still valid – any that are no longer valid need to be managed as risks to the project and will often result in a formal change request
- if a risk has changed in terms of its priority as calculated by combining an assessment of the likelihood and impact
- if a risk can be closed as it is no longer applicable due to the execution of risk management activities or a change in the project circumstances.

Any risk that has occurred should be copied into the project issue log and the specific risk management activities for that risk executed as a matter of urgency. Often this will involve a change request to be processed via '4.5 Perform integrated change control' due to the need for additional resources or time in order to execute risk response activities.

Risk monitoring and controlling tools and techniques

The following tools and techniques are commonly used by project managers, and often the PMO, to assist with the activities involved in monitoring and controlling risk.

- **Risk reassessment:** risk monitoring and control activities often result in the identification of new risks, reassessment of current risks and the closing of risks that no longer apply. Reassessment sessions need to be scheduled regularly and risk registers, status reports and risk action plans updated as a result.
- **Risk audits:** often performed by independent parties such as the PMO or internal risk department. These examine and document the effectiveness of risk responses.
- **Variance and trend analysis:** compares the planned results of risk responses to the actual outcomes to determine if the treatment of the risk yielded the expected impact reduction.
- **Reserve analysis:** compares the amount of risk reserves, or contingency, that remain at any point in time to determine if this is adequate based on the current risk ratings and expected cumulative impacts.
- **Status meetings:** project risk management activities and a review of the risk log should be on the agenda for all regular project status meetings.
- **Status reports:** risk ratings and trends should be included in project status reports for the high-priority risks.

RESEARCH AND REFLECTION ACTIVITY

PROJECT RISK MANAGEMENT

Take some time to reflect on the project risk management processes and examples of project failure that you have seen. How many of these failures were due to a major risk not being identified before happening, or were due to a failure to monitor and control project risks that were identified and stored in the risk log but never reviewed.

Conduct some online research into project risk management and read some interesting war stories by trying the following searches:

- project war stories
- project risk management stories.

REAL-WORLD EXPERIENCE

RISK MANAGEMENT FOR THE OLYMPICS

This is an edited extract from a blog post by Will Jennings – the full article can be found at the *Harvard Business Review*'s Blog Network website (http://blogs.hbr.org).

A lot of things didn't happen at the London Olympics in 2012. This was the result of extensive risk planning and risk management. Some of the things that didn't happen include a terrorist incident, a breakdown of the London rail system, power blackouts, volcanic ash clouds, flooding, an outbreak of infectious disease. The reason is that the London organising committee (LOCOG) and the International Olympic Committee (IOC) spent years thinking about every scenario they could imagine. Simulations of security incidents were rehearsed, and contingency plans for mass evacuations or emergency situations were put in place. Even so, there were numerous examples of incidents occurring that could have been avoided if more risk planning and management had been undertaken – for example, the transport workers strike and the much publicised failure to hire sufficient security staff.

Risk management is now at the heart of the governance model for the Olympic Games and the Olympics movement, and not only because of their growing scale and complexity. There is also the time horizon involved, which can be up to 20 years from the genesis of a host city's bid to the conclusion of the actual event. Long timelines mean greater vulnerability to emerging risks – that is, dangers with a large potential impact that are not well understood or easily quantified, or which emerge as the unanticipated result of disparate causal processes interacting. These risks can emanate from the realm of security, public health, natural ecology, technology or economics. In the run-up to the London 2012 Olympics, for example, the global financial crisis caused private developers for the Olympic Village project to withdraw, requiring a refinancing package backed by government.

Consider, too, that when threats materialise at large-scale events, the damage often spills over to other parties. Even before the official opening of London 2012, a mix-up with the flag for the North Korean women's football team had organisers scrambling to resolve a diplomatic spat. Other mega-events have sometimes taken their toll in business disruption, by interrupting supply chains, altering consumption, or giving rise to workforce absenteeism. The Olympics can bring a halt to 'business as usual' for the host government as well, as it diverts resources to support and police the event. Higher than normal volumes of population movements can create hazards for public health and cause traffic congestion. The influx of spectators offers a target for petty crime, and the symbolism of the Olympics presents a temptation for terrorists.

Managing risk involves a judicious mix of preventing the risks that can reasonably be controlled, learning to recognise the ones that can't be prevented, being prepared to react to limit damage, and having the resources to recover from the problems that do occur. Olympics organisers traditionally focused on reaction and recovery, using tools such as insurance (taken out for personal injury and property coverage), safety plans, and command and control structures. Since the 1980s, however, Games organising committees have increasingly invested in teams and systems dedicated to the management of risk through internal controls. Risk mitigation is now integrated into decision making and operations, and no longer treated as just an input into the calculation of insurance premiums.

Ensuring readiness for Games-time (in Olympic-speak) now involves strategic pre-emption through stress-testing and scenario planning. Table-top 'gaming' exercises at the top of the chain of command and practical training of personnel through rehearsals are routine across many of the diverse functions of Olympics operations. In the months leading up to London 2012, for example, visible military rehearsals were staged on the River Thames in addition to many test events performed on the main site. Ahead of Vancouver 2010, IT planning identified around 600 scenarios for rehearsals in a formal playbook which also documented procedures to follow in the event of an incident.

The rise of Olympics risk management is certainly evident at the level of the IOC, the guardian of the Games. It is understandably preoccupied with financial risk, since the event is effectively its only commercial asset, and with reputational risk, given that the Olympics 'halo' that derives from this is what makes that asset so valuable. Since the events of 9/11, the IOC has taken out insurance cover against event cancellation due to either terrorism or natural disaster (something which organising committees had done for many years before). More significantly, though, since the 1990s it has increasingly formalised its process of evaluation of bids and its monitoring of the readiness of preparations of host cities.

Olympics organisers and the IOC have wisely leveraged the business world's growing understanding of risk management. 'Risk-based' approaches to planning for the Vancouver 2010 Winter Olympics and the London 2012 Summer Olympics (confirmed through research interviews with senior officials) reveal the strong influence of the ideas and practice of risk management; for example, in the creation of risk registers (i.e. databases) and monitoring systems put in place to spot issues that pose potential dangers further down the line. The rise of Olympics risk management has touched not only on the most visible fields of finance and security, but a wide range of activities, such as in procurement and contract management, health and safety, the assessment of environmental impacts, and public health planning.

Source: Extract from the article: 'The Olympics as a Story of Risk Management' by Will Jennings, with permission Harvard Business Publishing.

Related processes from the PMBOK® Guide

4.4 *Monitor and control project work (monitoring and controlling):* The process of tracking, reviewing and regulating the progress made towards the objectives defined in the PMP. The project manager is specifically responsible for the monitoring and control of project work, sometimes with the assistance of a project management team or project management office for larger projects. Monitoring is an aspect of project management performed throughout the project, but it becomes more critical during the execution phase. It is closely linked to '5.6 Control scope', '6.7 Control schedule', '7.4 Control costs', '8.3 Quality control', '10.3 Control communications' and '11.6 Control risks'.

4.5 *Perform integrated change control (monitoring and controlling):* The process of reviewing all change requests, including approving or rejecting changes and managing the flow-on impacts on all project deliverables and all components of the PMP. All requested changes should be identified through '5.6 Control scope'. The activities within this process are critical to managing stakeholder expectations and to ensuring the highest chance of project success. They occur from project inception through to completion and are part of the monitor and control process group. It is important that only approved changes be incorporated into the project, as it is surprisingly common to see unapproved changes being inadvertently undertaken.

5.5 *Validate scope (monitoring and controlling):* The process of formal review and acceptance sign-off of completed project deliverables by the project sponsor and key stakeholders. Closely linked to '8.3 Control quality' and also to the successful completion of the project.

5.6 *Control scope (monitoring and controlling):* The process of monitoring the status of both the project and product scope. It focuses on managing any changes to the scope baseline and understanding the flow-on impacts on time, cost and quality via the related process '4.5 Perform integrated change control'.

6.7 *Control schedule (monitoring and controlling):* The process of monitoring the status of the project to update project progress and manage changes to the schedule baseline. It is closely linked to '4.5 Perform integrated change control' and '10.3 Control communications'. It is impossible to report on the progress of a project without first setting a baseline and then establishing processes and procedures for capturing work performance data along the way.

7.4 *Control costs (monitoring and controlling):* The process of monitoring the status of project expenditure. It involves updating the project budget with actuals, comparing performance against baseline and managing any changes. It is critical to monitor both the expenditure and the work performed for that expenditure. Any increase to the authorised budget can only be approved via '4.5 Perform integrated change control' and it is also closely linked to '10.3 Control communications'.

10.3 *Control communications (monitoring and controlling):* The process of collecting and distributing project performance and status information. This involves the periodic collection of actual performance data and comparing this against the planned baselines of the project. This enables the reporting of performance as well as reforecasting the future performance of the project.

CHAPTER SUMMARY

» Risks are uncertain events or conditions. If they occur they will have an impact (usually negative) on at least one project objective – scope, time, cost or quality.

» Project risk is always in the future. The more risks that are identified (and treated) at the beginning of the project then the more likely it is that the project will be successful.

» Many international, national and organisational standards exist to provide frameworks for project risk management. Unfortunately it is still a relatively weak area within project management due to the investment of time and resources that it requires and the natural tendency of many people to avoid thinking about possible negative outcomes.

» Good practice dictates that *all* assumptions documented in any of the planning processes are automatically placed into the risk log to enable effective monitoring and control.

» A project risk that has occurred can also be treated as an issue. Known risks are those that have been identified and analysed during project planning.

» Unknown risks may also occur during the project for which no risk planning has been conducted.

» For high-risk, large and complex projects a contingency is often added to cover responses to unexpected risks if they occur.

» Project sponsors, project managers and organisations will have different appetites for risk; these needs are to be taken into account when determining the contingency.

» One of the most important risk identification techniques is to start with standard risk categories. These are normally contained in a risk breakdown structure and help to ensure that all aspects of risk on a project are considered.

» Any assumptions that have been documented during the planning processes need to be analysed and included in the risk log. If any assumption does not prove to be true there will be impacts on project objectives so the risk of assumptions proving untrue must be evaluated.

» Qualitative risk analysis considers the likelihood and consequences of risks in order to determine their priority based on the extent of the negative impact they may have on the project. It is the most common type of analysis that is undertaken as it can be astonishingly accurate and requires less effort than quantitative risk analysis.

» Quantitative risk analysis involves estimating the measurable impact on project objectives, specifically cost, time, scope and quality.

» There are four standard approaches to risk response planning – avoid, transfer, mitigate and accept.

» It is important to monitor risks to determine if they have occurred, if the likelihood and impact has changed and to identify if any new risks have become apparent. Good practice dictates that the risks that have been captured in the risk log are reviewed on a weekly basis.

» Any risk that has occurred will require resolution via the execution of any risk management activities that have been predetermined for the risk.

» Any risk that has occurred should be copied into the project issue log and the specific risk management activities for that risk executed as a matter of urgency. Often this will involve the need for a change request.

REVISION QUESTIONS

Revision questions are divided into two sections. The first covers Certificate IV understanding and the second covers Diploma-level understanding. Both sections are relevant to Diploma students and teachers, while only the first section is relevant to Certificate students and teachers.

Certificate IV of Project Management

BSBPMG415A
performance
criteria questions

These questions relate to the performance criteria stated in 'BSBPMG415A Apply project risk management techniques'.

1   What is a project risk?
2   What is the purpose of the project risk log?
3   What are the typical contents of the project risk log?
4   What techniques can be used to identify project risks?
5   What is the purpose of the risk breakdown structure?
6   What are the primary risk analysis methods?
7   How is the project risk rating calculated?
8   How is the project risk rating used to determine the priority of the risk?
9   Which four specific treatment options can be applied to risks?
10   How often should risks be monitored?
11   What is risk contingency?

Diploma of Project Management

BSBPMG517A
performance
criteria questions

These questions relate to the performance criteria stated in 'BSBPMG517A Manage project risk'.

1   What is the difference between qualitative and quantitative risk analysis?
2   Who should be involved in the identification and prioritisation of project risks?
3   Who is responsible for managing risk on a project?
4   Who is responsible for managing specific risks and executing risk response/action plans?
5   What is residual risk and how is it calculated?
6   How can risk contingency be quantified?
7   How are the most appropriate risk treatment options determined?
8   Which of the four risk responses is the most difficult to implement and why?
9   In what circumstances would you accept a risk?
10   What are the typical contents of a risk response plan?
11   What is being looked for when risk monitoring and controlling activities are performed?
12   Do assumptions represent risks on projects?
13   How can risks be used to improve the execution of future projects?

DISCUSSION QUESTIONS

BSBPMG415A and
BSBPMG517A
performance
criteria questions

1   With all the standards that exist, why is risk management one of the most poorly executed project management functions?
2   What determines an individual's specific risk appetite?
3   Why should assumptions be considered risks?
4   What is the difference between a risk and an issue?
5   What is the concept of positive risk?
6   Should contingency be applied for each individual risk or across the overall project?
7   What is the difference between residual risk and risk contingency?
8   How often should risks be monitored and what do you consider to be part of the monitoring process?
9   What are the benefits of doing an overall project risk assessment during the initiation phase?
10 Why is the concept of positive risk rarely applied?
11 Should risk response plans be prepared for every risk in the risk log? If not, what criteria are used to determine which risks receive treatment plans?
12 Why are risks that have occurred treated as issues?

ONLINE RESOURCES

Visit the online companion website at http://www.cengagebrain.com to link to important additional resources, including templates, real-world case studies, revision quizzes and additional study material.

FURTHER READING AND REFERENCES

Bartlett, J. (2004). *Project risk analysis and management guide* (2nd ed.). Buckinghamshire, UK: APM Publishing Limited.

Galway, L. (2004). *Quantitative risk analysis for project management: A critical review.* RAND Corporation.

Jennings, W. (2012). *The Olympics as a story of risk management.* HBR Blog Network, accessed on 27 June 2013 at http://blogs.hbr.org/cs/2012/08/the_olympics_as_a_story_of_ris.html.

Kerzner, H. (2007). *Project management: A systems approach to planning, scheduling, and controlling* (9th ed.). Brisbane: John Wiley & Sons.

Kloppenborg, T. J. (2012). *Contemporary project management* (2nd ed.). Melbourne: Cengage Learning.

NASA. (2009). *Guidelines for risk management, S3001, Revision B.* Accessed 26 June 2013 at http://www.nasa.gov/centers/ivv/pdf/209213main_S3001.pdf.

Project Management Institute (PMI). (2009). *Practice standard for project risk management.* Newtown Square, PA: author.

Project Management Institute (PMI). (2013). *A guide to the Project Management Body of Knowledge* (PMBOK® Guide) (5th ed.). Newtown Square, PA. Chapter 11, pp. 30–354.

Protecht. (n.d.). Can residual risk be higher than inherent risk? Accessed on 27 June 2013 at http://www.protecht.eu/resources/articles/can-residual-risk-be-higher-than-inherent-risk.

Schwable, K. (2011). *Information technology project management* (revised 6th ed.). Melbourne: Cengage Learning.

Standards Australia. (2004). *Risk management guidelines companion to AS/NZS 4360:2004.* SAI Global.

Standards Australia. (2009). *Risk management standard – AS/NZS ISO 31000:2009.* SAI Global.

US Department of Transportation. (2013). *Risk and opportunity management plan* (revised 23 July). Lakewood, CO: Central Federal Lands Highway Division.

Project procurement management

LEARNING OBJECTIVES

IN THIS CHAPTER YOU WILL:

1   learn about the specific processes, tools and techniques and major deliverables related to the key knowledge area of Project Procurement Management

2   learn how to plan, conduct, administer and close procurement activities

3   review different types of procurement that can be used to fulfil different requirements

4   appreciate the importance of procurement policies and procedures

5   understand the various types of contracts used for the procurement of project resources

6   understand the steps within the tender process and the different tender approaches available

7   consider the importance of establishing requirements and selection criteria for major procurement items.

Context

According to the NSI Online Certificate IV and Diploma of Project Management materials, project procurement management includes processes to acquire resources (staff, equipment, products or services) from outside of the project team. It also includes the contract management and change control processes required to develop and implement purchase orders and contracts.

The project procurement processes of planning, conducting, administering and closing form the lifecycle of any contract that is established as part of that process. A complex project can involve managing multiple contracts or subcontracts simultaneously, while purchasing interactions with government departments and large organisations are often dictated by complex and formal procurement policies and procedures.

Project procurements often involve formal contracts, which are legal documents between a buyer and a seller that are mutually binding. Sellers are obliged to provide the specified products or services and buyers are obliged to provide monetary compensation. Some contracts are extremely complex and others can be very simple. They all include terms and conditions specified by the buyer and negotiated with the seller and normally require an extensive negotiation and approval process, including expert assistance from procurement and legal professionals.

Source: The Northern Sydney Institute, Part of TAFE NSW.

PMBOK® Guide processes for project procurement management

See PMBOK®
Guide Figure 12-2
Plan
procurements:
inputs, tools and
techniques, and
outputs

See PMBOK®
Guide Chapter 12
Project
procurement
management

The PMBOK® Guide processes for project procurement management are:
12.1   Plan procurement management
12.2   Conduct procurements
12.3   Control procurements
12.4   Close procurements.

12.1   ***Plan procurement management (planning):*** The process for identifying the procurement requirements for a project. This involves identifying all resources and equipment that must be purchased and utilised in order to complete the project, as well as specifying the procurement approach and selection criteria. It considers potential suppliers and the contractual arrangements that may be required to manage these external parties to achieve the project objectives.

12.2   ***Conduct procurements (execution):*** The process for obtaining seller responses, selecting sellers and awarding the contracts for all procurement requirements from outside the project. This is sometimes referred to as the *tender process* and can be repeated in more detail for major procurements once a shortlist of qualified vendors is identified.

FIGURE 14.1 PROJECT PROCUREMENT MANAGEMENT – A PROCESS PERSPECTIVE

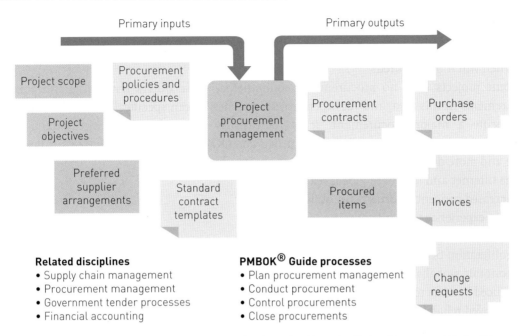

Source: Adapted from Project Management Institute, *A guide to the Project Management Body of Knowledge*, (PMBOK® Guide), fifth edition.

12.3 ***Control procurements (monitoring and controlling):*** The process of managing procurement relationships, monitoring contract performance and making changes or corrections as needed. Generally undertaken by both the buyer and the seller as both parties need to ensure that the other is meeting their contractual obligations.

12.4 ***Close procurements (closing):*** The process of completing each procurement activity that has been undertaken for a project. It involves the administrative activities related to handing over, claims, change requests and final procurement results.

Procurement planning

The purpose of the procurement management plan is to define the procurement requirements for the project and how these will be managed. It includes developing procurement documentation, such as tenders, through to contract negotiations and acquisitions, and on to contract closure or asset disposal.

Procurement decisions are generally made early in the planning phase in order to allow time for procurement activities to be conducted and then for the items to be sourced, built or shipped. There are seven key decisions made when determining if a procurement is required for a project:

1   Does the project have all the required resources: staff, equipment, systems, products, etc.?
2   Is procurement required?

3 What will be procured?

4 How will it be procured?

5 What type of contract will be used?

6 How much will be procured?

7 When will it be procured?

Some projects have no procurement requirements, while others have large and complex requirements in this area, and yet other projects may have been specifically established in order to execute a major procurement. It is increasingly important for project managers to understand how to plan for, and execute, procurement activities as project success is becoming more and more dependent on external procurements due to:

- the internet and increased global reach
- increased concentration on core activities
- more experience with outsourcing
- increased availability of outsourcing services
- proliferation of packaged software systems for standard business applications
- economic globalisation and open markets
- reduced barriers to trade; e.g. tariffs
- improved reliability and speed of transportation.

When a major procurement activity is required, it is common for this to be planned in a stand-alone procurement management plan. The contents of the procurement management plan are:

- identification of items to be procured
- procurement methods; e.g. tender, preferred supplier, comparison of quotations, etc.
- evaluation and selection criteria
- type of contract to be used
- contract approval process
- budget allowances
- timeframe requirements
- links to procurement planning policies and procedures
- links to procurement planning templates
- links to contract templates
- links to lists of preferred suppliers.

REAL-WORLD EXPERIENCE

PROCUREMENT PLANNING TABLE

I find it very useful to organise all the procurement information into a table I devised called the procurement planning table (see Figure 14.2).

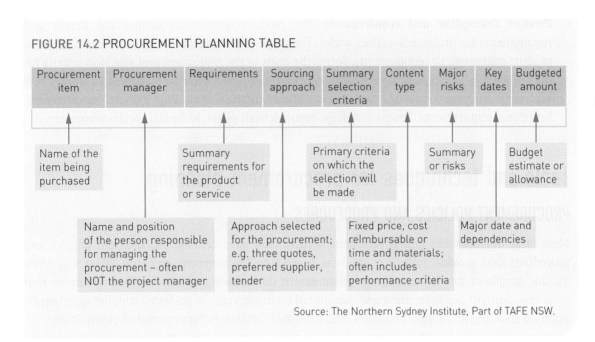

FIGURE 14.2 PROCUREMENT PLANNING TABLE

Procurement planning table template

Source: The Northern Sydney Institute, Part of TAFE NSW.

There are many sources of procurement requirements and many possible inputs into the procurement plan, such as:

- scope statement and baseline
- work breakdown structure (WBS)
- detailed requirements documentation
- project schedule
- risk register
- activity resource requirements
- activity cost estimates
- cost performance baseline
- marketplace conditions
- availability of equipment, products and services
- suppliers' past performance
- procurement planning policies and procedures
- procurement planning templates
- templates for standard contracts
- formal procurements policies and procedures
- preferred supplier agreements and list of suppliers
- outsourcing agreements.

The primary inputs are:

- **Project scope statement:** the project scope statement defines the deliverables that must be produced to meet the project's objectives. A clear and comprehensive scope statement makes it very obvious what cannot be produced with the existing project resources and determines if procurement activities are required to obtain or contribute to the major project deliverables and outcomes.

- ***Product description and requirements:*** the product description defines the details and requirements for major deliverables within the scope. If a deliverable is to be procured then the product statement, or requirements, forms the basis of the evaluation and selection criteria for the acquisition. Sometimes these requirements are contained within a statement of work. There are many different forms of requirements documentation including: systems requirements, functional requirements, design drawings, constructions plans, technical specifications, etc.

Tools and techniques for procurement planning

PROCUREMENT POLICIES AND PROCEDURES

Most large organisations and government departments have detailed procurement policies and procedures that provide guidelines on how to execute procurement processes. They will often include templates for the mandatory procurement documents and are designed to ensure that good procurement decisions are made. Additional inclusions can be preferred supplier agreements, purchase ordering and supply processes, and delegated authorities for approval of expenditure.

It is common for the procedures to be more rigorous as the value of the items to be procured increases. It is critical that project managers both seek out and follow these policies and procedures as the primary purpose is to increase the chance of project success and to reduce risk due to the legal aspects of most major procurements.

EVALUATING MARKET CONDITIONS

An important procurement activity is determining what sources are available to provide the needed products or services for the project. This may be the first time that the project organisation has procured the required item so there may be no knowledge of what is available on the market. There are times when there are many vendors, as the item is a commodity, and there will be other circumstances when the choices may be extremely limited due to scarcity or the innovative nature of the item.

An evaluation of the market conditions and overall availability is critical as it assists with early planning for funding of the procurement activities. Often some form of approval will be required for the funds before the procurement activities can be undertaken. This is necessary to ensure that the funds have been set aside. In many cases, this must be based on a prediction as the final price cannot be determined accurately until the selection and negotiation activities have been completed. The buyer will have less influence over the procurement outcomes and pricing if there is only a single vendor (monopoly) or a very limited set of vendors (oligopoly).

MAKE OR BUY ANALYSIS

This process determines whether particular work can be accomplished by the project team or must be purchased from outside sources. The capability may exist internally but may be committed to other projects, or it may be for something which the organisation doesn't have the background or experience to produce. With increasingly free market conditions and globalisation it is becoming more common for projects to procure items rather than make them. Factors which can influence these decisions include:

- budget constraints
- preferences for leasing over direct acquisition
- indirect costs, such as ongoing maintenance
- financial management practices for asset depreciation.

TABLE 14.1 MAKE OR BUY ANALYSIS

Reasons to make	Reasons to buy
No product available – restricted supply	Commodity
Research and development	No internal expertise
Protect intellectual property	Openly available supply
Less costly than buying	Less costly than making
Utilise in-house skills and staff	No staff available
Maintain control	Procurement risk reasonable
High procurement risk	Vendors available

EXPERT JUDGEMENT

Often large organisations have procurement departments or internal experts within the legal or finance departments who have responsibilities to oversee procurement policies and procedures and who can assist with both project and general organisational procurement processes. The types of assistance you can obtain from these internal experts includes contract selection, contract negotiations, oversight of tender processes and so on.

In the absence of internal procurement experts, then project managers often need to provide this expertise themselves, or for major procurement, they may be able to seek assistance from external experts such as lawyers, consultants, subject matter experts, professional associations or industry bodies.

PREFERRED SUPPLIER AGREEMENTS

Many organisations and government departments negotiate agreements with prequalified suppliers for resources, products or services that are regularly required in the execution of projects or general business outcomes. In these cases, the project manager needs to ensure that suppliers for any external resources, products and services are selected from a list of preferred suppliers. Predetermined preferred supplier lists have the major advantage of significantly reducing procurement risks. If they exist then any exceptions normally require approval from the procurement department or project sponsor.

Procurement approaches and contracts

There are many different procurement approaches that are available to the project manager and often these are prescribed by procurement policies and procedures based on the value of the item that is being procured. These approaches include those outlined in the following list:

- **Quotation:** usually requires the project manager to seek several quotes from which one is selected based on price and compliance with requirements. Normally used for procurement of commodities with a low value where there is little risk.
- **Previous supplier:** involves purchasing from a previously selected, well-performing supplier.
- **Preferred supplier:** as detailed above, this involves purchasing from a prequalified list of potential suppliers. There will often be different lists for various resources, products and services that are used regularly.
- **Tender process:** involves conducting a formal procurement process for major procurement items which will result in the negotiation of a contract to supply specified resources, products or services. In cases where there is good knowledge of the market and suppliers, or where preferred supplier lists are in place, then a closed tender (by invitation only) will often be chosen as this is faster and involves less risk. Open tenders are made available to any potential vendor in cases where there is little knowledge of the vendors or market conditions. The open tender process can take longer due to the need to go through several rounds of selection. Tender processes can be very complex and time consuming, so they are normally reserved for major procurement items over a specified monetary threshold.

Types of procurement contracts

There are many different types of contract structures that can be used for project procurement activities. The three primary categories of contracts are as follows:

1 **Fixed price:** these involve setting a total fixed price for a defined product or service and can often include financial incentives for achieving or exceeding objectives such as time, cost and quality. Suppliers assume much of the delivery risk and these are normally the most complex to negotiate and administer as each side seeks to clarify the scope of the product and services as well as any processes for any potential variations. There can be high degrees of tension between the buyer and the seller due to disagreements as to detailed requirements that are considered part of the fixed-price commitment as opposed to change requests.

2 **_Cost reimbursable:_** these involve paying the supplier for the actual costs incurred plus an agreed fee for profit. These contracts also often include financial incentives or penalty clauses for achieving, exceeding or missing objectives such as time, cost and quality. The delivery risk is shared between the buyer and seller and there is flexibility for the buyer to redirect the seller whenever the scope of work changes, as long as they are willing to incur additional costs. These are especially popular when it is difficult to define the detailed requirements, or on research and development projects which involve a high degree of uncertainty. Financial and legal penalties are harder to enforce if the contract conditions are not met but these contract types are significantly easier to negotiate and administer than fixed-price arrangements.

3 **_Time and materials:_** these are a hybrid containing aspects of both cost-reimbursable and fixed-price contracts. They are often used to acquire specialist human resources such as contract staff, consultants and subject matter experts. They are also common when the buyer cannot, or doesn't want to, specify the statement of work or requirements in detail as it gives them flexibility to redirect the seller whenever the scope of work changes (just like with cost-reimbursable contracts). Many organisations will establish formal end dates for these types of contracts in order to manage and monitor costs.

It can be difficult to determine the preferred contract type for a particular procurement and sometimes the preference may change as a result of the actual negotiation process. Most project managers need to seek advice from procurement, legal and finance experts in order to select the most appropriate contract throughout the negotiation.

REAL-WORLD EXPERIENCE

HOW NOT TO PURCHASE APPLICATION SYSTEMS

When I was responsible for developing and implementing a new financial services product, one of the major procurement items was the purchase and installation of a new software package to administer the new product. There were several industry-leading packages available as we proceeded with a tender process based on very detailed requirements. The software selection process went very smoothly with the chosen package meeting our requirements and it was easily tailored to handle the detailed product characteristics. It was configured, implemented and tested within our tight and fixed timeframe.

But how is this an example of poor procurement processes? Well, it wasn't until 12 months after the financial services product was launched that the contract for the purchase and ongoing support of the software package was finally executed. This, naturally, places enormous risk on the product once it has launched. Luckily, the project budget was not adversely impacted as the legal experts assisting in the negotiation were internal and not charged to the project.

The key issues and chronology were:
- the initial responsibility for the contract negotiation was assigned to the IT manager who had no accountability to myself as the program director as he reported to the IT director
- the IT manager had competing priorities and had no experience in this type of negotiation

- the contract was for the software license and also for software configuration services
- the organisation had comprehensive template contracts for software purchases which had onerous terms and conditions for performance which were too complicated for a contract of this low value with a small software vendor
- negotiations had progressed very slowly as the vendor was trying to have the standard terms modified to be more reasonable and applicable to their circumstances and the negotiators from the organisation felt they did not have the authority to make such changes
- when I became aware of the delays and issues, I worked with the IT manager and asked the legal department to provide a more senior resource to assist
- given the urgency and significant risks, we then proceeded to finalise negotiations by taking the vendor's standard contract as our base and worked the following six Saturdays to finalise the contract.

TABLE 14.2 CHARACTERISTICS OF CONTRACT TYPES

Type of contract	Description	Risks	Characteristics and applications
Fixed price	A flat fee for the purchased item where the seller assumes all responsibility for any price variations.	The seller assumes the risk.	» Most common contract type. » Requires detailed requirements and scope definition. » Often used for commodities that are locally produced.
Fixed-price incentive fee	A flat fee for the purchased item which includes terms and conditions allowing for incentive fees for the seller based on measures such as time, cost, scope and quality.	The seller assumes the risk but there are incentives to improve performance.	As above. » Where the seller has confidence that they can outperform expectations.
Fixed-price with economic price adjustments	A flat fee for the purchased item with terms and conditions allowing for price increases that may relate to movement in the economy, such as salaries, inflation, exchange rates, etc.	The seller assumes most of the risk but the buyer takes on risks relating to changes in agreed economic variables.	As above. » Normally used when the contract spans a number of years or requires significant imported components or offshore labour.

Type of contract	Description	Risks	Characteristics and applications
Cost plus fixed fee	Actual agreed costs plus an agreed fixed amount of profit margin for the seller.	Most of the risk is on the buyer.	» Additional costs are the responsibility of the buyer. » Used in cases where the buyer wishes to maintain some flexibility over the direction and scope of the project.
Cost plus percentage of cost	Actual agreed costs plus an agreed percentage-based profit margin for the seller.	One of the highest risk contract types for the buyer.	» Additional costs are the responsibility of the buyer and there is no cap on the incentive payment. » There is an incentive for the seller to exceed initial cost expectations due to the uncapped nature of the profit.
Cost plus incentive fee	Actual agreed costs plus an agreed profit margin for the seller which is based on some form of performance measures such a time, scope, cost and quality.	Most of the risk is on the buyer but there are incentives for the seller to perform well.	» Additional costs are the responsibility of the buyer but are tied to performance criteria on the part of the seller. » Used to share some of the risk with the seller and to encourage good performance against the contract terms.
Time and materials	This is a hybrid containing aspects of both cost-reimbursable and fixed-price contracts.	Most of the risk is on the buyer.	» Often used to acquire specialist human resources, such as contract staff, consultants and subject matter experts. » Also common when the buyer cannot, or doesn't want to, specify the statement of work or requirements in detail. » Doesn't normally result in the best price as the seller needs to include contingency.

FIGURE 14.3 PROCUREMENT CONTRACT RISK PROFILES

Contract type	Buyer's risk	Seller's risk
Time and materials	High	Low
Fixed price	Low	High
Fixed price with variations	Medium	Medium
Fixed price with penalties	Low	High
Guaranteed maximum price	Shared	Shared
Cost plus incentive fee	Medium	Low
Cost plus fixed fee	High	Medium
Cost plus percentage fee	High	Medium

PROJECT MANAGEMENT MASTERY

PROCUREMENT RISKS

Although the topic of project risk is covered in Chapter 13, there is merit in considering some of the unique risks that are possible when undertaking procurement. Procurement is often chosen as a strategy to *reduce* the risk of the executing organisation as they don't have to make or build the item when there is a lack of expertise or specialisation in the area. However, when a project is reliant on a third party for delivery, then an external dependency is created and this *increases* risk as the direct control over the deliverable is reduced or completely outsourced to the supplier.

The typical procurement risks and responses to these are outlined in Table 14.3.

TABLE 14.3 PROCUREMENT RISKS AND RESPONSES

Procurement risk	Management responses
The vendor may go out of business within the timeframe of the project without delivering, or only partially delivering on, their commitments.	» Conduct a financial background check on the vendor to ensure viability. » Build terms into the contract to allow the buyer to take over the delivery, in terms of hiring professionals to complete software development, having access to the plant and equipment to complete manufacturing, etc.

Procurement risk	Management responses
The vendor may take on too much work and not be able to meet the agreed deadlines.	» Build incentives and penalties into the contract to encourage good vendor performance or to provide additional funds should the vendor not meet their commitments.
The vendor may not correctly interpret the requirements and cause issues for project scope, time and cost.	» Document the requirements in as much detail as possible given the project team's level of skill and the timeframes involved. » Carefully manage the quality and completeness of deliverables along the way so that change requests and defects can be resolved early. » Build detailed change control processes into the terms of the contract.

Conducting procurement activities

Procurement activities are conducted during the execution phase in line with the procurement plan that is developed in the planning phase. Conducting procurements starts at the point where bids are being received from suppliers for items that need to be procured. Tender documentation, supplier briefing materials, requirements and selection criteria have all been developed during planning.

Figure 14.4 shows basic processes for the planning and conduct of procurements.

FIGURE 14.4 PLAN AND CONDUCT PROCUREMENT PROCESSES, SIDE BY SIDE

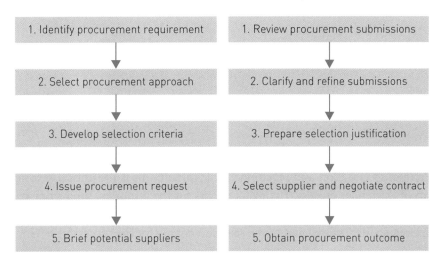

These can seem like simple processes, but for major procurements they can be very complex and time consuming.

RESEARCH AND REFLECTION ACTIVITY

PROCUREMENT POLICIES AND PROCEDURES

Most large organisations will have extensive policies and procedures governing the manner in which procurements are to be conducted. Review those of your own organisation and if you think they are weak then review the procurement frameworks that have been developed by various government departments to assist vendors in working with them.

Research both internal and external procurement frameworks and processes.

There are many potential steps that can be included in a tender process, depending on the preferences and policies of the purchasing organisation. Figure 14.5 brings together good practice and common standards for tender processes.

FIGURE 14.5 TYPICAL TENDER PROCESS STEPS

Source: The Northern Sydney Institute, Part of TAFE NSW.

- **Step 1:** Product specification and requirements definition: this is the critical first step and is the foundation of the tender process. The requirements for the resources, product or service need to be described in sufficient detail to enable the 'make or buy' decision. If a tender is required, then the detailed requirements form part of the selection criteria for the successful vendor.

- ***Step 2:*** Procurement process selection: once it has been decided to acquire the item then the specific procurement process needs to be determined. Common options include quotation, previous supplier, preferred supplier or tender process (open or closed). These are described earlier in the chapter.
- ***Step 3:*** Request for information (optional): in the event that an open tender process is selected, then it is common practice to issue a request for information which asks potential suppliers to provide information on their products or services, as well as their capabilities, financial status, other clients and so on.
- ***Step 4:*** Review potential suppliers and respondents: this formal review of potential suppliers and respondents is based on the initial qualifying criteria. It enables the purchasing organisation to determine a shortlist of potential vendors that will be invited to participate in the formal tender, which reduces the complexity and length of the tender process.
- ***Step 5:*** Prequalification briefing (optional): the purchasing organisation may conduct briefing sessions for shortlisted suppliers, or may run open briefing sessions for all potential suppliers so the suppliers can determine if they wish to proceed to the next stage based on a self-assessment of their capabilities against the requirements.
- ***Step 6:*** Issue request for tender: this involves the formal issuing of the tender documentation. For closed tenders this will be directly to each shortlisted supplier. For open tenders this could be via an advertisement in print media or on specialised tender websites. Potential suppliers may be able to download the tender themselves or may need to contact the purchasing organisation in order to receive a copy of the documentation. There are numerous templates for tenders available at many government procurement websites. The typical contents include background and objectives, detailed requirements, selection criteria, request for supplier information, checklists and self-assessment tables.
- ***Step 7:*** Briefing and question and answer sessions (optional): it is common practice, but not mandatory, for the buyer to provide opportunities for potential suppliers to clarify their understanding of the requirements and to ask detailed questions. These may be private or open sessions depending on the buyer's preference. It is good practice to run these as open sessions where all potential suppliers attend; this approach is not normally comfortable for potential suppliers but it helps to ensure that there are no advantages or disadvantages accidentally given to one supplier over another. It is important that all potential suppliers are treated equally in order to prevent any recourse from unsuccessful suppliers after the award of the tender.
- ***Step 8:*** Supplier submissions: this involves the formal submission of tender responses by potential suppliers. There is normally a process for submission that has been stipulated (e.g. hardcopy and/or electronic copies, standard templates, cut-off dates and times, etc.). Potential suppliers that do not comply with the submission process may be disqualified from

tendering. This is critical to ensure no advantages are given to some suppliers over others, perhaps by granting one supplier an extension over the others.

- **Step 9:** Review selection criteria: this process step involves the formal review of the tender submissions by experts nominated by the purchasing organisation. These will normally include the project sponsor, project manager, internal subject matter experts and sometimes representatives from internal finance, procurement and legal departments. Occasionally, external subject matter experts may be engaged to assist with the selection process for highly specialised items.

- **Step 10:** Announce selection: this involves the formal award of the tender to the successful supplier and the notification of this to the unsuccessful suppliers. Sometimes unsuccessful suppliers are offered the opportunity to obtain feedback on why they were unsuccessful.

- **Step 11:** Negotiate contract: this can be a difficult and long process that often requires assistance from procurement and legal professionals and starts with the establishment of the type of contract that will be used (see also Table 14.2).

Figure 14.6 shows the steps involved in assessing whether or not to respond to a tender from the seller's perspective.

FIGURE 14.6 SELLER'S PERSPECTIVES ON TENDERS

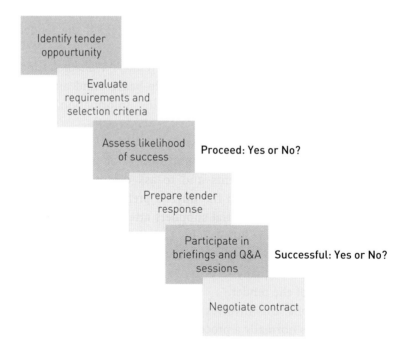

Administering procurements

The administration of procurements is the combination of all the monitoring and controlling processes and then applying these to the procurement activities. The primary activities which are performed include:

- management of vendor relationships
- assessment of vendor performance against the terms of the procurement contract
- assessment of the goods and services delivered against the specific requirements in the procurement contract
- execution of project and organisational obligations as the purchaser
- monitoring and controlling of procurement-related risks and execution of risk management actions if required
- initiation, review and approval of change requests related to procurement
- identification and review of defects for resolution
- management financial obligations, such as purchase orders, invoice payments and cost tracking
- applying specific project management processes to procurement management, including directing and managing, performance reporting, quality control and change control
- identification and execution of modifications to procurement contracts if required due to changed requirements or circumstances
- review of contract terms and conditions
- execution of legal action if procurement contracts are breached.

The primary outputs of this process are change requests, defects and performance reports. The tools and techniques that facilitate the administration and management of procurement activities are:

- change control processes as specified in each contract
- procurement and vendor performance reviews
- performance or status reporting
- independent inspections or audits as stipulated; e.g. review by independent quality surveyors of construction progress
- administration of claims made under the contract terms and conditions
- detailed records management systems and processes for correspondence, invoices, specifications, change requests and claims.

The major cause of variation and change requests in relation to procurement activities is due to unclear requirements leading to additional scope (which in turn creates pressure on quality, time and cost baselines). This is often a source of conflict between buyers and sellers. Buyers may lack the expertise or time to document the requirements clearly, or in sufficient detail, so as to avoid future misinterpretation, and sellers will normally position any issues around the requirements as change requests which would be at the client's cost, rather than defects which would be at their cost. Good practice is to deal with any of these as change requests as part of '4.5 Perform integrated change control'.

Many organisations treat contract administration as an administrative function separate from the project and it is carried out by a purchasing department or by a designated functional manager. Managing these relationships both internally and externally can be a very complex communication activity with its own processes and procedures that must be followed, often dictated by the terms of the contract and internal policies and procedures.

Closing procurements

This is a collection of activities that relate to the closing of procurements that were undertaken by a project. However, not all projects undertake procurement activities, so Table 14.4 summarises the various types of projects and common closing procurement requirements.

TABLE 14.4 CLOSING PROCUREMENT ACTIVITIES

Project examples	Typical procurement scope and activities	Procurement closure activities
Process improvement (Lean Six Sigma)	Many process improvement projects using the Lean Six Sigma approach require absolutely no procurement. The primary focus is on reducing defects, improving customer satisfaction and reducing time to delivery of products or services.	» Not applicable. » Final timesheets and accrual of costs for final invoices which may not have been presented. » Termination of personal services contracts.
Software package acquisition and installation	Normally require a formal request for tender and selection process. The contract may include both the software licence and installation services.	» Finalisation of contracts for installation services based on complete provision of the services. » Handover of the ongoing software contract to a systems owner who manages on-going licence and support payments.
Office building/ construction	Major procurement activities for design and construction services, equipment and materials. Many work packages awarded to subcontractors using formal tender processes.	» Complex procurement closure activities to finalise those procurement activities that conclude with the handover of the building and to initiate defect repair periods. » Potential disputed procurement items requiring mediation or legal processes. » Formal handover to building manager and tenants for on-going maintenance.

The closing of procurements involves either the completion of all contracts required for the project or the handover of contracts for ongoing administration for the life of the product or service that was purchased. Early termination of a contract is a special case of procurement closure and can occur by mutual agreement or when either the buyer or seller fails to meet agreed terms and obligations. This can result in legal action, as can any unresolved claims, such as defect repairs versus change requests.

Related processes from the PMBOK® Guide

4.1 ***Develop project charter (initiation):*** In practice, the high-level project scope is developed and documented during the initiation phase in the project charter. It forms the boundaries for subsequent scoping processes. Unfortunately, the PMBOK® Guide has the scope definition activities all occurring in the planning phase and is therefore out of sync with practice.

4.2 ***Develop project management plan (planning):*** This is the process of defining and documenting the actions necessary to prepare and integrate all subsidiary plans for each of the other key knowledge areas of project management. The PMP is the primary deliverable from the planning phase. Good practice dictates that the PMP is baselined at the end of the planning phase, particularly in the areas of scope, cost and time. It is progressively added to during project execution via the perform integrated change control process.

The planning for all the key knowledge areas is normally performed at the same time as this process, or expanded upon shortly afterwards. All key knowledge areas have discrete processes for planning that are defined in their process groups.

This process is closely linked to '8.1 Plan quality management', '9.1 Plan human resource management', '10.1 Plan communications management', '11.1 Plan risk management' and '12.1 Plan procurement management'.

4.5 ***Perform integrated change control (monitoring and controlling):*** The process of reviewing all change requests, including approving or rejecting changes and managing the flow-on impacts on all project deliverables and all components of the PMP. All requested changes should be identified through '5.6 Control scope'. The activities within this process are critical to managing stakeholder expectations and to ensuring the highest chance of project success. They occur from project inception through to completion and are part of the monitor and control process group. It is important that only approved changes be incorporated into the project, as it is surprisingly common to see unapproved changes being inadvertently undertaken.

6.4 ***Estimate activity resources (planning):*** The process of estimating the types and quantities of material, people, equipment or supplies required to perform each activity. It is closely linked to '9.1 Develop human resource management plan' and '9.2 Acquire project team' and the project procurement management processes.

6.5 ***Estimate activity durations (planning):*** The process of approximating the number of work periods needed to complete individual activities with estimated resources. Work periods may be hours, days, weeks, months and so on and different resources will exhibit differing productivity levels.

6.6 ***Develop schedule (planning):*** The process of analysing activity sequences, durations, resource requirements and schedule constraints to create the project schedule. This is best completed with the aid of project scheduling software such as MS Project.

7.2 ***Estimate costs (planning):*** The process for developing an estimate of costs to complete all activities required to finish the project. These estimates are a prediction based on the information known at any point in time and the assumptions that have been made for planning purposes.

9.2 ***Acquire project team (execution):*** The process of confirming human resource availability and selecting the team members necessary to complete the project activities. Project managers need to negotiate and influence in order to obtain the best team possible for the project, as they may not have direct control over resource selection due to industrial agreements, project sponsor preferences and internal HR policies. It is closely related to '6.4 Estimate activity resources' and '6.5 Estimate activity durations'.

9.3 ***Develop the project team (execution):*** The process for identifying skills development needs and improving competencies of the project team members. This also includes managing team member interaction and the overall team environment to enhance the performance and increase the probability of project success.

11.2 ***Identify risks (planning):*** The process for identifying the risks that may impact the project. It is useful to have a broad group of key stakeholders, project team members and internal experts participate in the risk identification session. Good practice dictates that as far as possible all major risks should be identified during the planning phase, although this is an iterative process as often risks are unpredictable and new risks become obvious during execution.

13.1 ***Identify stakeholders (initiation):*** The process for identifying the people, groups and organisations that are interested in, or impacted by, the project. They could in turn affect the outcomes of the project depending on their relative power. Their interests and influence are critical to project success.

CHAPTER SUMMARY

» It is becoming more common to acquire resources, products and services from outside of the project and the organisation executing the project.

» Procurement needs to be extensively planned as it involves a high degree of risk, is often expensive and results in a formal contract which is legally binding for both the buyer and the seller.

» Procurement management processes are complex and related to many other project management processes in other key knowledge areas. Many organisations and government departments have extensive procurement policies and procedures to help reduce the associated risks.

» A procurement planning table is useful as it helps develop an overarching understanding of all procurement requirements on a project and assists in keeping track of them.

» There are four main procurement approaches that can be selected: quotation, previous supplier, preferred supplier and tender.

» Tender processes can involve a request for information if the vendors and market conditions are not known.

» The typical steps in a tender process are requests for information, short list development, requests for tender, vendor briefings, submissions, selection and contract negotiation.

» Tenders can be open or closed. Closed tenders extend the invitation to specifically selected vendors and tend to be faster and therefore less risky.

» Subject matter experts are often available both internally and externally to assist with procurement activities, including legal, finance and procurement specialists.

» There are three main types of contracts that can be used for procurement: time and materials, cost plus and fixed price. There are many variations to the specific terms and conditions within these contracts that split the risks across the buyer and seller in different proportions.

» The primary activities involved in the administration of procurements include: management of vendor relationships, assessment of vendor performance against the terms of the procurement contract, assessment of the goods and services delivered against the specific requirements in the contract and monitoring and controlling of procurement-related risks and execution of risk management actions if required.

» Most procurements close when the contract is completed, although sometimes there is a need to hand over the on-going administration of assets acquired as a result of project procurement once the project is finished.

» The early termination of a procurement is normally the result of either the buyer or seller not meeting their obligations under the contract. This often results in serious losses, non-delivery of project outcomes and legal action.

REVISION QUESTIONS

Revision questions are divided into two sections. The first covers Certificate IV understanding and the second covers Diploma-level understanding. Both sections are relevant to Diploma students and teachers, while only the first section is relevant to Certificate students and teachers.

Certificate IV of Project Management

These questions relate to the performance criteria stated in 'BSBPMG416A Apply project procurement procedures'.

1 What are the project procurement management processes?
2 Where can you obtain direction and guidelines for the conduct of project procurement activities?
3 What tools and techniques can be applied to procurement planning activities?
4 What types of procurement approaches exist?
5 What are the three main types of procurement contracts?
6 What are the typical steps in a tender process?
7 What activities are carried out when administering procurements?
8 What activities are carried out when closing procurements?

BSBPMG416A
performance
criteria questions

BSBPMG518A
performance
criteria questions

Diploma of Project Management

These questions relate to the performance criteria stated in 'BSBPMG518A Manage project procurement'.

1. Under what circumstances do organisations normally decide to undertake project procurement?
2. What are the different approaches that can be taken for procurement?
3. What is the importance of the selection criteria?
4. What types of selection criteria are normally applied in addition to straight financial considerations?
5. What is the relative risk for both the buyer and seller of the different procurement contract types?
6. What is the purpose of building in penalties and incentives into procurement contracts?
7. What professionals and subject matter experts can be called upon to assist the project manager with procurement activities?
8. How are procurements closed and what occurs when there are disputes over delivery?

BSBPMG416A and
BSBPMG518A
performance
criteria questions

DISCUSSION QUESTIONS

1. What processes are used to manage defects and change requests and why might this generate conflict between buyers and sellers?
2. What are the relative pros and cons of the three major types of procurement contracts?
3. In what circumstances are tenders normally chosen as the procurement method?
4. What additional risks are placed on a project that requires a major procurement and how can these be managed?
5. What tensions exist between a buyer and seller with respect to the requirements in terms of defects versus change requests?

ONLINE RESOURCES

Visit the online companion website at http://www.cengagebrain.com to link to important additional resources, including templates, real-world case studies, revision quizzes and additional study material.

FURTHER READING AND REFERENCES

Clarke, N., & Howell, R. (2009). *Emotional intelligence and projects*. Newtown Square, PA: Project Management Institute.

Dobie, C. (2007). *A handbook of project management: A complete guide for beginners to professionals*. Sydney: Allen and Unwin.

Flannes, S., & Levin, G. (2005). *Essential people skills for project managers*. Vienna, VA: Management Concepts.

Fleming, Q. (2003). *Project procurement management: Contracting, subcontracting, teaming*. FMS Press.

Guth, S. (2009). *Project procurement management: A guide to structured procurements*. Guth Ventures LLC.

Hartley, S. (2008). *Project management: Principles, processes and practice* (2nd ed.). Sydney: Pearson Education.

Kerzner, H. (2007). *Project management: A systems approach to planning, scheduling, and controlling* (9th ed.). Brisbane: John Wiley & Sons.

Kloppenborg, T. J. (2012). *Contemporary project management* (2nd ed.). Melbourne: Cengage Learning.

Mulcahy, R. (2006). *PM crash course – Real-world project management tools & techniques.* Minnetonka, MN: RMC Publications.

Portny S. E., Mantel, S. J., Meredith, J. R., ... Sutton, M. M. (2008). *Project management – Planning, scheduling and controlling projects.* Brisbane: Wiley.

Project Management Institute (PMI). (2013). *A guide to the Project Management Body of Knowledge* (PMBOK® Guide) (5th ed.). Newtown Square, PA: author.

Schwable, K. (2011). *Information technology project management* (revised 6th ed.). Melbourne: Cengage Learning.

Tan, H. C., Anumba, C., Carrillo, P., ... Udeaja, C. (2010). *Capture and reuse of project knowledge in construction.* Chichester, UK: Wiley-Blackwell.

Verzuh, E. (2005). *The fast forward MBA in project management.* Brisbane: John Wiley & Sons.

Online references

ACT Procurement Solutions: http://www.procurement.act.gov.au/

Australian Association of Procurement and Contract Management: http://www.aapcm.com.au/resources/useful-articles

Australian Government tenders: http://www.tenders.gov.au

Australian Government procurement guidelines and information: http://www.treasury.gov.au/procurement/

Australian National Audit Office (ANAO): http://www.anao.gov.au/

Australian Procurement and Construction Council: http://www.apcc.com.au

Commonwealth Procurement Guidelines: http://www.finance.gov.au/procurement/procurement-policy-and-guidance/CPG/index.html

Defence Materiel Organisation – DPPM: http://www.defence.gov.au/dmo/gc/dppm.cfm

Department of Defence: http://www.defence.gov.au/

Department of Finance and Deregulation – Procurement: http://www.finance.gov.au/procurement

Federal purchasing policy: http://www.finance.gov.au/procurement/

Local Government Procurement Organisation: http://www.lgp.org.au/councils/tendering-resources

Northern Territory Government – Department of Business Procurement directions: http://www.dob.nt.gov.au/business/tenders-contracts/references/Pages/directions.aspx

NSW ProcurePoint: http://www.procurepoint.nsw.gov.au/

NSW Government tenders: http://www.tenders.nsw.gov.au

Queensland State procurement policy: http://www.hpw.qld.gov.au/supplydisposal/GovernmentProcurement/ProcurementPolicyGuidance/Pages/default.aspx

Small Biz connect has extensive and simple information on tendering at the following link: http://toolkit.smallbiz.nsw.gov.au/chapter/26/134

South Australian State Procurement Board: http://www.spb.sa.gov.au/site/home.aspx

Tasmania Purchasing: http://www.purchasing.tas.gov.au/

VIC Government tenders: http://www.tenders.vic.gov.au

VIC Purchasing Board: http://www.vgpb.vic.gov.au

Whole of Government Procurement Arrangements: http://www.finance.gov.au/procurement/wog-procurement/index.html

Project stakeholder management

Context

Project stakeholder management encompasses the processes that identify, analyse and manage stakeholders and their expectations. Recapping on the definition of project success, this occurs when the:

- expectations of the client are met
- agreed project objectives have been delivered
- business outcomes have been realised
- timeframe and budget have been met
- quality and scope requirements have been delivered.

The primary client for internal projects is the project sponsor while there is a 'genuine' client when projects are being delivered for a person or organisation that is separate to the executing organisation. There is never just one client, which is why the concept of stakeholders and their expectations is so critical to determining project success.

There is often confusion between project stakeholders and project team members. The distinction is clear. As mentioned in Chapter 12, project stakeholders are individuals or groups that are interested in, or may be impacted by, the outcomes of the project. Project team members are individuals who have been assigned specific accountability for the development and completion of assigned project deliverables.

Recapping from Chapter 11, project managers use the processes and techniques of project human resource management to direct and manage the project team, whereas they use the processes and techniques of project stakeholder management and change management to influence and manage stakeholders. Project communications management applies equally to both.

Stakeholders are defined as any person, group or organisation that is interested in, or impacted by, the project. For those who are only interested in the project, then the major approaches for managing their expectations come from the project communications processes. For those actually impacted by the project, then the major approaches for helping them to understand and adjust to the change come from the change management arena. Change management is considered a stand-alone discipline and profession in the area of human resource management and it is not to be confused with change control.

RESEARCH AND REFLECTION ACTIVITY

CHANGE MANAGEMENT

Conduct some online research into change management. Consider and review the frameworks and approaches that you find. Try search terms such as ADKAR, Prosci, Kotter, Heart of Change, Change management, Stakeholder management and so on.

- Do you think you could use these concepts to improve stakeholder management?
- Which concepts appeal to you over others?
- Does your HR management department provide experts or assistance in these areas?

PMBOK® Guide processes for project stakeholder management

The PMBOK® Guide processes for project stakeholder management are:

13.1 Identify stakeholders

13.2 Plan stakeholder management

13.3 Manage stakeholder engagement

13.4 Control stakeholder engagement.

13.1 **Identify stakeholders (initiation):** The process for identifying the people, groups and organisations that are interested in, or impacted by, the project. They could in turn affect the outcomes of the project depending on their relative power. Their interests and influence are critical to project success.

13.2 **Plan stakeholder management (execution):** The process of developing management strategies to engage stakeholders throughout the project lifecycle in order to satisfy their needs and improve the chances of project success.

13.3 **Manage stakeholder engagement (execution):** The process for communicating and working with stakeholders to meet their needs and manage their expectations. This includes change management activities such as training, communication and engagement.

13.4 **Control stakeholder engagement (monitoring and controlling):** The process for monitoring overall project stakeholder relationships and adjusting engagement approaches.

See PMBOK®
Guide Figure 13-2
Identify
stakeholders:
inputs, tools and
techniques, and
outputs

See PMBOK®
Guide Chapter 13
Project
stakeholder
management

FIGURE 15.1 PROJECT STAKEHOLDER MANAGEMENT – A PROCESS PERSPECTIVE

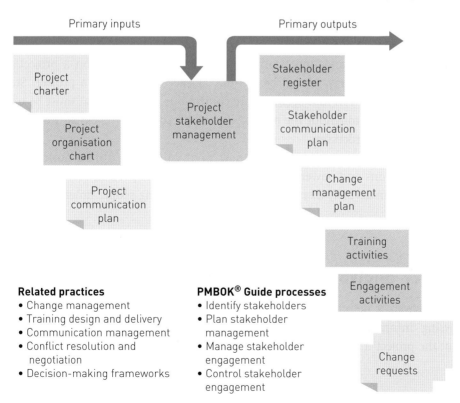

Source: Adapted from Project Management Institute, *A guide to the Project Management Body of Knowledge*, (PMBOK® Guide), fifth edition.

Stakeholder identification

This is the process of identifying all people and organisations involved in, or impacted by, the project. Stakeholders include diverse groups, such as customers, sponsors, impacted management, impacted staff, external organisations and sometimes even the public or media. These stakeholders can positively or negatively impact the project, hence it is important to understand their interests so these can be managed in order to increase the chances of success.

The project team and the project sponsor are also considered stakeholders but they tend to require different management to stakeholders, who are not on the project team. The project team is managed by the project manager using the processes, tools and techniques encompassed by the key knowledge area of Project Human Resource Management.

The project sponsor is the most critical stakeholder and they are almost always positive towards the project, given that they generally have the most to gain from the outcomes. There are, however, rare circumstances where the project sponsor can exert a negative influence over the project.

Stakeholders with positive expectations from a project will often assist the project, while the interests of stakeholders with negative expectations are often served by seeking to hinder the progress of the project or indeed attempting to have the project cancelled.

The project management team must identify both internal and external stakeholders in order to determine the project requirements and expectations of all parties involved. The project manager must then manage the influence and expectations of the various stakeholders to ensure a successful project outcome.

Identifying stakeholders and understanding their relative influence on a project is critical and can be difficult; they may not all be obvious at the beginning of a project. Stakeholder identification and expectation management are continuous processes that must be undertaken by the project manager throughout the project. It is also a good idea to enlist the support of the project sponsor in these processes.

Stakeholders can change over time and new ones can be identified during the project. Stakeholder expectations and power can also change during the project. Stakeholders identified later in the project can severely disrupt the project by impacting scope, timeframes and success measures.

See PMBOK® Guide Figure 2-6 The relationship between stakeholders and the project

Stakeholder analysis

Stakeholder analysis is defined by PMBOK® Guide as 'the process of systematically gathering and analysing information to determine whose interests should be taken into account throughout the project' (PMI, 2013, p. 563). This analysis identifies the interests, expectations and influence of the stakeholders, and considers stakeholders with both positive and negative feelings towards the project.

Positive stakeholders can be leveraged to enhance project success and negative stakeholders need to be encouraged to support the project, or at least be neutral in their impact.

Use the three-step process outlined in the PMBOK® Guide:

- **Step 1:** identify all potential project stakeholders
- **Step 2:** analyse the potential impact of each stakeholder
- **Step 3:** assess likely stakeholder reactions and plan to get support.

First, identify all the potential stakeholders and gather basic information about them, such as their role and position within the organisational hierarchy, their authority levels and any specific interests or expectations.

The key stakeholders are easily identified as they appear in the project governance and structure chart, if one has already been developed. This group includes anyone in a decision-making or management role who will be impacted by the project.

It can be difficult to identify all the stakeholders and additional stakeholders can often emerge later in the project. This always presents difficulties and often leads to delays as additional expectations are woven into the project. The more comprehensive is the stakeholder identification during project initiation, the better.

Stakeholders are often uncovered through discussions with the initial key stakeholders and the list should be expanded until all potential stakeholders are identified – for example, staff or customers impacted by the project, third party suppliers or finance and legal departments. It is a good idea to consult other experts within the organisation, such as the sponsor, other project managers and the PMO, who may be able to identify other stakeholders. (See Figure 2.7 on page 33.)

Developing the stakeholder register

The stakeholder register is a key deliverable during project initiation. The process of developing the stakeholder register carries on from stakeholder analysis and includes the identification of the power and interest of each stakeholder.

STAKEHOLDER POWER AND INTEREST

Introduce specific groups of stakeholders during this process but it is critical that they have a homogenous set of expectations – if not then they need to be called out individually. This stakeholder classification information is normally captured in the stakeholder power and interest grid. There are several different forms of this grid, but the recommended one is the power and interest grid (see Chapter 2, page 33) found in the PMBOK® Guide (see PMI, 2013, p. 397).

Once you have completed the stakeholder power and interest grid, the next step is to determine your specific approach to stakeholder management and communication for each key

See PMBOK® Guide Figure 13-4 Example power/ interest grid with stakeholders

stakeholder or group of stakeholders. The amount of effort and type of communication mechanisms will vary depending on their power and interest. Let's explore the four quadrants.

- *Manage closely:* the expectations of and relationships with this set of stakeholders are the most critical to achieving the project objectives. More effort will go into communicating with this group and more interactive communication methods will be used.
- *Keep satisfied:* this group are the next in order of importance due to their level of power. It is necessary to monitor their level of interest; if it increases then the level of attention and communication needs to increase. While in this quadrant, the emphasis will be on regular but less interactive communication. This is often called PUSH communication, as it is directly addressed to the recipient but doesn't always require a more time intensive form of interactive communication such as a face-to-face meeting. Choose PUSH mechanisms as the primary mode of communicating with this group and always offer to follow up with a meeting or phone call if they require more information or have questions.
- *Keep informed:* this group can often have very high interest but almost no power or influence over the project. They need to be monitored because if they move into the keep satisfied or manage closely quadrants then the approach to communicating with them and managing their expectations needs to be taken up a level. Generally, use a combination of PUSH and PULL communication mechanisms. Send them occasional specifically addressed emails (PUSH) but concentrate on providing them with the opportunity to self-serve information from a project-related website or online noticeboard.
- *Monitor:* this group can largely be left to satisfy their own communication requirements. It is best to meet with them irregularly and only if requested. Send this group general updates designed for public consumption that direct them to the PULL mechanisms provided for the keep informed group. It is critical, though, that this group is regularly monitored, especially if they move into the keep satisfied quadrant.

Stakeholder analysis matrix

Figure 2.9 on page 35 has identified and classified the key stakeholders according to their power and interest, so the next step is to assess their likely reactions to the project and to determine engagement strategies to leverage the positive influence of some, and to reduce the negative influence of others.

Stakeholder analysis matrix template

A stakeholder analysis template with instructions can be found online at

Take this opportunity to identify any major project risks that relate to stakeholders and to commence populating the risk register. The completion of the stakeholder analysis matrix is the first step in communication planning. Both of these are explained more in Chapters 3, 12 and 13.

Both the position of stakeholders on the power and interest grid and the content of the stakeholder analysis matrix can be very sensitive. It is strongly recommended that these deliverables are treated as confidential and only shared with the core project team, and potentially the project sponsor.

Managing stakeholder engagement

Stakeholder expectations need to be actively managed to increase the likelihood of project acceptance and success. In order to manage the expectations of the various project stakeholders, it is critical to have completed a detailed stakeholder analysis to determine their requirements for deliverables and activities in the areas of communication, training and engagement. The management of key project stakeholders, including the project sponsor and senior management involved in project governance (typically known as the steering committee), is primarily undertaken using the disciplines covered in Chapter 12. This section concentrates on the management of other stakeholders who are interested in, or impacted by, the project outcomes.

Stakeholder management is one of the most important and difficult roles for the project manager. See Chapter 4 (pages 81–3) for more details on managing expectations.

Most of the key inputs into this process are produced during the earlier communications planning activities and include:
- communications plan
- stakeholder register
- stakeholder management strategies.

The key skills required by the project manager to manage and anticipate stakeholder expectations are:
- intuition and judgement
- understanding of human behaviour and motivations
- political astuteness
- rapport building skills
- negotiation skills
- influencing skills
- problem solving skills
- active listening.

Good communication and training are used to assist stakeholders to understand and gain the necessary skills to continue to be successful after the project has delivered the outcomes. 'Engagement' is less easily understood and is often considered a loose concept or approach to managing expectations, but with some adjustment it is easy to see that engagement activities are both tangible and critical to the successful adoption of change. Figure 15.2 shows the relationships between the more commonly understood areas of communication and training and the critical area of engagement.

FIGURE 15.2 STAKEHOLDER ENGAGEMENT ACTIVITIES

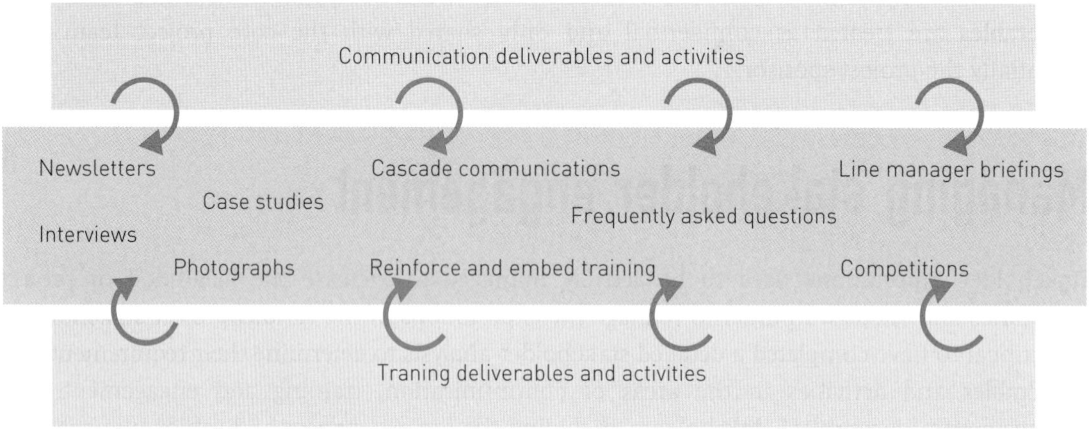

Communication deliverables and activities

Newsletters   Cascade communications   Line manager briefings

Case studies

Interviews   Frequently asked questions

Photographs   Reinforce and embed training   Competitions

Traning deliverables and activities

Causes of conflict on projects

One definition of conflict is:

> verb (used without object) 1. to come into collision or disagreement; be contradictory, at variance, or in opposition; clash: The account of one eyewitness conflicted with that of the other. My class conflicts with my going to the concert. 2. to fight or contend; do battle.
>
> noun 3. a fight, battle, or struggle, esp. a prolonged struggle; strife. 4. controversy; quarrel: conflicts between parties. 5. discord of action, feeling, or effect; antagonism or opposition, as of interests or principles: a conflict of ideas. 6. a striking together; collision. 7. incompatibility or interference, as of one idea, desire, event, or activity with another: a conflict in the schedule. 8. psychiatry: a mental struggle arising from opposing demands or impulses.

Source: http://www.Dictionary.Reference.com.

Wherever there are people there will be conflict. On projects conflict exists when two people wish to carry out acts which are mutually inconsistent. They may both want to do the same thing, such as deliver a project, but in fundamentally different ways. Or they may want to do different things that are mutually incompatible, such as increase scope or decrease the timeframe. The conflict is resolved when some mutually compatible set of actions is worked out.

The definition of conflict can be extended from individuals to groups (such as teams and organisations) and more than two parties can be involved in the conflict. With teams of people and various groups of stakeholders, conflict is inevitable and often good; for example, good teams always go through the forming, storming, norming and performing periods. And getting the most out of diversity means that the project manager will often need to deal with contradictory values, perspectives and opinions.

Conflict is often needed and can make a positive contribution to the achievement of the project. When managed positively it can:

- help to raise and address problems
- focus work on the most appropriate issues
- help people 'be real'; for example, it motivates them to participate
- help people learn how to recognise and benefit from their differences.

When conflict is poorly managed it can detract seriously from the ability of the project to achieve the assigned objectives, and in extreme circumstances it can even lead to early closure of the project. Conflict is a problem when it:

- hampers productivity
- lowers morale
- causes more and continued conflicts
- causes inappropriate behaviours
- causes delays or cost overruns
- causes scope or quality issues.

The primary causes of conflict on projects are:

1 ***Poor communication:*** often occurs when team members and stakeholders use different terms to describe similar activities and deliverables, or if communication around decision making is unclear, comes as a surprise or the rationale is not explained. Common side effects of poor communication are a lack of respect for project decision makers and a tendency for team members to believe rumours.

2 ***Poorly defined roles and responsibilities:*** these can lead to disagreements or confusion about specific accountabilities and can result in team members trying to execute deliverables in different ways or potentially refusing to undertake deliverables as they believe they are someone else's responsibility.

3 ***Interpersonal chemistry:*** clashes and misunderstandings can result from conflicting values and attitudes, and if certain team members have strong personalities or views that clash with other team members or even the overall project approach. This can be due to expectations created by previous project environments and organisational cultures.

4 ***Under-resourcing:*** conflict in teams is more prevalent when there is too much to do and everyone is working extra hours. This is usually because of insufficient resource allocation for the project team or a failure to backfill or reduce work expectations for stakeholders who need to spend time working on the project as subject matter experts.

5 ***Ineffective project sponsorship:*** project sponsors can be ineffective for many reasons; for example, they may be inexperienced with projects and not understand their role, they may have not wanted to be a project sponsor or they may lack sufficient authority and senior management support to resolve issues and make decisions.

6 *Incompatible goals and priorities:* this creates conflict as people are pulling in different directions in order to achieve their own goals and priorities above those of others or of the project. This is a surprisingly common issue and results from a lack of sharing of assigned goals and objectives.

Negotiation frameworks

Conflict is dynamic and each time you analyse a conflict situation it will be different. There are two primary types of conflict – latent and manifest. Latent conflict is covert and occurs when the participants are not openly expressing their concerns or disagreements. This form of conflict often manifests as poor morale and productivity and requires some form of catalyst in order to uncover the conflict so that negotiation and conflict resolution can commence.

Manifest conflict is out in the open and the perception of the conflict is shared and acknowledged by all participants. In this case negotiation and conflict resolution can commence immediately.

Negotiation is a sophisticated form of communication and is critical to the constructive management of conflict. It is important that conflict management skills are used throughout the negotiation process.

Common responses to conflict

According to Spegel, Rogers and Buckley (1998), there are five common responses to conflict.

1 *Competing:* is a style in which one's own needs are advocated over the needs of others. It relies on an aggressive style of communication, low regard for future relationships and the exercise of coercive power. Those using a competitive style tend to seek control over a discussion as they often fear that loss of control will result in solutions that fail to meet their needs.

2 *Avoiding:* also known as smoothing or appeasing, and is the opposite of the competing response. People using this style try to be diplomatic and often give way on their needs in order to appease others with more power. They may never openly state their needs as they see preserving the relationship as the critical outcome of the negotiation.

3 *Accommodating:* this is driven by a negative perception of conflict and those with this preference hope that the conflict will simply go away. Sometimes feelings get pent up, needs go unexpressed, and the conflict festers until it becomes too big to ignore, when perhaps it could have been more easily overcome if it had been addressed earlier. Relationships can completely break down and project goals can be severely impacted.

4 *Compromising:* in which participants gain and give in a series of trade-offs and negotiations. While it gets an outcome, compromise is generally not satisfying for all parties

as sometimes participants give way in order to reach agreement to the detriment of their goals or those of the project.

5 *Collaborating:* is the pooling of individual needs and goals toward a common goal and is often called 'win-win'. Collaboration requires assertive communication and cooperation in order to achieve a better solution than either individual could have achieved alone. It offers the chance for consensus, the integration of needs and the potential to exceed the original possibilities. It is considered the most positive form of conflict resolution but is the most difficult to achieve due to other factors such as limited timeframe and the emotionality and relative power of the participants.

Negotiation for conflict resolution

The Conflict Resolution Network (a not-for-profit that specialises in conflict resolution) suggests five basic principles of negotiation that facilitate outcomes:

1 be hard on the problem and soft on the person
2 focus on needs, not positions
3 emphasise common ground
4 be inventive about options
5 make clear agreements.

The following negotiation framework has been adapted from the NSW Government's community builders program. Their best practice recommendations are outlined below.

1 *Preparation:* do your homework and know as much as possible about yourself and the other parties. Think about the concept of a best alternative to a negotiated settlement (BATNA) for both yourself and on behalf of the other participant. Establish your best and worst case scenarios and the pros and cons of these.

2 *Create an appropriate environment:* in terms of the physical environment, all aspects of the location, venue, seating arrangements, etc. should be neutral, non-threatening, calm and supportive. Ensure that you select appropriate language which is understandable to both parties and consider using interpreters if necessary. With respect to the timeframe, it is important to be flexible and not to rush to an outcome as successful negotiations require time and effort.

3 *Establish the ground rules:* behavioural – not interrupting, taking turns, respect, no abuse. Procedural – clarify roles of various parties: facilitator, chairperson, experts, absent partners. Substantive – what can be discussed and decided, confidentiality, privacy, permission to speak to the media.

4 *Adopt conflict resolution strategies including:*
   • commit to a win-win solution
   • fight fair
   • manage your emotions

- be honest and authentic
- get your facts right
- focus on the issue not the person
- maintain the relationship (create empathy by seeing yourself and the other party from their point of view)
- identify unfair tactics and deal with them
- use active listening (noting non-verbal as well as spoken messages – facial expressions, voice inflexions, body language)
- use a variety of questioning techniques
- make it possible for parties to back down at any stage without feeling humiliated.

5 ***Confirm the authority the participants have to negotiate:*** it is important to ensure that all participants have the authority to negotiate and to make decisions, otherwise there may be little progress made as decisions can't be made nor agreements reached. It can be better to postpone the session until the participants with the appropriate levels of authority can attend.

6 ***Identify the non-negotiables:*** the negotiation will progress more smoothly if all participants are clear on the conditions on which they cannot compromise. Many people can find this concept difficult as they are concerned that it will erode their position, but it can assist to greatly reduce the timeframe and tension often associated with difficult negotiations.

7 ***Identify the issues and agree on them:*** it can be very useful to clarify the areas where you disagree so you can divide the issues into different categories. This enables you to address less difficult issues when the negotiations are stuck on more critical issues, to refocus on the issues and try to resolve them, and to explore best and worst alternatives to negotiating an acceptable agreement.

8 ***Clarify each party's needs and explore them:*** wants are not the same as needs, as they are often not negotiable. Exploring why the participants have their sets of needs and wants can greatly assist to end the conflict or finalise the negotiation. It can be beneficial to base the negotiations on the basic needs and true interests of each party.

9 ***Find the common ground and establish a common purpose:*** if possible, establish some objective and fair standards against which the final outcome can be judged. Negotiations based on principles can be more positive than those based on power.

10 ***Explore the options:*** be as inventive and creative as possible in suggesting and exploring all options, as this can generate innovative solutions that can lead to effective win-win outcomes.

11 ***Discuss possible solutions:*** do this in terms of possible viability and which solutions can provide the best outcome for all participants in terms of creating a win-win situation. It can be useful at this point to review the areas of agreement and common ground.

12 ***Select areas of agreement and commit to these:*** recap and clearly agree on what has already been decided. It is important to understand and confirm the agreements.

13 *Record these agreements:* ensure all parties have copies of the record of agreements to avoid back sliding on what has already been achieved.

14 *Decide on follow-up actions and timeframes:* negotiators will need to report outcomes to other stakeholders; to accelerate this process it can be helpful to decide on the spokesperson and the timeframe for the implementation of the agreement.

Source: Roslyn McDonald, Premier's Department, NSW 2002.

Change management frameworks
What is change and change management?

Change is when events occur that result in our normal environment being altered. This alteration then requires us to do something differently than we did before the change occurred. Change is constant, with us all the time and is accelerating in our modern age. Change is not predictable and does not always follow an exact pattern. Change varies in degree from a minor irritation to something with major impacts. Change makes individuals uncomfortable as it means uncertainty.

Change management is the application of a set of tools, processes, skills and principles for managing the people side of change to achieve the required outcomes of a project or change initiative. Change management can be used to develop both a holistic and structured approach for enabling and supporting individual change, as well as a customised approach based on the specific stakeholders being impacted. It enables individuals to make successful personal transitions resulting in the adoption and realisation of change.

REAL-WORLD EXPERIENCE

WHAT CHANGE MANAGEMENT IS NOT

Many inexperienced project managers, especially those from IT and engineering backgrounds, often confuse the concept of change management with other disciplines. This can create problems among the project team and stakeholders. The following list helps you to understand what change management is **not**:

- It is **not** change control
- It is **not** integrated change control
- It is **not** release management
- It is **not** configuration management
- It is **not** requirements traceability.

The benefits of change management

The goal of change management is to implement projects and business changes quickly so as to minimise disruption and maximise the benefits. The benefits of adopting a change management approach to the management of stakeholders within the context of a project are:

- employees have a solid understanding of why change is happening
- employees engage in both the solution and the change
- training is used to build knowledge after employees have made the personal decision to support the change
- resistance is identified and dealt with early in the process
- senior leaders demonstrate their own and the organisation's commitment to the change
- communications are segmented and customised for different audiences in order to answer the questions that they care about and to improve overall support.

When change is consistently managed well and change management practices are embedded into an organisation, then changes are less painful and momentum increases. The probability of achieving successful project outcomes increases and the organisation builds a history of successful change which, in turn, improves the likelihood of success for future projects and change initiatives.

Integrating project management and change management

Project management and change management are closely aligned. Change management is not an adjunct to a project, or a phase within the project, rather it is an activity that starts with the project and ends with the project. All projects cause change: 'A project is a change is a project'.

When an organisation introduces a change in a project, that change needs to be effectively managed on both the technical side and the people side. A technical-side focus ensures that the change is developed, designed and delivered effectively. The discipline of project management provides the structure, processes and tools to make this happen. Change management ensures that the needs of stakeholders are considered so that the change can be embraced and embedded so as to achieve the outcomes of the project.

Project management and change management both aim to increase the likelihood that projects deliver the intended results and outcomes. Integration of these will improve a project's chances of success. This is one of the major reasons that the PMBOK® Guide now has the new key knowledge area of Project Stakeholder Management. Unfortunately, it doesn't include sufficient discussion of change management tools and techniques.

Project managers and change managers often have competing priorities, but these can be combined to improve overall project success. This process is facilitated by:

- ensuring the project is accountable for delivering results and outcomes from both a technical project management perspective and also an effective people management perspective
- the change management resources defining their success in terms of the achievement of both the project results and the people outcomes, not just the execution of the change management activities
- clearly defining the differing roles, responsibilities and objectives of the project and change management teams, as well as providing clear frameworks as to how these roles need to work together and the physical deliverables that must be executed by each discipline
- applying a structured approach to change management which complements the structured processes and disciplines of project management.

PROJECT MANAGEMENT MASTERY

PROJECT AND CHANGE MANAGEMENT

Many inexperienced project managers do not appreciate the importance of planning communication and stakeholder management activities. They then find themselves with no time set aside to complete these activities, which increases their stress levels and reduces the chance of project success as not enough effort is being directed to this critical area. This is often due to a fundamental misunderstanding that all a successful project manager needs to do is manage the technical components of the project with a focus on scope, time, cost, quality, risk and procurement.

On small projects, the project manager often needs to take on some of the analysis tasks of a subject matter expert and also perform the communication and stakeholder management tasks that might fall to a change manager on a larger project.

According to recent research on IT-related projects from The Standish Group's *CHAOS Summary for 2010*, around 30 per cent of IT projects can be considered successful, with between 15 and 24 per cent considered failures, and the remaining 44 to 53 per cent having challenges whereby they have not delivered on all of the project objectives. Dr John Kotter, a prominent leadership and change management figure, states that his 30 years or research proves a 70 per cent failure for major change efforts in organisations. The common causes of failure in many of these studies relates to poor stakeholder management, inadequate communication and poor management of the project team. These are all the human factors of project management, and further advance the case to combine the disciplines of change management into the practice of project management.

For project managers who don't have the support of a change manager, then the solution is to selectively incorporate the major processes, deliverables and activities of change management into your project delivery approach and to ensure that you allow yourself sufficient time during execution to undertake these activities.

Kotter's change management approach

FIGURE 15.3 KOTTER'S EIGHT STEPS TO SUCCESSFUL CHANGE AND PROSCI'S 3-PHASE MODEL

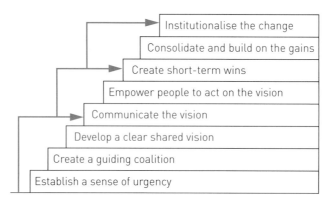

There are many theories about how to execute change and some of the most influential originated with John Kotter, a professor at Harvard Business School and widely acknowledged change expert. Kotter introduced his eight-step change process in his book *Leading change*. The following summary of his eight steps has been adapted to enhance the applicability of the framework for project delivery.

- Step 1 ***Create urgency:*** it helps to develop a sense of urgency around the need for change as this motivates stakeholders to get things moving. This requires open and convincing dialogue with the project sponsor and senior stakeholders about the need for the changes that will be delivered as a result of the project. The more project team members and stakeholders repeat a consistent message about the objectives, then the greater the sense of both commitment and urgency is created. Project managers should also seek to identify potential threats and scenarios that may detract from achieving the project outcomes.

- Step 2 ***Form a powerful coalition:*** you will require an influential project sponsor and a powerful steering committee in order to convince people that the change being delivered by the project is necessary. Project success is easier to achieve with strong leadership and visible support from senior people within the executing organisation. So, to lead change, you need to bring together a team of influential people. Once formed, your 'change coalition' needs to work as a team, continuing to build urgency and momentum around the project.

- Step 3 ***Create a strong vision:*** there will be many ideas, delivery approaches and solutions put forward during project inception. Document these clearly in the project charter as the project goals and objectives and seek agreement and support from both the project sponsor and the steering committee. A clear vision will help the project team and stakeholders to align behind the purpose of the project.

- Step 4 ***Communicate the vision:*** this involves formal project kick-off sessions/meetings and briefings as well as constant communications to ensure that the project team and stakeholders remain focused on, and aligned to, the project goals and objectives. The project team, project manager, project sponsor and steering committee must all remain consistent and supportive of the project vision by leading by example and motivating others to provide support.

- Step 5 **Remove obstacles:** once the project vision is clear and supported by all major stakeholders, then the project team should be motivated to commence work on delivering the outcomes. There are usually some stakeholders and project team members who will resist the change activities because of different views on how the objectives should be achieved or other common resistance factors. The project manager needs to review barriers regularly, and enlist the support of the project sponsor and steering committee to remove these barriers and maintain support for the project. Stakeholder analysis assists with identifying those who are, or are likely to, resist the changes. By being informed it is easier to address the needs and concerns of these individuals or groups.

- Step 6 **Create short-term wins:** project team motivation and stakeholder support is heightened by the achievement of interim goals along the way. Project managers can create short-term targets that build upon each other to meet the overall project outcomes. This is further supported by having appropriate reward and recognition schemes in place to acknowledge achievements and high performance along the way.

- Step 7 **Build on the change:** Kotter argues that many change projects fail because victory is declared too early. Quick wins are only the beginning of what needs to be done to achieve long-term business objectives once each project is completed. Each successful project provides an opportunity to build on what went right and to identify what can be improved to increase success on future projects. Project managers need to ensure that post-implementation reviews are conducted and the results shared, as well as capturing lessons learned along the way. There is a tendency to focus on what went wrong but it is equally important to capture the positive learnings so that these can be leveraged in the future.

- Step 8 **Anchor the changes in corporate culture:** to make any change stick it needs to become part of the organisation and culture. In project management terms this means ensuring that the project is transitioned to business as usual. Publically recognising key project team members and stakeholders who contributed to the achievement of the project objectives will help, as well as implementing plans for a handover from the project to business representatives to ensure on-going benefits are achieved.

Prosci's change methodology

The Prosci 3-Phase Change Methodology and ADKAR were created by Jeff Hiatt, the President of Prosci Research and founder of the Change Management Learning Center. Prosci was founded in 1994 and is a world leader in change management research. Prosci's early research revealed that the ineffective management of people throughout the change process was the number one reason cited for unsuccessful projects. This is supported by the *CHAOS Summary for 2010* published by the Standish Group. This biannual report consistently attributes project failure to poor communication, which could be translated as ineffective people management of the project team and stakeholders.

The three key principles underpinning the Prosci approach are:

1 change management requires both an individual and an organisational perspective
2 ADKAR presents an easy-to-use model for individual change
3 The 3-phase process gives structure to delivering change within a project lifecycle.

THE ADKAR MODEL FOR INDIVIDUAL CHANGE

Under the ADKAR model, the first step in managing change within an organisation is to understand how to manage change with a single individual. ADKAR is an effective tool for planning change management activities, diagnosing gaps, developing corrective actions and supporting managers as they lead their teams through the change. Prosci's research has repeatedly shown that employees respond most effectively to change messages that are delivered by their direct manager when the manager has obviously committed to the change themselves.

ADKAR stands for awareness, desire, knowledge, ability and reinforcement. For an individual to change they need:

- *Awareness of the need for change:* this is created by using communication from senior management to position the need for change. This needs to be supported by compelling arguments that address both the facts and the emotional benefits. These come via sharing customer feedback and market trends and conditions, as well as describing what will happen if the change cannot be implemented.
- *Desire to participate and support the change:* this requires the creation of a compelling vision and strong visible support by all areas of leadership. It helps if there are immediate and obvious consequences for senior leaders who do not actively support the change vision. Other enablers include the creation of future scenarios such as a 'day in the life of' which can help people to envisage the future state. It is a good time to harness the energy of early adopters and those who are dissatisfied with the current state.
- *Knowledge on how to change:* this is created via learning activities that provide people with the skills required to be successful after the change has been implemented. These learning activities include: access to information, face-to-face training, webinars, self-paced elearning, line manager briefings, frequently asked questions and so on.
- *Ability to implement required skills and behaviours:* this is the creation of both the environment and the opportunities for team members and stakeholders to apply their new skills and behaviours with support from line management in the form of coaching, mentoring and the removal of barriers.

- ***Reinforcement to sustain the change:*** this is critical and does not always have to be tied to money. It is possible to encourage the embedding of the new skills and behaviours through public recognition programs, as well as making revisions to employee objectives, incentives and performance management schemes that align to the post-change environment.

RESEARCH AND REFLECTION ACTIVITY

STAGES OF CHANGE COMMITMENT

The ADKAR model is a form of commitment curve. Commitment curves are regularly used by organisations when implementing change programs and major projects. The curves assess the commitment of employees to the changes and provide a path that is designed to increase overall employee commitment and thereby increase the business benefits that are associated with the change. There are many commitment curves that have been developed by organisations, academics and consulting firms. Conduct some online research and review the various commitment curves that exist and consider which of them appeals to you the most and may also be the most useful in your organisation or industry.

Try search terms such as:
- change commitment curve
- employee commitment curve
- commitment curve
- change curve.

PROSCI'S 3-PHASE CHANGE PROCESS

Prosci's organisational change management process was first introduced in 2002, after their third change management benchmarking study. It comprises three phases: preparing for change, managing change and reinforcing change. These change phases can be mapped to the five process groups in the standard PMBOK® Guide project lifecycle as shown in Figure 15.4. The Prosci phases kick off just after the PMBOK® Guide process groups begin, and the reinforcing change phase will often continue after the project has been formally closed.

FIGURE 15.4 PMBOK® GUIDE AND PROSCI PHASES

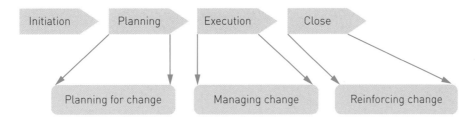

- ***Phase 1 – Preparing for change:*** this is aimed at getting ready and answers the question 'How much change management is needed for this specific project?'. It provides the situational awareness that is critical for effective change management. The outputs of this phase are as follows and almost exactly map to those recommended by PMBOK® Guide's process '13.2 Plan stakeholder management':
  - change characteristics profile
  - organisational attributes profile
  - change management strategy
  - change management team structure
  - sponsor assessment, structure and roles.
- ***Phase 2 – Managing change:*** this is focused on creating stakeholder management plans that are integrated into the project activities. Based on Prosci's research, there are five plans that should be created to help individuals move through the ADKAR model and these map to the outputs recommended by PMBOK® Guide's processes '10.1 Plan communications management' and '13.2 Plan stakeholder management':
  - communication plan
  - sponsor roadmap
  - training plan
  - coaching plan
  - resistance management plan.
- ***Phase 3 – Reinforcing change:*** this phase is critical but unfortunately it is often overlooked as it continues after the project has formally closed. It aims to help project teams create specific action plans to ensure the change is sustained. In this phase, project teams develop measures and mechanisms to see if the change has taken hold, to see if employees are actually doing their jobs the new way and to celebrate success. If not, then additional change management activities should be planned to address skills gaps or resistance factors. The major outputs of this phase are:
  - reinforcement mechanisms
  - compliance audit reports
  - corrective action plans
  - individual and group recognition approaches
  - success celebrations
  - after-action review.

Source: Change Management Learning Center © Prosci 1996–2013. Prosci and ADKAR are registered trademarks of Prosci Inc.

REAL-WORLD EXPERIENCE

IMPLEMENTING CHANGE MANAGEMENT PLANS

I have been working with the Prosci 3-Phase model over the last four years and find myself often adapting it to fit the context of delivering organisational and personal change within the constraints of project timeframes and budgets. The main adaptation I make is to extend Prosci's phase 2 (managing change) to include the planning and the execution of the communication, engagement and training deliverables and activities. I also align Prosci's phase 1 (preparing for change) with the PMBOK® Guide's planning phase; Prosci's phase 2 with PMBOK® Guide's execution phase; and Prosci's Phase 3 (reinforcing change) with PMBOK® Guide's closing phase. However, in my experience, many of the embedding activities need to be handed over to line managers and team leaders for delivery after a formal project closure.

INTERRELATIONSHIPS BETWEEN ADKAR AND THE 3-PHASE APPROACH

The ADKAR model focuses on the change process for an individual, while the 3-phase approach is designed to enable change to be executed as part of project delivery. Figure 15.5 illustrates the relationships between the two models.

FIGURE 15.5 ADKAR AND 3-PHASE INTERRELATIONSHIPS

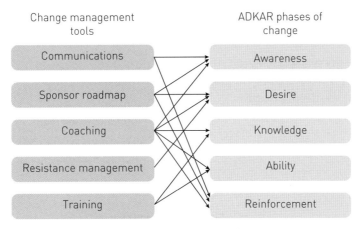

Connecting organisational and individual change management

Source: Change Management Learning Center © Prosci 1996–2013. Prosci and ADKAR are registered trademarks of Prosci Inc.

Controlling stakeholder engagement

Controlling stakeholder engagement is the process of communicating and working with stakeholders to address issues as they arise. Concerns need to be addressed as soon as they occur in order to prevent and minimise any negative impact. Specific issues need to be clarified, understood and resolved. This results in decisions, agreements and sometimes change requests, as well as adjustments to the stakeholder and communication plans that are being executed.

Many issues that arise during project execution are the result of a collection of factors in the stakeholder management discipline area that are often known as change resistance. Figure 15.6 provides a framework to assist in the understanding of different approaches that can be used to manage stakeholders that display varying levels of resistance.

FIGURE 15.6 DIMENSIONS OF STAKEHOLDER RESISTANCE

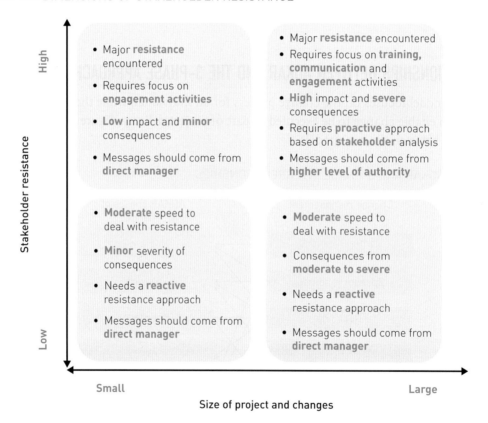

The stakeholder resistance grid in Figure 15.6 has been adapted from a Prosci grid designed to understand organisational change resistance. It has been adapted for use when understanding the behaviours of individual stakeholders and the resistance management approaches that can be applied. It can be used equally well to support the activities designed to control stakeholder engagement and to support the analysis of stakeholders, which is a critical component of stakeholder management planning. It is best explained by translating the various approaches into a table, as can be seen in Table 15.1.

TABLE 15.1 STAKEHOLDER RESISTANCE GRID

Quadrant	Pace of intervention	Severity of consequences	Approach to resistance	Best influencer
Stakeholder ready Small change	Moderate	Minor	Reactive	Project team or direct manager
Stakeholder resistant Small change	Slow	Minor	Proactive	Direct manager
Stakeholder ready Large change	Moderate	Moderate to severe	Reactive	Direct manager
Stakeholder resistant Large change	Quick	Severe	Proactive	Direct manager and highest authority

Propensity to adopt change

Individuals respond to change in different ways. Research into the uptake of innovations (which are themselves changes) can be very revealing in terms of understanding why different people seem to have a natural propensity to absorb and adopt changes, while others seem to find it more difficult. The following diagram shows the results of research into change adoption and change resistance that was carried out by Everett Rodgers (quoted in Robinson, 2009, p. 2).

FIGURE 15.7 CHANGE RESISTANCE AND ADOPTION

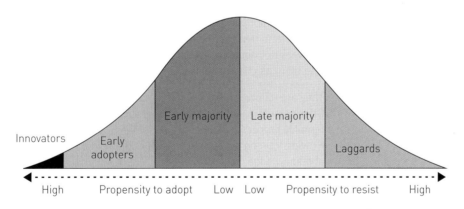

Source: Les Robinson, http://www.enablingchange.com.au.

Rodgers found that in any population people will fall into one of five categories in terms of their propensity to either resist or adopt change. These are outlined below.

- Innovators make up 2.5 per cent of the population and are the first to embrace change.
- Early adopters make up 13.5 per cent of the population and like to take on new challenges. They are often trendsetters and have high degrees of influence.

- The early majority at 34 per cent represent the equal largest group and are initially thoughtful about change and tend to become more positive.
- The late majority at 34 per cent are the other equal largest group and are sceptical about change, often only changing after being heavily influenced by their peers – the early majority.
- Laggards represent 16 per cent and are individuals who hold on to the past and actively resist change even after the vast majority of a population have accepted it. They will often choose to leave or be forced to leave due to poor performance.

The communication and change management needs of these different groups vary greatly and it is important to provide for the needs of all groups in order to maximise the success of the changes being delivered by the project. It is also important to realise that individuals may fall into different categories with each new change; i.e. they are an innovator on one project and a laggard on the next.

Table 15.2 provides guidelines on how to engage and communicate with people in the different categories.

TABLE 15.2 GUIDELINES ON ENGAGING WITH DIFFERENCE

Change adoption category	Tactics to improve engagement and reduce resistance
Innovators	» Provide them with support » Publicise their ideas » Use them as role models for others » Actively involve them with the project » Have them allocated to the project team if possible
Early adopters	» They are trendsetters and want to be associated with new ideas » Acknowledge their contribution and leverage their influence » Use them to test the changes and to provide feedback to generate answers to frequently asked questions » Use them as change champions and to deliver training
Early majority	» They are followers who are influenced by the early adopters » Offer competitions and prizes to get them engaged » Simplify processes to encourage uptake » Provide training and support to equip them with the required skills and knowledge
Late majority	» This groups dislikes risks and are uncomfortable with the change » Use the early majority as role models to promote success stories from this group » Respond to feedback and questions from the laggards to allay the concerns of this group » Provide an opportunity to submit questions and to review answers to frequently asked questions » Establish interactive question and answer sessions to address specific concerns

Change adoption category	Tactics to improve engagement and reduce resistance
Laggards	» Can be very anxious and stressed by the particular change » Provide many opportunities to up-skill in order to obtain the required competencies » Provide both training and reinforcement activities » Use their direct managers as coaches to improve performance » Communicate clearly about the consequences of not adopting the changes

What is change resistance?

Resistance to change is any behaviour or action that opposes the alterations that are underway. It can be covert or overt, conscious or unconscious, passive or aggressive, individual or organised by groups. Some individuals are very aware that they are uncomfortable or against the change and resist publicly and openly; others may unknowingly resist and be surprised by their own actions and behaviours; and yet others will be aware of their resistance and seek to undermine the change without others becoming aware (this is known as passive-aggressive behaviour).

Whatever form resistance to change takes, it threatens the success of the project or change initiative and can greatly impact the speed with which benefits can be achieved, and in its worst forms it can cause the cancellation of an entire project. Table 15.3 helps in understanding the characteristics of resistance to change by highlighting what it is and what it is not.

TABLE 15.3 CHANGE RESISTANCE IS/IS NOT

Change resistance is . . .	Change resistance is not . . .
Inevitable	Necessarily logical
A natural function of change	A sign of disloyalty
Manageable	Something to overcome or combat
An attempt by people to protect themselves	Aimed at an individual or to be taken personally
A sign that something important has been found	Designed to discredit your competence
A learning process	Indicative of poor performance
A sign of controlling the change process	A sign that the change process is out of control

Source: The Northern Sydney Institute, Part of TAFE NSW.

COMMON CAUSES OF CHANGE RESISTANCE

Understanding the likely causes of resistance to change provides important insights into how the resistance can be managed by controlling stakeholder engagement. The common causes of change resistance are given below.

1 *Loss of control:* many individuals feel resentful when change is imposed on them. A sense of control is essential to the self-esteem of many people. A sense of not having control is often cited as a primary cause of stress for people experiencing change. This factor will often manifest in attempts at overt or covert sabotage, or result in a marked increase in stress levels leading to conflict and abnormal workplace behaviours.

2 *Fear of the unknown:* when the future state is unknown this can result in fear which leads to resistance as employees seek to protect themselves, their position and their livelihood. This can be a particular problem on very large projects, where the change is so extreme or complex that most people are unable to see their own personal future state.

3 *Self-doubt:* in some cases individuals fear that they won't be able to learn the new skills that are required to be successful in the future state. This can become evident as some people will choose to leave the organisation before the change is implemented, or others may actively resist the adoption of new processes or techniques.

4 *Unexpected change:* people react negatively almost instinctively when decisions or demands are placed upon them without any forewarning or preparation. An individual who has had no time to think through their reaction will almost certainly react negatively and resist change. This can be a difficult factor to overcome in cases where it is critical to maintain confidentiality of particular actions, such as retrenchments or the disbanding of business units.

5 *Force of habit:* many people are habitual in their nature and resent any break to this routine. Naturally, change disrupts their routines and pushes them outside their comfort zone, often causing insecurities that lead to resistance behaviours such as nit picking to find fault with the changes and citing minor issues as reasons for why the change should be rejected.

6 *Ego and pride:* many people perceive that if something is to be changed then it implies that the way it was done before was inferior. This can be a particular challenge with inflexible individuals who were deeply involved in the design of the current state. They can often be deeply affronted and hostile if someone suggests that things can be improved. This is one of the most common forms of change resistance and can be difficult to overcome as it is not logical. Sometimes asking these individuals what things frustrate them and what they have always wanted to change can be enough to get them to move forward, especially if their suggestions are incorporated.

7 *Chaos theory:* changes occurring in a professional environment can have an impact on a person's personal life, just as changes in a person's personal life can reduce their capacity to absorb changes in the work environment. People undergoing stressful external circumstances, such as family illness, addiction issues, recent deaths of close family

members, divorce and so on, will often struggle to accept change. It is important to understand what is happening without prying and provide support if possible. Many organisations have employee assistance schemes which provide counselling and support services for those requiring personal assistance in order to remain productive at work.

8 ***Increased workload:*** the implementation of change, and the actual change itself, can lead to increased workloads. Employees often need to continue to perform the same volume of work in the old way while contributing expertise to the design of the future state and also learning the new skills and practices they will need once the change has been implemented. If they are not given relief in terms of reducing the expectations on productivity then they are likely to suffer high levels of stress. They may be simply unable to increase their workload to accommodate the expectations.

9 ***Previous experience:*** a history of failed project and change initiatives, or simple exhaustion from constant change (often known as change fatigue), can cause resistance. Given that around 50 per cent of IT projects fail (Standish Group, 2010), and up to 70 per cent of change initiatives (Kotter International, 2012), then this can be the most prevalent form of change resistance faced by project managers and change managers.

10 ***Personal job security:*** resistance is common when there are possibile job losses or retrenchments as a result of the change. If this is not expected then it is useful to communicate that no job losses are expected, but only if this is reasonably certain. If job losses are likely or certain, then it is often best to inform those concerned of the percentage of workers who will be affected, how the decisions will be made, when the decisions will be made, and what support will be provided to those who will be leaving. Fear of the unknown is often worse than clearly understanding the negative consequences that will occur.

11 ***Lack of compelling vision:*** change resistance is increased in cases where a compelling vision has not been created. The vision must clearly describe why the change is required in terms that all employees can understand. Some people will hope that if they ignore the changes then management will simply give up and things will go back to the way they were; indeed, they may have first-hand experience of this occurrence. It is important to create a sense of urgency and to describe the need for the change in a way that is backed up by facts as well as emotions. It can help to point out to employees the consequences of *not* changing; e.g. job losses or even going out of business.

12 ***Complacency:*** employees can resist change due to complacency, especially when they are comfortable with the current state and can see that the future state will significantly increase the expectations placed on them, or significantly decrease their status (money, recognition, personal power, etc.). It can help to emphasise that the current state is no longer an option and to clearly point out the consequences of not changing. In many cases it is best to quickly remove this layer (as it is often middle management) to give the organisation a chance to move forward, and clearly emphasise that everyone needs to support the change or face the consequences.

Figure 15.8 is a summary of the consequences of not addressing and managing resistance to change.

FIGURE 15.8 CONSEQUENCES OF NOT ADDRESSING RESISTANCE

What is originally desired by leadership...	Reallity of what employees are confronted with...	Outcomes IF 'human side' is not addressed
▸ Productivity increases ▸ New service concepts ▸ New processes or process redesign ▸ New organisational structures, cross-functional collaboration ▸ Radical cost cutting/headcount reduction	▸ Fear of job losses ▸ Potential loss of responsibillity and independence ▸ Change of responsibillity and decision authority ▸ Change of work location ▸ New and unknown leadership styles ▸ Inconsistent or incompatible leadership styles ▸ New expectations of superiors and peers ▸ Loss of status ▸ Requirements for additional skills and expertise ▸ New and unkown tasks ▸ New colleagues	▸ Resistance in teams or line organisation toward implementation ▸ Slow and/or incomplete implementation ▸ Lack of decision taking and/or frequent revisions of decisions ▸ Quality problems ▸ Reduced productivity ▸ Loss of 'high performers' ▸ Insecurity and increased risk avoidance ▸ Reduced individual commitment ▸ Negative word of mouth

Change management addresses the emotional impact of these issues

Source: Booz Allen Hamilton, 2004, p. 7. Booz & Company.

Resistance management approaches

ENGAGE LOGIC AND EMOTION

This is one of the most recommended approaches to avoiding resistance to change, but also one of the most difficult. It is central to Kotter's change steps and also underpins the approaches undertaken by major consulting firms, such as Booz Allen Hamilton. It is widely accepted (although with varying degrees of underpinning data) that up to 70 per cent of change initiatives fail and many of these are using a project-based approach to delivery.

There is a critical connection between the thinking and the feeling sides of change. Kotter believed that change is more successful when those affected can understand the change from both a logical and an emotional viewpoint. This is particularly powerful when a direct manager has a good working relationship with an employee. In this case, often a personal appeal such as 'I believe in this change. It would mean a lot to me if you could be supportive' is enough to get a reluctant employee to support a major change.

REAL-WORLD EXPERIENCE

LEADERS AND CHANGE

I have observed that change leaders (typically senior executives who are also sponsoring the project to deliver the changes) have already embraced the need for change and they try to use data and logic to convince their staff that the change is both worthwhile and necessary.

They fail to recognise that their people are emotional beings and may not support a change when the rationale is based on pure logic. It is necessary to embrace the 'heart' of change and tap into emotions in order to carry the change forward successfully.

I have seen many situations where insufficient effort and resourcing is devoted to the change management aspects of a major project due to the naive view of the project sponsor and steering committee that the outcomes and benefits of the project are so obvious that they speak for themselves. Senior stakeholders are often so convinced about the change that they can't imagine that any staff would resist. Here are some direct quotes from recent conversations I have had when trying to convince steering committees about the need for change management (including communication, training and engagement activities):

- 'They are accountants. They are used to complying with regulations.'
- 'Recent projects haven't been very successful as our staff didn't do what we asked them to do.'
- 'We just tell them and they do it' – this came from the same person who made the statement above!
- 'I don't like FAQs so I don't think that we need to spend the time on these.'
- 'We ran them through an overview at a recent conference. I can't see that they need any more detail.'

LISTEN TO OBJECTIONS

This approach requires a genuine interest in understanding objections to the change and then responding to the objections. It is not enough to simply allow individuals to complain. Each objection must be responded to in terms of how it has been considered, or not considered, in the design of the future state.

The power of true listening and empathy is often underestimated. In many cases, employees simply want to be heard and to voice their objections. Understanding these objections can often provide a clear path toward resolution. Listening can also help identify misunderstandings about the change that can be quickly clarified.

If there is insufficient communication then rumours will often be created to fill the void. Rumours and background conversations often produce incorrect or misinterpreted messages which create incorrect perceptions. Giving employees a voice via suggestion boxes, frequently asked questions and online blogs provides information about the accuracy of perceptions which can then be corrected via further communication.

It is critical that responses are not seen as arguing, convincing or defending. The goal of this technique is to listen, understand and provide clarity, not to convince employees to adopt the change.

WHAT'S IN IT FOR ME (WIIFM)

It can be very beneficial to consider the situation of different groups of stakeholders and exactly how they will be impacted – both negatively and positively. The positive side of the equation is often referred to as what's in it for me or WIIFM. This can then be reinforced in one-on-one conversations and via briefing sessions so that employees become aware of the positive outcomes rather than dwelling on the negative impacts of the change.

EMPOWER EMPLOYEES

Some types of changes can be effectively delivered by employees, as long as they are clear about the overall outcomes that are required and the constraints within which the solutions needs to be delivered; e.g. time, cost, plant and equipment. Just how much the project or change initiative can be left in the hands of individuals is dependent on the speed that is required, the type of change, size and complexity of the project, and the culture of the organisation.

Even if it is not appropriate to delegate completely to employees, it is still possible to empower them by seeking their input and suggestions, involving them in pilots, or actively getting them to work on the project as subject matter experts. The direct involvement of these individuals can then be publicised so that other employees are aware of the employee engagement in the changes.

REMOVE BARRIERS

The desire to change can be inhibited by obstacles or barriers. These barriers may be within the organisation, or external pressures that are influencing the behaviour of the individual. For example, sometimes projects or changes are implemented and a set of new competencies or behaviours is required. It can be hard for employees to be successful in this future state if the performance evaluation criteria have not been changed and still reward performance based on the previous skills or behaviours. To embed change it is critical that the performance measures are aligned to the new outcomes.

PROVIDE CLEAR CHOICES AND CONSEQUENCES

Providing people with choices will make them feel more in control. When choices can't be provided, then it is important that employees understand the consequences of not changing. Managers can facilitate this process by being clear about the choices employees have during change. In many cases, the actual change may be out of the control of frontline supervisors and managers. If so, managers must communicate in simple and clear terms what the choices and consequences are for each employee.

If the change is critical to the success of the project, then people who continue to resist may suffer the following consequences:

- increased personal stress
- reduced results and job performance
- reduced effectiveness
- reduced efficiency
- reduced job satisfaction
- illness and absenteeism
- may be forced to leave
- may elect to leave.

CREATE MOMENTUM

Most people respond positively to the opportunity for better things in the future. Momentum and a desire to move to the future state can be created by senior management sharing their vision and passion for the change, and providing details of specific things that will be better in the future. This approach works best in cultures of trust and respect, but is not as effective in highly power-oriented, command-and-control organisations.

PROMOTE BENEFITS AND EARLY WINS

Some people are less able to imagine a better future; they won't really believe it until they can actually see or experience it. Demonstrating the benefits of change in a real and tangible way can help to create desire in these individuals. This could include the promotion of quick wins from early phases, sharing case studies of other projects or organisations that have achieved benefits by making similar changes, sharing personal testimonials or inviting speakers to give briefings to staff, or visibly demonstrating the success of pilot programs or trials within your own organisation. Making the change real and demonstrating that success is possible can remove doubts and fears that some employees feel about change.

MAKE A PERSONAL APPEAL

This approach only works for leaders with open and inclusive styles where there is a strong relationship with employees and high levels of rapport. A prerequisite is honest, open relationships where there are high levels of trust and respect. This form of appeal may include phrases such as 'I believe in this change', 'This is important to me' and 'I want your support'.

BUILD ADVOCATES

This approach relies on working with influential employees who are openly negative about the change. Support them so that they become advocates for the change. Efforts to argue with them or to try to convince them to change their opinion will often be met with stronger resistance. But if you can convert them by involving them in the change, listening to them and responding to their objections, pointing out the consequences for them and for others, and potentially making a personal appeal, then they can become the strongest supporters. It is then possible to turn them into a spokesperson for the change and to publicise their personal case study in order to influence others to be more supportive.

Focusing on a few strong resistors rather than on large stakeholder groups can help to regain some control over the powerful background conversations or rumour mill, as well as utilise the natural influence that these individuals have over their peers.

CREATE A SACRIFICE

This approach involves removing obvious dissenters early in order to clearly show that the organisation is serious about achieving the change and that there are potentially severe consequences for those who are unable to support the change. Sometimes it is sufficient to remove one influential negative stakeholder, at other times it is necessary to remove an entire class of stakeholders who may be complacent and believe that by rallying together to resist the change then the organisation will give up the attempt. This was a very common approach to the corporate restructures that occurred in the late 1980s and again in the early twenty-first century. Many organisations removed entire layers of middle management in order to create change and reduce operating costs. This type of action shows that senior management is serious about the change, resistance will not be tolerated and there are consequences to not supporting the change. If used too often this can create a culture of fear among employees which can stifle productivity and innovation, but it can be extremely effective when used occasionally.

Common issues leading to change requests

Many project managers do not consider communications or engagement activities to be part of the project scope. However, the preparation and delivery of communication and engagement activities takes effort and results in deliverables that need to be included within the project scope in order to avoid change requests and pressure on timeframes and budgets.

Table 15.4 outlines some of the major causes of variations due to stakeholder engagement activities. If any of these arise, it is good practice is to make these change requests as part of '4.5 Perform integrated change control'.

TABLE 15.4 STAKEHOLDER FACTORS LEADING TO CHANGE REQUESTS

Change factor	Explanation and understanding
A critical group of stakeholders is overlooked	When insufficient analysis of stakeholders is undertaken in the initiation phase, it is common for additional groups of stakeholders to be revealed during execution. This will often result in additional communication or training activities that were not included in the original scope.
Stakeholder pressure may result in changes to scope	Sometimes assumptions made about scope inclusions and exclusions will be overturned due to pressure exerted by stakeholders during the planning or execution of the project. At other times a critical requirement of a particular stakeholder or group will have been accidentally overlooked. This type of change should be formally documented and managed via change control processes.
Stakeholder management activities are under-resourced	The effort and resourcing required to complete stakeholder management activities is often underestimated, resulting in the need to increase resourcing (and thus cost) in order to achieve the project's objectives. If additional resources are not allocated then the project may need to be extended or some of the objectives sacrificed.
Undeclared priorities	Stakeholders may have conflicting priorities that can impact the support and resources they are able to provide to the project. This can lead to the project manager not being aware of the other calls on the resource's time and to therefore overallocate them to activities in the project schedule.

Related processes from the PMBOK® Guide

4.1 **Develop project charter (initiation):** In practice, the high-level project scope is developed and documented during the initiation phase in the project charter. It forms the boundaries for subsequent scoping processes. Unfortunately, the PMBOK® Guide has the scope definition activities all occurring in the planning phase and is therefore out of sync with practice.

4.2 **Develop project management plan (planning):** This is the process of defining and documenting the actions necessary to prepare and integrate all subsidiary plans for each of the other key knowledge areas of project management. The PMP is the primary deliverable from the planning phase. Good practice dictates that the PMP is baselined at the end of the planning phase, particularly in the areas of scope, cost and time. It is progressively added to during project execution via the perform integrated change control process.

The planning for all the key knowledge areas is normally performed at the same time as this process, or expanded upon shortly afterwards. All key knowledge areas have discrete processes for planning that are defined in their process groups.

This process is closely linked to '8.1 Plan quality management', '9.1 Plan human resource management', '10.1 Plan communications management', '11.1 Plan risk management' and '12.1 Plan procurement management'.

4.3 **Direct and manage project work (execution):** The process of performing the work defined in the PMP in order to achieve the project's objectives. The project manager directs the execution of the planned activities, sometimes with the assistance of a project management team for larger projects. The PMBOK® Guide includes this process within the execution phase but there is merit in thinking of it as a separate process group having equal importance to monitoring and controlling.

4.4 **Monitor and control project work (execution):** The process of tracking, reviewing and regulating the progress made towards the objectives defined in the PMP. The project manager is specifically responsible for the monitoring and control of project work, sometimes with the assistance of a project management team or project management office for larger projects. Monitoring is an aspect of project management performed throughout the project, but it becomes more critical during the execution phase. It is closely linked to '5.6 Control scope', '6.7 Control schedule', '7.4 Control costs', '8.3 Quality control', '10.3 Control communications' and '11.6 Control risks'.

4.5 **Perform integrated change control (monitoring and controlling):** The process of reviewing all change requests, including approving or rejecting changes and managing the flow-on impacts on all project deliverables and all components of the PMP. All requested changes should be identified through '5.6 Control scope'. The activities within this process are critical to managing stakeholder expectations and to ensuring the highest chance of project success. They occur from project inception through to completion and are part of the monitor and control process group. It is important that only approved changes be incorporated into the project, as it is surprisingly common to see unapproved changes being inadvertently undertaken.

5.2 **Collect requirements (planning):** The process of defining and documenting the needs of the project sponsor and key stakeholders. Encompasses the requirements related to the specific functional and non-functional characteristics of outputs being delivered by the project. Occurs during the planning phase and is very closely related to project success measures, because if the end products do not meet the requirements then it is highly unlikely the project sponsor will sign off on the completion of the project.

8.1 **Plan quality management (planning):** The process for identifying the quality requirements and quality standards applicable to a project and documenting how these requirements will be achieved for each deliverable. This also includes the identification of the quality assurance and quality control techniques that will be used to check that each deliverable has met the required quality expectations.

9.4 **Manage project team (execution):** The process for tracking team member performance, providing feedback, resolving issues and managing changes to improve team performance. This requires the skills of influencing team behaviour, managing conflict, resolving issues and managing team member performance appraisals.

10.1 *Plan communications management (planning):* The process for determining the project stakeholder information needs and for developing tailored communication approaches to meet those needs. Other components can include defining the communication needs within the project team.

11.1 *Plan risk management (planning):* The process for defining how to conduct risk management activities for a project. This involves determining the risk management framework, including concepts such as the risk breakdown structure, likelihood and impact, and risk management approaches. Excellent international standards exist for risk management and many organisations have incorporated these into their own organisational processes.

11.2 *Identify risks (planning):* The process for identifying the risks that may impact the project. It is useful to have a broad group of key stakeholders, project team members and internal experts participate in the risk identification session. Good practice dictates that as far as possible all major risks should be identified during the planning phase, although this is an iterative process as often risks are unpredictable and new risks become obvious during execution.

12.1 *Plan procurement management (planning):* The process for identifying the procurement requirements for a project. This involves identifying all resources and equipment that must be purchased and utilised in order to complete the project, as well as specifying the procurement approach and selection criteria. It considers potential suppliers and the contractual arrangements that may be required to manage these external parties to achieve the project objectives.

CHAPTER SUMMARY

» Just under 50 per cent of business projects fail (*CHAOS Summary for 2010*, Standish Group) and around 70 per cent of all change initiatives fail (research from Prosci and Kotter). One of the most common causes of failure in both studies relates to poor stakeholder management, inadequate communication and poor management of the project team.

» Stakeholders are persons, or organisations, who are actively involved in the project, or whose interests may be positively or negatively affected by the performance or completion of the project.

» Stakeholders can exert positive and negative influences on the project.

» It can be difficult to identify all the stakeholders, but the key stakeholders are easily identified as they appear in the project governance and structure chart. Additional stakeholders can often emerge later in the project.

» Stakeholder analysis is the process of systematically gathering and analysing information to determine whose interests should be taken into account throughout the project.

» The power and interest grid and the stakeholder analysis matrix assist in planning approaches to managing stakeholder expectations.
» The position of a stakeholder in the power and interest grid determines their relative priority and therefore the effort that will be expended on managing their requirements. Those with the highest power and interest will require the most attention.
» Stakeholders will require a combination of communication, training and engagement activities to help them support the project and be equipped for the future state once the project is completed.
» When conflict is poorly managed it can detract seriously from the ability of the project to achieve the assigned objectives; in extreme circumstances it can even lead to early closure of the project.
» The three most common causes of conflict on projects are poor communication, poorly defined roles and responsibilities and interpersonal chemistry.
» There are five common responses to conflict in the Spegel, Rogers and Buckley model: competing, avoiding, accommodating, compromising and collaborating. Compromising is very common and collaborating provides the most positive results for all parties (but is sometimes infeasible).
» Understanding stakeholder preferences and behaviours with respect to conflict can greatly assist with negotiations, as can following a structured approach to the conduct of a negotiation.
» Change management is the application of a set of tools, processes, skills and principles for managing the people side of change to achieve the required outcomes of a project or change initiative.
» The goal of change management is to implement projects and business changes quickly so as to minimise the disruption and maximise the benefits.
» There are several major approaches to change management that can be integrated into project management in order to increase success, including Kotter, Prosci's 3-phase approach and ADKAR. Understanding a personal change journey within the context of delivering change as part of a project will increase success.
» Controlling stakeholder engagement is the process of communicating and working with stakeholders to address issues as they arise. Concerns need to be addressed as soon as they occur in order to prevent and minimise any negative impact. This results in decisions, agreements and sometimes change requests.
» Rodgers found that people fall into one of five categories in terms of their propensity to either resist or adopt change: innovators (2.5 per cent), early adopters (13.5 per cent), early majority (34 per cent), late majority (34 per cent) and laggards (16 per cent).
» Resistance to change is any behaviour or action that opposes the alterations that are underway. It can be covert or overt, conscious or unconscious, passive or aggressive, individual or organised by groups. It needs to be managed as it can threaten the success of the project and can greatly impact the speed with which benefits can be achieved.

REVISION QUESTIONS

Revision questions are divided into two sections. The first covers Certificate IV understanding and the second covers Diploma-level understanding. Both sections are relevant to Diploma students and teachers, while only the first section is relevant to Certificate students and teachers.

Certificate IV of Project Management

BSBPMG418A
performance
criteria questions

These questions relate to the performance criteria stated in 'BSBPMG418A Apply stakeholder engagement techniques'.

1   What steps are involved in identifying and analysing stakeholders?
2   Why is it often difficult to determine all the project stakeholders?

3   Who can help to identify additional stakeholders?

4   How does the power and interest grid help you to understand the needs of different stakeholders?

5   What techniques are used for stakeholders with high power and high interest?

6   What techniques are used for stakeholders with high power and low interest?

7   What techniques are used for stakeholders with low power and high interest?

8   What techniques are used for stakeholders with low power and low interest?

9   What interpersonal skills are used to communicate with and manage stakeholder expectations?

10   What are the common responses to conflict?

11   What steps are involved in negotiations?

12   What are the primary styles of negotiation?

13   Why do some stakeholders resist the changes being delivered by projects?

14   What types of communication needs will different stakeholders have?

Diploma of Project Management

These questions relate to the performance criteria stated in 'BSBPMG519A Manage stakeholder engagement'.

1   How are the communication, training and engagement needs of stakeholders determined?

2   What types of activities fall into communication?

3   What types of activities fall into training?

4   What types of activities fall into engagement?

5   How do you plan for stakeholders who have different requirements and different reactions to change?

6   What are the common causes of change resistance?

7   What change management approaches can be used to manage resistance?

8   What types of change requests may result from stakeholder management activities?

9   How is stakeholder engagement controlled?

10   What types of plans can be developed to manage stakeholder requirements?

BSBPMG519A
performance
criteria questions

DISCUSSION QUESTIONS

1   How can change management and project management be integrated?

2   What are the benefits of change management?

3   Why are projects and change so closely related?

4   Why is it necessary to understand stakeholder behaviours when planning and controlling stakeholder engagement?

5   Should project managers be responsible for change management activities?

6   What is the difference between communication, training and engagement? Give examples of physical deliverables in each area.

7   What are the major causes of change resistance and how can these be managed?

8   Why is it important to manage both conflict and change resistance on projects?

9   Why is it difficult to always achieve 'win-win' outcomes for negotiations?

BSBPMG418A and
BSBPMG519A
performance
criteria questions

ONLINE RESOURCES

Visit the online companion website at http://www.cengagebrain.com to link to important additional resources, including templates, real-world case studies, revision quizzes and additional study material.

FURTHER READING AND REFERENCES

Clarke, N., & Howell, R. (2009). *Emotional intelligence and projects.* Newtown Square, PA: Project Management Institute.

Cohen, D. (2005). *The heart of change field guide.* Boston: McGraw Hill.

Flannes, S., & Levin, G. (2005). *Essential people skills for project managers.* Vienna, VA: Management Concepts.

Hiatt, J. (2006). *ADKAR: A model for change in business, government and our community.* Prosci.

Hyatt, J. M. (2006). *ADKAR - A model for change in business, government and our community.* Prosci Learning Centre Publications

Keller, S., & Aiken, C. (2008). *The inconvenient truth about change management – Why it isn't working and what to do about it.* McKinsey and Company.

Kotter, J. (2012). *Leading change.* Boston, MA: Harvard Business Press.

Kotter, J., & Cohen, D. (2002). *The heart of change: Real life stories of how people change their organisation.* Boston, MA: Harvard Business Press.

Kotter International. (2012). http://www.kotterinternational.com/our-principles/changesteps. Kotter International, Inc.

Maurer, R. (2010). *Beyond the wall of resistance: Why 70% of all changes still fail and what you can do about it.* Austin, TX: Bard Press.

The McKinsey Quarterly. (2006). *Organizing for successful change management: A McKinsey global survey.* http://www.leadway.org/PDF/Organizing%20for%20successful%20change%20management.pdf.

Project Management Institute (PMI). (2013). *A guide to the Project Management Body of Knowledge (PMBOK® Guide)* (5th ed.). Newtown Square, PA . Chapter 13, pp. 391–416.

Robinson, L. (2009). *A summary of diffusion of innovations.* Enabling Change: author. www.enablingchange.com.au.

Schwable, K. (2011). *Information technology project management* (revised 6th ed.). Melbourne: Cengage Learning.

Spegel, N., Rogers, B., & Buckley, R. P. (1998). *Negotiation: theory and techniques.* Sydney: Butterworths.

The Standish Group. (2010). *CHAOS Summary for 2010.* Boston, MA: The Standish Group International, Inc.

Tan, H. C., Anumba, C., Carrillo, P., . . . Udeaja, C. (2010). *Capture and reuse of project knowledge in construction.* Chichester, UK: Wiley-Blackwell.

Verzuh, E. (2005). *The fast forward MBA in project management.* Brisbane: John Wiley & Sons.

Online references

Change Management Learning Center: http://www.change-management.com/

Kotter International: Change management and strategy: http://www.kotterinternational.com/

Les Robinson: http://www.enablingchange.com.au

NSW Government. (n.d.) Negotiation skills – A communitybuilders.nsw Toolkit. Accessed on 1 July 2013, http://www.communitybuilders.nsw.gov.au/331_2.html.

Prosci's 3-phase approach and ADKAR: http://www.prosci.com/

The Conflict Resolution Network: http://www.crnhq.org

Project integration management

1   become familiar with the relationship between project integration and the other key knowledge areas

2   appreciate the overarching project lifecycle and the processes involved in each phase: initiation, planning, execution, monitoring and control, and closing

3   learn how to develop the project charter as part of initiating a project

4   understand the importance of the project management plan and consider different approaches to constructing this deliverable

5   explain integrated change control and how this relates to controlling processes for scope, time, cost and quality

6   appreciate the benefits and different approaches for conducting post-implementation reviews

7   learn the importance of the project environment (both internal and external) in determining the most appropriate project methodology and approach

8   understand how to integrate and balance the overall project management functions of scope, time, cost, quality, human resources, communication, risk and procurement

9   appreciate the importance of aligning and integrating all project management functions to achieve the project objectives and meet the required success criteria.

Context

Project integration management includes the processes and activities needed to coordinate all the project management processes and activities included within the other key knowledge areas, across all phases and process groups within the project lifecycle as shown in Figure 16.1.

FIGURE 16.1 PROJECT MANAGEMENT LIFECYCLE

This is a complex group of processes which requires the project manager to manage the integration of all functions of project management, coordinate internal and external environments and implement project activities throughout the project lifecycle. The project manager needs to have an intimate understanding of the project management context and environment for each particular project, and to combine this with critical thinking skills in order to determine the project methodology and approach which will best achieve the outcomes of the project.

PROJECT MANAGEMENT MASTERY

PROJECT INTEGRATION MANAGEMENT

Think of project integration management as the conductor and the other key knowledge areas as the instruments in the orchestra. Project integration management is the consolidation of all project management activities that relate to successful project completion, delivering on stakeholder expectations and meeting requirements.

In this context, the project manager must:
- manage the integration and interdependencies of all functions of project management
- coordinate internal and external environments
- implement project activities throughout the project lifecycle
- make choices and trade-offs between competing objectives and alternative actions
- define and implement integrated change control processes
- direct and manage the project team through the execution of project deliverables
- monitor and control progress against the project management plan (PMP)
- resolve issues and respond to risks by implementing corrective actions and risk management plans.

Responsibilities of project team members

See PMBOK®
Guide Figure 3-3
Project
management
process
interactions

Only the project manager has the responsibility for managing the integrative processes of a project. This means they need to work across all of the functions and tasks involved in project management and ensure they are all working smoothly together. It often involves making trade-offs between competing objectives and alternatives to meet or exceed stakeholder needs and expectations.

FIGURE 16.2 PROJECT MANAGERS VERSUS PROJECT TEAM MEMBERS

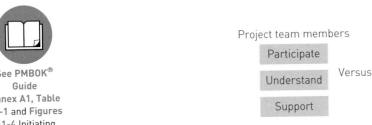

See PMBOK®
Guide
Annex A1, Table
A1-1 and Figures
A1-4 Initiating
process group,
A1-7 Planning
process group,
A1-32 Execution
process group,
A1-41 Monitoring
and controlling
process group
and A1-53 Closing
process group

Figure 16.2 depicts the main differences between the responsibilities of project managers and project team members. This distinction, between integration responsibilities and supporting responsibilities, is the key differentiating factor between the competencies expected in the Certificate IV of Project Management and the Diploma of Project Management.

The complexity of this process group and the interrelationships between all the key knowledge areas is depicted in Figure 3-3 Project management process interactions in the PMBOK® Guide (PMI, 2013, p. 53).

See PMBOK®
Guide Chapter 4
Project
integration
management

PMBOK® Guide processes for project integration management

See PMBOK®
Guide Figure 4-1
Project
integration
management
overview

The PMBOK® Guide processes for project integration management are:

4.1 Develop project charter
4.2 Develop project management plan
4.3 Direct and manage project work
4.4 Monitor and control project work
4.5 Perform integrated change control
4.6 Close project or phase.

REAL-WORLD EXPERIENCE

CONTEXT AND COMPLEXITY IN PROJECT INTEGRATION

The following diagram is the best I have found in terms of providing the context for the complexity of project integration. It is an excellent summary of the inputs, processes and outputs of project integration from the start to the end of a project.

FIGURE 16.3 PROJECT INTEGRATION MANAGEMENT SUMMARY

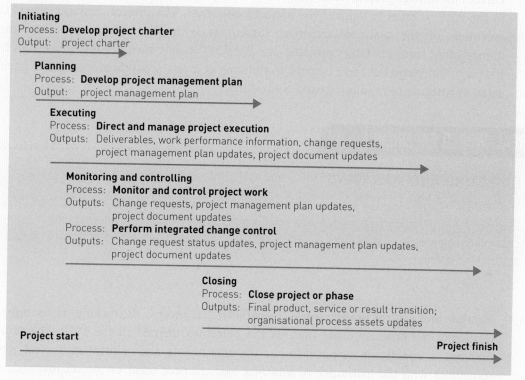

Initiating
Process: **Develop project charter**
Output: project charter

Planning
Process: **Develop project management plan**
Output: project management plan

Executing
Process: **Direct and manage project execution**
Outputs: Deliverables, work performance information, change requests, project management plan updates, project document updates

Monitoring and controlling
Process: **Monitor and control project work**
Outputs: Change requests, project management plan updates, project document updates
Process: **Perform integrated change control**
Outputs: Change request status updates, project management plan updates, project document updates

Closing
Process: **Close project or phase**
Outputs: Final product, service or result transition; organisational process assets updates

Project start

Project finish

Source: From Schawlbe. *Information Technology Project Management* (with Microsoft Project 2010 60 Day Trial CD-ROM), 7th edition, p. 131. © 2014 Brooks/Cole, a part of Cengage Learning, Inc. Reproduced by permission.

4.1 ***Develop project charter (initiation):*** In practice, the high-level project scope is developed and documented during the initiation phase in the project charter. It forms the boundaries for subsequent scoping processes. Unfortunately, the PMBOK® Guide has the scope definition activities all occurring in the planning phase and is therefore out of sync with practice.

4.2 ***Develop project management plan (planning):*** This is the process of defining and documenting the actions necessary to prepare and integrate all subsidiary plans for each of the other key knowledge areas of project management. The PMP is the primary deliverable from the planning phase. Good practice dictates that the PMP is baselined at the end of the planning phase, particularly in the areas of scope, cost and time. It is progressively added to during project execution via the perform integrated change control process.

The planning for all the key knowledge areas is normally performed at the same time as this process, or expanded upon shortly afterwards. All key knowledge areas have discrete processes for planning that are defined in their process groups.

This process is closely linked to '8.1 Plan quality management', '9.1 Plan human resource management', '10.1 Plan communications management', '11.1 Plan risk management' and '12.1 Plan procurement management'.

4.3 ***Direct and manage project work (execution):*** The process of performing the work defined in the PMP in order to achieve the project's objectives. The project manager directs the execution of the planned activities, sometimes with the assistance of a project management team for larger projects. The PMBOK® Guide includes this process within the execution phase but there is merit in thinking of it as a separate process group having equal importance to monitoring and controlling.

REAL-WORLD EXPERIENCE

DIRECTING AND MANAGING

The PMBOK® Guide includes this process (4.3) within the execution phase, while I prefer to think of it as a separate process group having equal importance to monitoring and controlling; hence my adaptation of the PMBOK® Guide standard project lifecycle and phases as depicted in Figure 16.1.

4.4 ***Monitor and control project work (execution):*** The process of tracking, reviewing and regulating the progress made towards the objectives defined in the PMP. The project manager is specifically responsible for the monitoring and control of project work, sometimes with the assistance of a project management team or project management office for larger projects. Monitoring is an aspect of project management performed throughout the project, but it becomes more critical during the execution phase. It is closely linked to '5.6 Control scope', '6.7 Control schedule', '7.4 Control costs', '8.3 Quality control', '10.3 Control communications' and '11.6 Control risks'.

4.5 ***Perform integrated change control (monitoring and controlling):*** The process of reviewing all change requests, including approving or rejecting changes and managing the flow-on impacts on all project deliverables and all components of the PMP. All requested changes should be identified through '5.6 Control scope'. The activities within this process are critical to managing stakeholder expectations and to ensuring the highest chance of project success. They occur from project inception through to completion and are part of the monitor and control process group. It is important that only approved changes be incorporated into the project, as it is surprisingly common to see unapproved changes being inadvertently undertaken.

4.6 ***Close project or phase (closing):*** The process of finalising all activities across all of the key knowledge areas. It is concerned with formally closing the project, or phase, so that work can cease and the project team can be disbanded. It represents the administrative closure of the project and the formal handover to ongoing operations. It mainly occurs during the closing phase but can also be performed at the end of each phase for large projects, depending on the methodology being used.

PROJECT MANAGEMENT MASTERY

THE ART OF INTEGRATION

Project integration represents a level of project management mastery that few project managers ever achieve. Truly mastering the art of integrating the scientific elements of project management (as represented by the key knowledge areas) is a prerequisite to successfully rising from the level of project manager to project or program director. As I have mentioned previously, project integration management is the conductor and the other key knowledge areas are the instruments in the orchestra.

Developing the project charter

The process of developing the project charter is fully examined in Chapter 2. For completeness, though, the key elements are summarised again here.

The project charter is the primary deliverable from the initiation phase. It formally defines and authorises a project by documenting the initial requirements that will satisfy the needs of the project sponsor and stakeholders. It establishes a partnership between the project sponsor, or client, and the project manager.

Depending on the industry, project charters are often known as either the project brief, concept paper, high-level plan or statement of work.

The following inputs are common when developing a project charter:
- project statement of work
- business need or rationale
- product and project description
- strategic plan
- business case
- regulations and standards
- contractual requirements
- methodologies, policies and procedures.

FIGURE 16.4 DEVELOPING THE PROJECT CHARTER

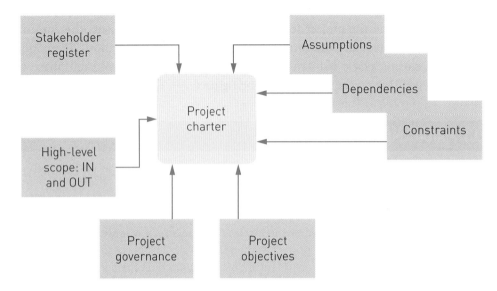

The specific contents of the project charter vary across methodologies, industries and templates. Many templates can be found online and this is a good place to start if you do not have a standard template. Inexperienced project managers will also benefit from reviewing several examples as previous content is often a useful guide.

The common contents of a project charter are:

**See PMBOK®
Guide Figure 4-2**
Develop project charter: inputs, tools and techniques, and outputs

- project background
- project description
- project purpose or justification
- project objectives
- high-level scope, including what's in and out of scope
- assumptions, dependencies, constraints
- unresolved issues
- high-level risks or overall risk analysis
- preferred timeframe
- estimated high-level budget
- high-level project structure.

A project charter template with instructions can be found online at www.cengagebrain.com.

Project charter template

Project objectives

It is critical that the project objectives (sometimes known as *success criteria*) are measurable, otherwise progress towards them is difficult to quantify and ultimately achieve (see Chapter 2, pages 17–19 for information regarding the SMART framework).

Defining project success seems simple; it is about delivering on time and on budget. These are important success criteria, but in most cases there are additional criteria that are of equal, or higher, importance to the project sponsor. It is often more important that the project deliver tangible business results, as defined by the project objectives.

Project success occurs when the:

- expectations of the project sponsor or client are met
- agreed project objectives have been met
- business outcomes have been realised
- timeframe and budget have been delivered
- quality and scope requirements have been delivered.

Source: The Northern Sydney Institute, Part of TAFE NSW.

Assumptions, dependencies and constraints

In Chapter 2, assumptions were defined as factors that, for planning purposes, are considered to be true, real or certain with no proof of certainty; they affect all aspects of project planning and involve a degree or risk. Dependencies were identified as being the relationships between the current project and other activities external to the project, whereas constraints were characterised as restrictions or limitations affecting the performance of the project; they can be internal to the organisation or imposed by external bodies, and they often relate to fixed timeframes or fixed budgets. For more information about assumptions, dependences and constraints, please see Chapter 2 (pages 22–5).

Source: The Northern Sydney Institute, Part of TAFE NSW.

In scope and out of scope

It is often more important, or at least of equal importance, to document what is out of scope as well as what is in scope. The concept of *out of scope* is vital to the setting and management of stakeholder expectations, especially those of the project sponsor. (See 'preferred timeframe' and 'indicative budget' in Chapter 2, page 27.)

Developing the project management plan (PMP)

Recapping from Chapter 3, this is the process of defining and documenting the actions necessary to prepare and integrate all subsidiary plans for each of the other key knowledge areas of project management. Good practice dictates that the PMP is baselined at the end of the planning phase. The planning processes for all key knowledge areas are normally performed at the same time, or expanded upon shortly after the completion of scope, time and cost planning.

The relationship to scope, time and cost is slightly different to the other areas of communication, risk, human resources, quality and procurement. There are no stand-alone scope, time or cost planning processes as they are contained within '4.2 Develop project management plan'. There are only three formal baselines required for scope, time and cost. The other key knowledge areas have discrete processes for planning that are defined in their process groups. The following diagram illustrates the discrete processes which create each of the three baselines.

FIGURE 16.5 PROJECT BASELINES

Scope baseline	produced during	5.5 Validate scope
Schedule baseline	produced during	6.6 Develop schedule
Cost baseline	produced during	7.3 Determine budget

Source: The Northern Sydney Institute, Part of TAFE NSW.

The PMP is the primary deliverable from the planning phase. It defines how all aspects of the project are to be undertaken through the execution phase and establishes the mechanisms to direct and manage, and monitor and control the project.

PROJECT MANAGEMENT MASTERY

CONTROLLING SCOPE CREEP

Once approved, the PMP can only be changed via a formal change request using the integrated change control process. It is worth recapping discussions in Chapters 5 and 7 by remembering that it is surprisingly easy for inexperienced project managers and project team members to expand the scope of a project, or absorb the impacts of an unexpected occurrence, without realising they are doing it. This immediately places a project in jeopardy of not delivering successfully.

It requires a sophisticated understanding of the interrelationships between the key knowledge areas and integrated change control processes, as well as strong project control disciplines, to ensure scope creep doesn't occur.

Composition of the project management plan

The PMP can be composed of subsidiary plans for the other key knowledge areas or, alternatively, it can be developed as one integrated plan. The latter is more common in Australia.

The following inputs are common when developing the PMP:
- project charter
- subsidiary plans developed in other planning processes
- industry standards and regulations
- organisational policies and procedures
- project management methodology
- project management tools
- planning templates
- knowledge from past projects
- expert judgement and advice.

Common inclusions in the PMP are:
- project lifecycle and project management processes
- selected tools and techniques
- project objectives and how these will be achieved
- change management plan
- baselines for scope, time and cost
- performance measurement and status reporting processes
- governance structure
- team structure
- subsidiary plans if required.

FIGURE 16.6 DEVELOPING THE PROJECT MANAGEMENT PLAN

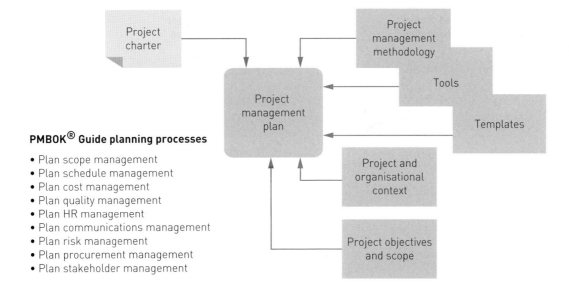

REAL-WORLD EXPERIENCE

PREFERENCES IN THE PMP

Over the last 20 years I have observed a distinct shift in preferences in the development of the PMP. I was working with a major IT consulting firm and there was a push to develop comprehensive PMPs with separate sections for each of the key knowledge areas. This was seen as a radical and extreme uplift in expectations as no formal PMPs had been produced prior to this. Several years later, when working for a telecommunications company, the expected practice was to develop a single integrated PMP. This is still the most common practice in Australia today.

In practice it is rare to have all components integrated into a single PMP. It is common to have the majority of key knowledge areas included and then to split out specific subsidiary plans (see Figure 16.7). Some of these ancillary plans are developed after the sign-off of the PMP at the commencement of the execution phase. This results in higher risk but means that execution and planning can run in parallel, so that near-term activities can be commenced for critical deliverables. Separate plans are still commonly produced for mega projects, particularly in the construction industry.

FIGURE 16.7 CONSTRUCTION OF THE PMP

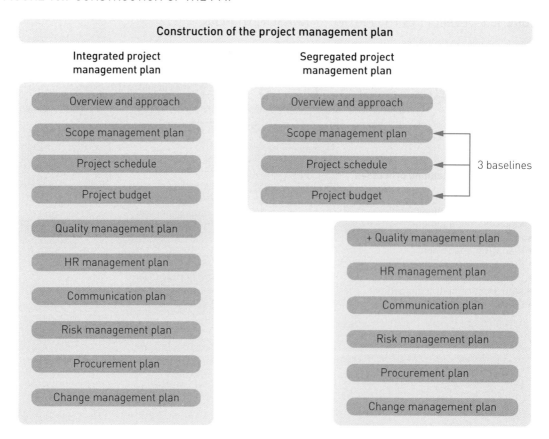

PROJECT MANAGEMENT MASTERY

PROCEDURES WITHIN THE PMP

Procedures often contained within, or referenced in, the PMP include:
- detail of the lifecycle selected for the project and the processes for each phase, typically tailored for each project
- descriptions of tools and techniques to be used by the project management team
- how work will be executed via different resourcing, team structures and contractual arrangements
- change control processes with detailed processes for integrated change control
- configuration management plan – often for larger IT, engineering and construction projects
- procedures for maintaining and amending baselines
- communications mechanisms and tools
- procedures for, and timing of, key management reviews, sign-off and approval.

RESEARCH AND REFLECTION ACTIVITY

INTEGRATED VERSUS SEPARATE PMPS

Conduct online research to find examples of PMPs in your industry and in others.
  Consider the pros and cons of integrated versus separated PMPs.

Determining the methodology and approach

One of the most important but unfortunately weak areas of project integration is the determination of the project approach and methodology. Many organisations will have adopted a particular methodology or standard for project delivery, such as Prince 2, Agile, waterfall, Lean Six Sigma and so on. Project managers will then be expected to follow the chosen methodology, regardless of the specific context of each project.

Small projects with low execution risk can often be weighed down by too much project management administration if the standard methodology is followed. These are normally designed for larger, more complex projects, as the primary reason to follow a standard methodology is to reduce delivery risk.

REAL-WORLD EXPERIENCE

UNDERLYING STANDARDS

I recommend that a fast path is designed that specifically caters for smaller projects.
It should highlight the minimum mandatory deliverables and practices.

In my view, the PMBOK® Guide is an underlying standard that can be applied no matter what delivery methodology is being used. The PMBOK® Guide is like vanilla ice-cream and the various methodologies represent different flavours. Just like you will choose various flavours depending on your mood, you should choose different methodologies depending on the requirements of each project.

PROJECT MANAGEMENT MASTERY

OPTIMAL DELIVERY APPROACH – COMBINING METHODOLOGIES

It takes an advanced level of expertise and also a high degree of critical thinking to create the optimal project delivery approach for each unique project and context. This involves selecting different methodologies, integrating them, tailoring them and combining them to form the specific combination that will increase the possibility of successful delivery.

It is also possible to incorporate methodologies and standards from other fields, such as change management, risk management and quality management. This requires a sophisticated level of understanding and experience.

REAL-WORLD EXPERIENCE

PROCESS IMPROVEMENT USING SIX SIGMA

I have been told, rather incorrectly, by some associates at another organisation that they use Six Sigma as their project management methodology so they don't need to worry about the PMBOK® Guide. I am a certified Six Sigma black belt and in my opinion Six Sigma is a wonderful process improvement methodology but it lacks the fundamental building blocks of a project delivery methodology. I recommend blending the Six Sigma DMAIC steps with the PMBOK® Guide's project delivery phases as shown in Figure 16.8.

FIGURE 16.8 PROCESS IMPROVEMENT USING SIX SIGMA WITH NO IT SYSTEM CHANGES

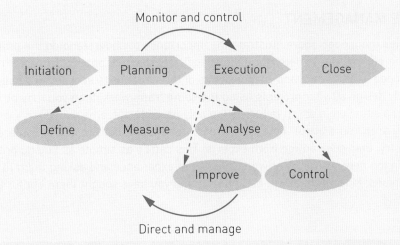

Source: Adapted from Project Management Institute, *A guide to the Project Management Body of Knowledge*, (PMBOK® Guide), fifth edition.

REAL-WORLD EXPERIENCE

INTEGRATING CHANGE MANAGEMENT INTO PROJECT MANAGEMENT

Another interesting challenge, particularly when projects have a significant organisational design component and will have major impacts on large groups of stakeholders, is to integrate change management approaches into the project delivery approach. I recommend blending Prosci's ADKAR approach with the PMBOK® Guide's project delivery phases (see Figure 16.9).

FIGURE 16.9 INTEGRATION OF PROJECT AND CHANGE MANAGEMENT

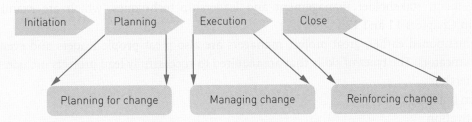

PROJECT MANAGEMENT MASTERY

FLEXIBLE MANAGEMENT

The examples mentioned above illustrate the importance of understanding the project context and environment in order to determine the specific approach to project delivery. Project managers need to be flexible and responsive to different contexts in order to be successful. If you doggedly design all your projects using the same framework, then you may be establishing a situation in which failure is the only possible outcome.

So, if you aren't sure about the best approach for a particular project, or you are entering a new industry, then seek advice from experts. This can be as simple as finding project managers in the new environment who have lots of experience and asking them to review your initial plans. Most of them will be flattered that you have sought them out for advice.

RESEARCH AND REFLECTION ACTIVITY

CHALLENGES TO TAILORING THE PROJECT DELIVERY APPROACH

- Which approach best suits your industry and projects?
- What challenges will you face when trying to tailor the project delivery approach, or incorporate approaches from other fields?

Directing and managing project work

This is the process of performing the work defined in the PMP in order to achieve the project's objectives. The project manager directs the execution of the planned activities, sometimes with the assistance of a project management team for larger projects. This involves a lot of people management, stakeholder management and leadership techniques, which are examined in detail in Chapters 11 and 12.

As mentioned earlier, great project managers are also great people leaders and even better communicators. The types of skills that are required to successfully lead projects include:

- leadership
- team building
- motivation
- communication
- influencing

- conflict resolution
- negotiation
- decision making
- cultural and political awareness.
  The direct and manage process group is concerned with the:
- creation of project deliverables
- management of the project staff and stakeholders
- acquisition, use and consumption of non-human resources
- implementation of planned processes and procedures
- communication
- monitoring and resolution of risks and issues
- implementation of process improvements
- collection and documentation of lessons learned.

Source: The Northern Sydney Institute, Part of TAFE NSW.

FIGURE 16.10 DIRECT AND MANAGE PROCESS PERSPECTIVE

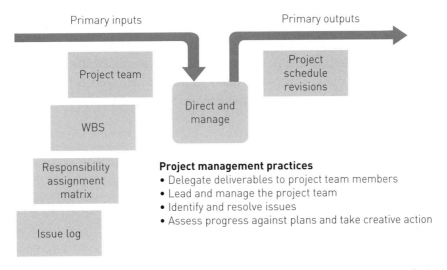

Source: Adapted from Project Management Institute, *A guide to the Project Management Body of Knowledge*,
(PMBOK® Guide), fifth edition.

An important aspect of directing and managing project work is the implementation of any approved changes to the project scope or objectives. It is closely related to the processes of '4.5 Perform integrated change control', '5.6 Control scope', '8.2 Perform quality assurance' and '8.3 Control quality'.

Three types of changes can occur during project execution:

- **corrective action**: required to adjust project performance back into line with the PMP
- **preventative action**: reduces the probability of negative consequences associated with project risks
- **defect repair**: required to repair or replace defective outcomes or components.

Source: The Northern Sydney Institute, Part of TAFE NSW.

Monitoring and controlling the project

This is the process of tracking, reviewing and regulating the progress made by a project towards the objectives defined in the PMP. The project manager is responsible for the monitoring and control of project work, sometimes with the assistance of a project management team or project management office for larger projects. Monitoring is an aspect of project management performed throughout the project.

As first mentioned in Chapter 5, continuous monitoring reveals the health of the project and any areas requiring special attention. This activity, when combined with directing and managing, can easily keep a project manager fully occupied during the execution phase. It is surprising that many project sponsors and project managers underestimate the time that it takes to keep a project on track. This often results in project managers being split across many projects at the same time which could contribute to less successful outcomes.

REAL-WORLD EXPERIENCE

BUSINESS PROJECT MANAGEMENT IN A LAW FIRM

I was hired to establish the PMO function and increase project delivery capability in one of Australia's largest commercial law firms. When I arrived I was astonished to learn that there were two project managers in the business and that they were each supposedly managing 20–25 projects at a time. I quickly pointed out that with that many projects each, all they were doing was watching the projects; they were neither managing them nor monitoring and controlling them. The result was that almost all projects exceeded the originally estimated timeframe by 100 to 150 per cent.

I immediately set about two courses of action. First, I held sessions with the senior management team to prioritise the current projects so that effort could be concentrated on the highest-priority projects in order to reduce the work in progress and improve project completion rates. This action is an example of the application of Little's law from the field of operations management (see also Chapter 10). Little's law states that *you can deliver more product by reducing work in progress*. I have found that it is directly applicable to the project pipeline.

Second, I started a concentrated up-skilling program with the middle managers. They were trained in basic project management techniques and provided with on-going coaching so they could deliver their own low-risk, low-impact projects. The two experienced project managers could then concentrate on the delivery of more complex, higher-risk projects with greater impact across the firm. In just 12 months of this new approach, 18 projects were completed.

The monitor and control process group is concerned with:

- comparing actual performance against the PMP
- assessing performance to determine corrective and preventative actions
- identifying new risks and monitoring existing risks
- identifying new issues and monitoring existing issues
- maintaining accurate and up-to-date progress and status information
- providing information for status reports
- the tracking and reforecasting of progress
- providing reforecasts of costs and timelines
- monitoring implementation of approved change requests.

Source: The Northern Sydney Institute, Part of TAFE NSW.

Monitoring involves the collection, measuring and distribution of project performance information, as illustrated in Figure 5.1 (page 94). Controlling, meanwhile, involves assessing actual progress against planned progress in order to take action to bring the project back on track. One key aspect of controlling is to ensure that when a risk or issue occurs on a critical path activity (as determined in the project schedule) then the project manager must ensure that it is resolved with the highest priority or the project will automatically be delayed.

As detailed in the NSI Online Certificate IV and Diploma of Project Management, the major outputs for this process are:

- change requests
- updates to project schedule management plan
- updates to project cost management plan
- updates to quality management plan
- changes to scope baseline
- changes to cost baseline
- changes to schedule baseline
- reforecasts
- performance and status reports (see Chapters 5 and 12, pages 94 and 319–21, respectively)
- updates to risks and issues logs.

Source: The Northern Sydney Institute, Part of TAFE NSW.

RESEARCH AND REFLECTION ACTIVITY

KEEPING PROJECTS ON TRACK

Take some time to reflect on the skills, experience and processes that you use to execute and monitor projects.

Discuss the approaches that other project managers use in your organisation and ask them about their key learnings around how to keep projects on track.

Perform integrated change control

As first mentioned in Chapter 5, integrated change control is the process of reviewing all change requests, including approving or rejecting changes and managing the flow-on impacts on all project deliverables and components of the PMP. Integrated change control occurs from project inception all the way through to project completion.

All requested changes should be identified through the '4.4 Monitor and control project work' and '5.6 Control scope' processes.

The following change activities are often undertaken:

- influencing stakeholders and the project team to ensure only approved changes are implemented
- reviewing, analysing and approving change requests quickly
- understanding the complete impacts of the approved changes and managing their implementation
- maintaining the integrity of project baselines for scope, time and cost
- coordinating changes across the entire project.

According to the NSI Online Certificate IV and Diploma of Project Management, the project manager has the primary responsibility for controlling scope and managing changes, although the project sponsor should review and approve or reject all change requests. It is dangerous for the project manager to take on accountability for this decision making and should be avoided.

It is important that everyone on the project team, as well as the project sponsor and key stakeholders, understand the change control process (see Chapter 5, pages 95–7) and are vigilant in identifying potential scope changes for review, rather than simply incorporating them into the project scope by accident. This phenomenon is prevalent on projects and can directly lead to project failure in terms of timelines and budgets. It is known as scope creep and is explained further in Chapter 7.

FIGURE 16.11 PERFORM INTEGRATED CHANGE CONTROL: INPUTS AND OUTPUTS

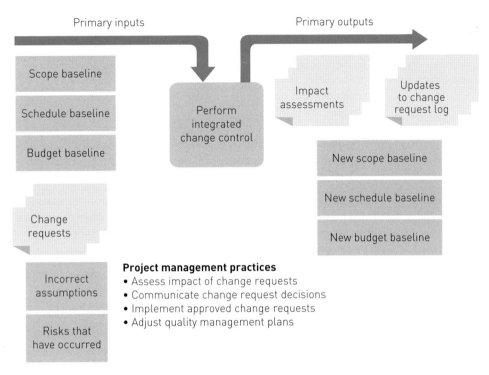

Source: Adapted from Project Management Institute, *A guide to the Project Management Body of Knowledge*, (PMBOK® Guide), fifth edition.

Causes of change on projects

As first mentioned in Chapter 7, changes are inevitable on projects and some project managers can create huge amounts of stress for themselves by ignoring this possibility or trying to deny requests for change. The point of change control is to consciously review and approve all positive or necessary changes and to review and reject all erroneous or unnecessary changes.

PROJECT MANAGEMENT MASTERY

SOURCES OF CHANGE

The most successful and experienced project managers understand that project changes come from many sources, not just changes to scope.

Based on my observations and experience there are many legitimate causes of changes in projects – a summary is included in Table 16.1. Also, poor change control and weak scope management can greatly increase the change of project failure. So, it is critical that strong scope management and change control processes are developed and implemented.

TABLE 16.1 SOURCES OF CHANGE

Change factor	Explanation and understanding
Requirements and business needs	As mentioned in Chapter 7, sometimes the requirements for the project will change due to changes in the market or business conditions. But most often they will change due to a critical requirement being overlooked during scoping and planning and it will need to be incorporated in order to deliver the project objectives and to realise future benefits. It is easy to overlook critical requirements if there has been inadequate involvement from the project sponsor and key stakeholders during the requirements definition activities.
Organisation and priority changes	Organisations may change their structure through transformation and efficiency initiatives, mergers and acquisitions. When this occurs the priorities of the organisation often change just as they do if overall project funding is reduced.
Assumptions are untrue	Any assumptions that are made during the planning phase may prove untrue through execution, in which case there will be flow-on impacts on the PMP and baselines that need to be managed.
Risks occur	Risks that actually occur during the project will have impacts on the PMP and baselines that need to be managed.
Innovation or technology change	Sometimes a new process, technique or technology improvement will open up opportunities to accelerate or improve project delivery. If so, then a good project manager will ensure that it is appropriately exploited in order to improve project outcomes.
Regulations or standards change	If any relevant regulation or standard applicable to the project changes during the project timeframe there will likely be impacts to be managed.
Insufficient planning	Sometimes there is a rush to complete planning and commence execution and this can lead to incomplete planning which in turn leads to omissions and changes down the track. Inexperienced project managers, and a lack of involvement from the project sponsor and key stakeholders, can lead to poor planning.
Changes to baselines	Any factor that changes the scope, time or cost of the project will impact on the project. Factors outside of the project manager's control may necessitate delivering the project more quickly, reducing the budget or changing (increasing or decreasing) the scope.
Changes to dependencies	There will be changes to a project whenever there are changes to other projects upon which it is dependent. Project delays or changes to scope will have flow-on impacts on dependent projects.

Change control process

Change requests are referred to many times in the project scope processes and are primary outputs of the validate scope and control scope subprocesses. Good practice dictates that change requests are created to document any event which will impact on the project. This is typically a form (hardcopy or electronic) that allows a project stakeholder to request a change to any aspect of the project, but most commonly to scope. They will need to provide details of the requested change and a rationale. In reality, it is the project manager who most often enters and completes change requests as they have the most vested interest in a formal and well-managed change control process.

It is also worthwhile using a change request log as part of the suite of project control logs – more discussion of this concept appears in Chapter 5. All change requests should be logged, even those that are rejected, as this can be very useful when managing the expectations of new stakeholder or project team members.

A recommended change control process is outlined in Figure 5.2 on page 96.

Since there is always a natural resistance to formal processes, the change control process should be kept as simple and streamlined as possible. It is extremely important to have a two-step approval process, where a change request is initially approved to proceed to the impact-assessment step and then considered for a second time once the impact assessment has been completed.

Many change control processes omit the first approval step and this has unseen but inevitable negative impacts on the project. Any effort that is spent assessing the impact of a change request is diverting resources away from the already agreed project deliverables and scope. This will incrementally increase costs and extend the timeline, often without anyone noticing, such that it is a surprise to both the project manager and sponsor when the team informs them that they can't complete the project according to the original time and cost baselines. And project sponsors really dislike nasty surprises!

In practice, the initial approval or rejection step prior to assessing impacts will sift out many erroneous or misaligned change requests. Only those with real merit will progress to the impact assessment. See Chapter 7 (pages 155–7) for more on change control processes, and Figure 5.2 on p. 98 for the change control process.

Project closure

Project closure is the process of finalising all activities across all of the process groups and key knowledge areas to formally close a phase or a project. The current version of the PMBOK® Guide provides little detail on this area and will be substantially supplemented in this chapter with good practices from real world experience. For example, most project management practitioners consider the post-implementation review to be the primary deliverable from the project closure phase, yet this document is not mentioned in the PMBOK® Guide.

Post-implementation reviews are strongly recommended at the end of a project to identify lessons learned that will assist the success of future projects.

PMBOK® Guide and best practice processes for project closure

The PMBOK® Guide has only two processes identified for project closure:

4.6   Close project or phase

12.4   Close procurements.

Best practice dictates that we also consider the following additional processes:

- gather stakeholder feedback
- identify and share lessons learned
- develop the post-implementation review
- develop the project transition plan
- perform accounting closure
- update estimating tools
- conduct project team performance reviews
- benefits realisation.

More details on project closure can be found in Chapter 6.

Related processes from the PMBOK® Guide

5.6   ***Control scope (monitoring and controlling):*** The process of monitoring the status of both the project and product scope. It focuses on managing any changes to the scope baseline and understanding the flow-on impacts on time, cost and quality via the related process of '4.5 Perform integrated change control'.

- ***Planning process group:*** The processes required to establish the scope of the project, refine the objectives and define the project delivery approach that will place the project in the best possible position to successfully deliver the defined objectives.

- ***Monitoring and controlling process group:*** There is at least one process in each of the key knowledge areas, with the exception of Project Human Resource Management, that relates to the monitoring and controlling of a project. These all work together to ensure that projects are kept on track and they deliver the required outcomes to the required level of quality. There is a relationship between all the monitoring and control processes and project closure.

CHAPTER SUMMARY

» The project charter is the core deliverable that initiates a project. It contains the high-level scope, most particularly the in- and out-of-scope items as well as assumptions, dependencies and constraints that provide the boundaries for the project.

» Project objectives can be translated into project success measures and provide clear goals for the project team.

» The PMP is the core deliverable from the planning phase. It involves the coordination of planning efforts across all key knowledge areas and can be produced as one integrated document or discrete and separate documents for each major planning area.

» Project managers need sophisticated people management and leadership skills in order to successfully direct and manage projects.

» The capturing of lessons learned on projects is also part of the directing and managing process group.

» Project status reporting is the primary output from the monitoring and controlling process group.

» Integrated change control is an expanded version of controlling scope; it ensures that all impacts of a change request are clearly understood and then fully implemented.

» Strong change control requires two approval points: one before the impact is assessed and another after impact assessment. This prevents wasted effort on impact assessments on changes that are unlikely to proceed.

» Project closure is the process of finalising all activities across all of the process groups and key knowledge areas to formally close a phase or a project. The primary output of this process is the post-implementation review, which is unfortunately rarely produced.

REVISION QUESTIONS

Revision questions are divided into two sections. The first covers Certificate IV understanding and the second covers Diploma-level understanding. Both sections are relevant to Diploma students and teachers, while only the first section is relevant to Certificate students and teachers.

Certificate IV of Project Management

These questions relate to the performance criteria stated in 'BSBPMG417A Apply project lifecycle management processes'.

1   What processes are involved in project integration?
2   What framework is useful to document project objectives?
3   What are the primary activities involved in monitoring and controlling a project?
4   What are the primary activities involved in directing and managing a project?
5   Why is the selection of the project methodology and approach important to project success?
6   Why are project logs important?
7   What typical project logs are set up for most projects?
8   What is integrated change control?
9   What are the typical contents of a change request?
10 Who needs to know the outcomes of change request decisions?
11 What activities are involved in project closure?

BSBPMG417A
performance
criteria questions

BSBPMG521A
performance
criteria questions

Diploma of Project Management

These questions relate to the performance criteria stated in 'BSBPMG521A Manage project integration'.

1   What factors are used to determine project prioritisation?
2   How are projects aligned to organisational strategy?
3   How is the project governance structure established?
4   What activities are involved in project planning and design?
5   What project baselines are recommended as good practice?
6   When are project baselines established?
7   What is the relationship between constraints on a project and the 'triple constraint'?
8   How is the project methodology and approach determined?
9   Who needs to review and approve the PMP?
10   What is the role of the PMO in assisting the project manager?
11   What is the difference between integrated change control and control project scope?
12   Why are approval steps recommended before and after the assessment of the impact of change requests?
13   Who is the primary decision maker when approving or rejecting change requests?
14   Under what circumstances might projects be closed early?

DISCUSSION QUESTIONS

BSBPMG417A and
BSBPMG521A
performance
criteria questions

1   Why is scope creep so prevalent on projects and what can be done to reduce this?
2   How can the 'triple constraint' be used to manage the expectations of stakeholders?
3   Why are projects sometimes undertaken that do not align to the organisation's strategies and goals?
4   Are all project governance structures the same? If so, what does this look like? If not, then how is it determined?
5   What are the pros and cons of an integrated PMP over separate subsidiary plans?
6   How does the project manager ensure that project work is being executed according to the plan?
7   Under what circumstances can the project baselines be changed and who has the authority to approve these changes?

ONLINE RESOURCES

Visit the online companion website at http://www.cengagebrain.com to link to important additional resources, including templates, real-world case studies, revision quizzes and additional study material.

FURTHER READING AND REFERENCES

Department of Defence. (2006). Competency standard for complex project managers, public release Version 2.0. Canberra: author, http://www.defence.gov.au/dmo/proj_man/Complex_PM_v2.0.pdf

Dobie, C. (2007). *A handbook of project management: A complete guide for beginners to professionals.* Sydney: Allen and Unwin.

Global Alliance for Project Performance Standards (GAPPS): www.globalpmstandards.org

Hartley, S. (2008). *Project management: Principles, processes and practice* (2nd ed.). Sydney: Pearson Education.

Kerzner, H. (2007). *Project management: A systems approach to planning, scheduling, and controlling* (9th ed.). Brisbane: John Wiley & Sons.

Kloppenborg, T. J. (2012). *Contemporary project management* (2nd ed.). Melbourne: Cengage Learning.

Mulcahy, R. (2006). *PM crash course – Real-world project management tools & techniques.*. Minnetonka, MN: RMC Publications.

NASA. (2011). NASA space flight program and project management requirements, NASA interim directive (NID) for NPR 7120.5D, http://nodis3.gsfc.nasa.gov/OPD_docs/NID_7120_97_.pdf

Portny S. E., Mantel, S. J., Meredith, J. R., . . . Sutton, M. M. (2008). *Project management – Planning, scheduling and controlling projects*. Brisbane: Wiley.

Project Management Institute (PMI). (2013). *A guide to the Project Management Body of Knowledge* (PMBOK® Guide) (5th ed.). Newtown Square, PA. Chapter 4, pp. 63–104.

Schwable, K. (2011). *Information technology project management* (revised 6th ed.). Melbourne: Cengage Learning.

Tan, H. C., Anumba, C., Carrillo, P., . . . Udeaja, C. (2010). *Capture and reuse of project knowledge in construction*. Chichester, UK: Wiley-Blackwell.

Verzuh, E. (2005). *The fast forward MBA in project management*. Brisbane: John Wiley & Sons.

Project management certification; professional bodies

The field of project management is in transition between a set of skills and a recognised profession (see Figure A1.1 below).

FIGURE A1.1 EVOLUTION OF THE PROJECT MANAGEMENT PROFESSION

Past	Present	Future
• Poor understanding of the key knowledge areas and competencies • Thought anyone who was highly organised could be a project manager • Emerging professional bodies • No formal standards • Anyone could call themselves a project manager	• Better understanding of the key knowledge areas and competencies • Strong professional bodies • Emerging standards and competencies • Formal certification and registration of project managers • Can still be a project manager without certification	• Formal acceptance of the key knowledge areas and competencies • Formal recognition of standards and competencies • Unable to be a project manager without certification • Specific skills, experience, certification and professional membership expected • Compulsory certification and continuing professional development • Unable to be a project manager without certification

Source: The Northern Sydney Institute, Part of TAFE NSW.

Defining and committing to a regime of performance standards and professional expectations is essential as the field of project management progresses into an acknowledged profession. Employers are increasingly seeking a project management qualification, certification or membership from the project management professionals they employ. For this reason, the background and focus areas of the two main professional bodies that operate within Australia are provided in this appendix:

- PMI – Project Management Institute **www.pmi.org.au**
- AIPM – Australian Institute of Project Management **www.aipm.com.au**.

Project Management Institute

The Project Management Institute (PMI) was founded in 1969 as a not-for-profit organisation with the purpose of 'building professionalism in project management'. They have over 700 000 members and 460 000 certification holders worldwide, with over 1800 members in the Sydney chapter alone.

The key components of their framework for promoting professionalism in the project management profession are:

1 professional certification
2 project manager competency framework
3 standards for professional practice
4 PMI code of ethics.

PMI professional certification

Certified project managers are generally accredited with the success of high-performing projects. According to PMI (2012) organisations with more than 35 per cent PMP certified project managers had better project performance, and according to the 2012 PricewaterhouseCoopers survey, 67 per cent of participants believe that PM training contributes to business performance. The same PwC survey found that the use of industry standard methodologies such a PMBOK® Guide and Prince2 had increased from 38 per cent in 2007 to 44 per cent in 2012.

The PMI offers the following levels of certification, which include three overarching qualifications and three specialised certifications:

- Certified Associate in Project Management (CAPM)®
- Project Management Professional (PMP)®
- Program Management Professional (PgMP)®
- PMI Agile Certified Practitioner (PMI-ACP)®
- PMI Risk Management Professional (PMI-RMP)®
- PMI Scheduling Professional (PMI-SP)®.

All of the PMI certifications involve an exam that tests knowledge on the particular standard associated with each level or specialisation of certification; the pass mark is generally well above 50 per cent. A more recent addition to the certification process is the submission of evidence via referees of a prescribed amount of continuous experience at the particular level under assessment. There are a prescribed number of professional development units that must be obtained in order to maintain certification. Figure A1.2 outlines the PMI accreditation framework.

PMI competency framework

In addition to the certification framework, the PMI has developed a competency framework that seeks to clearly define the capabilities and skills required for project managers to be successful. These are extremely useful in the recruitment, selection and performance assessment of project management professionals, and can be obtained for free, along with other PMI career framework materials by registering your organisation at www.pathpro.pmi.org.

PMI standards for professional practice

The PMI develops and publishes four foundation standards, details of which can be found on the PMI library of global standards webpage (http://www.pmi.org/PMBOK-Guide-and-Standards/Standards-Library-of-PMI-Global-Standards.aspx). The standards listed are:

1 *A Guide to the Project Management Body of Knowledge* (PMBoK Guide), 5th edition, 2013. This is recognised by the American National Standards Institute (ANSI) and the Australian Standards organisations as national standards.
2 *The Standard for Program Management*, 3rd edition, 2013.
3 *The Standard for Portfolio Management*, 3rd edition, 2013.
4 *Organizational Project Management Maturity Model* (OPM3), 3rd edition, 2013.

FIGURE A1.2 PMI ACCREDITATION FRAMEWORK

	CAPM®	PMI-SP®	PMI-RMP®	PMP®	PgMP®
Full name	Certified Associate in Project Management	PMI Scheduling Professional	PMI Risk Management Professional	Project Management Professional	Program Management Professional
Project role	Contributes to project team	Develops and maintains project schedule	Assesses and identifies risks and mitigates threats and capitalises on opportunities	Leads and directs project teams	Achieves an organisational objective through defining and overseeing projects and resources
Eligibility requirements	High school diploma/global equivalent AND 1500 hours experience OR 23 hours pm education	High school diploma/global equivalent 5000 hours project scheduling experience 40 hours project scheduling education OR Bachelor's degree/global equivalent 3500 hours project scheduling experience 30 hours project scheduling education	High school diploma/global equivalent 4500 hours project risk management experience 40 hours project risk management education OR Bachelor's degree/global equivalent 3000 hours project risk management experience 30 hours project risk management education	High school diploma/global equivalent 5 years project management experience 35 hours project management education OR Bachelor's degree/global equivalent 3 years project management experience 35 hours project management education	High school diploma/global equivalent 4 years project management experience 7 years program management education OR Bachelor's degree/global equivalent 4 years project management experience 4 years program management experience
Steps to obtaining credential	application process + multiple-choice exam	application process + multiple-choice exam	application process + multiple-choice exam	application process + multiple-choice exam	3 evaluations – application panel review + multiple-choice exam + multi-rater assessment
Exam information	3 hours; 150 questions	3.5 hours; 170 questions	3.5 hours; 170 questions	4 hours; 200 questions	4 hours; 170 questions
Fees	US$225 PMI member (US$300 non-member)	US$520 PMI member (US$670 non-member)	US$520 PMI member (US$670 non-member)	US$405 PMI member (US$555 non-member)	US$1500 PMI member (US$1800 non-member)
Credential maintenance cycles and requirements	5 years; re-exam	3 years; 30 PDUs in project scheduling	3 years; 30 PDUs in risk management	3 years; 60 PDUs	3 years; 60 PDUs

Source: Project Management Institute, Jordan Chapter.

There are also complementary practice standards and extensions to the PMBOK® Guide as follows:

1 *Practice Standard for Project Risk Management*, 2009
2 *Practice Standard for Earned Value Management*, 2nd edition 2011
3 *Practice Standard for Project Configuration Management*, 2007
4 *Practice Standard for Work Breakdown Structures*, 2nd edition, 2006
5 *Practice Standard for Scheduling*, 2nd edition, 2011
6 *Practice Standard for Project Estimating*, 2010
7 *Software Extension to the PMBoK Guide*, 5th edition, 2013
8 *Construction Extension to the PMBoK Guide*, 3rd edition, 2007
9 *Government Extension to the PMBoK Guide*, 3rd edition, 2006.

PMI code of ethics

The PMI Code of Ethics and Professional Conduct was developed by PMI volunteers. It aims to instil confidence in the project management profession and to help project professionals become better practitioners by committing to the achievement of high standards for project management practice and behaviour. The PMI Code is founded on:

1 responsibility
2 respect
3 fairness
4 honesty.

Each value is described as a mandatory requirement, which members must uphold or face a potential breach of the code, and an aspirational requirement, which members must strive to uphold. Breaches by a PMI member can be submitted by anyone to the PMI Ethics Review Committee and can result in the removal of membership and possible legal action. A copy of the PMI Code can be downloaded from the PMI website at http://www.pmi.org/About-Us/Ethics.aspx.

Australian Institute of Project Management

The Australian Institute of Project Management (AIPM) was formed in 1976 as the Project Managers' Forum. It is the largest professional project management institute in the Australasian region and has approximately 10 000 members. AIPM's mission is to foster professional applications of project management skills and techniques as the preferred process for delivering business outcomes. Their motto is to 'encourage excellence through professionalism in project management'.

The key components of their framework for promoting professionalism in the project management profession are:

1 project manager certification via the AIPM or the IPMA
2 professional competency standards
3 AIPM code of professional conduct.

In 2009 the AIPM became a member association of the International Project Management Association (IPMA). The IPMA represents over 50 project management associations around the world and the AIPM is now the IPMA's second-largest member association, which gives AIPM a strong voice within that global PM community. AIPM members are now able to undertake the AIPM's certification or the IPMA's certification, which are explained below.

AIPM professional certification

RegPM (Registered Project Manager) is AIPM's project management certification program. It involves an individually designed competency-based workplace assessment program where candidates are required to compile evidence that displays their competence in project management. The following certifications are offered:

- Certified Practising Project Practitioner (CPPP)
- Certified Practising Project Manager (CPPM)
- Certified Practising Project Director (CPPD)
- Certified Practising Portfolio Executive (CPPE).

None of the AIPM professional certifications involve an exam, but they do require the compilation of evidence. This evidence can be mailed to the AIPM for assessment or reviewed in the workplace by an accredited assessor. The AIPM has a prescribed number of continuing professional development points that must be accumulated in order to maintain certification.

IPMA professional certification

The IPMA certification levels are outlined in Figure A1.3 and are as follows:

- Certified Project Management Associate
- Certified Project Manager
- Certified Senior Project Manager
- Certified Project Director.

FIGURE A1.3 IPMA CERTIFICATION FRAMEWORK

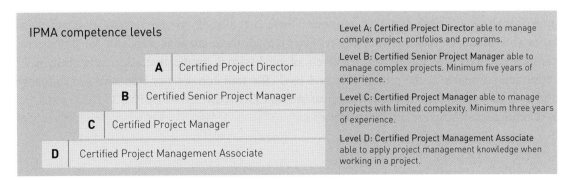

IPMA competence levels

A	Certified Project Director
B	Certified Senior Project Manager
C	Certified Project Manager
D	Certified Project Management Associate

Level A: Certified Project Director able to manage complex project portfolios and programs.

Level B: Certified Senior Project Manager able to manage complex projects. Minimum five years of experience.

Level C: Certified Project Manager able to manage projects with limited complexity. Minimum three years of experience.

Level D: Certified Project Management Associate able to apply project management knowledge when working in a project.

Source: Australian Institute of Project Management.

There are various ways that project managers can become IPMA certified through AIPM. These include:

- **full assessment** where individuals can undertake IPMA certification independently.
- **bridging assessment** where members who are currently RegPM certified can add IPMA certification to their credentials.
- **parallel assessment** where members can obtain both the RegPM and IPMA certifications concurrently.

IPMA certification is valid for five years from the date of issue and is maintained by undergoing a recertification assessment every five years. This differs from the AIPM regime which requires the maintenance of continuous professional development. Figure A1.4 compares IMPA and AIPM certifications.

FIGURE A1.4 COMPARING IPMA AND AIPM CERTIFICATIONS

IPMA certification	AIPM RegPM certification
Level D Certified Project Management Associate	**CPPP** Certified Practising Project Practitioner
Level C Certified Project Manager	**CPPM** Certified Practising Project Manager
Level B Certified Senior Project Manager	**CSPM*** Certified Senior Project Manager
Level A Certified Project Director	**CPPD** Certified Practising Project Director
	CPPE Certified Practising Portfolio Executive

*Not yet available

Source: Australian Institute of Project Management.

AIPM professional competency standards

The AIPM has developed a comprehensive set of competency standards for project management professionals at differing levels of seniority. These are aligned to the Australian qualification framework to ensure national consistency. Even though there are four standards for professional competency, there are still only three levels of professional certification. Currently there is no certification available at the project executive level. The four competency standards are as follows and are available at http://www.aipm.com.au/AIPM/CERTIFICATION/REGPM/3G/R/regpm.aspx:

1 Certified Practising Project Practitioner
2 Certified Practising Project Manager
3 Certified Practising Project Director
4 Certified Practising Project Executive.

AIPM Code of Professional Conduct

The AIPM Code illustrates the values and behaviours expected by the AIPM and is underpinned by the following principles:

- integrity
- competency
- impartiality
- accountability
- honesty.

    The Code has four key areas of responsibility:

1 professional conduct
2 personal responsibilities
3 project management
4 responsibility to the profession and to the institute.

Breaches of the Code may result in removal of the member's name from the register of members and/or the removal of name from the register of certified practitioners. See http://www.aipm.com.au/3G/C/code_of_ethics.aspx for more information.

Benefits of certification and membership

The benefits of membership for both the PMI and AIPM are:

- participation in conferences and networking events
- availability of recognised education and training opportunities
- eligibility for participation in project management awards
- provision of CPD and PDU opportunities.

    The primary benefits of PMI and AIPM certification are recognition within the industry for your particular level of competency and enhanced chances of finding employment above those that are not certified. Indeed, in the United States, securing a role within the project management profession without one of the PMP certifications is almost impossible. Comparatively Australia has not been so strict in certification, but the need for some form of formal project management training is usually expected.

    There are some unique benefits offered by each institute. The AIPM provides access to professional indemnity insurance and advertises project management roles. The PMI is more widely recognised internationally and more active in conducting global networking and educational activities via its various chapters. The PMI also provides free printing of five copies of the PMBOK® Guide with all memberships, access to online copies of other foundation standards, and use of an extensive library of members-only eBooks and articles.

Other professional bodies

There are many professional bodies within the project management profession. These mostly have prominence within their geographical area or country. Some are listed below.

- **ASPM** American Society for Advancement of Project Management (a member of the International Project Management Association) **www.aspm.org**
- **IPMA** International Project Management Association (a Swiss based not-for-profit association that is a federation of over 55 Member Associations. IMPA was initiated in 1965 and claims to be the oldest professional body in the project management profession. AIPM is a member association) **www.ipma.ch**
- **IAPPM** International Association of Project and Program Management **www.iappm.org**
- **APM** Association of Project Management **www.apm.org.uk**
- **Engineers Australia www.engineersaustralia.org.au**
- **Australian Computer Society www.acs.org.au**
- **AIM** Australian Institute of Management **www.aim.com.au**

References

PricewaterhouseCoopers. (2012). *Insights and trends: Current portfolio, programme and project management practices. The third global survey on the current state of project management.* Pricewaterhouse Coopers.

Project Management Institute (PMI). (2012). *Pulse of the profession: Driving success in challenging times.* Project Management Institute, Inc.

Projects, programs and portfolios

A career in the management of individual projects inevitably links to the more complex relationships between projects, programs and portfolios. Broadly, projects are related to programs and portfolios in the following manner:

- **Projects** are the lowest unit of delivery and can be collected together to form programs.
- **Programs** are a collection of projects, or one very large project, that must be broken down into large, discrete work packages that are assigned to several project managers, who in turn are responsible to the program manager.
- **Portfolios** are collections of projects and programs; a portfolio's collection of projects or programs are not necessarily interdependent or directly related.

Project professionals, who are just starting out in the industry, will find understanding these interrelationships useful as they may be responsible for delivering a small project within a larger program. Alternatively, their project might be closed out early due to other higher-priority projects within the portfolio. Reference information outlining some important features of these relationship types is found in this appendix.

Interrelationships between projects, programs and portfolios

The specific construction of programs and portfolios is dependent on the objectives of the organisation and the project management maturity level of the organisation. Figure A2.1 shows the continuum of goals for project management.

FIGURE A2.1 CONTINUUM OF PROJECT, PROGRAM AND PORTFOLIO MANAGEMENT

Program management
- Are we effective program managers?
- Do our programs deliver consolidated benefits?
- Do we make appropriate decisions about priorities?
- Are we delivering integrated scope?
- Are we delivering the required medium-term outcomes?

Tactical goals   Medium-term goals   Strategic goals

Portfolio management
- Are we effective portfolio managers?
- Do we prioritise and allocate funding based on these priorities?
- Are we making appropriate trade-offs between scope, time and cost across the portfolio?
- Are we delivering the required strategic outcomes?
- Do we construct our portfolios to deliver corporate objectives?

Project management
- Are we effective project managers?
- Are we on time and on budget?
- Are we delivering the required scope?
- Are we delivering the required short-term outcomes?
- Do our projects deliver success?

Source: Adapted From Schwalbe. *Information Technology Project Management* (with Microsoft Project 2010 60 Day Trial CD-ROM). 7th edition, p. 18. © 2014 Brooks/Cole, a part of Cengage Learning, Inc. Reproduced by permission.

The larger the project, program or portfolio, the higher the risk – generally, only organisations with higher levels of project management maturity should attempt to execute anything larger than a medium-sized project. Table A2.1 from PMBOK® Guide shows the complexity and flexibility of the possible structures within programs and portfolios.

TABLE A2.1 COMPARATIVE OVERVIEW OF PROJECT, PROGRAM AND PORTFOLIO MANAGEMENT

Organisational project management			
	Projects	**Programs**	**Portfolios**
Scope	Projects have defined objectives. Scope is progressively elaborated throughout the project lifecycle.	Programs have a larger scope and provide more significant benefits.	Portfolios have an organisational scope that changes with the strategic objectives of the organisation.
Change	Project managers expect change and implement processes to keep change managed and controlled.	Program managers expect change from both inside and outside the program and are prepared to manage it.	Portfolio managers continuously monitor changes in the broader internal and external environments.
Planning	Project managers progressively elaborate high-level information into detailed plans throughout the project lifecycle.	Program managers develop the overall program plan and create high-level plans the guide the detailed planning at the component level.	Portfolio managers create and maintain necessary processes and communication relative to the aggregate portfolio.
Management	Project managers manage the project team to meet the project objectives.	Program managers manage the program staff and the project managers; they provide vision and overall leadership.	Portfolio managers may manage or coordinate portfolio management staff, or program and project staff that may have reporting responsibilities into the aggregate portfolio.
Success	Success is measured by product and project quality, timeliness, budget compliance and degree of customer satisfaction.	Success is measured by the degree to which the program satisfies the needs and benefits for which it was undertaken.	Success is measured in terms of the aggregate investment performance and benefit realisation of the portfolio.

(Continued)

Organisational project management			
	Projects	**Programs**	**Portfolios**
Monitoring	Project managers monitor and control the work of producing the products, services or results that the project was undertaken to produce.	Program managers monitor the progress of program components to ensure the overall goals, schedules, budget and benefits of the program will be met.	Portfolio managers monitor strategic changes and aggregate resource allocation, performance results and risk of the portfolio.

Project Management Institute, *A guide to the Project Management Body of Knowledge*, (PMBOK® Guide), p. 8. Project Management Institute, Inc 2013. Copyright and all rights reserved. Material from this publication has been reproduced with the permission of PMI.

Program management

There are many definitions offered in various texts for the concept of a program. PMBOK® Guide defines a program as 'a group of related projects that are managed together in order to increase the overall benefits and to achieve the strategic objectives of an organisation'.

Other definitions for program include:

- A temporary, flexible organisation structure created to coordinate, direct and oversee the implementation of a set of related projects and activities in order to deliver outcomes and benefits related to an organisation's strategic objectives; a programme is likely to have a life that spans several years. (Managing Successful Programmes, UK Office of Government Commerce, 2007)
- A set of related projects and organisational changes put in place to achieve a strategic goal and to deliver the benefits that the organisation expects. (IPMA Competence Baseline, International Project Management Association, 2006)
- A group of related projects managed in a coordinated way to obtain benefits and control not available from managing them individually. Programs may include elements of related work outside the scope of the discrete projects in the program. (The Standard for Program Management, Project Management Institute, 2008)

This variety in definitions highlights that a program, and therefore program management, is a flexible concept applied by organisations in different ways in order to best achieve their strategic outcomes. Program management is essentially about how best to deliver the business strategy via projects. Usually, a single project alone will not achieve the overall results of an entire business.

Benefits of program management

Programs are often recognised to have inherently higher risks associated with their execution and delivery than individual projects. However, with high risk comes high reward, so, despite the additional complexity necessary, programs deliver more benefits than individual projects in isolation. Program management helps an organisation achieve transformation when there is high complexity, ambiguity and risk because it has a strong focus on the overall benefits and strategic alignment needed for change. The benefits of programs and program management are below.

- Programs contribute to the strategic objectives.
- Programs provide greater integration, management and visibility of the inter-dependencies between the component projects.
- Programs enable trade-offs between priorities and funding sources across a broader set of projects.
- Programs can deliver transformation change.
- Programs offer an opportunity to deliver in tranches so as to enable the absorption of the project outcomes into the normal operations of an organisation in increments.
- Programs provide a framework to resolve competing demands for resources.
- Programs enable risks to be managed across interrelated projects.
- Programs enable the maximisation of business benefits.
- Programs enable more effective engagement of stakeholders in the achievement of the overall strategic vision and objectives by showing them the entire picture or blueprint.

Portfolio management

Portfolio management ensures that projects, programs and change initiatives are: selected and supported by the appropriate level of senior management; contribute to strategic objectives and business priorities; prioritised in-line with strategic objectives and business priorities; and considered within the overall business constraints in terms of funding, risk, resource availability and the ability of the organisation to absorb change.

Benefits of project portfolio management

The benefits of project portfolio management include:

- greater financial benefits and measurable contributions to strategic objectives
- overall visibility through the optimisation of the project portfolio (via combining related projects, closing redundant or duplicate projects and promoting higher priority projects)
- integrated change control across the portfolio by managing the project pipeline (including dependencies, and resource and funding constraints)

- improved resource allocation and utilisation by focusing on the highest priority projects and programs
- improved project delivery practices through overarching project delivery frameworks, and the sharing of good practices and lessons learned
- enhanced transparency, accountability and governance
- improved stakeholder engagement and change management by ensuring that the changes of projects can be absorbed and integrated back into business in order to achieve the expected benefits
- better guidance and frameworks for decision makers to prioritise, plan, and control enterprise portfolios
- ability for the organisation to add further value and strengthen performance to improve business results and achieve strategic objectives
- reduced unplanned, negative events by providing formal portfolio oversight so that program and project managers have a process to identify potential problems earlier in order to take corrective action before they impact financial results
- built-in contingencies for the overall portfolio to provide flexibility in managing trade-offs, funding and resources
- ability to extend project management best practices across the entire organisation
- increased visibility and better understanding of future resourcing requirements to deliver business outcomes via projects.

Figure A2.2 shows the connection of organisational strategy to the portfolio.

FIGURE A2.2 CONNECTION TO ORGANISATIONAL STRATEGY

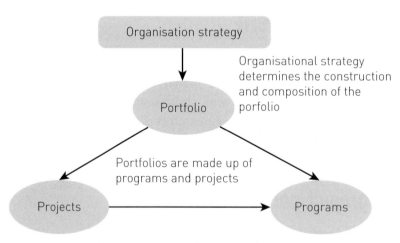

The role of the PMO

Portfolio management is the centralised management of multiple projects, programs and possibly sub-portfolios across a business unit or the entire organisation. Portfolio management typically requires the centralised management of processes, methods, and frameworks. It is widely becoming known as project portfolio management (PPM). PPM is often necessary for organisations that have large numbers of projects and programs, high levels of investment in the project portfolio and a need for improved governance or execution of the portfolio to maximise business benefits. If an organisation is large and sophisticated enough to apply PPM then it will usually also have a project management office (PMO), which is responsible for the overall management and governance of the project portfolio. PMOs are widely being referred to as P³MOs, which stands for project, program and portfolio management offices.

The PMO has responsibility for supporting the primary management functions included within PPM. According to the PMI's *Standard for Portfolio Management* there are five key knowledge areas involved in Portfolio management, these are:

1 portfolio strategic management
2 portfolio governance management
3 portfolio performance management
4 portfolio communication management
5 portfolio risk management.

Below lists the groups that are usually involved in PPM.

- **Senior management and executives** are responsible for setting the strategic direction, establishing the overall level of portfolio funding that will be available each year and directing the prioritisation of all projects within the portfolio.
- **Project management office (PMO)** is responsible for governing the overall portfolio in terms of prioritisation, funding allocation, resource planning, project delivery frameworks and performance reporting.
- **Functional managers** often assume the role of project or program sponsor for the various initiatives that relate to their business area. This group also includes other functions that assist in the delivery of the portfolio, such as human resource managers, finance managers and procurement managers. This group is responsible for the supporting the successful execution of projects and programs.
- **Portfolio managers** often are at the head of the PMO and are responsible for overseeing the processes and frameworks that govern the formation and execution of projects and programs within the portfolio. They usually are responsible for managing the portfolio approval and decision making functions of the senior management and executives, including prioritisation, funding allocation, performance reporting and integrated change control.
- **Program and project managers** are responsible for executing their assigned projects and programs in order to achieve the business objectives of the specific project or program. They are accountable to their project or program sponsor (usually a functional manager) and need to follow the project delivery processes prescribed by the PMO.

- **Project teams** are the groups of people assigned to each project or program to perform assigned tasks in order to produce the deliverables that form the scope of each project or program. They are accountable to the project or program managers.

The delivery outcomes of project, program and portfolio management for organisational strategy, business value and project objectives are shown below in Figure A2.3.

FIGURE A2.3 DELIVERY OUTCOMES VIA PORTFOLIOS

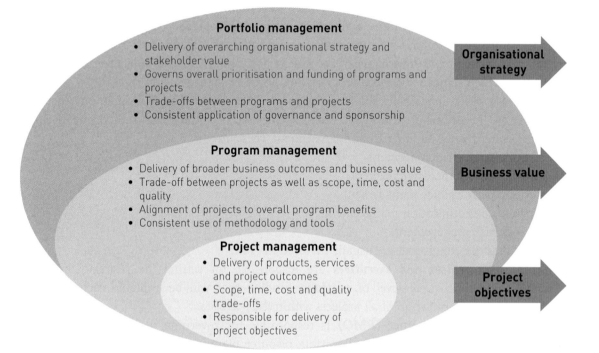

Portfolio management
- Delivery of overarching organisational strategy and stakeholder value
- Governs overall prioritisation and funding of programs and projects
- Trade-offs between programs and projects
- Consistent application of governance and sponsorship

Organisational strategy

Program management
- Delivery of broader business outcomes and business value
- Trade-off between projects as well as scope, time, cost and quality
- Alignment of projects to overall program benefits
- Consistent use of methodology and tools

Business value

Project management
- Delivery of products, services and project outcomes
- Scope, time, cost and quality trade-offs
- Responsible for delivery of project objectives

Project objectives

References

Project Management Institute (PMI), *A Guide to the Project Management Body of Knowledge* (PMBoK Guide), 5th edn, 2013, Newtown, PA.

Project Management Institute (PMI), *The Standard for Program Management*, 3rd edn, 2013, Newtown, PA.

Project Management Institute (PMI), *The Standard for Portfolio Management*, 3rd edn, 2013, Newtown, PA.

Global Alliance for Project Performance Standards (GAPPS), *A Framework for Performance Based Competency Standards for Program Managers*, 2011, Sydney.

Office of Government Commerce (OGC), *Portfolio, Programme and Project Offices: P3O, 2008*, Stationery Office, London, UK.

Glossary

accounting closure	The critical process of finalising the project budget and shutting down the project cost centres so that no more time recording, billing or invoices can be processed against the project. This typically occurs a few months after the project has formally closed to enable time for invoices to be received and contract disputes to be resolved.
active listening	A critical skill that helps ensure you have accurately understood the meaning and needs of others. It involves listening attentively and confirming your understanding of the meaning being conveyed. Positive reinforcement activities, such as nodding and paraphrasing, are important components.
activities	The specific steps that need to be executed in order to produce a deliverable.
activity resource requirements	A list of the resource requirements for each activity that is captured to assist with detailed planning and to ensure that the required number of resources and skills sets are acquired. This includes the human resources as well as other resources, such as funding, equipment, services, etc.
ADKAR©	ADKAR is an effective tool for planning change management activities as they relate to individuals, diagnosing gaps, developing corrective actions and supporting managers as they lead their teams through the change. ADKAR stands for awareness, desire, knowledge, ability and reinforcement. It is a model of personal change for an individual.
Agile	Development methods for highly flexible and interactive projects, using iterative methods of determining requirements and delivering tangible benefits in stages rather than waiting until all requirements have been delivered.
analogous cost estimating	Uses characteristics from past projects which are similar to a current project in order to accelerate overall planning and estimation of costs and timeframes.
assumptions	Factors that are considered to be true in order to complete project planning. They involve a degree of risk as they may be proven to be untrue once the project has commenced the execution phase. If they are untrue there are often significant impacts on the PMP which need to be managed via integrated change control. It is recommended that *all* assumptions are also included as risks in the risk log or risk register.
Australian Human Rights Commission	The Australian administrative body with the authority to investigate complaints of discrimination and human rights breaches.
backward pass	In the critical path method, this calculates the late end dates for all activities.
baseline	An agreed starting point used as a basis for comparison of performance or completeness. Project success is measured against the final agreed baselines for scope, time and cost. After the end of the planning phase, these baselines can only be changed via formal change control and approval from the project sponsor.

business case	A feasibility study of a proposed project that will outline the costs and benefits of a particular project in order to facilitate project prioritisation, project approvals and decision making.
change management	The application of a set of tools, processes, skills and principles for managing the people side of change to achieve the required outcomes of a project or change initiative. It is important that this is not confused with change control.
change request	A formal proposal to change any aspect of a project that will impact the timeframe, budget or scope. Change requests may result from untrue assumptions, risks that have occurred, poor planning or omissions from the scope or requirements. These are often referred to as variations in the construction industry.
closing procurements	A collection of activities which, according to the PMBOK® Guide, relate to the closing of procurements that were undertaken in the project. These include the finalisation of contracts, handover to business as usual, negotiation of disputes, etc.
collecting requirements	Defining and documenting the needs of stakeholders. The requirements provide more detail on the project scope and product, and can take the form of business requirements, functional requirements, quality requirements, technical requirements and so on.
communications management plan	Contains definitions of the communication resourcing, requirements and processes for the project. The emphasis is on defining the specific communication requirements for all project stakeholders and ensuring that these are delivered.
concept paper	An alternative name for the project charter which is the primary initiation document of a project. It can also be known as the project brief, high-level plan or statement of work.
constraints	These are limitations that are placed on a project which impact the planning and execution of the project. They are normally applied to the concepts of time or cost, when there is a fixed deadline or a limited budget for the project. They can also apply when the project must comply with specified regulations and standards.
control	Involves assessing actual progress against planned progress in order to take action to bring the project back on track as per the project baselines.
controlling scope	The process of monitoring the status of both the project and product scope. It focuses on managing any changes to the scope baseline and understanding the flow-on impacts on time, cost and quality.
crashing the schedule	Adding more resources to activities. This only works when an activity can be effectively undertaken by more than one resource, thereby shortening the duration of the activity.
critical path	The combination of activities that generates the shortest duration of the project by finding the longest path through the project schedule based on the unique combination of activity interdependencies that have been stipulated in the schedule.
deliverables	The physical outputs that your project must produce in order to meet the required outcomes and fulfil the project and product scope.

dependencies	These occur between projects and external activities as well as between the specific activities within a project. External dependencies are things which are outside of the project manager's control which may have an impact on the execution of a project. These need to be documented and carefully monitored as they represent risks to the successful delivery of the project.
DISC model of behaviour	The basis of this model is that normal human emotions lead to behavioural differences among groups of people and that understanding this can help people manage their experiences and relationships. The acronym stands for Dominant, Influencer, Steady and Cautious behavioural traits.
earned value management (EVM)	A technique that integrates the three key baselines of scope, time and cost; it measures the planned value, earned value and actual cost of each activity as it is being executed. This enables the measurement of the progress of the project against the three baselines of scope, cost and time.
fast tracking	A technique which involves running activities in parallel that would normally have been done sequentially. This is a common method of reducing the overall timeframe of a project and increases the execution risk.
forecasting	The technique of capturing cost data for activities from the bottom up and using experience gained from the work that has already been completed to estimate a revised cost forecast to complete each activity.
forward pass	In the critical path method, this calculates the early finish dates for all activities.
Four Absolutes of Quality Management	Crosby's approach to quality management which requires quality to be defined as conformance to requirements, quality to be caused by prevention and zero defect standards, and the measurement of quality to be the price of non-conformance.
free float	The amount of time an individual activity which is on the critical path can be delayed without impacting project duration.
GANTT chart	An illustration of the project schedule in bar chart form that shows start and finish dates for each element. The development of this critical visual management tool is accredited to Henry Gantt in the 1910s.
key knowledge areas	Areas of competency required by a project manager, as defined by the PMBOK® Guide. The fifth edition defines 10 key knowledge areas.
Kotter	John Kotter, a professor at Harvard Business School and widely acknowledged change expert, introduced his eight-step change process in his 1995 book *Leading change*.
knowledge management	Capturing and sharing knowledge to improve organisational performance and it is the key to success for professional services firms. It involves the capture, reuse and sharing of precedents, examples and templates.
high-level plan	This term is sometimes used to describe the primary initiation document of a project. May also be known as a project brief, concept paper, project charter or statement of work. At other times it is used to refer to a summary, or abbreviated, version of the detailed PMP.
human resource management	Encompasses the processes that organise, manage and lead the project team.

integrated change control	The process of reviewing all change requests that have been identified by the monitoring and controlling of project work. It includes the approval or rejection of change requests and the assessment of impacts across all key knowledge areas, and also ensures that approved change requests are successfully delivered.
International Organization for Standardization (ISO)	An international not-for-profit standard-setting body that defines quality as 'the degree to which a set of inherent characteristics fulfils requirements' (ISO9000:2000).
Lean Six Sigma	A process improvement framework that combines the concepts of Lean Manufacturing and Six Sigma. It focuses on delivering process efficiencies through the reduction of defects and the elimination of waste.
methodology	A set or system of methods, principles and rules for regulating a given discipline, as in project management, the arts or sciences (dictionary.com).
milestone	A significant event or point in a project that is tracked to indicate the achievement of major outcomes.
monitor	Involves the collection, measurement and distribution of project performance information.
monitor and control	The processes involved in the assessment of project progress, the resolution of issues to bring the project back on track, and the collection and distribution of project performance information.
Myers-Briggs Type Indicator (MBTI)®	A behavioural test that is designed to measure psychological preferences in how people perceive the world and make decisions. It was first published in 1943 and originally developed in the US by Katharine Cook Briggs and her daughter Isabel Briggs Myers.
non-verbal communication	The process of communicating through visual and other wordless cues such as body language, facial expressions, etc.
organisational charts	Hierarchical diagrams that show team members where the project fits within the overall organisational structure and that depict the structure and reporting lines for the project.
performance assessment	A human resource management activity which assess the performance of a team member or individual. For project staff this is typically performed by the project manager at the end of a project, but may also be required in line with the timeframes of the organisation's performance review cycle for all staff.
PERT charts	The Project Evaluation and Review Technique (PERT) is a graphical illustration of a project's schedule and shows the order in which activities need to be performed in order to deliver the project in the shortest possible time (the critical path). It was invented in the 1950s by the US Navy.
plan-do-check-act	Deming's four-step process for the definition and implementation of quality improvements. Many of these have been incorporated into Lean Six Sigma.
PMBOK® Guide	The Project Management Body of Knowledge – a project management standard developed by the Project Management Institute (PMI), a US-based professional organisation for project managers. The PMBOK® Guide is now available in its fifth edition.

portfolio	A collection of projects or programs that are grouped together to facilitate effective management or to meet strategic business objectives. The projects and programs within the portfolio do not always have inter-dependencies.
portfolio management	The centralised and co-ordinated management of projects and programs in order to achieve strategic business objectives.
post-implementation review (PIR)	This is the primary activity performed during the closure phase. It formally evaluates the performance of the project against the objectives and final baselines, as well as gathering lessons learned and critical project knowledge that can be used on future projects.
precedence diagramming method	One of the key techniques used to sequence activities in projects. It is a component of the critical path methodology that has become the industry standard and underpins the project management software that produces both GANTT and PERT charts. There are four interrelationships between activities – Finish-Start, Start-Start, Finish-Finish and Start-Finish.
preferred supplier	Suppliers for any external resources, products and services that have been through a selection and prequalification process in order to go onto a preferred supplier list.
Prince2	**PR**ojects **IN C**ontrolled **E**nvironments: a process-based methodological approach to project management. It was developed by the UK Government and is the accepted project management methodology in the UK.
procurement	The acquisition of goods, services or work from an external source.
procurement management plan	Defines the procurement requirements for the project including all items that must be sourced from outside of the project, such as equipment, contract resources, systems, materials, etc. It includes high-level information about the items to be procured for overall tracking purposes and specifies procurement processes to be used for the project.
product scope	The features and functions that characterise a product or service.
program	A group of related projects managed in a co-ordinated way to obtain benefits and maintain control.
program director	The position title for a project manager who is responsible for managing a suite of related projects in order to achieve overarching business outcomes. This is generally considered a more senior position than a project manager as the role is more broad and more complex.
program management	The centralised and co-ordinated management of a program to achieve the program's strategic objectives and benefits.
project	A temporary endeavour undertaken to create a unique product, service or result.
project audit	A special type of evaluation of a project that is carried out during the execution of the project, to determine if it should be cancelled (also known as a health check).
project baseline	According to the PMBOK® Guide, there are three specific baselines that should be set for a project. These are the scope baseline, schedule baseline and budget baseline. They are set at the end of the planning phase and should only be altered via formal change control.

project brief	The primary initiation document of a project and the major deliverable from the initiation phase. It sets the overall objectives and boundaries of a project. May also be known as the project charter, concept paper, high-level plan or statement of work.
project budget baseline	This is set at the end of the planning phase when the project budget is firm and all budgetary assumptions are clear. It is the version of the project budget which the performance of the budget is measured, and provides the basis for the monitoring of cost performance on the project. The project budget baseline should only be changed via formal change control with the approval of the project sponsor.
project charter	The primary initiation document of a project and the major deliverable from the initiation phase. It sets the overall objectives and boundaries of a project. May also be known as the project charter, concept paper, high-level plan or statement of work.
project closure	The process of finalising all activities across all of the process groups and key knowledge areas to formally close a phase or a project.
project coordinator	The position title for a project resource who provides administrative support on a project, including maintaining the project schedule and control logs. They typically report to a project manager or program director.
project execution	The process group that involves directing and managing the project team and resources in order to perform the activities that complete the deliverables that are required to deliver the project scope.
project health check	A special type of evaluation of a project that is carried out during the execution of the project, to determine if it should be cancelled (also known as a project audit).
project initiation	The process group that involves the inception of the project, including the definition of the objectives, scope and boundaries and the initial identification of key stakeholders.
project kick-off meeting	A critical session that sets the framework and objectives for the project and creates engagement for the project team at the beginning of the project.
project knowledge management	Knowledge management techniques specifically used to improve the success of projects. It requires the capture, sharing and management of project deliverables and examples that can be applied to future projects with similar characteristics.
project management	Both a profession and a set of tools and techniques that can be applied to the delivery of defined outcomes.
Project Management Institute (PMI)	A US-based professional organisation for project managers. It was started in 1999 and is known to have the largest membership of any project management body, with more than 600 000 members and 184 chapters worldwide.
project management plan (PMP)	The primary output of the planning phase, it is the result of a complex interplay between more than 20 project management processes and typically contains the activities and processes that must be executed in order to deliver the project scope and objectives. It normally contains sections for each of the 10 key knowledge areas as defined in the PMBOK® Guide but can also refer to subsidiary plans in areas such as risk, stakeholder management, communications and quality management.

project manager	The position title for a person chosen to lead a project. It implies advanced capabilities and understanding of project management disciplines, tools and techniques.
project phase	The lifecycle of a project is typically divided into several phases which represent a collection of related activities that result in the completion of one or more major project deliverables. The PMBOK® Guide defines four phases of a project – initiation, planning, execution and closing, with a related process group that assesses and manages project performance known as monitoring and controlling.
project planning	The phase of the project that delivers the PMP. It contains all the activities required to develop plans for all 10 key knowledge areas. It is also the primary function of the project manager in the early phases of the project management lifecycle.
project risk	An uncertain event or condition that, if it occurs, has a positive or negative effect on one or more project objectives such as scope, schedule, cost, and quality.
project scope	The work that must be performed to deliver a product, service or result with the specified features and functions; the work that must be performed in order to create all the deliverables that are required to deliver the project objectives.
project scope statement	A detailed description of the project including the objectives, major deliverables, assumptions, dependencies, constraints and end products.
project sponsor	The person, or position, for whom the project is being undertaken. Often they are funding the project or will directly benefit from the deliverables and outcomes of the project. They can be internal or external to the organisation executing the project. The project manager is accountable to this person for the successful delivery of the project.
project stakeholders	Individuals or groups that are interested in, or may be impacted by, the outcomes of the project.
project success	Occurs when the expectations of the project sponsor or client have been met; agreed project objectives have been met; business outcomes have been realised; and timeframe, budget, quality and scope requirements have been delivered.
project team charter	Often developed in the first team building session or during a project kick-off meeting, it is a list of positive team behaviours that is then agreed upon and upheld by the project team throughout the entire project. It assists with team engagement and increases productivity and cooperation in the early stages of a project.
project team members	Individuals who have been given specific accountability for the development and completion of assigned project deliverables.
project transition plan	A project management document that plans the formal handover of the project deliverables, outcomes or assets to the business owner for on-going operation.
Prosci ©3-Phase change methodology	A change management process comprising three phases: preparing for change, managing change and reinforcing change. Created by Jeff Hiatt, the president of Prosci Research and founder of the Change Management Learning Center. It is used to plan change management activities for project stakeholders that align to the delivery of a project.

qualitative risk analysis	Considers the likelihood and consequences of risks in order to determine their priority based on the extent of the negative impact they may have on the project.
quality assurance	Quality activities (e.g. reviews, process checklists and quality audits) that are built into the processes used to create the product and deliverables.
quality control	Quality activities (e.g. inspection and testing) performed at the completion of a product or deliverable; used to verify that deliverables meet the requirements and that they are complete and correct.
quality management plan	Defines the processes required in order to deliver the acceptable level of quality for a project in terms of the deliverables, products and outcomes that are to be achieved.
quantitative risk analysis	Involves estimating the measurable impact of a risk on project objectives, specifically cost, time, scope and quality.
RACI chart	A form of **R**esponsibility **A**ssignment **M**atrix that define roles as **R**esponsible, **A**ccountable, **C**onsulted and **I**nformed.
RASIC chart	A variation of the basic RACI chart that defines the roles as **R**eview, **A**ccountable, **S**ign-off, **I**nformed and **C**ontribute/consulted. This is generally easier for people to understand as there is often confusion between responsible and accountable in the RACI format.
requirements management plan	Defines the processes that are applied to the development, tracking and management of requirements throughout the project in order to ensure they are delivered within the final project outputs.
resource assignments	Lists of the skills and experience of each resource along with the specific deliverables for which they will be accountable.
resource breakdown structure	A hierarchical chart of resources required for the completion of a project. This includes people as well as other resources such as equipment, services and materials.
resource calendar	Where resource commitments are captured to ensure they are allocated to the specified project and made unavailable to other projects.
responsibility assignment matrix (RAM)	A structured table that relates the project organisation chart to the deliverables in the work breakdown structure to help ensure that all components of the project scope have been assigned to a project team or member for delivery. The original format is RACI: **R**esponsible, **A**ccountable, **C**onsulted, **I**nformed. A more recent improvement is the RASIC: **R**eview, **A**ccountable, **S**ign-off, **I**nformed, **C**ontribute/consulted.
risk acceptance	An approach to managing risk which involves accepting the consequences of an individual risk as the impact on project objectives is relatively minor.
risk avoidance	An approach to managing risk that involves avoiding the risk completely by replanning the project delivery approach or changing the project scope. This treatment is normally used for risks that have a high likelihood and high consequences.
risk breakdown structure (RBS)	A hierarchy chart that lists the categories and subcategories of risks that may arise for a typical project. It helps to ensure that important categories of potential risk are not overlooked.

risk log	A register of all the risks that have been identified, or have occurred, on a project along with key characteristics and management responses to those risks.
risk management plan	Documents the processes, tools and procedures that will be used to manage and control risks that may have a negative impact on a project.
risk mitigation	An approach to managing risk that involves changing the activities or approach of a project in order to reduce the negative impacts or the likelihood of a risk occurring.
risk owner	A person identified and assigned to a specific risk, to reduce the threat or mitigate the risk by ensuring monitoring and control happens.
risk transference	An approach to managing risk that involves shifting some or all of the ownership of a risk to a third party.
risk treatment	The particular approach that has been chosen to manage a particular risk in order to reduce its impact. Risk treatment approaches include mitigate, accept, transfer and avoid.
schedule baseline	The version of the project schedule that is locked in for the duration of performance tracking during the project. It is typically set at the end of the planning phase once the detailed PMP has been completed and after the schedule has been optimised via fast tracking or crashing. It should only be changed via formal change control if there are impacts on the overall end date.
scope baseline	The version of the scoping documentation that is locked in and is used to ensure that all the project requirements have been delivered. It is often set at the end of planning or at the beginning of execution, depending on when the detailed requirements documentation is being produced. It should only be changed via formal change control when there are impacts on project scope.
scope creep	The unintentional expansion of the project scope that occurs when change control processes are not formally followed. It erodes the successful delivery of a project as additional scope will need to be achieved without additional time, funding or resources.
scope management plan	Documents the project scope in detail and defines the processes for the definition, validation, control and management of the scope throughout the project.
Situational Leadership	Developed by Hershey and Blanchard, this is a people leadership framework that asserts that instead of using just one style, the most successful leaders adapt their leadership style based on the maturity, or capability, of each team member and the specific nature of the task they will be executing.
Six Sigma	A set of statistical tools and processes (used for quality management) that concentrate on the removal of defects from a particular business or manufacturing process.
SMART framework	The standard definition of measurable objectives: **S**pecific, **M**easurable, **A**greed, **R**ealistic, **T**imeframe. This is particularly useful in defining project objectives and also the performance objectives of team members.

stakeholder analysis	The process of systematically gathering and analysing information to determine whose interests should be taken into account and managed throughout the project.
standard	Something considered by an authority or by general consent as a basis of comparison; an approved model (dictionary.com).
statement of work	The primary initiation document of a project and the major deliverable from the initiation phase. It sets the overall objectives and boundaries of a project. May also be known as the project brief, concept paper, high-level plan or project charter. It can also be used to package a set of project deliverables together in order to outsource these to a third party.
steering committee	A management body or committee that is assigned oversight and governance responsibility for the project.
tasks	Substeps of activities.
team development	Bruce Tuckman's model of the stages of team development that include forming, storming, norming, performing and adjourning (mourning).
total float	The summation of the individual floats for each activity. Floats represent the amount of time an individual activity which is on the critical path can be delayed without impacting project duration.
triple constraint	Demonstrates the relationships between project time, project cost and project quality, all of which are related to, and constrained by, the overall boundaries of the project as defined in the project scope.
variance analysis	Looks more deeply at the root cause of positive or negative variances on activities, i.e. under- or overbudget amounts, to determine the impact they will have on the overall project budget.
VARK model	Classifies learning styles and preferences of individuals into either visual, aural, reading or kinaesthetic. Useful when determining stakeholder management approaches and developing project-related communication plans.
Waterfall (model)	A design process in which progress is seen as flowing steadily downwards (like a waterfall) through the phases of conception, initiation, analysis, design, construction, testing, production/implementation and maintenance.
work breakdown structure (WBS)	A deliverable-oriented hierarchical breakdown of the work to be executed by the project team to accomplish the project objectives and create the required deliverables.
WBS dictionary	A document that contains detailed information about each item in the WBS.
work package	A collection of related activities and deliverables that are assigned to a project team member or third party for execution. Very common terminology in the US and also the construction industry.
workstream	A subset of related deliverables and activities within a large project or program that are typically assigned to a project manager or a discipline leader (such as testing, change management, etc.) for delivery.

Index